NO MATTER HOW YOU SLICE IT—
home-baked bread puts the commercial
variety to shame! No wonder there's a
growing enthusiasm for bread-baking
—it's a healthy reaction against the
artificiality in our food and the
harmful additives they keep sneaking
into our lives.

Here's everything you need to know
to get you started. Discover what a
joyful, rewarding experience it is to

Bake Your Own Bread
And Be Healthier

"At last. A down-with-the-mystique-of-bread-
making book that does just that."—*Houston
Chronicle* ·

"A must for both health food enthusiasts and
traditional cooks."—*Florida Times-Union*

D0834546

Other SIGNET Books You'll Enjoy

☐ **JAPANESE COOKING by Peter and Joan Martin.** Here is a valuable addition to the kitchen bookshelf. Over 200 recipes have been carefully translated and thoroughly described so that any American cook can now experience the pleasures of authentic Japanese cuisine. Glossary, Index. (#Q4836—95¢)

☐ **COOKING WITH WINE by Morrison Wood.** The best of the world's most famous foods can now be prepared in your own kitchen. An expert shows how available ingredients are transformed into exotic fare by the creative use of American wines and liqueurs. (#Q4668—95¢)

☐ **COOKING AT THE TABLE by George Bradshaw.** Fun and flavorful recipes from soup to dessert that you can cook in ten minutes while your delighted guests look on, ranging from Japanese mizutaki to Viennese veal. (#Q4589—95¢)

☐ **CONFESSIONS OF A SNEAKY ORGANIC COOK . . . OR HOW TO MAKE YOUR FAMILY HEALTHY WHILE THEY'RE NOT LOOKING! by Jane Kinderlehrer.** A brightly written, excellent guide to healthy eating and cooking for the woman who doesn't want to make a big thing of it with her family. (#Q5119—95¢)

☐ **LET'S EAT RIGHT TO KEEP FIT by Adelle Davis.** Sensible, practical advice from America's foremost nutrition authority as to what vitamins, minerals and food balances you require; and the warning signs of diet deficiencies. (#E5379—$1.75)

THE NEW AMERICAN LIBRARY, INC.,
P.O. Box 999, Bergenfield, New Jersey 07621

Please send me the SIGNET BOOKS I have checked above. I am enclosing $＿＿＿＿＿＿(check or money order—no currency or C.O.D.'s). Please include the list price plus 25¢ a copy to cover handling and mailing costs. (Prices and numbers are subject to change without notice.)

Name＿＿＿＿＿＿＿＿＿＿＿＿＿＿＿＿＿＿＿＿＿＿＿＿

Address＿＿＿＿＿＿＿＿＿＿＿＿＿＿＿＿＿＿＿＿＿＿

City＿＿＿＿＿＿＿State＿＿＿＿＿＿Zip Code＿＿＿＿＿＿

Alow at least 3 weeks for delivery

Bake Your Own Bread

And Be Healthier

Floss and Stan Dworkin

A SIGNET BOOK
NEW AMERICAN LIBRARY
TIMES MIRROR

Copyright © 1972 by Floss Dworkin

All rights reserved, including the right to
reproduce this book or portions thereof in any form.

Library of Congress Catalog Card Number:
72-78104

This is an authorized reprint of a hardcover
· edition published by Holt, Rinehart and
Winston. Published simultaneously in Canada by
Holt, Rinehart and Winston of Canada, Limited.

Ⓞ

SIGNET, SIGNET CLASSICS,
SIGNETTE, MENTOR and PLUME BOOKS are
published by The New American Library, Inc.,
1301 Avenue of the Americas, New York,
New York 10019

First Printing, October, 1973

1 2 3 4 5 6 7 8 9

PRINTED IN THE UNITED STATES OF AMERICA

Contents

Bread baking is a lot like married love.
The first loaves of bread you make are not
the best you'll ever make, but they're better
than any you've ever bought.

PREFACE

Why We
No Longer
Use Margarine

Since finishing the manuscript for this book almost two years ago we've had second and third thoughts about the question of margarine versus butter.

Margarine was so much cheaper than butter, we used to keep it in the house for my baking classes. Well, that lower price is no bargain.

Butter is made from cream, a highly saturated fat. By churning, air is forced into this fat to make it solid. Sometimes salt is added (originally, no doubt, to preserve it, now because so many consumers are used to the flavor). Sometimes, especially in the winter when there is nothing green for our northern cows to eat, coloring is added to give it the look of summer cream (yellowish) rather than the look of winter cream (off-white). You can tell this colored butter because it does look so yellow—but there is no warning on the label. Undyed butter is widely available.

Margarine is a combination of vegetable oils and other ingredients—often, several chemicals. The oil used is usually not identified. Corn and soya oil are widely used and these unsaturated oils (if not tampered with) are good food. If, however, it is cottonseed oil, DDT residues may remain, because cotton, not considered a food crop, is heavily sprayed. If it is coconut oil, it is a very saturated oil to start with. This combination of oil and chemicals (and such other stuff as milk powder, salt, and water) is then hydrogenated (air is forced into it and the empty links of the molecules are filled by hydrogen) to make it solid—as solid as butter and as saturated as butter, and then dyed to make it look like butter.

There are so-called soft margarines, which contain more unsaturated oil—but often more chemicals. These too are dyed.

Neither butter nor margarine is essential to your diet. Some unsaturated fat is needed for those oil-soluble vitamins and for skin and hair tone.

Originally, we felt that either butter or margarine could be used for greasing the pans in our recipes. We have come to the conclusion that we were mistaken, and while it is too late to reset the type for all the recipes in *Bake Your Own Bread*, it is not too late to include this preface.

We now feel that the chemicals and dyes in margarine constitute a danger, and so we recommend that only butter be used to grease your baking pans.

To repeat: where our recipes read "For Greasing, melted butter or margarine," use melted butter only.

☞ 1 ☜
Down
with
the
Mystique

A BAS LE MYSTIQUE

Over the years a mystique has grown up around bread baking; a kind of mystery (in the old Greek sense of a secret religious society) which excluded the outsider who hadn't learned the rites at her mother's knee. Recently, however, there has been a renaissance of interest in home baking—probably a reaction to much of the artificiality in our food and a desire to eliminate some of the additives they keep sneaking into our lives. This interest in baking is part of the overall growth in interest in improving the quality of what goes into our stomachs.

This guide to the perplexed will steer you through the simplicities of bread baking, and through the complexities of improving your diet through baking your own bread.

It is not everything you ever wanted to know about baking but couldn't find out from your mother. Rather, it provides a foundation of techniques and recipes which, once mastered, will enable you to go on to virtually any bread, inventing recipes of your own, or adapting standard recipes to greater wholesomeness, improving your own and your family's health.

As for the mystique—there is none. Bread baking is a simple process, easily learned, quickly mastered by woman, man, or child, a satisfying and delicious pastime, a rewarding addition to everyday cooking, even profitable if you have the business sense.

Furthermore, bread you bake yourself is free from the chemical additives and free from the dirt introduced in any commercial bakery. (See Appendix B.)

Before going on to the recipes themselves, let me introduce you to the ingredients I use, to tell you where and how they fit into bread baking, and how they fit into a healthier diet.

THE INGREDIENTS

Flours

The flours and meals you'll be using in these recipes are the finely ground berries of various grasses (wheat, rye, corn) and beans (soy).

There are many other flours: buckwheat, barley, millet, peanut, ginseng, rice, even fish flour (not available in the States), to list a few. Any could be substituted for part of the flour listed in the recipes (you'll read about substitutions later on).

However, this is not a comprehensive but a basic book, and, basically, we'll be using wheat flour (white and whole), rye, corn, and soy.

WHEAT

The wheat berry (like all the grass berries) is made up of three parts: the coarse outer layer, the bran; the embryo or wheat germ (the part that, given the chance, would sprout into a new plant); and the inner part, or endosperm.

In the bran there are many vitamins and minerals, and proteins of a high quality (that is, proteins that are readily used by the body for the vital processes).

In the germ we have one of the richest sources of vitamin E, which is necessary for the absorption of vitamin A, and for general vitality. Experiments show that a lack of E can lead to heart disease. The germ also contains vitamin B, high-quality proteins, and oil high in food value and a good source of lecithin.

The endosperm is mostly starch with very little protein. It contains virtually no vitamins and minerals.

White flour is made exclusively of the endosperm.

When millers remove the bran and the germ from flour, they remove about twenty-five vitamins and minerals. When they enrich the flour before marketing it, they return four vitamins—and three of those in smaller amounts than what was removed.

Why?

Profit. And consumer preference.

In the mid-nineteenth century, when the invention of new milling techniques made it possible to produce white flour—prior to that, man was technologically too primitive to impoverish the food he ate—it was discovered that this new flour made a bread much finer in texture than whole wheat. There was an immediate demand for this "better" flour by the rich. (The poor took a while to catch up.) Millers and shopkeepers preferred it, too, because the removal of the germ meant that the white flour could be kept longer, there being nothing "live" left in it to go rancid.

After removal of the bran and germ came bleaching —a process wherein a gas is forced through the flour to whiten it further (and, incidentally, kill any last trace of vitamin E, etc., that might have remained).

The Minnesota Agricultural Experiment Station did an interesting experiment in the late 1940s. They took healthy, grain-fed cattle and began to feed them on grain from which the germ (and therefore the vitamin E) had been removed. The cattle continued to look just as healthy, but they began to drop dead of heart disease! After a while, the experimenters restored them to their former diet of whole grain. There were no more deaths from heart disease.

However, for all its nutritional deficiencies, there is no question that white flour gives you a finer textured bread than whole wheat does. It is lighter, fluffier, less absorbent, easier to shape, and easier to rise. I tried, as an experiment, to make Brioches with whole wheat flour. The flavor was good—but the texture? It just wasn't Brioches. The same is true of Challah—and of other light, airy breads as well. They were invented for white flour and, if whole wheat is used instead, they come out different breads.

What to do?

Our solution is to substitute raw wheat germ for some of the flour in every white bread we bake. (Our everyday bread is 100 percent whole wheat, or whole wheat mixed with other whole grains.)

In the recipes that call for white flour, use unbleached white flour—it, at least, has no chemical residues in it from bleaching, and does have a slightly higher
vitamin content. After you learn the texture and feel of
breads in their easiest form, I hope that you, too, will substitute raw wheat germ or whole wheat flour routinely for
part of the white flour.

Wheat flour comes in several varieties:

Whole wheat or graham flour. This should contain
all the bran and all the germ. It is rich in B and E vitamins
and contains many other nutrients. Sometimes you find a
cheaty graham flour, which is white flour with a little
bran thrown back. This is better than straight white, but
it is far from whole wheat.

Whole wheat flour should be *stone ground*—which
means that instead of being ground by high-speed (high-
heat) steel grinders, which tend to leave the wheat germ
oil in biggish clumps (and kill the vitamin E), the wheat
berries are ground between stone wheels which grind
the germ and oil particles up finely and distribute them
better throughout the flour. This helps the flour to keep
longer without going rancid.

Rancidity is a problem with whole wheat flour (and
all whole grain flours). You must sniff it when you buy
it—if it's off you can smell it. If possible, store flour in
the refrigerator to help keep it fresher. If, after you wet
it with the other ingredients, it smells rancid, throw it
out. Never eat flour that has gone bad; rancid oils have
a remarkable power to destroy vitamins.

Two caveats: (1) Be certain your source of flour is
a reliable one, and is not (as happened to me in a popular
health food store) selling you vitamin E-less, chemical-
ized, steel-ground whole wheat as the more expensive and
healthier stone ground. (2) Be certain that the whole
wheat flour you buy is not bleached or brominated. Brom-
inating (exposure of the flour to bromine gas) destroys
the germ, and so, much of the nutritive value. Pillsbury,
for example, markets a brominated graham flour.

Wheat germ flour. This is unbleached, enriched
white flour with the wheat germ returned after milling.
Nutritionally it is quite good, and some brands come from
Deaf Smith County, in Texas, where the mineral content
of the soil makes for especially nutritious grains. The

only trouble with this kind of flour is that it tends to be quite expensive. You can make your own wheat germ flour by using unbleached enriched white flour and substituting raw wheat germ as described in the recipes.

Unbleached enriched white flour. This flour gives you all the textural advantages of bleached flour without having gone through that last chemical treatment. It is only slightly more nutritious than bleached flour, but it is free of the chemical residues that bleaching can leave.

Bleached enriched white flour. As I said above, in this flour some twenty-five nutrients have been removed, and four returned, and they call that enrichment! There is also an unenriched white flour, but unless you have access to a commercial bakery, you shouldn't come into contact with it. Nutritionally it's on a par with library paste. And until recent pressure was brought by the federal government on the large companies, this nutrition-free junk was what all children's cakes were made of. Now, after being forced to add enrichment, the companies advertise: "Now Enriched!" as if they'd done something wonderful.

Gluten flour. "Gluten" is the protein part of the wheat berry, and gluten flour is about 50 percent protein. (Much of the starch has been removed.) It is usually reserved for people on special diets (diabetics, for example).

The gluten is that part of the flour which, by rubbing against itself in kneading, forms an elastic substance that holds the bubbles that the yeast makes. That's how yeast bread rises: by the elastic holding the expanding carbon dioxide bubbles released by the yeast. However, there are many flours that don't have any or much gluten—soy, for example. So, when I want to use a lot of soy (or any nongluten) flour in a recipe, I make sure to include some gluten flour to balance it out.

This flour does not have a good texture, but it can serve a good purpose.

Other wheat flours. If you shop around the health food stores (or mail order catalogues) you might well come across three other varieties of wheat flour: *whole wheat pastry flour, cracked wheat,* and *wheat grits.* All three of them are whole wheat (and so, good foods); all three of them are not suited to bread baking.

Whole wheat pastry flour is made from a different variety of wheat than the flour we use for bread baking. Also, it is more finely ground. If you try to make bread from it, the breads *will not rise,* and will have a "strange" flavor. You can use it for cookies, puddings, gravies, pastries, that sort of thing, but not bread.

Cracked wheat is the wheat berry cracked into large chunks, and you might as well try to knead bird gravel. While it is unsuitable as the *only* flour in a bread, it does make a nice textural addition—as does wheat grits (the wheat berry broken into smaller pieces). The commercial cracked wheat bread is made of white flour with some, though not much, cracked wheat added to it.

RYE

Rye is a very tasty flour, with very little gluten. A bread with a great deal of rye will have difficulty rising. One virtue of rye is that because it is not in great demand, it is available, I believe, only as a whole, stone-ground grain, unbleached, unenriched, unmucked about with in any way. But don't take my word for it. Read that label. If it doesn't say "stone ground" it's not stone ground. If it doesn't say "whole" or "100 percent whole" then something has been removed.

Rye also comes as a meal—a coarser grind of the same grain. If you can get it, do so, and use it instead of rye flour. The textural change is delightful.

CORN

There are cornmeals which are actually corn flours—the difference, again, is in the fineness of the grinding. The finer the grind, the more likely it is that the cornmeal will completely dissolve in the baking, leaving its flavor but not its texture.

Buying cornmeal can be tricky. For the most part, the cornmeals sold in supermarkets are enriched *degerminated.* They say it right on the box, "degerminated," in big letters, as if they were proud of it.

The germ of the corn—as the germ of the wheat or the rye—is the healthful part. If the germ is removed, all that is left are empty calories and a sprinkling of protein (not much, and poor-quality protein at that).

There is available in the supermarkets a brand of

white cornmeal that is stone ground and not degerminated: Indian Head. Of course, the health food stores
carry stone-ground yellow cornmeal that is complete.

SOY

As mentioned before, soy is not a grass like wheat or corn
or rye, it is a legume and, aside from gluten flour, the best
source of protein of any flour I use (about 40 percent protein). For vegetarians and others who don't eat much in
the way of animal proteins, soybeans are very important
in the diet because, like animal proteins, soybean proteins
are "complete."

When buying soy flour you have to watch out for
"defatted" or "low fat." Again, it is the oil (or fat) that
carries the lecithin (nutritionally very important); but
even low-fat soy flour is a good food.

Yeasts

Yeasts have been used by man since the dawn of his-
tory—and probably earlier. All fermented drinks are
changed from carbohydrate-rich liquids to part-alcoholic
liquids by yeasts. Robert Graves says that beer goes back
to pre-Hellenic times.

The Bible records that in the desert the children of
Israel had to make do with unleavened bread—so, clearly,
they usually ate leavened (yeast-risen) bread. The yeast
that rose their bread was of the wild or sourdough variety (see Chapter 5).

Skipping down the ages to relatively modern times,
brewers have kept their strains of yeast alive for genera-
tions—they are part of what give various beers their different flavors. For many years brewer's yeast was what
Grandma baked with—she simply went to the brewer
and bought a chunk.

Brewer's yeast (and a related strain called torula
yeast) is very high in B vitamins and protein. When dried
(and no longer alive) it is used as a dietary supplement,
an excellent idea these days when it's all but impossible
to get a broad range of B vitamins in our diet.

By the late nineteenth century Grandma was able to
buy prepackaged cake yeast, a live strain related, but not
identical, to brewer's yeast, with the yeast living in a

dryish—for yeast—medium that was mostly starch. By keeping this cake yeast as cool and dry as she could, she was able to keep a supply of it in her kitchen—until it went moldy.

One of the technological miracles to come out of World War II (along with DDT and nerve gas) was *active dry yeast*, which lasts for years in a dormant state (so long as it is kept dry: wetting it brings it to life).

Active dry yeast is superior in every way to cake yeast.

Cake yeast lives in its food and *is alive*—which means that unless you use it promptly either the yeast will eat all its food and die, or mold will take over. Active dry yeast is *dormant*, so may be kept for years.

Cake yeast is sensitive to temperature, doing its best at about the heat of tepid water, and being killed off by too much heat. Active dry yeast is operative through a broad range of temperatures—approaching 180°! This means that you can use quite hot liquid to start with, which in turn means much *faster* and *stronger* yeast action.

Cake yeast must be mashed in liquid and dissolved before it's ready to go into your recipe. Active dry yeast can be measured right into the bowl with the other ingredients; it begins working as soon as you add some liquid.

Cake yeast must be "proved": that is, after mashing and dissolving, it must be watched for bubbling, to make certain that it's still alive. With active dry yeast, there's no such problem.

So in all those old recipes (including Grandma's) that call for cake yeast, substitute! Where it says a cake of yeast, use a tablespoon of active dry yeast; Grandma will never know the difference.

(If, after all this, you insist on using cake yeast—and heaven knows there are stubborn people in this world—remember: 1 cake of yeast equals 1 tablespoon of dry; the cake must be mashed and proved; and all the liquids in the recipe must be lukewarm.)

I do offer this caution about active dry yeast.

I used to tell my students that there was no difference between either of two active dry yeasts: Fleischmann's, which was more expensive, but premeasured and in dated aluminum packets; and El Molino, available in quarter-pound to pound packages and thus much cheaper, but requiring refrigeration once the cellophane package was opened. Well, it's no longer true. Fleischmann's has taken to using a preservative in their yeast (why a preservative in a sealed packet of dried yeast, I can't imagine)—BHA, one of the preservatives restricted in England but not here. And I can only dis-recommend anything with chemical preservatives.

If you can't find El Molino yeast at a health food store near you, write for their catalogue: El Molino Mills, Alhambra, California. (Walnut Acres, Penns Creek, Pennsylvania, also sells a nonpreserved yeast in bulk.)

Sweeteners
COMPOSITION OF FOODS (100 GRAMS)

	Granulated sugar	Honey	Blackstrap molasses
Food energy (calories)	385	304	213
Protein (gm)	0	0.3	0
Carbohydrates (gm)	99.5	82.3	55
Calcium (mg)	0	5	684
Phosphorous (mg)	0	6	84
Iron (mg)	0.1	0.5	16.1
Sodium (mg)	1	5	96
Potassium (mg)	3	51	2,927
Thiamin (mg)	0	trace	0.1
Riboflavin (mg)	0	0.04	0.19
Niacin (mg)	0	0.3	2.0
Vitamin C (mg)	0	1	0

Based on U.S. Department of Agriculture Handbook No. 8, Composition of Foods.*

Before I say word one about sweeteners, make sure you've cast an eye at the preceding table.

The federal government bears me out—white sugar is, to all intents and purposes, nutrition-free. It has cal-

* Send $2 to: Superintendent of Documents, U.S. Government Printing Office, Washington, D.C. 20402. It's very worthwhile.

ories, it is almost pure carbohydrate, and *it is then value-less as a food.* In addition, once in your system, it will destroy B vitamins.

I urge you in the strongest terms possible to elimi-nate sugar entirely from your diet. My husband and I have.

We use only two sweeteners—for baking, cooking, desserts, beverages, everything—honey and blackstrap molasses.

HONEY

Honey is nectar gathered from flowers by bees (different flowers give you different flavors), predigested by the bees, and then evaporated by them to the thick consis-tency with which you're familiar. It is this predigestion which gives it unique properties. For example, honey can be digested by a stomach too damaged or too sensitive to digest anything else.

Honey has a flavor that far surpasses sugar, and con-tains in addition small amounts of a wide range of vita-mins and minerals—as well as having a *natural preserva-tive power* that can keep your breads fresher quite a long while. Commercial bakers are aware of this preservative power, and you will find commercial breads that contain honey among their ingredients—and no artificial pre-servatives. Sweet breads and cakes made with large amounts of honey can be stored indefinitely.

There are many therapeutic claims made for honey: I know several beekeepers who insist that honey keeps them well and young; other beekeepers have described its curative powers quite convincingly, and my husband has successfully used it as an antiseptic on several occasions.

BLACKSTRAP MOLASSES

Blackstrap molasses is closely related to the granulated sugar that can destroy vitamins in the body. They both come out of the same pot, so to speak.

There is nothing wrong with cane sugar in the cane. It has many vitamins and minerals and, aside from wreak-ing havoc on the teeth, might be highly recommended. However, once that cane sugar is harvested and thrown into the pot for boiling down, what happens is this: the heavier particles, the ones that contain the minerals, sink to the bottom. From the topmost layer—the nutrition-free layer—they take sugar, crystallize it, "refine" it further, and granulate it. This is the valueless part.

From the next layer, they take light molasses—still not worth much nutritionally. From the next layer they take a darker (better) grade of molasses. And from the bottom layer they take blackstrap. It's this bottom layer that contains all the nutritional goodies—huge amounts of all the good minerals and all the vitamins except those that are heat-sensitive.

You can find the lighter grades of molasses in all supermarkets, and the blackstrap in all health food stores. If you decide to buy a lighter grade, at least make certain that you get unsulfured molasses. The sulfuring is a chemical additive that does you no good.

Blackstrap molasses will not extend the freshness of your bread, but it has other remarkable properties: aside from liver, there is no richer natural source of iron available to us, and blackstrap contains traces of copper, which enables the body to absorb that iron; apart from the food values in the table, which show blackstrap also to be a good source of B vitamins (absent from most foods), blackstrap also contains a very wide range of minerals which it's almost impossible to get elsewhere—all this with only two thirds the calories and almost half the carbohydrates of sugar.

Blackstrap molasses has a licorice flavor that doesn't appeal to everyone; however, it's a taste well worth acquiring, and, when used in baking, a taste that disappears into the whole.

OTHER SWEETENERS

There are other sweeteners you may run across in your shopping:

"Raw" or Turbinado sugar. The only thing raw about this is the deal you get. This is sugar with a tiny bit of the minerals re-added—all of 2 percent. That's right, Turbinado sugar is 2 percent better than white sugar—at about three times the price.

Brown sugar. This comes in two grades, light and dark. This sugar is slightly better than white because the color is gotten by adding some molasses to the refined sugar—but then why not use molasses?

Maple sugar. This is quite rich in minerals, but very expensive and not widely available. If you can find it and afford it, by all means use it.

Molasses—other grades. As I said, blackstrap isn't the only grade of molasses. There are two other grades (light and dark—with the dark more nutritious than the light), neither of which is as good as blackstrap, but both of which are tremendously better than white sugar, and there is Barbados molasses, which is absolutely delicious and has virtually no food value (hardly better than white sugar).

In adapting other people's recipes, remember that all sweeteners are interchangeable. If it says 2 tablespoons of sugar, you can substitute 2 tablespoons of honey or of blackstrap. (Actually, honey is slightly sweeter than sugar, so 0.9 honey for 1 sugar would be more accurate.)

You can substitute blackstrap for the honey in any of my recipes that call for a tablespoon or two of honey without much affecting the flavor, but you will affect the color—blackstrap darkens a batter.

Milk

Calcium absorption takes place only in the presence of fat, therefore, children should have whole milk. If a child drinks whole milk, the fat is right there and there is no problem of absorption. If a child drinks nonfat milk, how does he manage calcium absorption?

Just what is whole milk? Certainly not the stuff that passes for whole milk in your supermarket dairy case. Americans stopped drinking really whole milk when pasteurization pushed raw milk off the commercial market.

There were good reasons for pasteurization—what with the diseases that could be spread through milk—but there were alternatives that were ignored because pasteurization was commercially feasible and the alternatives were expensive.

Pasteurization, aside from killing some of the bacteria in the milk, destroys vitamins A, B, and C, enzymes, and calcium, and anything else in the milk that happens to be heat sensitive—including the lecithin which helps our bodies deal with the cholesterol of the fats.

Wherever it's available, children should be given *certified raw milk*—that is, milk which has been neither pasteurized nor homogenized (in homogenization the milk is forced through thin tubes against a hard surface, breaking up the fat molecules permanently, and giving the milk a shelf life of up to ten *days*), and which comes from certified herds. This means that local and federal health departments have inspected the cows, the procedures, and the workers, and found them free from disease—and certified them as such. Certified milk contains fewer bacteria than pasteurized milk. It's a fact.

And that is really *whole* milk.

Adults, conversely, should have nonfat milk.

There is a good deal of medical opinion around that American adults drink *too much* whole milk. Doctors have connected high milk consumption with kidney stones in adults. An old Viennese physician told us of an experiment interrupted by the *Anschluss* which indicated that adults who drank large amounts of milk had lower resistance to disease than adults who didn't. My husband stopped drinking whole milk from that day, and certainly *his* resistance has improved enormously.

Good skim milk is much easier to find than certified raw milk. Most health food stores carry non-instant, low-heat, spray-dried, nonfat milk. The low heat means that much of the goodness is still intact after processing. In the more widely distributed instant skim milks, the milk is dried by a high-heat process which leaves even less vitamin and mineral content than pasteurization.

So, for drinking, by all means try to get the low-heat, spray-dried, nonfat milk.

For baking, however, I use the instant, high-heat, nonfat milk, available in any supermarket. I use powdered milk because of the convenience. It measures so easily (I don't even have to reconstitute it, just pour it right into the bowl), and I never have to worry about warming it up out of the fridge (see Temperature of Ingredients, pp. 18–19).

Fats

So far as the *chemistry* of bread baking is concerned, all fats are interchangeable: oil or butter or margarine or hydrogenated shortenings or lard; for bread baking it makes no real difference. For your health, however, there is more than a little difference.*

You can't live without fats and oils. That's not an exaggeration. The fatty acids the body manufactures from the fats and oils you eat are absolutely vital to your life processes. But not all fats and oils are equally usable.

This brings us to saturated and unsaturated fats.

Think of fats as little charms. The body links these charms together into a charm bracelet called fatty acids. If the links of the charm are open and unattached, they can easily be linked up in these fatty acid chains. If the links are filled already (with hydrogen or oxygen), they cannot be formed into fatty acid chains. Those fats with open links are called unsaturated and are desirable. Those fats with filled links are called saturated and are undesirable.

Margarine is an example of a saturated fat. Most margarines start out as vegetable oils—naturally unsaturated, useful, wholesome. However, to make the margarine solid at room temperature, it is hydrogenated (that is, those once-open links are filled with hydrogen), which makes the fats saturated and undesirable. The situation with lard and "Crisco"-type shortenings is even worse: lard is so heavily "stabilized" today that it needn't even be refrigerated; and "Crisco"-type shortenings are hydrogenated and full of chemicals. (Also, read your margarine box; most margarines have chemicals too.)

There are several breads in this book made without any shortening at all. They are lower in calories than breads made with shortening, but are not of as smooth a texture and dry out faster.

When recipes call for shortening I use and recommend only unsaturated vegetable oils (corn, soy, safflower, etc.). Besides being healthier, vegetable oils are more convenient than hard shortening: they can be measured in the same cup as the honey, without cleaning, they never have to be creamed, and they blend quite easily with the flour.

In buying liquid oils, be careful about preservatives and other additives (some brands have as many as half

---

* While butter and margarine are about the same in terms of saturation, butter is the more desirable because of the chemicals in margarine.

a dozen chemical additives). Read the labels. Just because an oil is liquid doesn't mean that it's wholesome.

Vegetable oils can be among our richest sources of vitamin E (which the federal government has recently conceded is necessary for good health). But the commercial hot-pressing process kills most of the vitamin E—leaving us something unsaturated, but also vitaminless. Baking also tends to kill much of the vitamin E. So, even though we use any type of vegetable oil in our baking, we make certain to use some *cold-pressed oil* every day (unheated, as in a salad dressing), to get some vitamin E.

Eggs

Eggs are a good food. They are fine protein and an excellent source of lecithin. (Did you stop eating eggs when cholesterol became famous? Well, lecithin enables the body to deal with the cholesterol the eggs contain.)

Have you been wondering why the shells on your eggs are so much thinner than they used to be?

The last time you bought eggs directly from a farmer, you may have noticed that not only were the shells thicker but the eggs *tasted* better than supermarket eggs.

It's not your imagination. They have done something to the eggs; or, rather, something to the chickens.

For, no doubt, sound economic reasons, the large-scale chicken farmers from whom most of our eggs come do not allow their chickens to run around and scratch for their food. They are kept in chicken houses that get little daylight or fresh air, and have never a bit of dirt to scratch in. They get a supposedly balanced feed with just enough minerals to produce an egg with just enough shell not to break in transit, an egg that's nutritionally poorer than the ones you had as a kid.

In order to lay a normal egg with a normal shell and normal food values, a chicken has to be able to get out in the sunshine and dirt and scratch around for its food.

That thin shell is symptomatic of what's wrong with so many of our foods today. Chemical feeds and fertilizers are no substitute for good husbandry. Food taken from heavily chemicaled soil and animals is poorer in vitamins and minerals than food taken from plants and animals grown organically.

Occasionally I have the opportunity to get organic eggs from a beekeeper. Not only are the shells thicker but the yolks are yellower, and the taste is vastly superior. I wish you the same opportunity.

In these recipes when I call for eggs, I mean large eggs. One size away—medium or extra large—will not make much difference, but if small eggs happen to be a good buy, substitute small eggs at the rate of three for two.

Salt

Does it seem to you that the salt has lost its savor? Well, in part it has. There are so many chemicals in the free-flowing salt that you buy in your neighborhood supermarket that there is, literally, less salt in the salt.

What is there instead?

Here's the label from the last box of supermarket salt I bought:

CONTAINS SALT
SODIUM SILICO ALUMINATE
DEXTROSE 0.1%
POTASSIUM IODIDE
YELLOW PRUSSIATE OF SODA
SODIUM BICARBONATE

And if that doesn't shake you, what does?

Salt, plus *five* chemicals (though iodine is necessary for health). I had one of my classes taste a ~~bit of that salt~~ and a bit of sea salt—and every student said that the sea salt was saltier. Those chemicals are there in large enough amounts to affect the saltiness of the salt, and you take them at every meal, every day.

You know, I hope, that federal law requires that packagers list ingredients in descending order by amount: that is, the ingredient there is most of comes first. If you'll look at that list again you'll see that "sodium silico aluminate" is listed second, and is therefore the second largest ingredient. I know of no use the body can make of aluminum at all!

What are your options? If you don't want sodium silico aluminate and yellow prussiate of soda and so forth, what can you do?

Our solution has been to switch to sea salt.

Sea salt is evaporated from seawater and comes

either as (relatively) pure sodium chloride (with traces of sea minerals quite vital to life) or as sodium chloride with magnesium carbonate added (both are naturally iodized).

Eating magnesium carbonate is okay because magnesium is needed by the body to help absorb calcium* and most of us—except for those living in Deaf Smith County, Texas, where the high magnesium level of the soil prevents tooth decay and bone fractures—have chronic magnesium deficiencies from eating food grown on chemical fertilizers.

Another option you have is to switch, at least in part, from salt to granulated kelp. Kelp is seaweed, and ground and dried kelp is nutritious and quite tasty—and a little salty as well as particularly high in iodine and calcium. I keep it in a shaker and use it on eggs and meat and any other food where I once used salt.

(Kosher salt, a *coarse* salt good for sprinkling on top of baking breads or pretzels, has only one chemical—polysorbate 80, whatever that is. It is used for the koshering of meats and poultry—that is, the rubbing down of the steak, for instance, to absorb and eliminate blood.)

All the recipes in this book were standardized to the tastes of my students, using saltier salt—sea salt. If you're using four- or five-chemical supermarket salt, you may want to slightly increase the amount called for. Whatever salt you use, don't hesitate to change the amount if it doesn't suit your taste.

Salt has a role in baking aside from bringing out flavors: because salt, in goodly amounts, will destroy microorganisms (including yeast), it functions as a stabilizer in retarding yeast growth.

So there it is: my white flour is unbleached enriched white; my whole grains are stone ground; my milk is powdered skim milk; I use only honey or blackstrap molasses for sweetener; my salt may be saltier than yours; my oil is only vegetable oil, unsaturated and unpreserved; and my yeast is active dry yeast.

* For those of you who want to know more about such things as why magnesium and calcium have to balance, and what a complete protein is, and which vitamins you are likely to be deficient in, I suggest you read Adelle Davis's *Let's Eat Right to Keep Fit*, available in paper from Signet Books.

SOME GENERAL PROCEDURES

The different kinds of breads we'll bake, though all of them yeast breads, have similarities and differences in preparation. The differences will be described in the specific chapters, but here, for easy reference, is a list of some procedures used in making almost any bread.

At the end of the procedures to *do*, you'll find a short list of procedures to *don't*. I would suggest you read that —it may surprise you.

Measurements

I don't own a measuring spoon. You don't need one either, not to bake the breads in this book. A teaspoon or a tablespoon will do equally well. I must admit that I do use a measuring cup—but you don't have to. You could use a teacup for your measuring, and so long as you used the same cup for liquid and flour, the proportions would be correct and the bread would come out fine.

As for whether the cups are level or heaped, packed or loose, it hardly matters. There is no absolute amount of flour, even if you repeat the same bread day after day. The amount of flour will vary according to humidity and temperature, when, where, and how the strain of wheat was grown, and according to how muscular you feel. So any of my recipes that call for a specific amount of flour should have the word "about" in parentheses.

Baking is not an exact science, and those who say "exactly . . ." are kidding you or themselves. Baking deals with physical changes that take place within a very broad range—a broad range of temperatures, and a broad range of chemical proportions.

Temperature of Ingredients

More battles for happy bread baking are won or lost on this battlefield than any other. When we discussed active dry yeast, I told you that it was much more heat resistant than the old cake yeast, and could be stimulated to faster growth by higher temperatures. That's not just an interesting fact. It is a key.

I got a call from a student one day (all my students

get permanent consultation privileges) complaining that a Challah refused to rise. After some questioning (Nero Wolf and I never leave our homes to solve a case) I found that she had used milk from the refrigerator. I reminded her that in class we had used hot water to make up the Challah. "But I let it come to room temperature!" Room temperature for that day was about 70°—roughly half the temperature of the water we had used in class. I told her to give the bread more time and to put it in a warmer place. The Challah eventually rose, and she finally had a successful bread.

So, if you change any of my water recipes to milk, or any cold liquid, heat it—certainly not to boiling, but to the temperature of hot tap water.

Eggs should be at room temperature. If you forget to take them out of the fridge beforehand, put them in a bowl of hot tap water for a few minutes and the temperature will be fine.

Oil should be at room temperature if you are using more than a few tablespoons.

Any cold—or even *cool*—ingredient will slow down the yeast.

That doesn't mean that you are to heat up everything to boiling. If you must heat an ingredient on the stove, stick a finger in to make sure the temperature is bearable. If it doesn't burn you it won't kill the yeast.

All this is especially true when you deal with my New Method Breads. They just won't work if you use cool ingredients.

Rising Dough

Yeast breads rise. The yeast plants make bubbles of carbon dioxide and the elastic gluten expands like balloons filling. Then, in the baking, after the yeast has been killed off, the heat expands the air bubbles further and you get more rise. Some breads rise just in the bowl, like Nan. Some breads rise just in the pan, like Method Breads. Most breads rise both in the bowl and as loaves, like 100 Percent Whole Wheat Bread or Brioches.

If left to their own devices, the yeast plants would make carbon dioxide at a leisurely pace—or, if your kitchen is cool, a quite slow pace. To encourage the yeast to work faster, the dough should be put in a very warm place. For me, the pilot light on my gas range is that place. (For a country friend, a large warm rock out in the summer sun is that place.) I put the bowl of dough on a trivet, cover the bowl, and there the yeast, stimulated by the heat, gases away at a satisfactory rate. So much for dough in the bowl. But what about dough after it has been shaped into loaves? That pilot just isn't big enough for three loaves of whole wheat bread, or two huge Challah. What then? If it's winter there's no difficulty. I put a piece of fieldstone on my kitchen radiator, and put the covered loaves on the stone.

But what about the warmer weather? Here's where you have to be inventive. I rise by hot water, and here's how.

Loaves in pans (especially New Method Breads). I make certain the water is good and hot, and then I run a few inches of water into my sink or bathtub (that's right—I said bathtub). I stand or float the pans of dough in this hot water, and then I take a towel and tent over the sink. (If your bathtub is deep, you needn't tent it over —just make sure the windows and doors are shut against drafts.) Breads will rise in their pans very quickly this way because the warmth surrounds them.

Free-standing loaves on baking sheets. Most baking sheets are too shallow to stand directly in water, so what I do is run the same few inches of water into the sink or bathtub, and invert heavy cups or some similar objects for the baking sheets to balance on—just out of the water. I then tent over as before.

Don't panic if a little water gets onto a loaf or into a pan: just pour it off. I have seen completely drowned loaves bake up very satisfactorily.

You can also rise on the top of the stove—if, like mine, yours gets very hot on the work surface. I light my stove and put my covered loaves on top, then shut the oven off after 15 minutes. Of course, that isn't practical if the particular type of bread you are baking must go into a cold oven. Free-standing loaves risen this way (or by any intense bottom heat) have a tendency to rise *wide* instead of *high*.

Dough can be risen out of the kitchen—on the back of a television set, radio, or hi-fi (but not solid state sets;

they don't generate the heat), or on top of an old-fashioned refrigerator.

If none of these works for you, figure out your own method.

Order of Ingredients

There is nothing sacred about my order of ingredients. I've found it quick and simple, but there is no need to follow it if you prefer some other. Of course, if you decide to put the flour in first or the yeast last, you might have some difficult experiences.

Greasing

You have to grease your loaf pans, casseroles, baking sheets, and so forth, or your breads won't come out. I grease with melted margarine or butter—not *oil*. The vegetable oils (which I use exclusively within the recipes) are polyunsaturated—they have small molecules. The hardened fats, like butter and margarine, are saturated and have *large* molecules. These large molecules make for better greasing because they don't absorb as readily into the bread. This means that more of the grease stays on the pan or baking sheet. Oil's small molecules get absorbed into the bread, which means poor lubrication (and more sticking), and that you actually consume more of the grease.

I brush on the melted margarine with a pastry brush, and find this method very satisfactory. But, if you prefer, you can rub directly with the stick (though this often leaves ungreased spots), or with greased fingers, or with the greasy butter wrapper.

Tests for Doneness

I test for doneness with a thin clean knife, a cake tester (a piece of wire the length of a broom straw), or, occasionally, a toothpick, and here's how I do it.

First of all, turn the bread out of its pan. (This turning out means gripping the rim of the pan with a potholder and turning it upside down onto a clean towel held in your free hand or spread out on some surface. If the bread is stubborn and sticks, work a thin knife around the edges of the pan, then try again.) I turn my breads out (with a few exceptions) so as to test through the bottom of the loaf. You could test through the top, but testing through the bottom leaves the top unscarred, and there's something very satisfying about that "perfect" loaf brought to the table.

Now that you have your turned-out loaf, stick a thin, clean (the *clean* is important—dough sticks to anything) knife or cake tester through the palest part of the bottom, all the way *almost to the top.* If there is any unbaked dough, it will most likely be near the top, so you have to go all the way in. Give the knife or tester a little wiggle from side to side (to enlarge the hole slightly), draw it out, and really give it a squint. You have to distinguish between unbaked dough—which comes out in lumps and if allowed to stay on the knife will harden—and water vapor, which wipes right off. Water vapor is fine, but any unbaked dough means that the loaf must go back to the oven.

I use a toothpick on breads like Brioches and Challah and Method Sally Lunn—and I test these breads through the top. The Challah gets tested at a juncture of a center braid, a Brioche gets tested right at the neck, and Sally Lunn gets hers through any pale place on top (Sally is glazed during baking, and you can't turn her out).

Bottom color can be an indication of doneness, if you know what it should look like. Though I prefer to think of it as a *clue* to when to test.

Thumping is sometimes recommended. You take the turned-out loaf in one hand and thump the bottom with the other. A hollow sound is supposed to say "done." It works sometimes. But sometimes it leaves you with a lovely hollow of undone dough in the middle.

So, for me, knife or cake-tester testing is the only sure way. *And you must test.* There is nothing so disappointing as bringing a lovely-looking loaf to the table and cutting in to find so much mush.

There are few detection devices as good as your nose for telling when a loaf is *approaching* doneness. For as it bakes, the aroma of baking gets quite strong. Even if you think the bread can't possibly be done yet—if it begins to smell good, check it. It may be that a hot spot is scorching one loaf and you'll want to turn it, or the bread may be done. So, if you can smell it—take a look.

Glazes

Glazes are put on a bread to change the taste, color, or texture of the crust, or (most important) to hold on seeds or whatever you sprinkle over the top.

Melted butter or margarine glazes. These should be brushed on when the loaf is removed from the oven and are put on a loaf to give it a shinier look. If you put them on early in the baking, they will give you a browner top, but no shine.

Egg glazes. These can be put on at any time up to the last few minutes of baking (they do require a few minutes of cooking on the loaf) and still come out beautiful. Just smear the egg (yolk or white or whole, according to the recipe) over the surface with your fingers or a pastry brush. An egg glaze can make a loaf *look* done before its time. Don't be fooled.

Honey-and-fruit-juice glaze. This glaze should be spooned over the loaf as soon as it's out of the oven.

Milk glaze. This glaze will give a browner crust to pale breads and rolls; it gets brushed on at the beginning, and can have the effect of softening your crust.

If you forget to put a glaze on at the beginning, don't worry—the middle of the baking will do, too.

If you forget to glaze as soon as the loaf comes out of the oven, don't worry—you can put it on 10 minutes later and still get a shiny effect.

Whisk Cleaning

I like to use a wire whisk to beat the batter in the early stages of mixing. Not that a spoon doesn't do the job—a whisk does it faster. But a whisk (or the beaters of your electric mixer) can be a cleaning problem, with all the batter sticking. Here's what to do. Keep some of the flour to be used handy in a measuring cup. When you want to switch from whisk (or beaters) to spoon or hand, dip the whisk into the flour and wipe everything off into the mixing bowl. The batter and flour wipe off easily and completely.

Pans

You don't have to own every size pan, casserole, and ring mold called for in these recipes. Any recipe for a ring mold will go into small pans, too. But you should be aware that the volume of a pan goes up enormously with only a little change in the dimensions: a pan $8\frac{1}{2}'' \times 4\frac{1}{2}'' \times 2\frac{1}{4}''$ holds 50 percent more than a pan $8'' \times 4'' \times 2''$. So, don't move to another size pan without changing the number of pans. If you don't have two large pans, three small pans will do.

Cooling on a Wire Rack

As a loaf of bread fresh from the oven cools, it gives off water vapor. The vapor from the sides and top goes off into the air. Fine. The vapor from the bottom will also go into the air *if the loaf sits on a wire rack.* If the loaf sits on a dish, table, board, or any similar surface, the condensing water will absorb back into the loaf, making the bottom a little soggy, instead of crisp as it should be. Observe your first loaf on the rack. You'll see the water drops on the surface below—a good reason for keeping the rack off any surface likely to water-stain.

DON'T

Don't Sift Flour. You would sift only if you were afraid of lumps or you wanted an exact measurement. No commercially packaged flour is lumpy today, and in bread baking you don't care about exact measurements. So don't make extra work for yourself. Worse yet, if you were to sift whole-grain flours you could be discarding some of the healthiest parts.

Don't "Pre-soften" Yeast. The only yeast I recommend in this book (apart from grow-it-yourself sourdough) is active dry yeast. Only cake yeast needs to be presoftened or proved or made into a sponge—which I won't explain here because you don't need to know it. Active dry yeast goes right into the bowl, dry. If you dissolve it in water first, you're wasting time and effort, and will only give yourself an additional dish to wash. I hate washing dishes—which is one reason most of the recipes in this book are one-bowl recipes.

Don't Break Eggs into a Separate Bowl. That's a hangover from the good old days when the chances were that in any dozen eggs you'd find one that was bad. It's been fifteen years since I've had a bad egg. Again, it's just extra work and extra dishes.

Don't Scald Milk. Unless you bake with raw milk, don't scald milk. Scalding was done to destroy certain milk enzymes that retarded yeast growth. The milk was heated to just below boiling, and then cooled to room temperature. Pasteurization gets rid of most of those same enzymes, if you insist on using whole milk. But I do strongly recommend powdered milk instead. It's much easier.

Don't Preheat Oven. Unless the recipe specifically says so, don't preheat. The baking times I give (and God knows they'll be different for your oven anyhow) are, except for those recipes that call for preheating, for cold ovens—that is. starting *below* 200°.

☞ 2 ☜

New
Method
Breads

*Though this be madness, yet
there is method in't.*

Color it 5 P.M. Color dinner for 6:30. Color yourself with
the sudden desire for fresh bread with dinner. What can
you have? Brown-and-serve rolls? Something from the
bakery? Baking powder biscuits?

No! You can have fresh, homemade, steaming-from-
the-oven yeast bread, made on the spot by you *in an hour
and a half or less*, without kneading, without special equipment, without special skill—and without preservatives or
chemical additives. You can have New Method Breads,
*and still have plenty of time to cook the rest of dinner,
even if you've never baked before!* These breads are so
simple it's hard to believe.

I discovered this method by mistake, in one of my
baking classes.

The class was running late and a Cheese Batter Bread
was last on the agenda. After the batter was beaten (I
was watching the testing of a Pumpernickel that refused
to get done), a student poured the batter directly into
greased pans instead of setting it in a bowl to rise. (This
rising in the bowl is a procedure common to all Batter
Breads and Kneaded Breads.) I "rescued" the batter and
put it to rise for the prescribed hour ("then punch down
and rise for 30 minutes . . ."). Well, as I'd feared, the
session broke up before the bread was baked, and everyone left with a complete disinterest in Batter Breads.
After all—this was a class with three weeks experience

in Kneaded Breads. They enjoyed kneading, were good at it, and found it satisfying. If a bread was going to take that long—they'd rather do a Kneaded Bread, thank you very much.

Later, I got to wondering what would have happened if I hadn't fixed that mistake. In fact, why should I rise the batter at all?

And the only reason was that recipes for batter breads say so.

Well, that wasn't reason enough. Recipes tell you to do all kinds of things you don't have to do.

So, I tried a batch and didn't rise the batter in the bowl at all. Just as that student had done accidentally, I turned the batter into baking pans as soon as I'd beaten it, then gave it just a 20-minute rise in the pans. And the result was a Cheese Method Bread, completed in less than 1½ hours—*the time it originally took just to rise the batter bread.*

Kneaded Breads, Batter Breads, and New Method Breads—just what are the differences?

Every bread starts with a "batter"; that's the sticky glop in your bowl when you've mixed in all the ingredients except, perhaps, the last bit of flour.

If you add that last flour and knead it on a board, then shape the dough, you have Kneaded Bread—and, believe me, there's nothing in the world like Kneaded Bread for evenness of texture and "picture-perfect" loaves.

If, to return to that sticky glop in your bowl, you didn't add that last bit of flour, but beat the batter, and let it rise once, twice, even three times for from 1½ to 3 hours—you have Batter Breads—very good, especially if you can't—or won't—knead.

If you beat the batter and then pour it directly into a greased baking pan to rise for 20 minutes, and then bake it, you have New Method Breads: every bit as good as Batter Breads that take three times as long to prepare, and without the work of Kneaded Breads.

Don't mistake me, these are not no-work breads. These are yeast breads, and all yeast breads must be worked somewhat to develop the gluten—the protein part of the flour that makes it elastic or rubbery when you handle it. This elasticity holds the air bubbles formed by

the yeast and allows yeast breads to rise. Either beating
or kneading will develop the gluten. Both are work.
Kneaded Breads must be worked for anywhere from 10 to
20 minutes—Method Breads are *beaten* a total of 4 to 6
minutes.

In the next chapter we'll take up kneading, but now,
even before you've kneaded a single bit of dough, you
can follow these four quick and easy steps that take you
from a great idea to a delicious light yeast bread:

1. Mix and beat the ingredients in one bowl with
one spoon.

2. Dump this resulting batter into greased baking
pans immediately.

3. Leave these pans in a warm place to rise for only
20 minutes. (This allows rising action to begin—rising will
finish during the next step.)

4. Put them in a cold oven and bake.

Details of what you'll see during the baking (yes, you
can open the oven during baking without collapses) ac-
company the individual recipes. Here are a few general
hints.

GENERAL HINTS

☞ In all the recipes, you'll notice that I call for
vigorous beating of the batter *before* all the flour is in.
The why is very simple; it's much easier to beat a thin
mixture with 3 cups of flour than a heavy, almost solid
mixture with $4\frac{1}{2}$. The gluten is developed in the thinner
batter, and it does save muscle power.

To save even more muscle, you might want to use an
electric mixer for this part of the work. There's no real
time saving. You substitute 1 minute of electric beating
at a medium speed for 3 minutes of hand beating, but
then you have to clean the beaters. (Dip them in some of
the remaining flour and rub the batter off with your
fingers.)

☞ Fill your pans *less than half full* of the batter.
Unless it is a very small pan, filling more than halfway
leads to possible sagging and, in any case, to an increase
in baking time.

☞ All these recipes for New Method Breads make (as you might guess) New Method Rolls. Use a muffin tray—or trays—greasing them and filling each mold with a ball or lump of dough a little more than halfway (yes, that's okay for rolls—they never sag), and bake for about 25 minutes in a slow (325°) oven.

☞ Do not preheat your oven. It is basic to Method Breads that they start in a cold oven; in this way the yeast is given a last chance to grow before baking kills it off. However, the dough continues to rise even after the yeast is dead—the heat expands the bubbles that have already been made.

If you have been using your oven before you begin your bread making, shut it off for a while and leave the door open; bring the temperature down below 200° before you put in your bread and relight.

HERB METHOD BREAD

If there is a *basic* Method Bread, this is it. We give the recipe here as an Herb Bread, but: if you omit the herbs, you have plain White Method Bread; if you substitute whole wheat flour for some of the white, you have Tan Method Bread; juggle the herbs, spices, and flavorings and you have a sweeter or spicier loaf.

The web (the arrangement of holes you see in the slice of bread) has a coarse, homemade look that is most satisfying, and the loaf has a rough texture unlike any packaged or bakery bread.

Since it cuts well (even slicing thin when cool), it is good for making hearty sandwiches. Or, hot, tear it apart as you would a Garlic Bread.

Hot or cooled, sliced or torn, this one is an exciting introduction to Method Breads.

HERB METHOD BREAD

For the Batter:
   2 tbsp. active dry yeast
   1 tsp. dill seed
   1 tsp. savory
   ½ tsp. dill weed
   1 tbsp. sea salt
   2 tbsp. honey
   2 cups hot water
   ⅔ cup skim milk powder
   4½ cups unbleached white flour
For Greasing:
   butter or margarine
Equipment:
   mixing bowl, mixing spoon, 2 loaf pans 8½″ × 4½″ ×
   2½″ (also, if you like, wire whisk and rubber spatula)

Mixing

Measure the **yeast** (2 tablespoons of yeast is the same as
2 packages of yeast is the same as ½ ounce of yeast),
herbs, salt, honey, hot water, and **skim milk powder** into
one large bowl and stir with a spoon or wire whisk until
the honey is dissolved. (The mixture will look quite
strange—a murky white with flecks of green herbs ap-
pearing and disappearing.)

Add the **first 3 cups of flour,** a cup at a time, stirring
gently until you have wetted the flour; the flour will fly
all over the kitchen if beaten energetically while still dry.

When you have the 3 cups of flour all wet, beat the
resulting batter *vigorously* for about 3 minutes, or beat it
lazily for 5 minutes (or with an electric beater at medium
speed for 1 minute). It's the number of movements that
counts, not the violence. You don't have to exhaust yourself to make good bread. Remember, we beat now to save
some hard work later.

Add the **next cup of flour,** about ¼ cup at a time, and
beat for another minute or so, even though it's harder now.
If you've been using a wire whisk, you'll want to shift at
this point to a spoon. If you find the batter too stiff to
beat with a spoon, work it with your bare hand for a
couple of minutes, squeezing the batter through your
fingers. Don't be afraid to touch it; getting sticky can be
fun.

Work in the **last ¼ cup of flour** well.

(The dough is ready when, as you pull the spoon or your hand from the batter, the mixture forms into rubbery sheets.)

Filling the Pans

Grease well two baking pans 8½″ × 4½″ × 2½″ (don't get thrown by the figures—that's a standard size). Don't forget to grease the top rim, we want the loaves to turn out of the pans easily.

Dump half the batter into each pan, dividing as equally as you can.

It's not easy to get the batter out of the mixing bowl and divided—it's very cohesive now and still sticky, and has to be helped out of the bowl and then poked into the corners of the pans. Corners that aren't filled now stay unfilled, making air pockets. I find the back of a greased spoon (or just a bare greased hand) handy for poking into unfilled corners and for smoothing out the top of the loaf. You can't make the top perfectly smooth; a rough top is one of the marks of this kind of bread.

Unless you are using very small pans, fill your pans *less than half full*. If you have too much batter for your two pans, grease a muffin pan and use the excess to make some Method Rolls.

Resting the Batter

Once the batter is turned into the pans, cover them with a clean towel and put them in a very warm place for 20 minutes (see Rising, pp. 19–21).

Baking

After 20 minutes—the batter has risen slightly—put the pans into a *cold oven* and light a low flame. (If your oven has a thermostat, set for 200°–250° for the first 10 minutes, and then raise to 350°–375°.)

Bake for about 50 minutes, total.

If, like mine, your oven has hot spots, look at the loaves after about 20 minutes and, if they are browner on one side, rotate them.

When done, the tops of the loaves should have an even, chocolate-brown color and the bottoms and sides should be golden brown.

Turn the loaves out and test for doneness (see pp. 21–23).

When finished, cool the loaves on a wire rack or bring them right to the table steaming hot, and tear apart or cut gently with a serrated knife. (They are easier to cut when cooled, but taste better when hot.)

Options

☞   As soon as the loaves are removed from the oven and turned out, brush the tops with **melted butter or margarine** for a shiny, happier look.

☞   If you're baking for children, use **2 cups of whole milk** instead of the water and skim milk powder. Richer yet, use whole milk *and* milk powder. (See pp. 12–13.)

☞   To make Tan Method Bread, substitute **2 cups of whole wheat flour** and **2 cups of white flour** for the 4½ cups of white in the recipe. That ½ cup is left out because whole wheat flour absorbs more water than white.

☞   Another excellent herb combination is **1 teaspoon basil, 1 teaspoon oregano,** and **½ teaspoon tarragon.** Or **caraway** can be substituted happily for the dill seeds.

☞   You can substitute **celery salt, garlic salt, dill salt,** or any **seasoned salt** to your liking for half the salt in the recipe.

☞   **Half a teaspoon of fresh-ground pepper** added to your favorite herb batter makes a delightful Pepper Herb Bread.

☞   Try any combination, using between 2 and 3 teaspoons of your favorite herbs: only you know what you like.

☞   Add **2 tablespoons of any unsaturated vegetable oil** to the recipe to improve its keeping power—though, in our house, keeping this bread is never a problem: it's always eaten within two days.

☞   Substitute **½ cup of wheat germ** for the last ½ cup of flour.

HERB METHOD BREAD—SUMMARY

    A. 2 tbsp. active dry yeast   B. 4½ cups flour
       1 tsp. dill seed
       1 tsp. savory
       ½ tsp. dill weed
       1 tbsp. sea salt
       2 tbsp. honey
       2 cups hot water
       ⅔ cup skim milk powder

Measure A into a large mixing bowl and stir.

Add 3 cups of B, 1 cup at a time, and beat vigorously for 3 minutes by hand (1 minute by electric beater).

Add fourth cup of B, ¼ cup at a time, and beat for another minute or so.

Work last ½ cup of B in well.

Grease two 8½″ × 4½″ × 2½″ loaf pans.

Scrape in the batter, poke it into all the corners, smooth the top with greased fingers or spatula.

Rise in hot water or in a warm place, covered, for 20 minutes.

Bake for 10 minutes at 200°–250°, then for 40 minutes at 350°–375°.

Knife-test for doneness.

Cool on a wire rack and eat hot.

PEANUT METHOD BREAD

This may be the world's fastest bread. The last loaf I baked took me just one hour and five minutes from start to finish, not including the time it takes to shell enough peanuts for half a cup. I recommend my no-work method for shelling—I get my husband to do it. (Since all nuts keep best in the shell, don't shell them too long before your baking.)

I grind the nuts right into the mixing bowl with a Mouli grater—really excellent for this—leaving whatever chunks leap out of the grater right there in the bowl.

To save time, you can use a half cup of peanut butter. In some stores you can buy fresh, ground-while-you-wait peanut butter—much healthier than the homogenized commercial kinds whose oils are hardened to keep longer

on the shelf. The healthier fresh-ground kind is not homogenized: it doesn't keep as long (all healthly oils have
a relatively short life and require refrigeration), but is
much better for you and your children.

If you use salted nuts—the last resort—reduce the
salt in the recipe by a half teaspoon. (The salt doesn't so
much keep the nuts from going rancid as it keeps you
from tasting the slight rancidity of the peanut oil.)

Peanut Method Bread is best finished by hand. Beat
in the first 2½ cups of flour by spoon, whisk, or electric
beater; then work in the last ½ cup of flour by squeezing
the batter between your fingers; then continue by hand
for an additional 2 minutes. This is quite a dry batter, and
it will divide easily and go into the baking cans without
trouble.

You'll see in the recipe that this is a tan bread—half
whole wheat and half unbleached white flour. This, together with the peanuts (which are high in protein), makes
it an ideal bread for children: it's healthy, and the coffee-
can shape of the loaves makes attractive—and different
—round sandwiches.

If you've got a problem eater, this bread may be a
partial solution, especially if you use the dough scraped
off your hand to make his initial on the top of the loaf.
The scrapings are enough for one fat initial.

PEANUT METHOD BREAD

        For Batter:
            2 tbsp. active dry yeast
            ¼ cup honey
            2 tsp. sea salt
            1¼ cups hot water
            ½ cup shelled peanuts
            1½ cups whole wheat flour
            1½ cups unbleached white flour
        For Greasing:
            butter or margarine
        Equipment:
            large bowl, mixing spoon, two 1-pound coffee cans

Mixing

Measure the **yeast, honey, salt,** and **water** into a large
mixing bowl and stir well, dissolving the honey.

Grate in ½ cup of shelled, roasted peanuts. Stir.

Add **1 cup of whole wheat flour,** and mix in.

Add **1 cup of white flour,** and mix in.

When the flours are thoroughly wet, beat vigorously by hand for 2 minutes, or moderately for 3 minutes (or by electric mixer for 1 minute).

Add the last ½ cup of **whole wheat flour** and stir.

Add the last ½ cup of **white flour** and work in by hand (one hand is enough), squeezing the dough and turning it to get in all the flour.

Continue to work by hand for another 2 minutes.

Filling the Cans

Grease well two 1-pound coffee cans. It is especially important to grease coffee cans generously because the ridges tend to hold the bread in.

Divide the batter in half and put half into each coffee can—filling less than half full: below the second ridge of a 3-ridge can.

The claylike dough you scrape from your hand is enough to make an initial (or design) on top of one loaf. By now the dough will roll easily between your palms.

Resting the Batter

Cover the cans with a clean towel and put into a very warm place to rise for 20 minutes.

There will be little evidence of rising: don't panic.

Baking

Put into a cold oven, set at medium (about 375°), and bake for 30–35 minutes.

If you peek after 10 minutes, you'll see some rising. In all, the dough about doubles before it's finished.

One sign of approaching doneness is a browning of the top. (Don't forget that this is a tan bread to begin with.) If after 30 minutes the top hasn't begun to brown —let it go for a while longer.

When the top has begun to brown, turn a loaf out of its coffee can and test through the bottom for doneness (see pp. 22–23). When the loaf is done, the sides and bottom have a dark, golden brown look.

If you've made an initial or design on the top, it will stand out beautifully because it bakes darker than the rest of the top.

Cool the loaves on a wire rack or eat them hot.

This bread slices beautifully, and has an even, fine web—honey won't drip through.

Options

☞ If your family really loves peanuts, use **more nuts** in the recipe and include more unground nuts.

☞ You might try another nut altogether—say, **filberts or walnuts.**

☞ If you use a 1½-quart casserole you'll get an even crisper crust because the thick sides of the casserole hold the heat. In this case, you'll have enough dough left over for a couple of rolls. The casserole takes 20 minutes longer to bake: 45–50 minutes at the same temperature. The rolls (dropped onto a greased cookie sheet or muffin pan) should be ready in less than 25 minutes.

☞ For an even higher-protein and lower-starch bread, substitute gluten flour for the white flour (see Gluten Flour, p. 5). If you do, double the salt in the recipe.

PEANUT METHOD BREAD—SUMMARY

A. 2 tbsp. active dry yeast
¼ cup honey
2 tsp. sea salt
1¼ cups hot water

B. ½ cup shelled peanuts

C. 1½ cups whole wheat flour

D. 1½ cups white flour

Measure A into a large bowl and stir.

Grate in B.

Mix in 1 cup of C.

Mix in 1 cup of D. Beat vigorously for 2 minutes by hand (1 minute by mixer).

Stir in last ½ cup of C.

Work in last ½ cup of D by hand, then work for 2 more minutes.

Grease well two 1-pound coffee cans.

Cheese Method Bread makes up into a wet-looking batter. In fact, the batter stays so relatively thin that it's possible to use a wire whisk throughout. When you're ready to dump the batter into the coffee cans and/or casseroles, you merely spoon the mixture in.

But this doesn't mean that the batter is not elastic. It is. It will show that rubbery-sheeting look when you dip out the spoonfuls. If it doesn't, beat it some more.

CHEESE METHOD BREAD

For Batter:
2 tbsp. active dry yeast
3 tbsp. honey
1 tbsp. sea salt
2 cups hot water
⅔ cup skim milk powder
2 tbsp. vegetable oil
2 cups unbleached white flour (more to come)
1 large egg
6 oz. cheese (grates to 2 cups)
3 more cups unbleached white flour
For Greasing:
butter or margarine
Equipment:
mixing bowl, spoon or whisk, cheese grater, two 1-pound coffee cans and 1½-quart casserole

Mixing

Measure the **yeast, honey, salt, water,** and **milk powder** into your mixing bowl and stir well.
minute.

Mix in the **oil.**

Add **2 cups of flour** and stir well until you have a smooth, creamy mixture.

Beat the **egg** in well.

Cut the **cheese** into grater-size chunks and grate directly into the bowl. Don't mind if some bits of the cheese remain chunks instead of getting grated. Stir the cheese in well.

Add the **third cup of flour** and beat for 1 minute.

Add another ½ **cup of flour** and beat for another

Add the **remaining flour** ½ cup at a time and work in well with your spoon or whisk. Because of the amount of flour, this recipe takes longer to work up than, say, Peanut Method Bread did, but it should still take less than an hour and a half altogether.

By the time you've worked in all the flour well, the batter is ready to turn into pans for baking. The batter will still look wettish—especially compared to the Peanut Method.

Filling the Cans

Grease well two 1-pound coffee cans and a 1½-quart casserole, filling each about one third full. If you don't have a casserole, make four 1-pound coffee can loaves, or simply use loaf pans.

Resting the Batter

Cover with clean towels and put into a very warm place to rise for 20 minutes. (Try the hot-water technique, p. 20. The two coffee cans will fit in a large spaghetti pot.)

There will only be a little rise after 20 minutes; not to worry.

Baking

Put into a cold oven and bake at a medium temperature (about 350°).

The 1-pound coffee cans take about 30 minutes, and are done when the top of the loaf begins to go brown. But test, don't guess (see pp. 21–23).

The casserole takes about 40 minutes to bake and forms a lovely golden-brown top when it's done. Again, turn the loaf out when you think it's done and test it.

Cool on a wire rack or bring it right to the table and tear it apart. You'll be glad you made more than one loaf.

Options

☞ Use more or less **cheese** to your taste; or try another kind of cheese.

☞ Try a Tan Cheese Bread, by using **2 cups of whole wheat flour** and 2½ cups of white for the total flour in the recipe.

☞ Substitute ½ cup of wheat germ (preferably raw) for ½ cup of the flour.

CHEESE METHOD BREAD—SUMMARY

A. 2 tbsp. active dry yeast
   3 tbsp. honey
   1 tbsp. sea salt
   2 cups hot water
   ⅔ cup skim milk powder

B. 2 tbsp. oil

C. 5 cups flour

D. 1 large egg

E. 6 oz. cheese

Measure A into a large mixing bowl and stir.
Add B.
Add 2 cups of C and mix well until smooth.
Add D and beat in well.
Grate in E and stir in well.
Add 1 cup of C and beat vigorously for 1 minute.
Beat in ½ cup of C for 1 minute.
Work in remains of C, ½ cup at a time, working in well.
Grease well two 1-pound coffee cans and a 1½-quart casserole, filling each about one third full.
Cover and rise in a warm place for 20 minutes. (Hot water recommended.)
Set in a cold oven and bake at 350° for 30 minutes for the coffee cans and 40 minutes for the casserole.
Knife-test for doneness.
Cool on a wire rack, or bring to the table hot.

METHOD SALLY LUNN

For flavor, texture, and seniority Sally Lunn is without doubt the queen of the Batter Breads.

Sally Lunn was an Englishwoman who is supposed to have sold these "cakes" in the resort town of Bath, sometime around the end of the eighteenth century.

And very like a European coffee cake it is: light and spongy in texture, yellow in color, with a flavor that is distinctively its own; it can be eaten plain, but is all the better for a sweet glaze; it is also one of the best toasters you will ever find. Or serve it with fruit preserves or honey and butter—even ice it as a cake.

Sally cuts well when hot—just use a serrated knife and saw gently; she even slices thin.

This is a perfect Method Bread for ring molds, or for long loaf pans. This recipe makes enough for two good-sized loaves or three rings.

One caution: Sally Lunn works up somewhat stickier than other New Method Breads. I handle this problem with a greased spoon and poke Sally into place and smooth the top easily.

Sally takes no longer than any other Method Bread—in fact, the last time I made it I made one ring and one large loaf: the ring was out in an *hour and fifteen minutes* from first measurement to turning out.

So by all means try this jewel of a Method Bread—and let your family eat cake.

METHOD SALLY LUNN

For Batter:
>   2 tbsp. active dry yeast
>   1 tsp. sea salt
>   ⅓ cup honey
>   1 cup hot water
>   ⅓ cup skim milk powder
>   ½ cup vegetable oil
>   2 cups unbleached white flour (more to come)
>   3 large eggs
>   2 more cups unbleached white flour

For Greasing:
>   butter or margarine

For Glaze:
>   1 tbsp. honey
>   juice of ½ orange
>   peel of ½ orange, grated

Equipment:
>   large mixing bowl, small bowl, 3 ring molds (or loaf pans), spoon

Mixing

Measure the **yeast, salt, honey, hot water,** and **milk powder** into a large bowl and mix well.

Stir in the **oil.**

Add **2 cups of flour,** mixing the whole into a paste.

Break in the **eggs** and mix until it's all smooth. (See Temperature of Ingredients, pp. 18–19.)

Add a **third cup of flour** and beat by hand for a few minutes, as vigorously as you can, or for 1 minute with an electric beater at medium speed.

Add the **remaining flour** ½ cup at a time, working it in very well. This working-in by spoon takes the place of beating, so don't skimp on it—there should be no excess flour visible on the bottom of the bowl or on the sides. When all the flour is worked in, the mixture should be elastic and ready; it will show that rubbery-sheeting look mentioned earlier. If you find the mixture too difficult to stir by spoon—*handle* it. All Method Breads are the better for extra handling.

Filling the Pans

Grease your pans well: three 8½″ × 4½″ × 2½″ pans, or three 9-inch diameter by 2-inch depth ring molds, or two 12¾″ × 4½″ × 2½″ pans—or some combination of pans and rings.

Turn the batter into the greased pans—which is easier said than done. This is a most cohesive batter and requires a great deal of urging to come out of its bowl. However, you can help the batter out with a greased spoon or spatula, or you can even use your greased hand.

With the same greased spoon, spatula, or hand, poke the batter into the corners of the pan. If you don't, you'll get air pockets—no great tragedy, but not desirable.

Try to smooth the batter out; tap down those peaks. If you leave them you get a rough top—also no tragedy.

With Sally Lunn it's especially important to remember to fill the pans *less than half full*. Sally rises. And the fuller the pan, the heavier the result.

Resting the Batter

Cover with a clean towel and put in a warm place for 20 minutes. The rising will be noticeable.

Baking

Start in a cold oven, set for medium-low, 350°.

Baking times will vary with the pans you use, from 30 minutes for ring molds, to 45 minutes for large pans.

Test with a toothpick for doneness (see p. 22).

Glazing

While the loaves are in the oven, gather together and combine into a small bowl **1 tablespoon of honey,** the **juice of ½ orange,** and the **peel of ¼ orange,** grated.

When you have stirred the glaze ingredients together, pull the racks half out of the oven and spoon the glaze over the loaves. Do be gentle. Sally is a lady in a delicate condition at this stage, very susceptible to denting from rough handling. The glaze can go on any time during the baking—or afterwards if you forget. It doesn't really matter.

Return the rack to the oven to conclude the baking.

When done, the loaves will look a mixture of yellow, brown, and gold on top. So don't depend on color—test.

Cooling

Allow to cool in the pan for a few minutes, then turn out directly onto a serving plate, for serving hot.

Sally can bake while you are eating your dinner—and be served hot for dessert.

Options

☞ Use **1 cup of whole milk** instead of the hot water and skim milk powder, but if so, *warm the milk.*

☞ You might prefer **lemon** to orange for your glaze.

☞ For Method Holiday Bread (any holiday) add **4 ounces of chopped dried fruits** (pineapple, apricots, figs) to the batter after all the flour is in.

☞ **Raisins** and **chopped dates**—½ cup of fruit per loaf—make a Method Dressy Bread. If you use this combination, then glaze before baking: the glaze protects the raisins from burning.

☞ **Chopped nuts** can be added to Method Holiday Bread or Method Dressy Bread.

☞ Glazing is not mandatory; Sally is quite able to stand on her own, a delicate and sweet—but not too sweet—girl.

you something that looks like real bread, and something that even feels like real bread (with a crisp crust), but for flavor bakery loaves don't compare to the French Bread you can make at home. You have to go to France to get French Bread this good (and I understand it's getting tougher to find good bread there, too).

The ingredients used in a commercial bakery just aren't as wholesome as those you use at home. They cut corners for profit; you don't have to. They use preservatives and chemical substitutes; you can use natural, wholesome ingredients. Furthermore, they make a loaf to suit the general public; you can make a loaf to suit your own taste.

Of course, the commercial baker has some advantages over the home baker, too. His oven gives uniform heat; I know mine and yours don't. He gets ample heat from the top as well as the bottom. We don't. And the baker of French Bread can use live steam in his oven—and this we can only approximate. But we'll do our best.

And our best will be pretty good.

We'll spray our loaves with water three times to give crust, and keep a pan of water in the bottom of the oven to raise the humidity during baking.

We'll use cornmeal on the baking sheets to give the loaves good, crunchy bottoms (that being the only part we can't spray).

We'll start with a cold oven to give the long strips of shaped dough plenty of chance to rise into high, light loaves.

All of which is considerably less trouble than it sounds. Especially for a bread which is not only tasty and a treat for the eyes, but the lowest calorie bread in this book.

FRENCH BREAD

For Dough:
    1½ tbsp. active dry yeast
    1 tbsp. honey
    1 tbsp. sea salt
    2 cups hot water
    6–7 cups unbleached white flour
For Greasing:
    melted butter or margarine
    sprinkling of cornmeal
Equipment:
    large mixing bowl, mixing spoon or whisk, kneading
    board, 2 baking sheets

Mixing

Into a large mixing bowl, measure the **yeast, honey,** and **salt.** Mix. (As soon as yeast meets either honey or water, you're making bread.)

Add the **hot water** (straight from the tap, if your tap gives good hot water), and stir. The yeast hasn't dissolved yet, but it is swelling and multiplying and making the water cloudy.

Add about **2 cups of flour** and stir in with a whisk or spoon.

Mix in **2 more cups of flour.** By now that spoon or whisk is a hindrance, so clean it off into the bowl (see pp. 12–13).

Add the **fifth cup of flour** and work it in with your hand.

Dump the **sixth cup of flour** onto your kneading board, spread it around, and scrape the dough out of the bowl onto this flour. A rubber or plastic scraper is handy for this transfer.

Kneading

Knead in this sixth cup of flour.

When the 6 cups of flour are worked in, you must decide if there is enough flour in the dough—and so we approach the moment of truth.

When there is enough flour, the dough will tend to *stop sticking to your hands* and will allow itself to be formed into a cohesive mass, something you can hold in one hand, palm down, while it falls slowly to the board.

When there is enough flour, the dough will have a smooth feeling as you rub your hands over its surface.

If you feel the dough wants more flour (and if your hands aren't sticking I'd say it doesn't—for this light bread we want to use as little flour as we can get away with, not as much flour as we can force in), dump another ½ cup onto the board and work it in. This recipe should hold no less than 6 cups of flour—and no more than about 7 cups. If you go past 8 cups you're on your way to Italian Bread (delicious, too, but something else, as you'll see when we get to it).

When the dough has enough flour, continue to knead for another 10 minutes. The dough should work easily. A light dusting of flour on the board now and then is a help—but that means a light dusting of flour, not a thick layer. Just enough to keep your dough from adhering to the board.

As you knead, you'll feel the resistance of the dough change from soft as pudding to something that actually seems to be pushing back against your hands. From being utterly pliant, it becomes something that wants to keep its own shape.

When you feel resistance grow, you're getting there.

After 10 minutes, the dough should have quite a smooth feel to it, and should show, when you look at a surface, the characteristic "wrinkles" that indicate when a dough has been kneaded enough. These "wrinkles" make the surface of the dough look somewhat like a textured paint job—not rough or coarse, just faintly textured.

If you're not sure after 10 minutes, knead for a few minutes more and look again. You can't hurt a bread by kneading too much, but if you don't knead enough, the dough won't hold its shape well in the loaf—it will sag, which seems a rather drastic way to find out that you haven't kneaded enough.

First Rise

After you've admired your kneaded ball of dough for a little while, pour a few drops of oil (or melted butter or margarine) into the same mixing bowl (you needn't wash it); put the ball of dough in; turn the dough over to oil the other sides; cover the bowl with a clean towel; and place it in a draft-free, warm place to rise for about an hour (see Rising Dough, pp. 19–21).

The rising time will depend on several variables (the general temperature of your kitchen, the warmth right under your bowl, the heaviness of your dough—to name a few), so rather than depending on a specific timing, use these guides: (1) look at the ball of dough—it will look much risen, taking up more than twice as much room in the bowl; and (2) when it looks that much bigger, use the finger test.

Finger Test

Gently insert into the dough (not in the center but near the side of the bowl where there is less surface tension and things are less dry) one or two fingers, halfway to the first knuckle—about half an inch. Wiggle them gently— to free them from the sticky dough—and draw them out again. Now watch. If the indentation you've made remains more or less intact, the dough has risen enough to "punch down." If the hole gradually fills itself, re-cover the bowl and let the dough rise for a while longer (say, 15 minutes).

If you attempt to bake bread that hasn't risen suffi- ciently, you'll get hard, heavy stuff—great for doorstops and for heaving through windows during riots, but no treat for you or your family. (There are places you can skimp in baking—I know I cut a lot of time corners in my classes because I've just got to get all the breads on the schedule finished before it gets late. But one place I have learned never to skimp is in the time for the first rise.)

Make certain, when you're finger testing, that you don't poke too strongly or too deeply. If you do, it will be like puncturing a balloon and you'll have to knead it all down and begin to rise your dough all over again.

OK, that's no tragedy. It can happen that a cat sits on the towel and punches it down for you prematurely. As long as your dough is still clean, you have lost nothing but time. Work it back to its original size and let it rise until it passes the finger test.

Remember, the speed of this first rise depends on the bowl being kept warm and out of drafts (the towel helps keep the drafts out and the heat in): in a cool place it can take all day to rise. So, if you wish, you can deliberately leave your dough in a nonwarm place and go out to the movies, expecting it to be sufficiently risen by the time you get back. Bread making doesn't chain you to the oven.

It happens sometimes, while you are at the movies, that your dough will rise as much as it wants, and then fall of its own accord. (You can tell because the dough adheres to the sides of the bowl, but sags in the middle.) Fine. Bakeries sometimes use this voluntary collapse to tell when their dough is ready to punch down. If that happens to you, you can skip the finger test because the dough has done it for itself.

Punching Down

When the dough has risen enough, make a fist and punch it down. When I say "punch it down," that's what you really do; make a fist and punch down through the risen dough. The dough will make a soft hissing noise as the gas is forced out, and that's what you're trying to do—get out most of the gas that's just been released into the bread from the yeast action.

Knead out the rest of the gas bubbles—either in the bowl or on your kneading board. (The dough shouldn't be sticky, but a light flouring of the board will help if it is.) This should take no more than a minute or so. Now you're not *kneading* to develop the gluten, but, rather, *squeezing* to get rid of the larger bubbles—all this to give you an even texture.

Shaping the Loaves

This recipe will make four fair-sized loaves. Cut the dough into four pieces. Don't be misled by the apparent smallness of the pieces of dough—they will really rise.

With your hands starting in the center, roll the pieces in long, thin "baguettes" about 1½ inches thick, the traditional shape for French Bread.

If you prefer, make some other shape that appeals to you: round for Portuguese Bread, eight small pieces for individual loaves, or even smaller for *Petits Pains* (see Options, pp. 58–59).

Grease two baking sheets and then sprinkle them

lightly with **yellow cornmeal,** shaking the pan from side to side make an even layer.

Place the shaped loaves onto these sheets, leaving plenty of room for them to rise and spread. You don't want the loaves to touch in the baking.

Again cover with clean, dry towels, and again put them into a warm, draft-free place to rise.

Second Rise

This bread, as any classic kneaded bread, takes a second rise after being shaped into loaves. Given the same warmth, this second rise takes about half as long as the first.

I don't use a test to tell me whether or not the loaves are risen enough; when they are ready *they will look almost twice as large*—taking up about twice as much room on the sheets. (Some experts recommend using a finger test on the loaves, but that finger mark stays in the finished loaf, and I don't like to mar my loaves. Besides, *this* rise can be skimped a little—if really necessary.)

The loaves get quite large in the rising—even larger in the baking—and if they touch each other (I warned you about leaving room) better not try to separate them; you're more likely to punch them down—which means more rising time. If, by mischance, they do get punched down, just reshape them into loaves and start again from there.

These re-starts don't mean that you double your rising time. The yeast is still growing, which means that *each subsequent rising takes less time.* (Gourmets like their bread to have three or even four risings in the bowl—and each is faster than the previous rise.)

When the loaves are risen you'll want to slash them and slather on cold water. You slash with a very sharp or serrated knife, making your cuts diagonally (to make the loaf rise up in the baking, rather than out—Viennese Bread is a long, oval loaf slashed down the center to grow very wide; don't do that here), three or four cuts per loaf. Make your slashes *very gently,* cutting only about $\frac{1}{8}$–$\frac{1}{4}$ inch into the loaf—with a serrated knife, just a bit more than the depth of the serrations. If you cut deeply, you'll burst that balloon again. (If you're making round loaves, slash them in the shape of a cross, or like tic-tac-toe, or like the spokes of a wheel.)

Once the cuts are made, slather the surface with cold

water, sprayed from your plant sprayer or laundry sprayer or applied gently with your fingers or a clean brush. This water helps in crust and color formation.

Baking

Boil up a cup or so of water and put it in an open container in the bottom of the oven (I use an old cake pan). The evaporation of this water (simulating steam in a brick oven) also helps in crust formation.

Put the loaves into a *cold* oven (this gives the yeast an extra chance to do its thing), nearer to the top than the bottom, light, and set your flame for about 400°—medium-high if you don't have a thermometer or thermostat.

Bake for about 30–40 minutes.

During the baking (after 10 minutes and again after 15 minutes) slide the loaves forward from the oven for two more sprayings or brushings of cold water. (This gives you a chance to admire how nice and big they are now.)

Bottom color is a better guide to doneness for this loaf than top color. You can get a brown top by reflectance. If you are using aluminum baking trays, the shiny bottom of the upper one reflects heat down onto the top of the lower tray, and the lower loaf can get a browner crust from this reflection.

When the bottom of a loaf shows darkish golden brown, take a loaf out of the oven and turn it upside down on a clean towel and knife-test it for doneness (see pp. 21–23).

If the loaves test done but are too pale for you, put them under the broiler flame or coil (at high) for 30 seconds—a minute will probably be too long, so watch that second hand—and the loaves will have brown tops, too.

Stand the loaves on a wire rack to cool.

By all means eat the bread hot, tearing off chunks in the French manner. This bread is never again so good as it is when hot from the oven.

Options

☞ The first thing to learn about this or any bread is that the taste to please is yours and that of your family. And one of the most variable tastes is that for salt. By all means, if you like a saltier loaf, add **more salt** to the recipe or use **salty water** for your spraying.

☞   This is a water bread, but the "water" you use can vary enormously; it can be **vegetable water** as well as tap water. If you boil vegetables the water winds up with most of the vitamins anyhow, so it makes good sense to use it for cooking. And don't think it has to be bland or thin "water" either. I've used a rich **chicken soup** for "water" and been very happy with the result.

Of course, if you're using a salty "water," adjust the amount of salt you use in the recipe.

☞   Another method for achieving the crust on French Bread uses the same recipe, but when the loaf has been in for about 20–25 minutes (about 15 minutes before the loaf is done), glaze the tops with an **egg white,** then sprinkle **sesame seeds** over the glazed surfaces.

☞   **Whole wheat flour** can be substituted for about two thirds of the white flour—though it works up best half and half. Put in the white first, then add the whole wheat flour a cup at a time. You'll find that you use less flour in total for the same amount of liquid—whole wheat flour absorbs more liquid than white. (See Chapter 4.)

☞   By all means substitute **1 cup of raw wheat germ** for the white flour: you'll be putting back much of what the miller took out. If you aren't sure how you'll like this change, substitute only half a cup of wheat germ the first time. But do substitute or you will get heavy bread. (Put the wheat germ in as the fourth or fifth cup.)

☞   **Petits Pains** (literally, little breads) are individual small loaves, made up exactly like the larger breads. (It's really a great moment when you can set one at each guest's place for a dinner party.) When the dough has completed its first rise, divide it into twelve pieces (rather than four), and shape each piece into an oval loaf about 6 inches long. Space them out on the baking sheets (remember, they will spread), rise them, spray, and bake, just like the full-sized loaves. They will bake up sooner—but only a *little* sooner.

Another method for getting color on the *Petits Pains* is to use an egg-white and water glaze (1 egg white mixed with 1 teaspoon of water). As soon as the *Petits Pains* are shaped into loaves, brush them with the egg glaze and sprinkle with **sesame seeds.**

The finished little breads will thump hollow, but do test at least one or two from each tray to make certain.

☞ This bread gets stale rather quickly (3–4 days); that's a characteristic of water breads. So you might want to bake only a part of the dough, and save the rest for later in the week. Nothing is simpler. Put the dough you didn't bake into the fridge in a covered bowl. The dough will rise, even in the cold, but that's all to the good: the more risings the better the texture. When you want the dough, take it from the fridge, punch it down, knead out the larger air bubbles, and allow it to come to room temperature before shaping into a loaf (or, you can shape immediately and allow extra time for the cold loaf to rise).

☞ If you add **2 tablespoons of vegetable oil** to the recipe, your bread won't stale quite as fast.

FRENCH BREAD—SUMMARY

A. 1½ tbsp. active dry yeast   B. 6–7 cups flour
 1 tbsp. honey
 1 tbsp. sea salt
 2 cups hot water

Into a large bowl measure and mix together A.

Mix in the first 5 cups of B.

Spread sixth cup over board, dump batter onto board, and knead with as much additional flour as required to stop sticking.

Knead another 10 minutes after all the flour is in.

Return to oiled bowl, cover, and set to rise in a warm place for an hour.

Finger-test.

When sufficiently risen, punch down, knead out the larger air bubbles.

Cut the dough into four pieces, shape into loaves, and place on greased, cornmealed baking sheets.

Cover loaves with a clean towel and put in a warm place to rise until doubled in size. (Do not test.)

Slash the loaves and water them.

Boil water and put it in the bottom of the stove. (Do not preheat oven.)

Put to bake for about 40 minutes at about 400°—medium-high.

Water again after 10 and after 15 minutes of baking.

Test by knife.

Cool on a wire rack. Eat hot—tearing rather than cutting.

ITALIAN BREAD

We use the words "French Bread" and "Italian Bread" as if these were the sole breads ever eaten in France and Italy. Actually, there's a wide spectrum of French and Italian Breads (see Brioches, pp. 154–162, for example). In a way, these two breads are poverty breads—that is, they are made of the cheapest ingredients (no expensive grains, no expensive additions).

Although they are presented here separately, the breads of these two nationalities have much in common, as you'll see in this recipe. The true national difference is the amount of flour—that is, the French generally work with soft and the Italians with stiff dough.

Italian Bread is work. Don't fool yourself that it's not. This is a bread that I have my husband knead for me. But if you want a substantial, dense, and delicious peasant bread, here it is.

If you are buying olive oil for this bread, or for any other part of your Italian dinner, watch out—you have to read the label. If the label says "virgin" you're all right, because many of the original vitamins will be intact. If the label says "pure" it is a more processed oil and is missing important nutrients. However, olive oil is used largely for flavor. For nutrition pick an oil higher in linoleic acid—say corn or soy oil.

This is the most difficult kneading of any of the breads in this book: it is the driest dough. And yet it should rise without difficulty.

ITALIAN BREAD

For the Dough:
    2 tbsp. active dry yeast
    1 tbsp. honey
    2 cups hot water
    1½ tbsp. sea salt
    ¼ cup vegetable (or olive) oil
    8–9 cups unbleached white flour
For Greasing:
    melted butter or margarine
    cornmeal for sprinkling
Equipment:
    large mixing bowl, mixing spoon, 2 baking sheets,
    would you believe an electric fan?, and an optional
    rolling pin

Mixing

Into a large mixing bowl measure **2 tablespoons of yeast** and **1 tablespoon of honey.**

Add **2 cups of hot tap water** and **1½ tablespoons of salt,** and stir until the salt is dissolved. (The yeast will probably look clumpy: don't fret, we've a long way to go.)

Add **¼ cup of vegetable (or olive) oil** and stir in.

Mix in the **first 4 cups of flour,** 2 cups at a time, stirring in with your spoon or a wire whisk.

Mix in the **next 2 cups of flour,** right in the bowl, though you'll probably want to switch to working with your hand rather than a spoon. It's at this point that we start kneading.

Dump a **seventh cup of flour** onto the board, and scrape the batter out of the bowl, onto the flour. Knead in well.

Measure **an eighth cup** and dump it on the board. Knead in well. No, I'm not kidding. The dough will take that eighth cup and more.

If you can manage it, add another **½ cup of flour** and knead in. (If you can't manage it, the bread will still be Italian.) If it's a damp day, add flour all the way to 9 cups —be a hero.

Once this last flour is well kneaded in, you already have cohesion, that is, you can hold up the dough ball in one hand, palm down, and it won't fall; now knead for another 5 or 10 minutes.

This is a very resistant dough—one you can almost stand on. And that resistance gives the clue to when it's ready. Shape the dough into a rough ball and press it against the board. If, despite your pressure, the ball wants to stay a few inches thick, then it's ready to put to rise. At this point, *the dough should stick to nothing.*

First Rise

Pour a few drops of oil (or melted butter or margarine) into the same bowl, drop in the ball of dough, turn it over a few times to make sure it's oiled all over, cover with a clean, wet towel, and put into a very warm, draft-free place to rise for *about* an hour (see pp. 19–21).

When the ball of dough looks quite risen, give it the finger test as described in French Bread, p. 54.

Punching Down

If the dough is ready, punch it down and knead gently for a moment to get rid of the larger air bubbles. The dough should feel easier to handle.

Shaping the Loaves

Learn the following procedure for getting a good web with this heavy bread, and you can use it to improve any kneaded bread you care to make.

Divide the dough into three pieces and shape each piece into a ball.

Lay a piece on your kneading board and, poking it

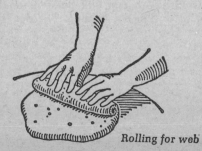

Rolling for web

with your fingers stiff, begin to flatten it into a rectangle. This whole process can be done with your bare hands, poking and pressing the dough thinner and thinner until it's about 10 by 12 inches and ½ inch thick; or, once you get the dough reasonably flat, you can switch to a rolling pin. Turning the dough over every so often makes it easier to handle, and less likely to stick.

Now, starting from the longer side of the rectangle, roll as tightly as you can manage, rolling the dough into a long, thick cigar. (The loaf will probably be about 2 inches thick and long enough to stretch right across your baking sheet.)

When you've got the cigar, pinch the ends closed and tuck them under (to look neat) and pinch the seam closed (otherwise the bread will unroll in the baking). Repeat to make the other two loaves.

Grease a pair of large baking sheets and sprinkle them with **yellow cornmeal**, shaking the sheets from side to side to get an even layer.

Lay the loaves on the sheets seam side down, as far apart as possible, to leave room for spreading and rising.

With a sharp knife, slash to a depth of almost ½ inch, three or four long diagonal slashes.

Using your fingers or a pastry brush or a sprayer, wet the surface of the loaves.

Cover with clean, dry towels and put to rise in a very warm place for one half to three quarters of an hour.

Baking

When risen (the slashes will gape wide), put a cup or so of water on to boil.

Once again spray or brush the loaves with cold water. Don't drown them, but do give them a good wetting.

Put a shallow pan in the bottom of your oven and pour in the boiling water, as with French Bread.

Put the loaves in the oven, and now light. For this heavy bread the yeast must have every chance to work.

Bake in a medium oven, around 350°–375° for 30–40 minutes.

Twice during the baking (at 10 and at 15 minutes) pull the loaves forward and again spray or brush them with water.

Crackling

When the loaves test done (see pp. 21–23), remove them from the oven and stand them on a wire rack. Now, believe it or not, if you want that crackled crust that is so typical of Italian Bread, cool the loaves in the breeze from an electric fan!

Eat the bread as hot as you can get it after the fanning. And don't worry about that old wives' tale about the unhealthiness of eating hot bread. It's true that when a loaf is very hot, and you cut it open with a dullish knife, or you press a bit of the dough between your fingers, it seems raw. But it isn't; raw dough looks drippy. There is still a good deal of moisture in a fresh-baked hot loaf, but it can't do you any harm at all.

So do eat your bread hot, when it's at its tastiest.

Options

☞ Substitute **1 cup of raw wheat germ** for a cup of white flour. (Make the substitution for any of the first 6 cups.)

☞ Substitute **whole wheat flour** for any amount of white, up to about 50 percent. (As the whole wheat flour is more absorbent, expect to use a total of about 7½–8½ cups of flour.)

☞ For a small adventure you might try a bread I call "Soychick" Bread. In this Italian Bread recipe, substitute for the water either **chicken soup** or the water left after cooking up a pot of chick peas (**chick-pea water** is quite flavorful). Then, substitute a cup of **soy flour** for a cup of white flour—late in the kneading (say, about cup no. 7). This is very rich for a water bread, high in protein from the soy, a mellow color, and one of the best toasters you'll ever find.

☞ Parma Bread. Add to the bowl **6 tablespoons of grated Parmesan cheese.**

If you want cheese in only one or two loaves, knead in 2 tablespoons of cheese per loaf after dividing into loaves. Make sure you knead the cheese in well.

After the final spraying, that is, after 15 minutes of baking, sprinkle the loaves with additional Parmesan.

☞ **Egg glaze** (see French Bread, p. 58). With this bread, the seeds for the glaze can be either sesame or poppy. Whenever I glaze, I seed: it's a waste to have that sticky egg surface and not put seeds on it. I prefer poppy seeds for Italian Rolls (follow the directions for *Petits Pains*, pp. 58–59).

☞ *Pane di San Giuseppe* (Saint Joseph's Bread) is made by adding **6 tablespoons of anise seed** after the hot water (and you've got to like anise for this one), and then shaping the loaf to resemble a patriarch's beard. (Though no one will stop you from making more conventional loaves and using a simple egg glaze.) On March 19, bring your beard-shaped loaf over to the *Festa di San Giuseppe* for blessing (most of us can use all the help we can get).

☞ Bread sticks are popular with young and old, and easy to have on hand because they keep better than loaves. Tear off walnut-sized balls of risen and punched-down dough. Roll these balls into strips a little thinner than your little finger. Pinch the ends smooth and lay on a greased baking sheet to rise (about half the time of the previous rise). Brush with milk, for color; and sprinkle on coarse salt—kosher salt or coarse sea salt. Bake at about 350° for 12–15 minutes or until a satisfactory golden-brown color. Eat one or two to make sure they are done.

☞ The most common Garlic Bread is made with a finished loaf of bread. Simply slice the loaf through lengthwise (that is, parallel to the cutting board) and smear the halves with **garlic butter** (made by mashing 1 or 2 cloves of garlic in ¼ cup of butter or margarine). Roll in aluminum foil and bake until heated through, about 10 minutes.

To make a Garlic Bread *baked with garlic*, add 2 tablespoons (or more) of **dried garlic flakes** after the hot water, and make up as you would the normal recipe.

ITALIAN BREAD—SUMMARY

A. 2 tbsp. active dry yeast   B. 8–9 cups flour
   1 tbsp. honey
   2 cups hot water
   1½ tbsp. sea salt
   ¼ cup oil

Into a large bowl measure and mix A.
Mix first 6 cups of B into a bowl, 2 cups at a time.

Spread another cup on kneading board and scrape out dough onto board.

Knead in the eighth cup.

Knead in as much of the last cup as you can, until the dough is very stiff and very resistant to kneading, then knead for another 5 or 10 minutes.

Cover with a clean wet towel and put to rise for about an hour.

When risen (as shown by a finger test), punch down, and shape into three long loaves.

Grease two baking sheets and sprinkle with cornmeal.

Lay the loaves on the sheets and slash three or four times per loaf, diagonally, almost ½ inch deep.

Spray with water and put to rise, covered, in a very warm place.

Boil up some water, and put in a shallow container on the bottom of the oven.

When the loaves are risen, spray again. Bake at about 350°–375° for 30–40 minutes.

Spray a third and fourth time after baking for 10 minutes and 15 minutes.

Test. Cool on a wire rack in a draft (for the Italian crackle). Eat hot.

REFRIGERATOR RISE BREADS

For some of my students, this is the basic bread: it's the only one their kids will eat, because it's the one that looks most like what they've been conditioned to by television.

Refrigerator Rise Bread is a favorite bread with people on a tight schedule. It can be made up (just kneaded and shaped) in the evening, kept in the refrigerator overnight (where it rises—hence, the name Refrigerator Rise), and in the morning popped into the oven to have hot and fresh with breakfast.

This isn't an original concept with me: Robin Hood flour has an entire leaflet devoted to it and Fleischmann's yeast has a recipe for a Cool Rise Bread in its recipe booklet. You can also make up your own Refrigerator Rise recipes, or adapt this or others to your likes.

We'll do two of these breads in this section: Wheat Germ Refrigerator Rise, and Oatmeal Refrigerator Bread, which, with the options, covers quite a bit of ground. In addition, see Refrigerator Rye in Chapter 7.

These are moist doughs, made with oil. In fact, whatever other options, changes, and variations you try, *don't leave out the oil*, because it's the oil that makes this kind of bread possible. It's the oil that allows the little bit of dough you put into the fridge in a baking pan to expand to almost three times its size by the time you take it out of the oven, and it's the oil that enables it to rise so well in the fridge.

Let me fill you in on the mechanics of this kind of bread.

First, you mix and knead it, like any kneaded bread, keeping a soft, moist dough, but one that doesn't stick.

Second, you divide it into loaf pans and put the loaves into the fridge to rise (a minimum of 5 hours, a maximum of 24).

Third, you take the loaves out and bake them.

As you can see, it's a simple procedure, with no testing or guessing about whether or not the bread is sufficiently risen—you can see it's risen, and you can know that if it's been rising for 5 to 24 hours, it's risen enough.

These breads have coarser webs than kneaded breads with two rises. French Bread has small, fairly even bubbles—we say that it has an even or smooth web. The pattern of the bubbles in Refrigerator Rise is uneven; largish bubbles tending toward the top of the bread and the smaller ones toward the bottom—making a coarse web. Occasionally these bubbles form right under the skin of the rising dough. When such blisters do form, prick them with a sharp fork, or pinch them between your fingers before baking the bread.

A shortcoming of Refrigerator Rise is that if you leave it too long in the fridge it may collapse; then it must be kneaded down and re-risen—which can take a while.

In my refrigerator I find the loaves subject to all kinds of minor accidents—a zucchini falls from an upper shelf, or my husband drops a loaf while taking something out of the refrigerator. But then, perhaps you're more careful than we are. Any zucchini marks, or what have you, stay in the bread.

When you put the loaves in the fridge, cover them

with oiled plastic wrap or waxed paper. If you don't grease the papers they will stick to the tops of the loaves and partly punch them down. Which means either you re-shape and re-rise or you settle for flat-topped bread. So, grease.

WHEAT GERM REFRIGERATOR RISE

For the Dough:
> 2 tbsp. active dry yeast
> 2 tbsp. honey
> 1 tbsp. sea salt
> 2 cups hot water
> ⅔ cup instant skim milk powder
> ½ cup vegetable oil
> 4 cups unbleached white flour
> 1 cup raw wheat germ
> 1–2 more cups unbleached white flour

For Greasing:
> melted margarine or butter

Equipment:
> large mixing bowl, mixing spoon or whisk, kneading board, 3 baking pans (8½″ × 4½″ × 2½″), plastic wrap or wax paper

Mixing

Into a large bowl mix together **2 tablespoons of yeast, 2 tablespoons of honey, 1 tablespoon of salt,** and **2 cups of hot tap water.** Stir to dissolve the salt.

Add ⅔ **cup of instant skim milk powder** (or ⅓ cup of the non-instant) and stir.

Mix in ½ **cup of vegetable oil.** (Here I would not recommend olive oil—unless you really enjoy the flavor.)

Stir in the **first 4 cups of flour,** 2 cups at a time.

When that's all wetted, stir in **1 cup of raw wheat germ.**

Kneading

Spread **1 cup of flour** over your kneading board, scrape the batter from the bowl onto the board, and work the flour in.

When this is all worked in, you will probably want to knead in, say, ½ **cup more,** plus sprinklings on the board to keep it from sticking. This should end up as a soft (not sticky), moist dough, so don't force flour to the point where it is dry: stop as soon as the dough can be handled without sticking.

When you have enough flour in the dough, knead for an easy 10 minutes.

Let the dough rest on the board while you grease three 8½″ × 4½″ × 2½″ baking pans with melted butter or margarine. *Don't substitute oil for greasing with this bread: the oil gets absorbed during the long rise, and the bread will stick.*

Cut the dough into three pieces and shape three loaves to fit the pans. (You can use the same flattening and rolling technique that we discussed in Italian Bread on pp. 56–57.)

If you want good, smooth end slices, chop down with the edge of your hand as near as possible to the end of the loaf. This karate chop will leave a small ridge of dough. Fold this ridge under, and repeat for the other side.

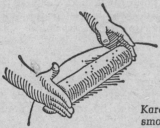

Karate chop for smooth end slices

Oil (or grease with melted butter or margarine) three pieces of plastic wrap to fit over the pans, and cover loosely.

Rising

We don't put these loaves into the usual "warm, draft-free place" to rise; we put them into a *cold*, draft-free place—your refrigerator.

Be sure that there's some room above the pans, for the dough will rise above the top, and then some.

Also, put the pans in a position where they **won't**

have to be moved around. A fingerprint made in the dough stays there (though even dented loaves come out looking beautiful).

Allow to rise for a minimum of 5 hours and a maximum of 24 hours. Like almost everything else in baking, this is an approximation: I have baked Refrigerator Rise after only 2 hours in the fridge; and I have occasionally seen it hold its shape for as much as 36 hours in the fridge—but don't count on it.

Baking

Remove from the refrigerator, take off the plastic gently, light your oven, and put the loaves in. It is not necessary to bring them to room temperature, but you may.

Bake at 325°–350° for about 50 minutes. But since this bread has a tendency to bake in more or less time than one expects, keep your nose peeled (see pp. 22–23).

When the crust is dark brown, test for doneness (see pp. 21–23). This is a taller bread than most, so be certain you get that knife all the way *almost* to the top.

Cool on a wire rack and serve warm.

Options

☞ Substitute up to half **whole wheat flour** for the white, remembering that since the whole wheat is more absorbent, you'll wind up using less flour for the same amount of liquid.

☞ Substitute **2 cups of whole milk** for the milk powder and hot water if you are baking for kids. Or use super-milk, that is, 2 cups of whole milk *plus* milk powder. As I've said before, you have to have *hot* liquid for good yeast action, so heat the milk.

☞ A **half cup of raisins** or more for the recipe, kneaded in when shaping the loaves, makes a very nice addition.

☞ The addition of ¼ **cup of sesame seeds** or **sunflower seeds** is a good variation.

WHEAT GERM REFRIGERATOR RISE—SUMMARY

A. 2 tbsp. active dry yeast
2 tbsp. honey
1 tbsp. sea salt
2 cups hot water

B. ⅔ cup skim milk powder

C. ½ cup vegetable oil

D. 5–6 cups flour

E. 1 cup raw wheat germ

Combine A into a large mixing bowl and stir.
Mix in B, then C.
Stir in 4 cups of D (2 cups at a time).
Work in E.
Spread fifth cup of D on kneading board; scrape out batter onto board, and knead in.
Knead in as much of a sixth cup as wanted.
Knead for 10 minutes more.
Divide and shape into three loaves.
Grease three 8½″ × 4½″ × 2½″ baking pans.
Put the loaves into the pans, cover each with a piece of greased plastic wrap, and put into the refrigerator to rise for 5–24 hours.
At baking time, remove plastic, bake at 325°–350° for about 50 minutes.
Test, cool on a wire rack, and eat warm.

OATMEAL REFRIGERATOR BREAD

With this bread we use yogurt as a baking ingredient for the first time.

I use homemade yogurt. It's easy to make and inexpensive.

Begin with a container of plain yogurt whose flavor you like (one without preservatives); mix a cup of it with a cup of reconstituted powdered milk, and put it in a warm place to "work." The yogurt will have solidified overnight and you'll have 2 cups of yogurt, which either has to be refrigerated or put to "work" again. Now, anytime you want to increase your yogurt, add milk again and put the mixture over gentle heat, and there it is—yogurt as good as the commercial kind and for pennies a cup. Make your own buttermilk the same way.

Go on—drive the dairy trust wild.

The recipe calls for 5 to 5½ cups of flour, but the amount of flour will depend on the brand of oatmeal you use (different brands have different absorptions).

Be sure not to use instant—the recipe has been worked out with real oatmeal. In fact, avoid all instant foods. That instant stuff has been precooked, or pre-softened, using heat that destroys whatever vitamins are left after the first processing.

OATMEAL REFRIGERATOR BREAD

For the Dough:
    1½ cups oatmeal (not instant)
    1½ cups boiling water
    ⅓ cup vegetable oil
    ⅓ cup honey
    2 tbsp. active dry yeast
    1 tbsp. sea salt
    1 cup yogurt (or buttermilk)
    5–5½ cups unbleached white flour
    ¼ cup raw wheat germ
For Greasing:
    melted butter or margarine
Equipment:
    large mixing bowl, mixing spoon or whisk, kneading board, 3 baking pans 8½″ × 4½″ × 2½″, plastic wrap

Mixing

Over 1½ cups of oatmeal, pour 1½ cups of boiling water and stir to wet down all the oatmeal.

Into the same cup measure ⅓ cup of vegetable oil and ⅓ cup of honey. Pour over the oatmeal and stir in, scraping the cup to get out all the liquid.

Stir in 2 tablespoons of yeast, then 1 tablespoon of salt and 1 cup of yogurt or buttermilk.

When the first seven ingredients are well mixed, add the first 4 cups of flour, 2 cups at a time, working it in well.

Mix in ¼ cup of raw wheat germ.

Pour 1 cup of flour (#5) onto the kneading board, scrape the batter onto the board, and work the flour in. This is a stickier batter than the Wheat Germ Refrigerator Rise, but resist the temptation to use large amounts of additional flour. Scrape your hands clean of batter, if necessary, and knead.

When the dough stops sticking, it has enough flour. Now knead for another 10 minutes.

Grease three 8½″ × 4½″ × 2½″ baking pans.

Divide the dough into thirds and shape three loaves.

Put the loaves into the pans, cover each loosely with a piece of greased wax paper or plastic, and put into the fridge.

Rising

Allow the loaves to rise in the fridge for 5–24 hours, without handling or punching them down.

Baking

When risen, take from the fridge, remove the plastic wrap, and bake at 350°–400° for around 40 minutes.

Test for doneness (see pp. 21–23).

Cool on a wire rack. Eat some warm; the rest will be good for days.

Options

☞ Like its near relative, Wheat Germ Refrigerator Rise, this bread can take ½ cup of raisins or ¼ cup of sesame seeds or sunflower seeds, kneaded into the loaves just before shaping.

OATMEAL REFRIGERATOR BREAD—SUMMARY

A. 1½ cups oatmeal
   1½ cups boiling water

B. ⅓ cup vegetable oil
   ⅓ cup honey

C. 2 tbsp. active dry yeast
   1 tbsp. sea salt
   1 cup yogurt
     (or buttermilk)

D. 5–5½ cups flour

E. ¼ cup raw wheat germ

Into a large mixing bowl combine A and stir well.

Add B and mix in.

Add C and stir.

Measure in first 4 cups of D, 2 cups at a time.

Work in E.

Spread another cup of D over the board and scrape batter onto the board. Knead in, adding as much more as required to keep dough from sticking.

Knead 10 minutes more.

Grease three baking pans, $8\frac{1}{2}'' \times 4\frac{1}{2}'' \times 2\frac{1}{2}''$.

Shape the dough into three loaves and put into the pans.

Cover with greased plastic wrap and set in the refrigerator to rise for 5–24 hours.

When you want to bake, remove plastic, and bake at 350°–400° for about 40 minutes.

Test for doneness.

Cool on a wire rack. Eat warm.

4

Whole
Wheat
Bread

Like a canoeist who has passed over some rocky shoals without getting a hole punched in his bottom, I breathe a deep sigh and pass from white breads that have to be made healthy, to Whole Wheat Breads. This is where we live.

These breads need no help—so long as you buy whole wheat flour which is untreated (not brominated, for example) and which is stone ground. These two conditions met, your whole wheat flour should have a broad range of vitamins and minerals and proteins, from both the germ and the bran.

We consider these our everyday breads, and so, I hope, will you. They are certainly tasty enough to be a daily favorite, and very healthful.

There are a few differences in handling whole wheat dough that are worth mentioning. For one thing, the raw whole wheat dough tends to form a crust easily, and so must be kept covered with a wet, clean towel while rising in the bowl. (Soak a towel with hot tap water and wring it out.) This will keep a damp atmosphere around the dough and prevent the surface from drying out. You could use a damp towel over all doughs, but for whole wheat it's a must.

Whole wheat flour is more absorbent than white flour (even than wheat germ flour), and so you'll use less flour for the same amount of liquid—keep that fact in mind when you are adapting or inventing your own recipes.

In kneading Whole Wheat Bread there is a different feel to the dough. White flour dough is more or less equally moist on the surface and inside the dough ball. But with whole wheat, the outside can feel dry, sticking

neither to the board nor to your hands, yet if you poke
your fingers inside it's sticky enough that you begin to
wonder if you don't need at least another cup of flour to
dry it out. Well, *don't dry it out!* It's supposed to feel
moist inside. If you were to force in enough flour to make
it feel like white flour dough, you'd wind up with a hor-
ribly heavy bread.

Whole Wheat Breads don't rise as high as white
breads, so don't expect them to. Nor can they give you as
fine and delicate a texture. But these are kneaded breads,
and, as kneaded breads, will give you good texture (just
not quite as fluffy as white). Because of this tendency toward heaviness, we like to give our Whole Wheat Breads
a bit of extra kneading. By doing this, and by working on
the wet side, you can wind up with a surprisingly light,
all-purpose bread.

If you've tried one or two other kneaded breads these
Whole Wheats should be no trouble for you. If you've
never kneaded before, see pp. 52–53.

When breads are made with half whole wheat and
half white flour—so many whole wheats in cookbooks are
just that, which is why I call my favorite bread "100
Percent"—they have some qualities of both. For example,
Tan French Bread will be not quite as high as the white,
but the crust will be just as crunchy and the flavor better!

100 PERCENT WHOLE WHEAT BREAD

I call this bread 100 Percent Whole Wheat Bread, but
actually it might be called 100 Percent Whole Wheat
Bread II as there are three 100 percent whole wheat
breads in this book: Dark Whole Wheat Raisin Method
Bread back in Chapter 1, this one, and Rich Whole Wheat,
which follows.

This is a water bread, and like any water bread will
dry out in a few days. But because of the preservative
power of the honey in it, it never *tastes* stale and resists
mold like crazy. I've eaten this bread after it has been
around the house for weeks, and though dry, the dryness
is like cold toast, not like stale bread—tasty and crunchy.

This recipe makes three moderate-sized loaves, either
standing free on baking sheets, or in pans. Since I often
bake more than one batch of bread at a time, I prefer

the pans, for convenience; but one gets a feeling of virtuosity from free-standing whole wheat loaves: the choice is yours. But for sandwiches, use pans: the loaves can only rise up, not out.

For all us calorie counters, this is the second-lowest calorie bread in the book.

100 PERCENT WHOLE WHEAT BREAD

For the Dough:
    2 tbsp. active dry yeast
    ¼ cup honey
    1 tbsp. sea salt
    3 cups hot water
    6½–7½ cups whole wheat flour
For Greasing:
    melted margarine or butter
Equipment:
    large mixing bowl, mixing spoon or whisk, kneading board, 3 baking pans 8″ × 4″ × 2″ (or 2 baking sheets)

Mixing

Into a large mixing bowl measure **2 tablespoons of yeast, ¼ cup of honey, 1 tablespoon of salt,** and **3 cups of hot tap water.** Stir to dissolve the salt.

Add the **first 4 cups of flour,** 2 cups at a time, wetting thoroughly before continuing.

Mix a **fifth cup of flour** into the bowl and work in.

Spread a **sixth cup of flour** on your kneading board and scrape the batter onto the board. Knead in.

Add another **½ cup of flour** to the board, and knead in.

Use as much of another cup as you require for good cohesion (lift the dough ball in one hand, palm down) and to make the dough stop sticking to the board.

When you have worked in enough flour, knead for an easy 15 minutes—or a vigorous 10 minutes. To keep the dough from sticking again during this kneading, you are entitled to flour the board lightly, even after you have "enough" flour in.

When those characteristic light wrinkles appear on the surface of the dough, it's ready. (If you aren't sure, knead for another 5 minutes. The first time you do this bread, do be sure you've kneaded enough.) Drip a few

drops of oil (or melted butter or margarine) into your
mixing bowl (no need to wash it first) and drop in the
dough ball. Turn the dough over a few times to oil all
sides. Cover with a wet, hot, clean towel, and put in a
warm, draft-free place to rise.

First Rise

On a warm day this rise should take about an hour,
though don't be surprised if it's more. This is whole wheat
flour, remember, and heavier than white.

At any rate, don't count on a specific timing for the
rise—use the finger test (see p. 54).

Shaping the Loaves

When ready, punch down and knead gently for a minute
to get out the larger air bubbles.

Divide the dough into three equal parts and shape
into three loaves. At this stage, if you opt to, you can
knead in grated orange rind or raisins (see Options).

Grease three 8″ × 4″ × 2″ baking pans (that's the
size of those disposable pans—but don't dispose of them;
they're good for many re-usings).

To make the loaves you can flatten and then roll up
the dough (as on pp. 62–63) and use that karate chop for
smoothing the ends (see p. 69)—or you can just shape
into loaf shapes as best you can. Just be sure that any
seam is on the bottom.

Fit the loaves into the pans (you can give them a
little patting here to even them off—you'll get a more
even rise that way; that is, your loaf won't hump as much
in the middle if the top is flat to begin with).

If you wish to use baking sheets to get free-standing
loaves, use two sheets and shape the dough into the same
three loaves. But once you've arrived at a shape, don't
even it out. Free-standing loaves are supposed to have
fat middles and tapered ends.

Rising the Loaves

This second rise can be more trouble than the first. Often,
where you have room for a bowl of dough in that warm

place, you don't have room for three loaf pans or two baking sheets. Be sure you've read Rising Dough, pp. 19–21. This bread is well-suited to on-top-of-the-oven rising, because it doesn't care whether it goes into a hot or a cold oven.

At any rate, once the dough is in the pans, re-cover with the same towel (now barely damp), and put in a very warm, draft-free place to rise for about half the time of the first rise.

Baking

The loaves will rise *well above* the rim of your pans by the time they are ready for baking.

Bake in a moderate oven, 350°–375°, for about 40 minutes.

Make certain your breads test done before you pull them from the oven.

If the bread tests undone, but the crust shows signs of scorching, shut the oven off and allow the bread to stay there for another 5 or 10 minutes *with the flame off*.

Cool on a wire rack and by all means eat hot.

Options

☞ For lots of added iron, you can change the honey in this, and most breads, to **blackstrap molasses.** This gives you a darker colored bread with more vitamins and minerals—but the molasses has no preservative power. Only honey has that magic something. Maybe you'd like to try half honey, half molasses?

☞ For an extra little zing to the taste of this bread, add the **grated peel of half an orange,** kneading it in well when you shape the loaves. If you're out of oranges try some lemon peel.

☞ My husband is crazy for **raisins.** We use a big juicy kind called Manukka (or Manoukka), which we get from a health food store where they are sold as unsprayed and unsulfured. I use a full cup of raisins for the batch, but if you are only mildly fond of raisins, you might start with ½ cup.

☞ Add **1 cup of skim milk powder** (½ cup of the non-instant) for a little calcium.

☞ For a whole batch of other options, see the end of the next bread.

---

100 PERCENT WHOLE WHEAT BREAD—SUMMARY

A. 2 tbsp. active dry yeast   B. 6½–7½ cups whole wheat
   ¼ cup honey   flour
   1 tbsp. sea salt
   3 cups hot water

Combine A into a large bowl and mix.

Combine the first 5 cups of B, 2 cups at a time.

Spread another cup (#6) on the kneading board, and scrape batter onto the board. Knead in.

Add another ½ cup to the board and knead in.

Add more as required (up to 1 more cup).

Knead for another 15 minutes.

Drip a few drops of oil into the same bowl. Oil the dough.

Cover with a clean, hot wet towel and put to rise in a warm place.

Finger-test.

Punch down and knead gently for a minute.

Shape into three loaves.

Grease three 8″ × 4″ × 2″ baking pans, drop loaves in, re-cover with the same towel, and rise again in a warm place.

Bake in a moderate oven (350°–375°) for about 40 minutes.

Test. Cool on a wire rack and serve hot.

RICH WHOLE WHEAT BREAD

This, too, is a 100 percent whole wheat bread.

It's easy enough to see why we call this Rich Whole Wheat. It has lots of eggs, milk, oil—and the calories that go with them. But what a delicious and healthful way to get those calories.

Unlike the previous bread, this one will keep—it may not last, but if it lasts, it will keep.

Near the end of the chapter, we'll discuss a lot of healthful substitutions and additions for the recipe. So don't skip the Options, they're really important to this chapter.

Be sure you use a large mixing bowl for this bread, as the dough will climb right out of it in the rising. Forewarned is forearmed—and it's messy cleaning up dough from around your pilot light. I know.

If you are beginning with Rich Whole Wheat, be sure you take a few minutes to read what was said about kneading whole wheat dough on pp. 74–75.

RICH WHOLE WHEAT BREAD

For the Dough:
2 tbsp. active dry yeast
1 tbsp. sea salt
¼ cup vegetable oil
¼ cup honey
2½ cups hot water
1 cup skim milk powder
2 cups whole wheat flour
3 large eggs
6–7 more cups whole wheat flour
For Greasing:
melted margarine or butter
Equipment:
large mixing bowl, mixing spoon or whisk, kneading board, 3 baking pans 8½″ × 4½″ × 2½″

Mixing

Into a large mixing bowl measure **2 tablespoons of yeast, 1 tablespoon of salt,** and (measured in the same cup) **¼ cup of oil** and **¼ cup of honey.**

Add **2½ cups of hot tap water** and stir briefly.

Mix in **1 cup of instant skim milk powder** (or ½ cup of non-instant).

Add **2 cups of whole wheat flour** and stir until the batter is fairly smooth. (This 2 cups of flour will help you mix the eggs into the batter more easily.)

Mix in **3 large eggs**, at room temperature. (See p. 15 and p. 19.)

Add the next **5 cups of flour,** 2 cups at a time, making certain it's all wetted before going on to the next 2 cups.

Dump another **cup of flour** (#8) onto the board and scrape the batter over it. Knead in, adding small amounts of flour as required, until the dough stops sticking.

Knead for another 10–15 minutes. The oil in this dough makes it easier to handle than 100 Percent Whole Wheat.

First Rise

When the dough is kneaded (you will see those satiny wrinkles), pour a few drops of oil back into the original bowl, drop the dough ball in, turning it over a few times to make sure it's all oiled, cover with a clean, hot, *wet* towel, and put in a warm, draft-free place to rise (about an hour or a little more).

Finger-test (see p. 54).

Rising the Loaves

If, after testing, that hole doesn't fill, punch the dough down, knead it for a moment to get rid of some of the bubbles, divide into three pieces, and shape into loaves.

By this time the dough feels absolutely lovely, is very easy to handle, and wouldn't dream of sticking to anything.

Grease three $8\frac{1}{2}'' \times 4\frac{1}{2}'' \times 2\frac{1}{2}''$ baking pans and drop the loaves in. Use your fingers to level off the loaves.

Re-cover with that same towel, and put into a very warm place to rise again (about $\frac{1}{2}$ hour).

Baking

When the loaves are well risen, put them to bake in a moderate oven (350°–375°) for about 40 minutes.

Test with a clean knife for doneness. These are fairly high loaves, so, inserting through the bottom crust, make sure your knife goes almost to the top, without piercing the top crust.

Cool on a wire rack.

This bread will keep, so don't be afraid to make more loaves than you can use today and tomorrow.

Options

SUBSTITUTIONS

In these whole wheat recipes you are entitled to a full cup of substitutions, though you can use less. By this, I don't mean additions, like raisins or sunflower seeds, I mean *substitutions*. As in earlier recipes we have substituted wheat germ for white flour to make a white recipe healthier, here we can substitute various flours to make these whole wheat breads healthier and more varied.

If you wish to juggle the various flours around, using ½ cup of this and ¼ cup each of this and that—go ahead. The only limit is your imagination—and that 1 cup. (Actually, if you don't mind heavy bread, you can substitute even more than 1 cup.)

☞ You can make "super-bread" by substituting **wheat germ** for 1 cup of whole wheat flour.

☞ **Soy flour or meal** is highly recommended by many nutritionists, because it has so much good protein and lecithin. If you want to use more than 1 cup of soy flour, you have to compensate by including some **gluten flour** to make up for the lack of gluten in the soy: for example, 2 cups of soy and 1 cup of gluten flour as a substitute for 3 cups of whole wheat.

☞ Also recommended are such coarse grains as **cracked wheat, wheat grits, rye meal,** and **cornmeal.** (For rye–whole wheat combinations, see Pumpernickel, Sour Pumpernickel, and Snack Breads.)

☞ Certain healthful cereals such as **Granola, Familia,** or **Wheat Germ Cereal** (though they contain sugar) are acceptable substitutions. (We used to breakfast on such cereals extensively—and expensively—but since we've been baking our own whole grain breads, we make our own "bread-cereal": whole grain bread crumbled and tossed with a little raw wheat germ, cut-up apple and/or other fresh fruit, seeds, a bit of dried fruit—add milk and it's great. And no sugar.)

☞ **Buckwheat flour** has a strong flavor, but you might want to experiment with small amounts.

☞ By all means try some **bran** or **rice polish**— these outer coverings are rich in B vitamins.

☞ **Millet** is worth trying, and **oatmeal,** while not as healthful as whole wheat, is good for variety.

☞ Other possible substitutes, if you can find them, are: **brown rice flour, barley flour, sunflower seed meal, flaxseed meal,** and **carob powder** (this last is a substitute for chocolate that kids will accept).

☞ So-called **eating yeast** fits in here, too, and is good, healthful stuff. Until you know how you like its strong flavor—it's an acquired taste—start out with a small amount—substituting, say, 3 tablespoons for 3 tablespoons of flour for the entire batch. It is also called torula yeast or brewer's yeast. Unlike the yeast we bake with, it is not alive when you buy it.

☞ And let's not forget the substitution of **blackstrap molasses** for all or part of the honey, as we discussed with 100 Percent Whole Wheat Bread.

ADDITIONS

☞ As with the last bread, knead the **grated rind of half a citrus fruit** into the loaves.

☞ Knead in **1 cup of raisins,** as you shape the loaves, or ½ cup to 1 cup of any **dried fruit, nut,** or **seed** combination that strikes your fancy or your palate. Sunflower seeds combined with raisins are great for this bread.

☞ For a crazy crunch, you might try adding ½ cup of well-drained **bean sprouts** (home-sprouted, I hope—they are infinitely superior to canned).

☞ For a pleasantly shiny **glaze,** brush the hot crust with melted butter or margarine as soon as the bread is out of the oven.

The possible combinations are vast in number, and can all add to the interest or, more important, the healthfulness of this already nutritious bread.

WHOLE WHEAT ROLLS

This Rich Whole Wheat dough is a natural for Whole Wheat Rolls, because the things that make it rich also make it easy to handle. But the 100 Percent Whole Wheat Bread dough (or any kneaded dough in the book) can also be used for these rolls. (If you are using a water dough, keeping it in the fridge for a day or so will make it easier to handle.)

These rolls are very simple to shape; the same recipe that makes three loaves of Rich Whole Wheat Bread makes about two dozen Whole Wheat Rolls. But what I like to do is bake two loaves of bread and put a third of the kneaded dough aside in the fridge until the loaves are gone, and then bake up the rolls (or vice versa). This dough will keep quite well in the fridge for 2 weeks.

To make these rolls, shape the dough into hockey puck rounds, about 1 inch by 3 inches, and lay the rounds on a greased baking sheet (if you make up the whole batch, you'll need two sheets) so that they don't touch.

Now, take a metal-handled knife, and press the handle firmly and evenly all the way across each roll, pressing almost down to the sheet, and wiggle it. This will divide the rolls almost in half. Don't fold the rounds.

Shaping Whole Wheat Rolls

Cover with a clean towel and put into a very warm place to rise for half an hour. They won't rise much, but that's all right.

Mix a thin **egg-yolk glaze** (1 egg yolk stirred with 1 tablespoon of water) and brush over the surface.

Sprinkle with **poppy seeds** while the glaze is still wet.

Bake in the same moderate oven for 20 minutes. The tops will turn a lovely golden brown.

These take so little time and planning (especially if you've reserved a part of the dough from your other baking) that they are great dinner rolls, coming to the table right from the oven, to be eaten at once. Rolls tend to get stale faster than a bread of the same dough, but these rich dough rolls keep quite well.

If you are using dough that's been kept in the fridge, do take it out a couple of hours ahead of time to allow it to come to room temperature. Or if you haven't time, not to worry—just allow a few more minutes for that rise in a warm place.

Remember, any of the options we offered for the bread hold for these rolls, too.

RICH WHOLE WHEAT BREAD—SUMMARY

A. 2 tbsp. active dry
   yeast
   1 tbsp. sea salt

B. ¼ cup vegetable oil
   ¼ cup honey

C. 2½ cups hot water

D. 1 cup skim milk powder

E. 2 cups whole wheat flour

F. 3 eggs

G. 6–7 more cups whole wheat
   flour

Into a large mixing bowl measure A.

Measure B into a cup and stir into A.

Add C and stir.

Mix in D.

Add E, and mix until fairly smooth.

Stir in F.

Add 5 cups of G, 2 cups at a time.

Dump another cup (no. 8) over the kneading board, and scrape batter out onto board. Knead in.

Add as much of ninth cup as necessary to stop dough from sticking.

Knead for another 10–15 minutes.

Oil the ball in the bowl, cover with a clean, wet towel, and put to rise in a very warm, draft-free place.

Finger-test.

When risen, punch down and shape into three loaves. (At this point make any seed, fruit, or nut additions.)

Grease three 8½″ × 4½″ × 2½″ baking pans.

Put loaves into pans, cover again with wet towel, and put again to rise in a very warm place.

Bake for about 40 minutes at 350°–375°.

Knife-test.

Cool on a wire rack.

Eat hot—but any left over will keep.

5

Sourdough—
Trapping
the
Wild
Yeast

What with television, the word "sourdough" must be familiar to everyone—the sourdoughs were Alaskan prospectors.

They were called sourdoughs because while prospecting they carried around with them a bit of homemade yeast (a "sourdough starter") which had begun life as a mixture of soured milk and flour and which they had, no doubt, bought from or been gifted by some earlier sourdough. They would carry this starter (mostly dry from the addition of flour) wrapped up inside their packs or inside their shirts to keep it from freezing. When they camped they would mix it with water and flour to make dough, saving a bit of it as a starter for next day's camp. Thus, even though no supermarket was around with prepackaged yeast, they were able to have yeast-risen bread—that is, Sourdough Bread.

On the West Coast and in Alaska, it's claimed that some of those original strains of sourdough (which may have come over with the Russian settlers of Alaska) are still alive. But you'll find sourdough breads on the East Coast and in-between coasts, too. So-called sour ryes incorporate sourdough, so do some English Muffins, and the various sourdough breads labeled as such.

BORNE FREE

What is sourdough? Actually, it's *free yeast*.

There are in the air, all around us, microscopic organisms. The three main groupings are bacteria, molds, and yeasts. Some are harmful to human beings, some are friendly, and many are indifferent. Any of them, when they chance upon a favorable medium, a welcoming environment, grow and multiply. (For example, yeasts like a wetter environment than molds do; if you set out something just moist, you are likely to see the visible mold colonies in a couple of days.)

If you can encourage wild yeast to grow in a favorable medium (such as a wet and warm mixture made from milk and flour) they will multiply and act for you like prepackaged yeast—with the major difference that the taste is a "sour," winey, rich flavor which can really turn your taste buds on.

We'll use it here in a half-dozen recipes with many possible variations: Sourdough French (tan or wheat germ or white), Pumpernickel, English Muffins, Sour Rye, Pan Loaves, and Snack Breads.

It's not that these breads, with some change in the recipes, can't be made with the same old reliable active dry yeast; it's that Sourdough Breads are altogether something else to taste. So, for flavor, variety, and economy— if you need justification—it's worth the bit of extra planning necessary to make Sourdough Breads.

(If you already own some sourdough starter, or have a friend who will give you some, skip this next section and go on to Doubling, p. 89.)

TRAPPING THE WILD YEAST

There are several ways of obtaining sourdough starter: you can buy good strains of starter in many health food stores or by mail from Walnut Acres, Penns Creek, Pennsylvania, or El Molino Mills, Alhambra, California; or you can get yours the same way I got mine—by trapping the wild yeast into a favorable medium.

I started with a cup of reconstituted powdered skim milk. Even if you use whole milk for everything else, I suggest you start with skim milk. It's not that it sours more quickly (though it often seems to), it's that with homogenized milk, because the fat molecules are so evenly distributed, it's not as easy to tell when the milk has begun to go sour.

Covering the cup of milk with a bit of cloth (only

to keep out dust and wandering bugs) I left it on my sideboard for almost two days, until it smelled sour.

Once it soured, I added a cup of flour, then stirred the mixture and covered it loosely again. (Note: 1 cup of milk plus 1 cup of flour makes about 1 cup of mixture.)

Within a couple of days the mixture had begun to make bubbles (a sure sign that yeast is in residence) and had taken on a spongy look. Don't worry if the liquid separates out on top—you can stir that right back in.

If you get no bubbling action by the fifth day of your project—start over.

If you get various colored molds on top—throw it away and start over. (Probably your medium was too dry and so more inviting to wandering molds than wandering yeast.) All you've wasted is a cup of milk and a cup of flour—less than the cost of a packet of yeast.

(There are, in various cookbooks, recipes for making "sourdough" starter using tame yeast and flour and milk, or tame yeast and flour and milk and a shot of vinegar. It's not the same—it's not even close. Tame yeast is tame, and only wild yeast gives you that great sourdough flavor.)

If you bake with your new starter the first week, you may be surprised at how bland it is *that first week*. It seems that sourdough culture likes to mature for a few weeks before it hits its full flavor stride. It will raise your bread immediately, but the flavor needs maturing, at least until the second week.

DOUBLING

Now you have a cup of starter. But since most sourdough recipes call for at least a cup of starter, you have to double—unless you want to go through the process of obtaining a new culture every time you bake.

Here's how to double: to your 1 cup of starter you add 1 cup of milk and 1 cup of flour. You stir the mixture together until it's fairly uniform, then leave it out at room temperature (loosely covered) for a few hours, then, when it looks spongy, refrigerate. What you now have is 2 cups of sourdough starter.

CARE AND MAINTENANCE

I keep my sourdough starter in plastic containers in the fridge with the covers on loosely. The starter is a live and lively yeast, and it is in the nature of yeast to make bubbles. And if it goes on making bubbles (as it does) and you've put the cover on that container good and tight—something's got to give.

There is an alternative: you can keep your sourdough starter in a ceramic crock (avoid metal altogether—the chemical reactions can be unhealthy) with a strong clamp.

Whichever way you store it, it must be stored cold, otherwise the culture would soon destroy itself in its own waste products.

Even in the fridge the life processes go on, though slowly, and if you keep your starter for a month without using it, you have to divide it and double again (providing fresh food for the remaining half). You can throw away the other half, or give it to a friend, with instructions on doubling.

A friend of ours freezes his sourdough starter (an old California strain) for six months at a time—taking it out of the freezer every six months (when he hasn't baked with it) for thawing, doubling, and refreezing.

GENERAL SOURDOUGH TECHNIQUE

Sourdough breads are not quick to make. They don't require any more work or watching than other breads, but they do require more time and a little more planning.

All of the following sourdough recipes give instructions on a "first day–second day" basis. There is no magic in the passing of a night, it's just that sourdough yeast is a much slower-acting yeast, and requires about 12 hours to grow enough to use.

The first day, or early in the morning of the baking day, you put together a very wet mixture which, because of the bubbliness of the yeast, is known as the sponge.

Of course, if your kitchen is quite cool, the sponge could take longer than twelve hours, and if your kitchen is hot or it's the middle of a heat wave, it could take hours less.

The sponge is made with a part of the flour, the honey (or molasses), and all of the liquid. We don't put salt in the sponge because it tends to retard the yeast action.

Once the sponge is risen, which means that the wild yeast has permeated every part of the flour and liquid mixture, you add the rest of the ingredients and then knead it. This is just the opposite of the pattern you learned for other kneaded breads, where first you knead and then rise, *for sourdoughs you rise in the sponge and then knead.*

Here, again, you need extra time after shaping. Sourdough loaves generally require 2–3 hours to rise. And, if your kitchen is cold, they may require even longer.

Most of these sourdough recipes call for the use of baking soda (bicarbonate of soda). The soda provides a bit of extra rising help. The starter is acid, the soda is base, and the chemical reaction when these two meet is to make bubbles as the starter neutralizes the soda.

But never use more than the amount of baking soda called for in my sourdough recipes. Any unneutralized soda will leave an unpleasant metallic taste, and, what's worse, will destroy some of the body's vitamins.

If you wish, the soda can be omitted altogether, leaving you with a slightly lower bread and a slightly more acid flavor.

SOURDOUGH FRENCH BREAD

Remember that basic water bread (our convertible French-Portuguese-Cuban Bread) back in Chapter 3? Well, here it is again, just as lovely to look at and with as fine a texture, but with a delicious difference in flavor. I won't describe the difference here; it's better if you make up your own superlatives.

I recommend quite strongly the substitution of wheat germ for some of the white in this bread (see p. 95), but you may prefer Sourdough Tan French (p. 95), which is quite good, too. It's a matter of taste.

Don't expect Sourdough French to rise quite as high as did our earlier French Bread. The sourdough yeast doesn't have as big a rising "kick" as does active dry yeast. But the difference is quite small.

SOURDOUGH FRENCH BREAD

The First Day:
  1 cup starter
  1½ cups hot tap water
  1 tbsp. honey
  3½ cups unbleached white flour
The Second Day:
  1 tbsp. sea salt
  ½ tsp. baking soda
  2–3 cups unbleached white flour (only enough to knead comfortably)
For Greasing:
  melted butter or margarine
  sprinkling of cornmeal
Equipment:
  mixing bowl and spoon, kneading board, 2 large baking sheets, sharp knife

The First Day

Prepare your sponge by mixing together in a large bowl: **1 cup of starter, 1½ cups of hot water, 1 tablespoon of honey, and 2 cups of flour.** Stir until the mixture is smooth, then add **1½ cups of flour** and stir again.

The sponge will not be creamy smooth at this time, and you don't have to try to make it so. Just make sure that all the flour is mixed in.

Cover with wax paper or plastic and a clean towel and put aside, out of drafts and *at room temperature,* until tomorrow morning—at least 12 hours. (The towel provides a tent to keep drafts off the top of the bowl.)

The Second Day

When you take the towel off, you may find that the sponge has risen to the paper and stuck to it. No worry, just scrape off the sticking batter and throw it back into the bowl. Or you may find that a crust has formed over the surface. This is quite normal; all you have to do is stir the crust under, and it will soon disappear into the batter.

But, crust or no, stir down the batter to about its original size.

Sprinkle over the surface of the stirred batter **1 tablespoon of salt** and a **scant ½ teaspoon of baking soda,** and mix these in with your spoon—even though the batter may be a little resistant to stirring.

Add ½ **cup of flour** to the bowl and stir it in until most of it disappears.

Dump **1 cup of flour** onto the center of your kneading board and spread it around a bit.

Empty the bowl onto this flour. (Do scrape out the bowl when you empty it.) Pour another ½ **cup of flour** over the top of the dough, and you're ready to begin kneading. (If you've never kneaded before, see pp. 52–53.)

Of course, the dough will be very wet to begin with, offering little more resistance than jellied consommé, but as you work in more flour, you'll approach something that feels like dough.

At this point your judgment comes in. You have used, so far, 5½ cups of flour—the minimum for this kind of bread. Is this enough? Or should you add another cup, up to the maximum? (Or, conceivably, beyond it?)

There is no *perfect* amount of flour. Some bakers like a "wet" dough which they feel produces lighter bread—others prefer a dry dough to get a solid, substantial bread. The amount of flour must depend on your feel for the dough, on that particular day, for that particular bread—and it's hard to be wrong.

When you've added as much flour as you think is necessary, knead the bread well for 10 minutes.

Even though you have "enough" flour in your dough, it may be necessary to add sprinklings of flour to the board to keep it from sticking while you knead. Don't think of this as adding to the total—it should be a very thin layer.

Shaping the Loaves

When those "wrinkles" appear (see p. 53), knead for a few more minutes to make sure, then leave the dough on your board and grease two large baking sheets.

Sprinkle the sheets with a small amount of **cornmeal** (this is to help with bottom crust), and then shake the sheets from side to side to distribute the meal uniformly.

Cut the dough in half, and roll each half on the board to shape a long, thin loaf (if you start rolling with your hands in the middle and move toward the ends, you're more likely to come up with something even). At this point the loaf should be about 1½–2 inches thick and long enough to stretch diagonally across your baking sheet.

If you don't have two sheets that are large enough, divide the dough into three pieces and shape three loaves, each about 1½ inches thick (put two on one sheet, one on another), and long enough to stretch the length of the sheet.

Cover with a clean towel or two, to keep the loaves both warm and clean, and put in a warm place to rise (see Rising Dough, pp. 19–21) for 2–3 hours—or until the loaves are *considerably* larger.

Frenching

Now we come to those things that make this "French" Bread.

When the loaves have risen sufficiently, put a couple of cups of water on to boil; this will eventually make steam in the oven.

Meanwhile, spray the loaves with water. You can use any kind of sprayer or sprinkler (though if you use a flit gun, watch out for rust), or you can sprinkle with your fingers, or brush on the water with a pastry brush (so long as you are very gentle). And don't be stingy—it's this water that gives the loaves a good crust.

Now it's time for surgery. With a very sharp or serrated knife, slash diagonally, three or four slashes, to a depth of about one-eighth inch. Be very careful not to slash too hard. If you do, the loaf will fall, and you'll have to wait for it to rise again—very frustrating. If you want to slash *before* spraying, go right ahead—it won't matter. And be sure you do slash diagonally, not lengthwise—that would spread the loaf wide; we want it to rise up.

Baking

French Bread—this or any other made in a home oven—must go into a cold oven (that is, under 200°: if you've been using it, let the oven cool down to this temperature). Pour the water you've been boiling into a pan and place it somewhere in the oven, out of the way of the bread.

Now light your oven. This bread will bake, eventually, at 350°–375°, and you can set your oven for that (medium-low). I say "eventually" because you will have to open the oven after 5 minutes of baking to spray the loaves again, and 5 minutes after that to spray for a third time, and this repeated opening and spraying cools the oven down.

Even with the spraying and opening of the oven, this bread will bake in 30–35 minutes, and take on a beautiful golden tan.

But remember, ovens vary, and yours and mine are sure to have different hot spots. Know your own oven and its baking times. Don't assume a loaf is done because it looks done—test (see pp. 21–23).

If these loaves test done, put them onto a cooling rack for a few minutes before you tear one open.

Options

☞ The main option you have with this bread is to make it a lot healthier. While unbleached flour contains more vitamins than bleached, it is still nutritionally scant pickings. So I recommend the substitution of ½ **cup of raw wheat germ** for ½ cup of the flour. Make this substitution the second day, adding the wheat germ instead of the *last ½ cup of flour that goes into the bowl*. We routinely make all our white breads with raw wheat germ.

☞ Sourdough Tan French is excellent. Substitute **whole wheat flour** for all the flour used the second day. Actually, you can substitute whole wheat for *half* the total white flour used in the recipe—which means you would use some whole wheat in making up the sponge the first day.

☞ If you would like a crust of a deeper color, use an **egg-white glaze.** In the last 5 or 10 minutes of baking, spread the surface of the loaves with stirred egg white (mixed with a teaspoon of water if it feels too thick to handle easily) and then sprinkle the tops of the loaves with **sesame seeds.**

SOURDOUGH FRENCH BREAD—SUMMARY

A. 1 cup starter
   1½ cups hot water
   1 tbsp. honey
   3½ cups flour

B. 1 tbsp. sea salt
   ½ tsp. baking soda

C. 2–3 cups flour

The night before (or early the same day) combine A into a large bowl.

At least 12 hours later, stir down and sprinkle B over the surface of the sponge and mix in.

Stir in ½ cup of C.

Flour the board with 1 cup of C, and knead in as much of the remainder as required to make a comfortable dough.

Knead for 10 minutes.

Shape into two long loaves and place on greased and cornmealed baking sheets. Cover with a clean towel, and put aside to rise for 2–3 hours.

When well risen, slash the loaves and spray them with water.

Put a pan of boiling water into the bottom of the oven.

Put the loaves into a cold oven and bake for 30–35 minutes at 350°–375°.

Spray again with water after 5 and after 10 minutes of baking. Test for doneness, cool briefly on a wire rack, and serve hot.

SOURDOUGH PAN LOAVES

Notice that in this bread the wheat germ is not an "option" but one of the regular ingredients: it's the wheat germ that makes this bread as tasty as it is.

This is a moister recipe than most of the Sourdough Breads, and therefore makes for a livelier batter, so be sure to use a bowl large enough both to hold the mixture as it expands and for kneading in later on. For this bread you don't even require a kneading board—*you'll knead it right in the bowl.* This will enable you to have a moister dough than is possible on a board (where you must keep adding flour to keep the dough from sticking), and so a lighter bread.

As the name states, these are not free-standing loaves but loaves made in a pan. I use a pan 9½″ × 5½″, and get two large loaves out of the recipe. They rise well, so if you want to use smaller pans, divide the dough into three loaves.

The dough you finish with is much softer and somewhat wetter and stickier than most you've been used to (that's why it's in the pan), so don't try to make this one conform—leave it soft and wet, or you'll wind up with a heavy bread.

This is a coarse, country-looking loaf, whose pan shape makes it excellent for sandwiches, while the combination of sourdough and wheat germ gives it a full, hearty flavor.

SOURDOUGH PAN LOAVES

The First Day:
    1 cup starter
    2½ cups water
    2 tbsp. honey
    5 cups unbleached white flour
The Second Day:
    3 tbsp. vegetable oil
    1 tbsp. sea salt
    1 scant tsp. baking soda
    1 cup raw wheat germ
    1½–2 cups unbleached white flour
For Greasing:
    melted butter or margarine
Equipment:
    large mixing bowl, mixing spoon, 2 loaf pans 9½″ × 5½″

The First Day

In your bowl, mix together the **starter**, the **water**, and the **honey** until fairly smooth. Then stir in the **flour** 2 cups at a time.

Cover with a clean towel and put aside in a draft-free place to rise at room temperature overnight or for 12 hours. (Actually, what you're doing here is giving the yeast of the starter a chance to "sour" as much of the flour as possible. If you were to put in all the flour to begin with, the sponge would be too dry; yeast grows best in a wet environment.)

The Second Day

Stir the sponge down, mixing in the crust that has most likely formed.

To the sponge add **3 tablespoons of oil, 1 tablespoon**

of salt, and a scant teaspoon of baking soda, and stir in until blended.

Add **1 cup of raw wheat germ** (the toasted will do if you can't get raw, but it's more expensive and poorer in vitamins) and mix in.

Add in the **flour,** $\frac{1}{2}$ cup at a time, kneading in all the visible flour before adding the next $\frac{1}{2}$ cup.

Unless the dough is uncomfortably wet, stop after $1\frac{1}{2}$ cups of flour. At any rate, only when the day is very humid are you likely to want more than 2 cups (a *total* of 7 cups of flour).

Kneading

Knead in the bowl for 10 minutes or so.

If you've never kneaded in a bowl, the technique is even simpler than board kneading. Just make sure the bowl is in a comfortable and relatively secure position at about arm's length, and then press the dough with your closed fist, then squeeze it with your fingers.

This bread will never stop sticking to your hands as you knead—though as time goes on it will tend to stick less. However, the dough ball will show cohesion when you pick it up and let it hang from your hand.

If you're not sure, knead some more.

Shaping the Loaves

Grease two $9\frac{1}{2}'' \times 5\frac{1}{2}'' \times 2\frac{3}{4}''$ loaf pans.

Divide the dough into two equal portions and form each half into the rough shape of a loaf.

Drop each half into a pan, and, with your fingers, even off the loaves so that the tops are fairly level. Any bumps or peaks will tend to stay as they are.

Rising the Loaves

Cover the loaves with a clean towel and put to rise in a warm place for $1\frac{1}{2}$–2 hours. The dough will rise to almost fill the pan.

Remember, sourdough is slower to rise than tame yeast doughs, and rising time will depend a great deal on the vitality of your starter.

Baking

When the dough about fills the pans, put them into your oven and bake for about 45 minutes at 360°–400°, medium-high.

When done, turn out onto a cooling rack and let cool for several minutes before slicing.

This is a bread with a grand crust—you'll enjoy it.

Options

☞ Substituting **1 cup of cornmeal** for the wheat germ gives a satisfying crunchiness—for those who like a bit of backtalk in their bread. For those who like crunchiness and wheat germ, use ½ cup of cornmeal and ½ cup of wheat germ.

☞ Substituting **1 cup of oatmeal** for the wheat germ gives you Oatmeal Sourdough Bread.

☞ Brushing the tops of the loaves with **melted butter** or **margarine** as soon as they are turned onto the cooling rack will give you a shiny glaze. But for my money that's strictly Madison Avenue. There is no taste difference.

SOURDOUGH PAN LOAVES—SUMMARY

A. 1 cup starter
   2½ cups water
   2 tbsp. honey
   5 cups flour

B. 3 tbsp. oil
   1 tbsp. sea salt
   1 scant tsp. baking soda

C. 1 cup raw wheat germ

D. 1½–2 cups flour

The first day make your sponge by combining A into a large bowl until smooth. Cover and put into a draft-free place to rise.

The second day stir down the sponge and work in B.

Add C and mix until completely wetted.

Add D to the bowl a ½ cup at a time.

Knead in the bowl for about 10 minutes.

Grease two 9½″ × 5½″ × 2¾″ pans with melted butter or margarine.

Divide the dough in half, shape into loaves, and put in pans.

Cover and allow to rise in a warm place for 1½–2 hours. The dough will rise to about fill the pans.

Bake for about 45 minutes at 360°–400°.

Turn out, test, and cool.

SOURDOUGH ENGLISH MUFFINS

This one's really kicky—you can get the whole family in on it.

I understand that you can't get English Muffins in England—there you have to ask for scones (to rhyme with "on"). But scones are heavy, and these Sourdough English Muffins are as light as you could wish for; and they taste better than the commercial variety.

Apparently, these muffins are called "English" because they are fried in a griddle on top of the stove, which is the way the English cook everything. Whatever the etymology, this is a bread cooked *without the oven*—what a break for the summer months!

In making English Muffins, pay special attention to the size of the flame under your griddle. The directions call for a low flame, and when I say *low* I mean *simmering low*. It will take an extra 5 minutes for the griddle to preheat, but once it's heated, the muffins will take only 8–10 minutes per batch to cook (4–5 minutes per side). This will give you a muffin still moist but done. But, as with any bread, there is only one ultimate test—break one open and look at it.

I find it very easy to cook four muffins at a time in the center of my 10-inch square griddle. With an electric frying pan you ought to be able to do better than that, since you'll have even heat in the corners of the pan. With an ordinary frying pan (a last resort) you're probably back to four at a time.

Butter the griddle only once (and that lightly), before putting up the first batch.

The cornmeal that you sprinkle on the wax paper and over the rising muffins serves two purposes: it makes the raw muffins easier to handle, that is, less likely to stick to the paper; and it gives them, after cooking, a bit more crunchiness, which is very much to the good.

This, like all sourdough breads, has to be started the night before, so try to get that "I-want-English-Muffins-for-breakfast!" feeling before you go to bed.

This recipe makes about 30 muffins, if you use a 3-inch cutter. If that's too many for your family, reserve a third or half of the kneaded dough and put the rest in the fridge for tomorrow—or next week. When you want your next batch of muffins, just let the dough come to room temperature before rolling it out. Or, you can cook up the whole batch, freeze as many as you like, and take them out of the freezer and toast them when they're wanted.

SOURDOUGH ENGLISH MUFFINS

The Night Before:
    1 cup starter
    2 tbsp. honey
    2 cups reconstituted skim milk (or whole milk)
    4 cups unbleached white flour
The Morning After:
    1 scant tsp. baking soda
    2 tsp. sea salt
    1–2 cups unbleached white flour
    cornmeal for sprinkling
Equipment:
    mixing bowl and spoon, kneading board, wax paper, rolling pin, 3" cutter (an empty tuna-fish can will do), griddle (or frying pan), pancake turner

The Night Before

Mix together **1 cup of sourdough starter, 2 tablespoons of honey,** and **2 cups of reconstituted skim milk** (if you're making these for kids, use whole milk). Just swish these together in the mixing bowl until they are smooth.

Add **4 cups of flour,** 2 cups at a time, and mix in. There's no need for any gluten development now, so do not whip—just get all the flour thoroughly wet.

Cover with a clean towel and leave at room temperature in a draft-free place.

The Morning After

Uncover your mixture and stir it down (it will have risen considerably). If it has risen too high and fallen, no problem, just stir it down the rest of the way.

Sprinkle a **scant teaspoon of baking soda** and **2 teaspoons of salt** over the surface of the dough and work in.

Flour your board with a **cup of flour,** and dump the mixture onto your kneading board.

You'll want to knead in this 1 cup of flour or more (up to 2 cups), until the dough is medium stiff—stiff enough to roll out.

Once you have enough flour in (when the dough no longer sticks to your hands), give it a 5-minute kneading— that's enough because in this dough we're not all that concerned with gluten development since the muffins are so small.

Up to this point you've been doing fairly familiar things with your dough. In fact, you could throw away the rest of the recipe, knead for another 5 or 10 minutes, divide into loaves, and make Sourdough Sandwich Bread (see p. 104).

Shaping the Muffins

Bring on the kiddies.

Flour the board lightly and roll the dough out to a half-inch thickness. (I use a rolling pin, but I begin by patting the dough somewhat flat.) Try to get the dough pretty close to a half inch; thinner and it will make too many muffins; thicker and the muffins will require more time to cook—coming close to burning on the outside and barely done inside.

Take a 3-inch round cutter (there's really no reason why you can't use a larger cutter, or a square or oblong cutter—or any shape you wish; it's just that commercially made muffins are cut about 3 inches and so that's what most people are used to) and cut as many rounds as you can from your rolled-out dough.

Spread wax paper on a couple of baking sheets or platters or trays and sprinkle with **cornmeal.**

As you cut out each round, lay it on the cornmealed wax paper—don't let the raw muffins touch each other, they'll stick.

When you've cut out all the rounds possible the first time through, squeeze the remaining dough into a ball, and roll it out again into that same half-inch thickness. Again cut your 3-inch rounds. And so on, until you've used up all your dough, and the muffins are laid out neatly on the wax paper.

Now sprinkle some additional cornmeal over the tops —not a lot.

Cover with a clean towel and put into a warm place to rise for about a half hour—that is, a half hour from when the first round was cut out. If your children are cutting the muffins and doing it slowly, the first set may be ready to cook by the time the last set is cut out. If, after half an hour, you don't see any rising, your place is probably too cool, so re-cover and let them go another half hour.

Cooking

When the muffins are ready to cook (don't test them, just look: they will be about three quarters of an inch thick now), preheat your griddle by putting it over a *low* flame for about 5 minutes, or until a drop of water will skitter on it.

I grease my griddle before preheating, only once for the whole batch. If you're using a frying pan, you'll need more greasing as you work.

Use a pancake turner or a spatula to loosen the muffins from the wax paper and to transport them to the griddle. Do not raise your flame. Try to keep them from touching each other on the griddle until they've cooked for a couple of minutes.

Cook on each side for 4–5 minutes, depending on the thickness of the raw rounds. If you managed to roll them a half inch thick, 4 minutes per side should do; thicker muffins require 5 minutes per side.

Here, in cooking, timing, and turning the muffins, is another perfect opportunity to use my no-work method— I give my husband the stopwatch and let him sit at the stove and do it. But even a large child would do.

These muffins are turned only once, so be sure to let them get done on that first side.

If your muffins rise to look like baseballs, you may flatten them *slightly* by pressing *gently* with your pancake

turner when you turn them over to do the second side.
This squares off the shoulders a bit; but don't lean on
them.

By all means test the first muffin to come off the
griddle. Tear it open and look for raw spots, then taste it.
Remember, though, these are fresh and not yet toasted—
the way that most of us are used to eating English Muffins.
If you want to, split and grill them right now.

Options

☞ To make these healthier, as well as even more
delicious, you can substitute ½ **cup of wheat germ** for
white flour (in which case you can knead it in with the
last of the flour), or you can substitute **whole wheat flour**
for the last 1–2 cups of flour in the recipe.

☞ If you want to make Sourdough Sandwich
Bread, divide the kneaded dough and put it into two
greased 8-inch pans, and allow to rise for about an hour
in a very warm place. Then bake in a moderate oven
(about 350°), for 40 minutes.

SOURDOUGH ENGLISH MUFFINS—SUMMARY

A. 1 cup starter
   2 tbsp. honey
   2 cups reconstituted
   skim (or whole) milk
   4 cups flour

B. 1 scant tsp. baking soda
   2 tsp. sea salt

C. 1–2 cups flour

The night before, combine A into a large bowl until
smooth.

Cover and put into a draft-free place to rise.

The next morning stir down and mix in B.

Flour your board with 1 cup of C and dump mixture
onto board. Knead in as much of C as necessary to make
dough non-sticky.

Knead for 5 minutes more.

Flour board lightly and roll or pat out dough to half-
inch thickness.

With a 3-inch cutter, cut rounds from the dough, re-
rolling until all the dough is in rounds.

As rounds are cut, place them on cornmealed wax paper. Sprinkle lightly with cornmeal.

Cover and allow to rise in a warm place for a half hour.

Preheat griddle (simmering low) for 5 minutes.

Cook 4–5 minutes per side, *turning only once.*

If necessary, press gently with pancake turner on second side to even off shape.

SOUR PUMPERNICKEL

I wish I knew what magic there is in bought bread that sets the standard for what bread is supposed to look like. So many times my students tell me of having to all but force their families into that first taste of homemade bread (which, of course, is always gobbled up after the first bite) simply because it doesn't look exactly like the bread that comes from the supermarket or bakery.

Well, here's a bread that bakes up to look so much like bakery bread that you can fool anyone—up to the first bite, that is, because the taste is like nothing you get in a bakery.

"Robust" is the word that best describes Sour Pumpernickel. Pile on the strong cheese and the onions and mustard—this bread still keeps its character and flavor.

It is, of course, sour—though not as sour as some breads—with the additional fillip of the flavor of rye and whole wheat, plus the added healthiness of blackstrap molasses.

The texture of the loaf is medium-light—just right for a sandwich, as well as excellent for toasting.

For this bread we use an egg-yolk glaze about 10 minutes before the loaves are finished baking; this serves two purposes: first, it helps to give that grand final dark color that is so traditional for pumpernickel; and, second, the egg helps to hold the final sprinkling of caraway seeds.

I find this Sour Pumpernickel easier to make than the standard Pumpernickel you will make in Chapter 7. Perhaps it's because of the overnight rise, but I find the dough ready to shape into loaves with much less kneading.

SOUR PUMPERNICKEL

The First Day:
1 cup starter
2 cups reconstituted skim milk
2 tbsp. blackstrap molasses
¼ cup vegetable oil
1 cup unbleached white flour
1 cup whole rye flour
2 cups whole wheat flour

The Second Day:
1 tbsp. sea salt
½ scant tsp. baking soda
½ cup whole rye flour
1–1½ cups unbleached white flour
1 tbsp. caraway seeds

For Greasing:
melted butter or margarine
white cornmeal for sprinkling

For Glazing:
egg yolk
caraway seeds

Equipment:
large mixing bowl and spoon (or whisk), 2 baking
sheets, pastry brush (optional)

The Night Before

Make up your sponge by combining in a large bowl **1 cup
of starter, 2 cups of reconstituted skim milk, 2 tablespoons
of blackstrap molasses, ¼ cup of vegetable oil, 1 cup of
white flour, 1 cup of rye flour, and 2 cups of whole wheat
flour.** I find it easiest to blend the whole if I stir in the
flour 1 cup at a time. A whisk is very handy for this
session.

Stir until it's smooth, then cover with a wet towel
overnight, in a draft-free place.

The Morning After

At least 12 hours later, stir the sponge down to its original
size.

Over the surface of the sponge sprinkle **1 tablespoon
of salt** and a scant **½ teaspoon of baking soda.** Stir in.

Add **½ cup of rye flour** and stir in.

Kneading

Pour **1 cup of white flour** onto your kneading board and dump the batter onto it.

Knead in.

This dough never stops being sticky, so you can expect to use about another ½ **cup of white flour** to sprinkle the board as you knead. We want a dough that can just be handled. (You may even have to flour your hands to shape the loaves.)

Once you have that cup of white flour kneaded in, however, the bread requires only about another easy 5 minutes of kneading.

During this last 5 minutes, knead in **1 tablespoon of caraway seeds**—enough to let the eater know there is caraway in the bread without making it a "caraway bread."

(If you want caraway in only one or two of the loaves, divide the dough—after the required 5 minutes of kneading—into three parts, and knead a teaspoon of caraway seeds into each loaf that you want seeded. Knead just enough to disperse the seeds.)

Grease two baking sheets. (The loaves rise and spread too much to fit all three of them on one sheet.)

Sprinkle some **white cornmeal** over the sheets and shake to spread evenly. (I use white cornmeal instead of yellow because the New York bakeries I know use white cornmeal for their pumpernickels—perhaps for the contrast.)

Shaping the Loaves

Divide the dough into thirds and shape the three pieces into three loaves. I recommend oblong rather than round loaves—they rise a bit better and make better sandwiches.

Lay the loaves on the greased and cornmealed baking sheets, well apart.

With a sharp knife slash each loaf diagonally with three slashes, ¼–½ inch deep. (You don't have to worry about making the loaves fall as you did when slashing French Bread—there hasn't been any rise yet.)

Rising

Cover the loaves with a clean towel, and put into a warm, draft-free place to rise for 2–3 hours.

When the loaves are well-risen—and they will look

well-risen, with the slashes gaping wide—slash again, right into the same slashes. Only this time be careful: slash gently so as to avoid making the loaves fall.

Now, as with the French Breads, spray or brush the loaves with water. We want to make certain the crust is good and thick.

Spray again after the bread has been in the oven for about 10 minutes.

Baking

Bake in a moderate oven (about 350°–375°) for about 40 minutes, then, when and if the bread tests *almost* done, shut the oven off and allow it to stay in the closed oven for another 10 minutes. This is to prevent the scorching that Pumpernickels are prone to.

By the way—after about 25 minutes, you might want to reverse the top and bottom trays to prevent scorching.

After the loaves have been baking for 30 minutes, remove them from the oven and glaze with an **egg yolk** diluted with a tablespoon of water, brushed on with a pastry brush or your fingers. As soon as you've put the glaze on a loaf, sprinkle it with **caraway seeds,** if desired.

Return to the oven and finish baking.

Cool on a wire rack and serve hot.

Be sure to let your family see you take these loaves out of the oven—it's the only way you'll convince them they didn't come from the bakery.

SOUR PUMPERNICKEL—SUMMARY

A. 1 cup starter
   2 cups reconstituted skim milk
   2 tbsp. blackstrap molasses
   ¼ cup vegetable oil
   1 cup white flour
   1 cup rye flour
   2 cups whole wheat flour

B. 1 tbsp. sea salt
   ½ scant tsp. baking soda

C. ½ cup rye flour

D. 1–1½ cups white flour

E. 1 tbsp. caraway seeds

The first day make up the sponge by combining A into a large bowl. Cover and put into a draft-free place to rise.

The second day stir down the sponge, sprinkle B over
its surface, and work in.

Stir in C.

Spread most of D over kneading board and dump
batter onto the board, adding flour to the board as necessary during the kneading.

Knead for 5 minutes or so, working in E.

Grease two baking sheets; then sprinkle them with
white cornmeal.

Divide the dough into three parts, shape into loaves,
lay on the sheets, and slash three or four times to a depth
of almost a half inch.

Rise for 2–3 hours.

When risen, slash again, gently.

Spray with water before going into the oven and
again after 10 minutes baking.

After 30 minutes of baking, glaze with an **egg-yolk-
and-water glaze** (1 yolk to 1 tablespoon of water) and
sprinkle with additional **caraway seeds.**

Bake at about 350°–375° for about 40 minutes, then
test for doneness. If almost done, shut off the oven and
leave the loaves in for another 10 minutes.

Cool on a wire rack.

SOUR RYE

Here is a traditional bread, adapted for a bit more nutritive value without losing a bit of its delicious flavor or
good looks.

"Sour Rye" is what it says when you buy the packaged bread in a market, or it may be known as Jewish Rye,
or even New York Rye, but it's all the same bread.

You'll notice that the recipe calls for 2 cups of milk—
or any liquid. That's quite literal. You could use plain
water or fruit juice or chicken soup or beer. The liquid
used makes only a small difference to the final flavor (but
then, the difference between something good and something special is only a small difference). I like to use soup
stock.

Rye flour tends to make for a heavyish bread, so you
don't want to force in more of the white flour than the
minimum required to handle the dough. I remind you

that whole grain doughs tend to feel wetter inside than all-white doughs. So, don't strive for a dry dough; let the dough be as moist as it can be, just this side of too sticky.

This bread is kneaded more than the Sour Pumpernickel (a very close cousin) because the proportion of rye flour is higher. Remember, rye flour has almost no gluten, and so you must work the wheat flour until its gluten is developed enough to carry both itself and the rye—an ideal situation which in reality you never quite achieve.

A reason that some bought rye breads seem quite light and fluffy compared to home baked (apart from being machine-kneaded and aerated that way) is that some commercial bakers use very little rye flour and substitute caramel or some other coloring matter to get the look of rye—a solution that doesn't have my sympathy.

SOUR RYE

The First Day:
: 1 cup starter
: 2 cups milk—or any liquid
: ¼ cup vegetable oil
: 2 tbsp. blackstrap molasses
: 2 cups whole rye flour
: 2 cups unbleached white flour

The Second Day:
: 1 tbsp. sea salt
: ½ scant tsp. baking soda
: 1 cup whole rye flour
: 2–2½ cups unbleached white flour (enough white to knead)

For Greasing:
: melted butter or margarine, white cornmeal for sprinkling

Equipment:
: mixing bowl and spoon, kneading board, baking sheets

The First Day

In a large mixing bowl, stir together **1 cup of starter, 2 cups of milk** (or any liquid), **¼ cup of oil, 2 tablespoons of blackstrap molasses, 2 cups of rye flour,** and **2 cups of white flour,** until all is smooth.

Cover with a wet towel, and put into a draft-free place to rise overnight (or 12 hours).

The Second Day

Stir down the risen sponge.

Sprinkle over the surface of the stirred-down sponge **1 tablespoon of salt** and a **scant ½ teaspoon of baking soda,** and stir in.

Add the remaining **rye flour (1 cup)** to the mixture in the bowl and work in, wetting all the flour.

Kneading

Pour **1 cup of white flour** onto your kneading board and dump the batter onto it. Until you've worked in this cup, the dough will seem very loose.

Add another **cup of white flour,** and knead it in.

When you've kneaded in enough flour, sprinkle on your board only enough additional flour to keep this normally sticky dough manageable.

Knead for about 10 minutes, until the dough feels springy—resistant to your push—or until you can see the wrinkles on its surface.

When your dough is ready, grease two baking sheets and sprinkle them with **white cornmeal.**

Shaping the Loaves

Divide the dough into three equal parts and shape the loaves until the top surfaces look smooth, then place on the sheets.

Slash diagonally with a sharp knife about a half inch deep (three or four slashes per loaf), cover with a clean towel, and put in a warm place to rise for 2–3 hours. The slashes will gape wide open when the bread is ready.

Baking

Bake for 40 minutes at about 350°–375°, and then, if it tests almost done, in the oven with flame off for another 10 minutes.

Cool on a wire rack.

For best slicing, wait until the bread is fairly cool.

Options

☞ If you want a thicker crust, **spray** the loaves with water before putting them in the oven, and then again after they've been in for 5 minutes.

☞ If you like the shininess of the bakery loaf (they achieve it by glazing with a cornstarch solution), you can **glaze** with a smearing of **thinned egg** (1 tablespoon of egg to 1 teaspoon of water) 10 minutes before you shut off the oven. (Then use the remaining egg for scrambled eggs.) Don't glaze too thickly or you'll get yellow streaks.

☞ When you apply the glaze you can sprinkle on some **caraway seeds.** The glaze stays wet for a moment or two—time enough to sprinkle the seeds.

☞ If you want to add **caraway seeds, dill seeds, Russian caraway,** or **sesame seeds** to the bread proper, use a tablespoon of seeds for the entire batch, kneaded in when you've added the flour; or a teaspoon per loaf, kneaded in when you shape the loaves.

SOUR RYE—SUMMARY

A. 1 cup starter
   2 cups milk (or other liquid)
   ¼ cup oil
   2 tbsp. blackstrap molasses
   2 cups rye flour
   2 cups white flour

B. 1 tbsp. sea salt
   ½ tsp. baking soda

C. 1 cup rye flour

D. 2–2½ cups white flour

The first day mix A into a large bowl, until smooth.

The second day stir down the sponge, and mix in B.

Add C and work in.

Pour 1 cup of D onto kneading board, dump batter onto board, and knead.

Knead in another cup of D—and as much more as required to keep the dough from sticking.

Knead for 10 minutes.

Shape into three loaves.

Grease two baking sheets and sprinkle with **white cornmeal.**

Lay loaves on sheets and slash to a depth of a half inch, diagonally, three or four slashes per loaf.

Cover and rise in a warm place for 2–3 hours.

Bake in a 350°–375° oven for 40 minutes, then for another 10 minutes with the flame off (if the bread tests almost done).

Allow to cool for best slices.

SNACK BREADS

If you're looking for a light, airily textured bread, with a delicate flavor—just perfect for watercress and cucumber sandwiches—*keep looking because this is not it.*

But, if you're looking for a chewy, strong-flavored sour bread that's great with cheese or salami or tongue or liverwurst or hors d'oeuvres—you've arrived!

I invented this bread for my husband's thirty-fifth birthday party, making it right to his order: sour-ryish but chewier, with plenty of seeds, in long thin loaves, just right for a buffet.

Snack Bread comes only in this small size because it's too heavy a bread for large sandwich loaves—though if you like a heavy sandwich, go ahead and try it.

This is a backward bread, really: instead of working for lightness and rise and good texture, as with almost every other bread, here we are looking for a solid toughness that would mark failure in any other recipe.

You can use various kinds of seeds in Snack Breads —caraway, dark caraway (also known as Russian caraway or *tchernetsa*), dill, poppy, celery—it's up to you. Our favorite is the burnt flavor of the dark caraway, and I use plenty. But you've got to please yourself, so adjust the seeds to your own taste.

Risen in a warm place for about half an hour, these loaves will show some expansion, but not much; so don't expect these to double in size before baking. This is a *heavy* bread—deliberately.

SNACK BREADS

Yesterday:
    1 cup starter
    1¾ cups hot water
    2 tbsp. honey
    4 cups whole wheat flour
Today:
    2 tbsp. sea salt
    2 tbsp. seeds (caraway or dark caraway or dill or fennel, etc.)
    1 cup whole rye flour or rye meal
For Greasing:
    melted margarine or butter
Equipment:
    mixing bowl and spoon, kneading board, baking sheets

First Day

The night before you plan to bake the bread, make up the sponge: into a large mixing bowl measure **1 cup of sourdough starter** (whole wheat starter if you have it, but white is fine), **1¾ cups of hot tap water,** and **2 tablespoons of honey,** stirring it all to dissolve the honey.

Stir in **4 cups of whole wheat flour,** until your mixture is smooth.

Cover the bowl with wax paper or plastic wrap and set it aside in a draft-free place overnight. (If you get the inspiration early enough in the morning, you can make these breads the same day, because this sponge needs only 8 or 9 hours to work.)

Second Day

Uncover the sponge and stir it down.

Stir into the sponge **2 tablespoons of salt** and **2 tablespoons** of your favorite **seeds.** (More if, like my husband, you're a real seed freak; less if your tastes run milder.)

Kneading

Spread a **cup of rye flour or rye meal** on the kneading board, and dump the sponge onto it.

Knead in the rye flour (if more than a cup is needed

to make it stop sticking to the board, use additional **whole wheat**—you don't want to use more than one cup of rye). Remember, this is a whole grain bread; the finished dough is supposed to feel *moister* than the finished dough of a white bread. So don't keep adding flour until the dough feels dry.

This is one bread where skimping on the kneading won't matter at all, so knead only a couple of minutes more.

Shaping the Loaves

When you've finished kneading, divide the dough into four pieces and roll out the loaves.

Flour the board lightly—just to keep it from sticking, not to add more flour—and, starting in the middle, roll the dough into a single strand an inch thick. (That should make it just long enough to fit onto a large baking sheet—if your sheet is too short, cut off the excess and make five shorter loaves.)

As each loaf is rolled out, lay it on a greased baking sheet, two per sheet.

When the four loaves are rolled out, put the sheets into a warm place, cover, and allow to rise for ½–¾ hour.

Baking

There will be little discernible rise in the loaves, but, if there is none at all, allow to rise for another 15 minutes.

We don't slash this bread—so don't be shocked when it cracks along the side.

Bake at about 350° for 30–40 minutes, and, when you think they're done, test. Don't allow the small size of the loaf to fool you into thinking that it must be done. There is no must about it. Whole grain breads—especially rye breads—can be stubborn that way, taking longer to bake on a damp day, or just because you're in a hurry.

Cool on a wire rack, and when you come to slicing it, slice it thin with a serrated knife: the crust is a tough one and a plain knife could easily slip.

SNACK BREADS—SUMMARY

A. 1 cup starter
   1¾ cups hot water
   2 tbsp. honey
   4 cups whole wheat flour

B. 2 tbsp. sea salt
   2 tbsp. seeds

C. 1 cup rye flour or
   rye meal

The first day combine A in a large bowl until smooth. Cover and put in a draft-free place to rise overnight.

The second day stir down, then add B, mixing in thoroughly.

Spread C on your kneading board, dump sponge onto board, and knead in. (If more flour is required to flour board, use whole wheat.)

Knead for a few more minutes.

Grease two baking sheets.

Divide the dough into quarters and shape each quarter into a long, thin loaf—about 1 inch thick.

Lay the loaves on the greased sheets.

Rise for ½–¾ hour.

Bake 30–40 minutes at about 350°.

Test, then cool on a wire rack.

Cut with a serrated knife.

6

Spiral
Breads

Here's a bread that can keep your family interested day after day, because, like Cleopatra (a noted Egyptian bread baker), custom cannot stale its infinite variety.

It is called Spiral Bread because the dough is rolled out to a thickness of about one quarter inch, and then rolled up into the shape of a loaf. We spread the flattened dough with various fillings, so that when sliced the spiral is evident to the eye and the palate.

There is virtually no limit to the variations you can try with this bread. Different herb combinations give you a bread to complement (or contrast with) any main course; small bits of meat or shrimp give you a bread that's a main course in itself; various sweet combinations give you a dessert bread.

Don't be afraid to let the kids help you here. Their imaginations are particularly fertile in dreaming up combinations, and they will get a big kick out of helping to roll out the dough and sprinkling on the herbs. And don't worry about their using too much of an herb; there are very few herbs that can be "too much" in this bread. You'd be surprised how much of most herbs you need to really maintain the flavor after baking.

This is also a rich dough, though, without eggs, not quite as rich as the Rich Whole Wheat. But it's just as easy to handle—a necessity for this bread.

It is also a great dough for rolls. I'll describe Kaiser Rolls (Hard Rolls) and Knots after we've made the bread.

Before we get on to the baking let's talk about the fillings.

Herb Fillings

In class, I usually plan one herb filling, and then put out all my herbs and seeds for the class to invent a combination of their own. The planned filling is invariably grated Parmesan cheese (enough to cover the whole of the rolled-out dough with a thin layer), oregano, fennel seed, and basil. With this, as with all herb fillings, I butter the rolled-out dough with melted margarine or butter before scattering the cheese. This greasing helps the separate swirls of the spiral to stand out after baking.

As for the invented fillings, they are always different, and always interesting and tasty: minced onion or garlic; celery seed and celery salt and grated cheese; seasoned salt and thyme and tarragon; dill seed and dill weed and savory.

The list could go on and on. There is no herb you can't use, no combination you shouldn't try.

Main Course Fillings

This is not my favorite way to use these breads, so I don't emphasize them in class, but they are fine with bits of raw shrimp and fennel seed spread over the buttered surface, or with bits of chopped meat, or even with certain unnamable unhealthy things like sausage.

Just roll them up and bake like any other bread.

Sweet Fillings

Here's where the compliments get extravagant.

The recipe makes three loaves, and after the planned herb loaf and the invented herb loaf, my class makes the third loaf with cinnamon honey.

To make cinnamon honey, mix 4 teaspoons of cinnamon with 1 cup of honey (or maple syrup or maple sugar, if you have it). This is more than you will use for one loaf of bread (or even two loaves), but it can be kept in a covered jar for the next time you bake Cinnamon Spiral— and you will bake it again—or for cinnamon toast, or for spooning over hot cereals.

We don't butter this one. Just brush the cinnamon honey over the rolled-out dough.

Two of my students invented a delicious healthful alternative to this bread: Honey-Carob Spiral. For those of you who don't know carob, it is ground-up dried St. John's bread (a seed pod from a tree), and it is a healthful substitute for chocolate.

Take a brush and spread about 3 tablespoons of honey over the rolled-out dough and then sprinkle about 3 tablespoons of carob powder over the honey. Add nuts if you like.

I don't recommend jam because it is made with white sugar, but one of my students swears by a thin jam filling.

Make up your own combinations.

SPIRAL BREAD

For the Dough:
  2 tbsp. active dry yeast
  2 tsp. sea salt
  2 tbsp. honey
  2 cups hot water
  ½ cup skim milk powder
  ¼ cup vegetable oil
  1 cup raw wheat germ
  5–6 cups unbleached white flour
For the Filling:
  (whatever you like)
For Greasing:
  melted butter or margarine
Equipment:
  large mixing bowl, spoon or whisk, kneading board, rolling pin, optional pastry brush, 3 baking pans

Mixing

Into a large mixing bowl measure and combine **2 tablespoons of yeast, 2 teaspoons of salt, 2 tablespoons of honey,** and **2 cups of hot tap water.** Stir.

Mix in **½ cup of skim milk powder** (¼ cup if noninstant).

Stir in **¼ cup of vegetable oil.**

Mix in **1 cup of raw wheat germ** and the first **4 cups of flour,** 2 cups at a time.

Kneading

Spread a **fifth cup** over the kneading board and scrape the batter out onto the flour. Knead in. The dough will be very wet.

A little bit at a time, add as much of the remaining cup (#6) as required to make the dough stop sticking.

After that, use only light sprinklings during kneading: this dough should be light.

Knead for a brisk 5 minutes (or a lazy, easy 10 minutes).

First Rise

When fully kneaded (at which point the wrinkles should show beautifully on this bread), drip a few drops of oil (or melted butter or margarine) in the scraped-out bowl; drop in the dough ball; turn over a few times to oil all sides; cover with a clean, dry towel; and put in a very warm, draft-free place to rise.

This dough is likely to rise somewhat faster than most; if the day is warm, the rise can be finished in 45 minutes. But don't go by the clock: finger-test (see p. 54).

If your fingerprint stays in the dough, punch down, and knead gently for a minute to get rid of the larger bubbles.

Rolling Out

Divide the dough into three equal pieces.

At this point, when baking for myself, I put one third in a bowl and stick it in the fridge for a later bread or for Pizza (ah! the magic in that word—I only have to write the word "Pizza" and my husband comes into the room), set another third aside for Rolls, and make the third into a Spiral Bread. But you know your appetite.

I'll describe the making of one Spiral loaf, and you can repeat it for as many loaves as you wish.

Sprinkle a thin layer of flour onto your board. You may have to make a few such sprinklings through the course of the rolling. Put the ball of dough on the floured board and begin to flatten it out by pressing it with your hand or pushing it with your fingers. Turn the dough over and repeat.

You'll want to turn the dough over several times in the course of this flattening—it helps keep it from sticking. If you do all your patting and rolling on one side, I guarantee that the dough will stick and pull apart when you try to roll it up.

If the dough shows any sign of sticking when you turn it, give it a little sprinkling of flour.

As you poke and flatten try to keep the shape of the dough roughly rectangular.

Now, take your rolling pin and roll the dough out to a rectangular shape, a quarter of an inch thick. Watch out for the edges; they tend to want to be thicker. Continue to turn the dough over between rollings. Keep the shape rectangular.

If, despite your best efforts, the shape insists on having some nonrectangular portions, cut them off and throw them onto another piece of dough. (Should you need to cut and patch, water applied with your fingertips becomes the glue to hold the sections of dough together.)

When you achieve the ¼-inch thickness, turn the dough over, and put on your fillings (see pp. 117–119), right out to the edges. Be generous: this is a loaf of bread, not a piece of toast. (With sweet fillings, however, it's better not to be too generous: they come out very sweet.)

Rolling Up

We now have a slab of dough about ¼ inch thick, and spread with a combination to suit our taste. So, take a deep breath and relax.

The way you roll this loaf depends on the pan you want to put it in. Sometimes, my students like to put a Spiral Bread into a ring mold. In that case, we start rolling from the long side of the rectangle of dough, to get as long a loaf as we can. Sometimes the loaf goes into a regular loaf pan, in which case we start rolling from the short side of the rectangle, for as short a loaf as we can get. Spiral Breads can even be done free-standing on a baking sheet—in which case, roll it any way you please.

The secret of a successful Spiral is to roll tightly, making sure there are no air spaces as you roll. Roll slowly and evenly, not letting any part get too far ahead, checking often for air pockets, pushing the dough along with the flats of your fingers. (As you roll, you may have to pull out the edges of the dough to keep the rectangle.)

If the dough insists on sticking to the board a little, don't worry and don't force it. Take a scraper or a knife and gently loosen the dough. If, as instructed, you've turned the dough over during the rolling-out, the sticking won't be serious.

When you've rolled the entire filled rectangle (it's

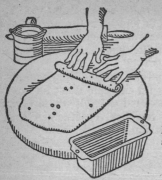

Rolling from the short
side to fit a loaf pan

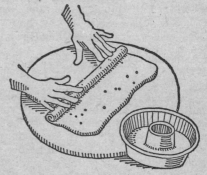

Rolling from the long
side to fit a ring mold

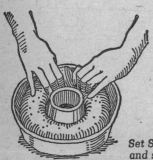

Set Spiral in ring mold
and seal the ends together.

easier than it sounds), wet your fingers and pinch all the seams closed, along the length and at both ends. Sweet fillings will run out if the seams aren't sealed. For a ring mold don't seal the ends; join the ends and seal them to each other.

Now, grease your pan and put the loaf in, seam side down. If the loaf is too short for the pan, don't be afraid to give it a gentle pull to make it longer. If it's too long, don't be afraid to push it together. Procrustean as it seems, you can do all this without losing the spiral.

Rising the Loaf

If you are doing a Cinnamon Spiral, spray the top with a little water and dribble over a bit more cinnamon. For Honey-Carob Spiral, spray and top with more carob powder.

For Cheese-Herb Spiral, butter the outside of the loaf (or smear it with egg white) and, if you like, sprinkle on additional cheese.

Cover with a clean, dry towel and put in a warm, draft-free place to rise for about half an hour.

The loaf will by no means double, but it will swell appreciably. (If you're rushed, this rise can be skimped a little.)

Baking

When risen, bake in a 350°–360° oven for 30–40 minutes.

Test with a clean knife for doneness (see pp. 21–23).

There is a problem with testing the sweet Spirals. Whether your filling is cinnamon and honey, honey and carob, jam, or some other sweet, the melting of the sweet can give a knife test that seems to indicate rawness.

You have to inspect your knife quite carefully; is that streaking really raw dough, or is it simply wet honey and carob?

Sometimes, the only way to tell is by cutting a loaf in half.

Try to serve this one hot.

A warning: Make certain your dough is rolled out to ¼-inch thickness, and that you roll it up tight. If your dough is thick and/or your roll too loose, the bread will come apart in the baking, and form internal arches—good for catacombs, but disappointing in bread.

Options

☞ If you are making all herb breads from this recipe you may want to add some **herbs** right into the dough. If so, put them in the mixing bowl after you add the hot water.

☞ You can double the **milk powder** to a full cup. No further adjustments will be required. Or make the bread with **whole milk**. If Spirals are your children's favorite, use super-milk—that is, whole milk plus milk powder. If you don't warm the whole milk, triple the rising time.

☞ If you wish, you may omit the buttering of the Herb Spirals—the difference is a subtle one.

KAISER ROLLS AND KNOT ROLLS

These two rolls have no real relationship to Spiral Breads: they are included here because this dough is particularly good for making rolls. Kaiser and Knot Rolls can be made from any kneaded dough. There's nothing to stop you from using, say, the Rich Whole Wheat dough and making yourself a brown Kaiser.

Kaiser Rolls

Kaiser Rolls are made very much like a pinwheel.

The entire recipe makes about 24 rolls. Or you can make 8 rolls with a third of the dough and refrigerate the rest.

Pinch off handball-sized bits of dough (or divide your third of the batter into eight parts), roll them into balls, then flatten them into rounds 4 to 4½ inches across. (You may have to flour your board lightly.)

Take one edge of the circle, lift it, and bring it into the center of the round. With your finger, press down the right side of the triangle you've just made.

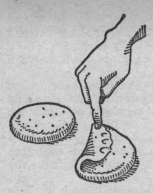

Press firmly along the
inside of the flap.

Lift the point . . .

And press it into the center.

Continue around, clockwise,
pressing only the right side
of each flap.

Press the last point
firmly into the center.

Move to the right, and lift the point which you've just created by pressing that seam and bring this point into the center, slightly overlapping the first fold.

Once again, with your finger, press down the right edge.

And again, moving to the right, lift the point end of the seam, and slightly overlap the points you've already made, and press down on the right side of the dough with your fingers.

The process is performed six times in all; the sixth time you don't press down the side of the triangle, but you do press firmly in the center, to make certain the roll doesn't open in the baking.

Set the rolls to rise for about half an hour, covered with a clean towel.

Put a couple of cups of water up to boil, because we're going to treat these rolls as if they were French Bread, so as to get a nice, crisp, crackling crust.

When risen, spray the rolls with water.

Put a shallow container into the bottom of the oven and pour in the boiling water.

Put your rolls in the oven and set it at 350°.

After 5 minutes, spray again.

After 15 minutes, take them from the oven, brush with **egg white,** and sprinkle on your favorite seeds. (I prefer **Russian caraway seeds,** but the delicatessens usually feature **poppy seeds.**)

Bake for a total of 25–30 minutes. (These rolls take this long because you remove them from the oven to glaze. If you omit sprayings and glazing, 20 minutes will do.)

Knot Rolls

These rolls are easy to make and very professional-looking.

The recipe will make about four dozen small rolls.

In your hands, shape a bit of dough until it's about 8 inches long and about $\frac{1}{2}$–$\frac{3}{4}$ inch thick. Then twist this rope into a simple overhand knot. You know, make a little loop and pass one end through.

Put to rise for half an hour, then treat just like the Kaiser Rolls. Or forget about the seeds, if you prefer.

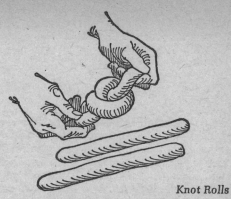

Knot Rolls

SPIRAL BREADS—SUMMARY

A. 2 tbsp. active dry
    yeast
    2 tsp. sea salt
    2 tbsp. honey
    2 cups hot water

B. ½ cup skim milk powder

C. ¼ cup vegetable oil

D. 1 cup raw wheat germ

E. 5–6 cups flour

Combine A into a large mixing bowl and stir.

Dissolve in B.

Stir in C.

Mix in D and the first 4 cups of E, 2 cups at a time.

Spread another cup of E over kneading board. Scrape batter onto board and knead in. (Add more until dough stops sticking, then sprinkle as needed.)

Knead briskly for 5 minutes.

Rise.

Finger-test and then punch down.

Pat and roll out dough into a rectangle, turning frequently and flouring board as required, until dough is ¼ inch thick.

Spread desired filling over dough.

Roll up tightly and evenly.

Seal seams with wet fingers.

Grease appropriate pan and put loaf in it. Cover and put to rise.

Wet top of loaf lightly and sprinkle on more of filling.

When risen, bake at around 360° for 30–40 minutes.

Test with a clean knife. Serve hot.

7

Rye
Breads
and
Pumpernickel

Rye is a low gluten (but not a nongluten) flour, which means that in an all-rye bread you would have to work like blue blazes to develop elasticity enough to hold some rise—and would still wind up with a bread two inches high.

Then why bother with Rye Bread at all? Well, if you ask that question, you've never tasted Rye Bread. I don't mean the kind of 1-cup-of-rye-to-3-cups-of-white bread that you'll find in most bakeries; that only gives you the barest hint of the great taste. Rye Breads are in a class by themselves when it comes to flavor (a class rivaled but not surpassed by Sourdough Breads).

Rye Breads are traditionally Northern European breads —German, Scandinavian, Russian. There is some difference between the breads made in Europe and the breads made here. Different strains of rye and wheat grow here. (Even the same strains take on somewhat different characteristics when grown in different soil.)

Russian peasants make a "black" bread from very dark flour, coarsely ground. But there is no equivalent flour in this country—and probably not in Russia today —so, to get a "black" bread I use blackstrap molasses: the federal government permits commercial bakers to use a whole string of chemical colorings.

While the four breads that make up this chapter aren't by any stretch of the imagination black, they are dark, and our Pumpernickel is quite dark. They are all delicious, with a delightful aroma, but by no means easy to make: in fact, two of them are out-and-out hard.

Rye flour is harder to handle than wheat. It looks

different and it feels different. It's stickier, which makes for more difficult kneading—yet it must be kneaded longer. Rye doughs are more moist, which means that to have a light-textured bread we never get the dough as dry as we do with wheat flour. (Do you remember what we did with Italian Bread to get a better web? Flattening the dough out and rolling it up? Well, *don't try that here*— rye dough will stick to the board!)

Of the four Rye Breads presented here, Potato Rye is the hardest to make up because it has the most rye flour; Refrigerator Rye is the easiest because it uses half white flour.

Pumpernickel is harder to make up than Refrigerator Rye, but easier than Swedish or Potato Rye. (Pumpernickel gives a higher and lighter loaf than the latter breads, with all the chewiness and flavor that makes it such a favorite in my classes.)

All the breads in this chapter require a great deal of kneading. Even after all the flour is in, you'll want to knead for another 15 minutes or more to develop as much of the gluten as you can.

If you've never made a kneaded bread before and want to try a rye bread first, start with Refrigerator Rye (but read pp. 129–130). It bears the closest resemblance to a "normal" bread, kneading up more quickly, with no worry about when the first rise is finished.

There are other problems with Rye Breads. For one, with Potato Rye and Swedish Rye you can't depend on the finger test to tell you when the dough is sufficiently risen. The dough of these two breads develops a minimum of gluten, and will hold a fingerprint *as soon as you finish kneading*, because of the low level of elasticity. So, for these two breads, don't use the finger test. Assume a rise (in a warm place, of course) of $1\frac{1}{2}$–2 hours, and keep looking at the dough. Much as I hate to resort to that old catch phrase, the dough has risen enough when it has "doubled in bulk," which means that it will take up about twice as much room in the rising bowl. Be sure you take a good look when you put the dough to rise—remember its size and level in the bowl.

With Refrigerator Rye and Pumpernickel you can use the finger test.

There is another problem with Rye Breads. Rye

dough tends to "draw wet," which means that the bread
can be baked enough to be fit for eating, and still show
streaks when you test it with a knife for doneness. (Refrigerator Rye isn't as much a problem this way as the
others.) Use the knife test by all means. It will still show
you whether or not you have gobs of unbaked dough. But
if the knife draws out a few *streaks* (not dough), tap the
loaf on the bottom. A done loaf will give quite a hollow
tom-tom sound.

I know this sounds inexact—but so much of baking
is.

Remember—you can always cut a loaf open to see
if it's done. If it's not, you can put it back in the oven.
The cut will not heal, but the bread will finish baking.

Share the making of these breads with a friend—
someone to relieve you and take over part of the kneading; I never make a Rye Bread without my husband.

If you don't have someone to help, knead in spurts,
covering the dough with the mixing bowl while you rest.
The dough doesn't care if it's kneaded in five 3-minute
chunks, or in one 15-minute sprint.

More than other breads, Ryes like an occasional
flouring of the kneading board—even after "enough"
flour is in.

Also, you'll have to clean your hands off more often;
as I said, rye is stickier. Spill a little flour between your
palms and rub away as much dough (onto the dough
ball) as you can. Then take a spoon or a scraper and
scrape away what remains. (You'll see what I mean
within the first minute of kneading Potato or Swedish
Rye.)

Are you discouraged? Don't be. These are rewarding
breads, healthful and great-tasting—and like nothing
you'll find in a bakery.

POTATO RYE

Potato Rye, and Swedish Rye which follows, should be
rated "X"—for adults only; the flavors are too definite
for kids.

Potato Rye is an old, traditional recipe, with European—especially German—roots, combining two peasant standbys, flour and potatoes.

This is quite different from any other bread in the book. It has no sweetener, neither honey nor molasses. The mashed potatoes and potato water are what feed the yeast. Of course, the flour will feed the yeast, too, but that is a slower process, while the carbohydrates in the potato are quickly converted, although not as quickly as honey or molasses.

Because it is such a great yeast-feeder, this water that the potatoes have cooked in should never be thrown away: it is an excellent bread-baking liquid.

The potato also helps to solidify the texture, making for a satisfying, crusty, heavy, solid bread—though by no means too heavy.

Both the mashed potato and the potato water should be hot when they are used, as hot as the hot tap water which we've used in most other recipes, so unless you have just cooked up the potatoes, heat them. If you use them cold, you'll slow down the rising time by hours. But, when you heat them, don't allow the water to boil. One of the few times I ever killed yeast was with this bread—bringing the potato water (with the potatoes in it) to a boil, and then not waiting for it to cool before throwing in the yeast. To avoid this, stick your finger in the water before you add it to the yeast. If you can hold your finger in it for a few seconds (no heroics, please), fine. If it feels too hot, wait a while or cool it down with a little cold potato water. Better to be safe than have dead yeast.

This bread is not a high riser. It is certainly higher than all-rye breads, but not nearly as high as the other loaves we've been working with.

But that's the nature of rye, and it still makes good toast and great eating.

POTATO RYE

For the Dough:
> 2 tbsp. active dry yeast
> 1 tbsp. sea salt
> 1 tbsp. caraway seeds
> 2 cups hot potato water
> 1 packed cup hot mashed potatoes
> 4 cups whole rye flour
> 2–2½ cups whole wheat flour

For Greasing:
> melted butter or margarine
> cornmeal

Equipment:
> large mixing bowl, mixing spoon, kneading board, large baking sheet

Mixing

Into a large mixing bowl, measure **2 tablespoons of yeast, 1 tablespoon of salt, 1 tablespoon of caraway seeds,** and **2 cups of hot** (but not boiling or near-boiling) **potato water,** and stir.

Add **1 cup of hot mashed potatoes.** Mix until the mashed potato has been distributed fairly evenly throughout.

Stir in the **4 cups of rye flour,** 2 cups at a time. (The mixture will appear grayish—don't worry.)

Add **1 cup of whole wheat flour** to the bowl and mix in.

Kneading

Spread **1 cup of whole wheat flour** over your kneading board, scrape the batter onto the flour, and knead it. There will be very little resistance or cohesion until you have the whole cup well in.

Continue to knead for 15 minutes, adding as much of an additional ½ **cup of whole wheat flour** to the board as necessary to handle the dough.

Remember, this dough never really gets dry. On the surface (if you don't dig your fingers into it), it will be rather less sticky, but it should never really dry, staying even wetter than the Whole Wheat Breads we've done.

If, after 15 minutes, you are not feeling resistance

when you knead, knead for another 5 or 10 minutes. It is very important to develop all the gluten you can.

First Rise

When the dough shows signs of good resistance as you knead, stop, scrape the dough off your hands, drip a few drops of oil into the scraped-out but unwashed bowl, drop the dough in, oil all sides, and put to rise in a very warm, draft-free place, covered with a hot, wet towel. (Like whole wheat dough, the rye will crust if the towel isn't wet and warm.)

You'll want it to rise for about 1½–2 hours, or until the dough has about doubled in volume. (Don't skimp on this rising time.)

Remember, the finger test doesn't work for this bread.

Shaping The Loaves

When doubled, punch down and knead out any large air bubbles, right in the bowl.

Dump the dough ball onto your kneading board, and cut in half.

Knead each half into a smooth ball, then shape into a loaf, about 8 by 4 inches, and as high as you can make it.

Grease a baking sheet large enough to hold your two good-sized loaves (they will swell), and sprinkle with **cornmeal** (for a good bottom crust).

Lay the loaves on the sheets, spaced well apart, and, with a sharp or serrated knife, slash each loaf with three or four diagonal slashes to a depth of about one-half inch.

Rising the Loaves

Cover with a clean, dry towel (a moist towel would stick to the loaves, causing them to fall when you removed it), and put back in that very warm, draft-free place to rise for 30 minutes to an hour (about half the time of the first rise).

The slashes will gape wide when the bread is well risen, and the loaves will look considerably larger. If you aren't certain the loaves have risen enough, wait a bit more.

When risen, remove the towel and spray, brush, or sprinkle the loaves with water, to help get that marvelous, crunchy crust. Spray again after 15 minutes of baking.

Baking

Bake the loaves in a moderate oven (350°–375°) for 50 minutes, then leave in the hot oven *with the flame off* for another 10 minutes. After a knife test has shown you there are no large clumps of dough, thump the bottom crust for hollowness.

Here's something I've found helpful: if the bottoms are showing signs of getting burnt before the baking time is up, and the knife test shows signs of raw dough—turn the loaves over and let them bake for a few minutes *topside down*.

When done, remove from the oven, allow to cool on a wire rack for a half hour, and eat warm.

Options

☞ In all Rye Bread recipes, the substitution of all or part **rye meal** for the rye flour will give you a pleasant chewiness.

☞ If you want to include **wheat germ** or **bran** in this recipe (or the following recipes), substitute for the rye flour, not the whole wheat. We need all the gluten we can get.

☞ You could make the recipe easier to work (and less nutritious) by substituting **unbleached white flour** for all or part of the whole wheat. If you do, be sure to substitute ½ cup of wheat germ for an equal amount of rye.

☞ The kind and amount of **seeds** are very much a matter of taste. My husband, for example, thinks that 1 tablespoon of caraway seeds isn't enough by half. You may want to try **dark caraway seeds** for this bread, or **fennel seed** (as in the Swedish Rye that follows).

☞ After the spraying you could sprinkle a teaspoonful of **seeds** over the surface of each loaf.

POTATO RYE—SUMMARY

A. 2 tbsp. active dry yeast
   1 tbsp. sea salt
   1 tbsp. caraway seeds
   2 cups hot potato water

B. 1 cup hot mashed
   potatoes

C. 4 cups whole rye
   flour

D. 2–2½ cups whole
   wheat flour

Combine A into a large mixing bowl and stir.

Add B and mix in.

Add C, 2 cups at a time. Stir in.

Mix in 1 cup of D.

Spread another cup of D over kneading board, scrape batter onto board, and knead in.

Add as much of remaining ½ cup as required to permit kneading, then knead for 15 minutes more.

Oil the dough in the mixing bowl, cover with a wet, hot, clean towel, and set to rise until doubled: about 1½–2 hours. Do not finger-test.

Punch down, knead out bubbles, then dump dough ball onto board and divide in half.

Shape two loaves, approximately 8 by 4 inches.

Grease a large baking sheet, sprinkle with cornmeal, and lay the loaves on the sheet, well apart.

Slash each loaf three or four times, a half inch deep.

Cover with a clean, dry towel, and replace in a warm, draft-free location for 30 minutes to an hour. (Look for the gaping of the slashes and for the increase in loaf size.)

When risen, spray with water. (Spray again after 15 minutes baking.)

Bake about 50 minutes at 350°–375°, then 10 minutes with flame off.

Thump the bottom for doneness. If done, the loaf should sound very hollow.

Cool on a wire rack for a half hour.

SWEDISH RYE

This is definitely the tastiest rye in the book, but really too savory for breakfast.

This is a traditional Swedish recipe (but made with

blackstrap molasses instead of corn syrup because I can't bring myself to use sugar syrups when molasses is so much better for me), and quite different from most of the kneaded breads we've made together.

Instead of slashing, we'll repeatedly prick the surface of the molded loaf with a fork.

Instead of working for a crisp crust, we'll try for a soft one, brushing the loaf tops with milk toward that end.

Instead of the standard loaf shape for whole grain breads, we'll shape these loaves like the French Bread baguettes.

When you shape the loaves, give a good bit of kneading to the individual thirds and shape them into smooth balls before you roll the dough out to long loaves. If there are folds in the dough, they won't disappear, and the bread might open along such a seam.

Although potato water is the liquid called for in this recipe, you have a wide range of liquids to choose from: skim milk or buttermilk are very Scandinavian; and beer is a popular liquid with Rye Breads. (See Options for amounts.) Whatever liquid you use, make certain it is hot (but not boiling). If you do not use potato water, increase the salt by 1 teaspoon.

This bread is slightly easier to work up than the Potato Rye. For one thing, there is a higher proportion of wheat flour in the recipe. For another, we use a $\frac{1}{4}$ cup of oil. That doesn't sound like much, but it does make a difference in ease of handling. But that doesn't mean you can skimp on the kneading. Don't.

The recipe tells you to mash the fennel seed in the mixing bowl with the back of a spoon, assuming that you don't own a mortar and pestle. If you do, by all means crush your fennel there and pour it into the bowl.

By the way, don't—unless you're desperate—use ground fennel. (If you do, use $1\frac{1}{2}$ tablespoons.)

SWEDISH RYE

For the Dough:
  2 tbsp. fennel seed
  2 tbsp. active dry yeast
  ¼ cup blackstrap molasses
  ¼ cup honey
  2 cups hot potato water
  2 tsp. sea salt
  grated peel of 1 orange
  ¼ cup vegetable oil
  3 cups whole rye flour
  3½–4 cups whole wheat flour
For Greasing:
  melted margarine or butter
  cornmeal
For Crust:
  milk
Equipment:
  large mixing bowl, spoon or whisk, kneading board, 2
  baking sheets, pastry brush (optional)

Mixing

Drop **2 tablespoons of fennel seed** into your mixing bowl,
and crush it with the back of the bowl of a spoon. It's not
necessary to grind it up fine—just break the seeds open to
release the flavor.

Add **2 tablespoons of yeast, ¼ cup of blackstrap molasses** plus **¼ cup of honey** (measured into the same cup),
and **2 cups of hot potato water** (not boiling). Stir, to mix.

Add **2 tablespoons of salt**, the **grated peel** (just the
zest, the outer peel) **of 1 orange**, and **¼ cup of vegetable
oil**. Stir.

Mix in well, **3 cups of rye flour**.
Mix in **3 cups of whole wheat flour**.

Kneading

Spread **¼ cup of whole wheat** over the kneading board and
scrape the batter onto the flour. Knead in.

Continue to knead for 15 minutes, using as much of
the remaining **¼ cup of flour** as necessary for kneading.
Try not to go beyond 7 cups altogether.

First Rise

When well kneaded, drip a few drops of oil into the scraped-out bowl; drop in the dough ball, oiling all surfaces; cover with a hot, wet, clean towel; and set in a very warm, draft-free place to rise for about 1½ hours.

Again, the finger test won't tell us when the dough is risen, so look for it to double in volume.

Shaping the Loaves

When risen, punch down, and knead in the bowl for a minute to get rid of those big air bubbles.

Turn the dough onto the board and cut into three pieces. Roll the dough into three smooth balls. Roll the balls out into three loaves, about 2 by 14 inches. I know these look quite thin, but they will swell—though never as much as French Bread loaves.

Grease two baking sheets with melted butter or margarine, and sprinkle with a thin layer of **cornmeal**.

Lay the loaves out, two on one sheet, one on another. Prick all over the top surface with a fork. (This gives quite a different look to the loaf than slashing.)

Rising the Loaves

Cover with a clean, *dry* towel, and set in a very warm, draft-free place to rise for 30–45 minutes. The loaves should look considerably risen before you bake them.

When risen, brush the tops with a bit of milk (skim or whole—it doesn't matter), using either a pastry brush or your fingers. Whichever you use, be careful—these loaves are very easy to knock down. (If you used *beer* as your liquid, don't brush with milk, brush with beer.)

Baking

Bake in a 350°–375° oven for about 30 minutes.

Try using the knife test—sometimes it works for this bread. At any rate—tap the bottom for the hollow sound.

Cool on a wire rack for a few minutes and serve hot. The taste of the fennel seed and orange is mind-blowing.

Options

☞ If you want to use **beer** for your liquid, be sure it's warm (and increase the salt by 1 teaspoon). Use either 2 cups of beer, or 1 cup of beer and 1 cup of another liquid. Don't worry about curdling the **milk** or **buttermilk**. Bread doesn't care. Any **vegetable water** will do excellently in this bread (or in any bread, for that matter).

☞ Reducing or cutting out the **honey** will lower the calories. It will also reduce the keeping power of your bread.

☞ **Anise seed** is another traditional Scandinavian herb, so feel free to substitute anise for the fennel seed. But crush it, and don't use the ground stuff—it has no texture.

☞ If you prefer a **hard crust** to the soft one that is characteristic of this bread, spray twice with water (as with the Potato Rye) instead of using milk.

☞ **Rye meal** substituted for rye flour makes for a nice chewiness.

☞ As with Potato Rye, if you are substituting **wheat germ** or **bran,** do so for part of the rye flour.

SWEDISH RYE—SUMMARY

A. 2 tbsp. fennel seed

B. 2 tbsp. active dry
   yeast
   ¼ cup blackstrap
   molasses
   ¼ cup honey
   2 cups hot potato water

C. 2 tsp. sea salt
   grated peel of 1
   orange
   ¼ cup vegetable oil

D. 3 cups whole rye
   flour

E. 3½–4 cups whole
   wheat flour

   milk

With the back of a spoon, crush A in your mixing bowl.

Add B and stir.

Mix in C.

Add D and mix in.

Stir in 3 cups of E.

Spread another ½ cup of E over the board and scrape batter onto board. Knead in.

Knead for 15 minutes, adding as much of remaining flour as necessary for kneading.

Oil the dough ball in the bowl; cover with a hot, wet, clean towel; rise in a warm place for about 1½ hours. Do not finger-test.

When risen, punch down, and knead for a few minutes in the bowl.

Dump onto kneading board and divide into three.

Roll each third into a smooth ball, then roll out into three long loaves, about 2 by 14 inches.

Lay loaves on greased and cornmealed baking sheets. Prick all over top surfaces with a fork.

Cover with a clean, dry towel and rise for 30–45 minutes.

When risen, brush surface of loaves with milk.

Bake 350°–375° for about 30 minutes.

Thump the bottom for the hollow sound indicating doneness.

Cool on a wire rack, serve hot.

REFRIGERATOR RYE

If Potato Rye and Swedish Rye are rated "X," there's no doubt that Refrigerator Rye is rated "G." This bread is mild flavored—for a Rye—and made in loaf pans for a sandwich shape.

If this is your first experience with a Refrigerator Rise Bread, you might want to refer back to Chapter 3, where a couple of them are discussed.

This is the easiest of the Rye Breads we'll do. The gluten in the white flour makes it quicker to work up cohesion, and gives it a higher rise than the other rye doughs. Also, it requires less kneading, with less dough sticking to your hands, and less need to flour the board.

All in all, a good, simple Rye Bread without particular problems to watch for.

REFRIGERATOR RYE

For the Dough:
  2 tbsp. active dry yeast
  1 tbsp. sea salt
  ⅓ cup blackstrap molasses
  ¼ cup vegetable oil
  2 cups hot water
  3 cups whole rye flour
  3–3½ cups unbleached white flour
For Greasing:
  melted butter or margarine
Equipment:
  mixing bowl, mixing spoon or whisk, kneading board,
  3 baking pans 8″ × 4″ × 2″, plastic wrap

Mixing

Into a mixing bowl combine **2 tablespoons of yeast, 1
tablespoon of salt, ⅓ cup of blackstrap molasses, ¼ cup of
vegetable oil,** and **2 cups of hot water.** Stir.
  Add **3 cups of whole rye flour** and mix in.
  Add **2 cups of white flour,** and mix that in.

Kneading

Spread **another cup of white flour** over the kneading board
and scrape the dough out onto it. Knead it.
  Add as much of the remaining **½ cup of white flour** as
is necessary to make the dough stop sticking (as little
as possible).
  When the dough stops sticking, knead for another 10
minutes. The dough will be quite cohesive and gets quite
springy as it approaches readiness.

Shaping the Loaves

As with the other Refrigerator Rise Breads, *this bread gets
no rise in the bowl.*
  When sufficently kneaded, divide the dough ball into
three equal parts and shape each part into a loaf to fit an
8″ × 4″ × 2″ loaf pan.
  Grease the three pans with melted butter or margarine, and put a loaf into each.
  With your fingers, level out the top of each loaf.

Now, take three pieces of greased plastic wrap and cover each pan. Grease the whole piece of plastic—the bread will fall if the plastic sticks. Don't make the plastic taut and don't try to fasten it to the sides; you want it movable, to rise as the dough rises.

Rising

When the loaves are covered, set them in the refrigerator, in a place where they won't have to be moved around, and where they will have room to rise well above the pans. (Remember, don't poke the breads—pokes will stay in the loaf, even if they don't punch the dough down.)

Allow to rise in the fridge for 5–24 hours. (The last time I baked this bread I took the loaves from the fridge after 6 hours and they were beautifully risen.)

Baking

When you want to bake them, take the loaves from the refrigerator, gently remove the plastic wrap, and bake immediately in an oven set for 350°–375° (medium flame) for about 45 minutes.

Knife-test for doneness (see pp. 21–23).

Cool on a wire rack, and by all means try it warm.

Options

☞ Again, you can use **any liquid** for the water in the recipe. Try **skim milk powder** (⅔ of a cup)—just add it to the recipe after the water—or substitute **whole milk,** heated. Any **vegetable water** is a welcome addition; if it's salty, reduce the salt in the recipe. Or any combination of these. Just because you use salty vegetable water doesn't mean you can't use milk powder in the same batch, and so on.

☞ **Caraway, fennel,** or **anise seeds** are an interesting addition to any Rye Bread. You can add a tablespoon to the mixing bowl, or knead in a teaspoon per loaf when shaping the loaves.

☞ By all means substitute some **bran** or **wheat germ** for some of the rye flour.

REFRIGERATOR RYE—SUMMARY

A. 2 tbsp. active dry yeast   B. 3 cups rye flour
    1 tbsp. sea salt
    ⅓ cup blackstrap molasses   C. 3–3½ cups white flour
    ¼ cup vegetable oil
    2 cups hot water

Combine A into a bowl.

Add B, and mix in.

Add 2 cups of C, and mix in.

Spread another cup of C over kneading board, scrape batter from bowl, and knead in.

Knead in as much of remaining ½ cup as necessary to stop sticking.

Knead for 10 minutes more.

Divide into three loaves.

Grease three baking pans, 8″ × 4″ × 2″, and set a loaf in each.

Cover the pans with greased plastic wrap and set in refrigerator to rise for 5–24 hours.

When risen, gently remove plastics, and bake about 45 minutes at 350°–375°.

Knife-test for doneness. Eat warm.

PUMPERNICKEL

This traditional bread is of German origin and combines rye, whole wheat, and white flours in a chewy, flavorful loaf. Occasionally you will see "pumpernickel flour" on sale. That's a laugh; there's no such thing. It will be a mixture of two or more kinds of flour. A particular favorite with my students, Pumpernickel requires a good deal of kneading, which makes it another "friend bread."

By way of getting a "black" peasant bread, there are recipes that call for burnt crumbs mashed up in the dough (to me they just taste burnt), others that call for chocolate, still others that use chemical colorings.

We'll use blackstrap molasses and Postum (or instant coffee). Postum, for those of you who don't know it, is a coffee substitute, a roasted cereal beverage with no caffeine, but with a taste and look close to coffee (though it does contain sugar). We'll also use it for the glaze, to finish the dark color. But you are welcome to try roasted chicory or coffee for the same effect.

Pumpernickel loaves are generally free-standing, either oval or round, but if you prefer a loaf pan, there's no reason you shouldn't try it.

PUMPERNICKEL

For the Dough:
3 tbsp. active dry yeast
2 tsp. sea salt
¼ cup blackstrap molasses
1 tbsp. Postum (or instant coffee powder)
2 cups hot water
¼ cup vegetable oil
2 cups whole rye flour
2 cups whole wheat flour
1–2 cups unbleached white flour
For Greasing:
melted butter or margarine
white cornmeal
For Glaze:
1 tsp. Postum
2 tsp. water
Equipment:
large mixing bowl, mixing spoon or whisk, kneading board, 2 baking sheets, pastry brush (optional)

Mixing

Combine in your large mixing bowl **3 tablespoons of yeast, 2 teaspoons of salt, ¼ cup of blackstrap molasses, 1 tablespoon of Postum,** and **2 cups of hot water.** Stir, mixing it all together.

Mix in **¼ cup of vegetable oil.**

Add **2 cups of whole rye flour,** and mix it in.

Add **2 cups of whole wheat flour,** and mix it in.

Kneading

Spread **1 cup of white flour** over the kneading board, scrape the batter out onto the board, and knead.

Add as much of the remaining **1 cup of white flour** as necessary to stop the dough from sticking—though, remember, this is mostly a whole grain bread, and it will always be stickier than an all-white bread.

Knead for 15 minutes more.

First Rise

When kneaded (and you should see those wrinkles), drip a few drops of oil into the bowl; drop the dough ball in; turn it to oil all surfaces; cover with a clean, hot, wet towel; and set in a very warm, draft-free place to rise (about 1–1½ hours).

You can use the finger test on this dough—it's mostly wheat and has plenty of gluten and lots of elasticity.

Shaping the Loaves

When risen, punch down in the bowl, and knead for a moment to get out the larger air bubbles.

Dump the dough onto the kneading board, and cut into three pieces.

Shape each piece into a loaf, either round or oval.

Grease two large baking sheets with melted butter or margarine, and sprinkle on some **white cornmeal.**

Place two loaves on one sheet (leaving plenty of room for rising) and one loaf on the other.

Cover with a clean, dry towel, and set again in that warm, draft-free place to rise. (You'll notice that we don't slash or prick our Pumpernickel loaves. We want them to be dense.)

When the loaves are well-risen (½–¾ hour), brush the top surfaces with a **glaze** made from **1 teaspoon of Postum** dissolved in **2 teaspoons of water.** You can use your fingers or a pastry brush, but, either way, be careful not to punch the loaf down, as you'll just have to reshape and wait for it to rise again.

Baking

Bake in a moderate oven (350°–375°) for 50 minutes to 1 hour. If the loaves seem close to scorching after 50 minutes, but still test raw, shut the oven off for the last 10 minutes of baking.

The knife test for doneness isn't fully reliable for this

Rye Bread, so thump the bottom for that telltale hollow sound.

Allow to cool on a wire rack, and eat warm.

Pumpernickel is a good keeper.

Options

☞ I like to use seeds in my Pumpernickel, a tablespoon of either **caraway, anise, dill,** or **fennel,** tossed into the mixing bowl after the water, or a teaspoon of any seed kneaded into each loaf when you're shaping it. You may want to make one loaf without seeds and two with, just to see what you like.

☞ Again, you can substitute *any liquid* for the water in this recipe: **milk, beer, vegetable water,** what have you. If you want to use **skim milk,** add ⅔ cup of instant powder (⅓ cup of non-instant) right after the hot water.

☞ **Raw wheat germ** or **bran** can be substituted for part of all three flours (¾ cup of raw wheat germ and/or bran substituted for ¼ cup of each flour).

☞ **Rye meal** is especially recommended as a substitute for the rye flour in this bread. It makes the texture even more interesting.

☞ If you forget to glaze the loaf before baking, you can glaze it any time—up to and including the moment you take it from the oven. However, if you glaze it after taking the bread from the oven, the taste of the Postum is recognizable as Postum; the flavor disappears in the baking.

☞ **Yellow cornmeal** instead of white is fine for sprinkling too.

PUMPERNICKEL—SUMMARY

A. 3 tbsp. active dry yeast
2 tsp. sea salt
¼ cup blackstrap molasses
1 tbsp. Postum (or instant coffee)
2 cups hot water

B. ¼ cup vegetable oil

C. 2 cups whole rye flour
2 cups whole wheat flour

D. 1–2 cups unbleached white flour
1 tsp. Postum in 2 teaspoons water

Combine A into a large mixing bowl.

Mix in B.

Mix in C, 2 cups at a time.

Spread 1 cup of D over kneading board, scrape batter onto board, and knead in.

Knead in as much of the remaining cup as required to make the dough stop sticking.

Knead for an additional 15 minutes.

In the same mixing bowl, oil the dough, cover with a clean, wet towel, and set to rise in a warm, draft-free place for 1–1½ hours.

Finger-test.

Punch down, knead for a moment, then dump the dough onto the kneading board.

Cut into three pieces, and shape each piece into a loaf.

Grease two baking sheets with **melted butter** or **margarine** and **sprinkle with white cornmeal.**

Lay the loaves on the sheets, leaving room for the rise.

Cover with a clean, dry towel, and let rise for 30–45 minutes in that warm, draft-free place.

When risen, glaze with **1 teaspoon of Postum** dissolved in **2 teaspoons water.**

Bake for 50 minutes to 1 hour at 350°–375°.

Thump bottom of loaf and listen for hollow sound indicating doneness.

Cool on a wire rack. Eat warm.

8

Challah
and
Brioches:
The
Great
Egg
Breads

These oily-eggy breads are incredibly easy to handle. That's probably what inspired the French to shape theirs into a crown or topknot, and the Jews to braid theirs into Challah—because with these doughs you can! Brioche dough is even oilier than Challah, though they share a delightfully silky look and feel.

CHALLAH—THE GREAT BRAID

If you were to poll the students in my baking classes, Challah would come out in front by far.

Challah is the traditional braided Jewish Sabbath loaf. This yeast bread, rich with eggs and oil, is delicious cooled, but even better eaten warm from the oven, with pieces torn rather than cut from the loaf.

The Challah one sees in bakeries is most often made from six strands of dough (one quarter of the mixture made into a small braid of three strands, set atop a larger braid of three strands made from the remaining three quarters of the dough). But to have a loaf symbolic of the Sabbath, you need a seven-strander (one strand for each day of the week), made up of a small three atop a large three, interwoven or crowned by a single strand, signifying the Sabbath—the crown of the week.

However, the number of strands do not affect the flavor and texture of this very satisfying bread. You might want to make three- or four- or six-strand braids during the week, and bake a seven-strander Friday to greet the Sabbath on Friday night.

Challah dough is a pleasure to handle. The combination of oil and eggs gives it a feel that some students have compared to a baby's bottom and others to a woman's breast—indicating the kind of rapture experienced kneading and braiding Challah.

This bread slices beautifully when cold, and makes the best toast and French toast I know. Also, it's a fine keeper, so you don't have to be afraid of having an extra loaf around for a few days.

CHALLAH

For the Braids:
- 2 tbsp. active dry yeast
- 4 tsp. sea salt
- ¾ cup honey
- 1¾ cups hot tap water
- 2 cups unbleached white flour (more to come)
- 1¼ cups vegetable oil
- 3 large eggs
- 5–6 more cups unbleached white flour

For the Glaze:
- 1 egg
- poppy seeds

For Greasing:
- melted butter or margarine

Equipment:
- large bowl, mixing spoon or wire whisk, kneading board (if you have a marble slab—great), large baking sheet (or 2 small ones)

Mixing

Measure the **yeast, salt, honey,** and **hot water** into the bowl and stir.

Mix in the first **2 cups of flour.** (All egg breads take

part of the flour early to give the eggs something to hold onto.)

Mix in the **oil** and **3 large eggs.**

Kneading

Add **4 more cups of flour** gradually. As soon as working with the spoon or whisk becomes heavy going, clean it into the bowl (see p. 23) and switch to mixing the flour in with your bare hands. (You've begun kneading right in the bowl.) This dough is easy to knead because it is soft and yielding.

Dump the dough out onto your floured kneading board (a rubber spatula will be handy in scraping out the sides of the bowl) and knead in some of the **remaining flour.** *Don't force in every last bit of flour* that you can—this dough *must remain silky.* Because Challah dough is oilier than most that you've been used to handling, the temptation is to force in more flour to make the dough conform to what you're used to. *Don't.* Challah is a nonconformist.

Of course the exact amount of flour you use will vary from day to day, especially depending on the moisture in the air. So, if the dough is still *sticky* (not oily, but actually sticking to your fingers) when you total 8 cups of flour, all right—add a bit more. And if you've reached a cohesive ball after only 6½ cups, stop! Baking is such an inexact craft.

After all the flour is in, 8–10 minutes more kneading should bring out those faint, satiny wrinkles on the surface.

First Rise

Put your ball of kneaded dough into a greased bowl; turn it over (to grease all sides), cover with a clean towel, and let stand in a very warm place for about a 1-hour rise.

After an hour, finger-test for sufficient rise (see p. 54). Don't go by its looks in the bowl because Challah more than doubles its volume. It can fill your bowl and still not be ready. If your finger test is at all doubtful, let it rise longer: a *full* first rise is vital to light Challah.

When the rising is complete, punch down, turn the dough out onto your board and knead for a couple of minutes to get rid of the larger gas bubbles—you can feel them pop as you squeeze the dough.

If you are working on marble you may not have to flour at all, but if you are using a wooden kneading board, *flour very lightly.*

Flour your hands as little as possible for this kneading and for the shaping. The oiliness of the dough takes care of most of the sticking.

Braiding

Cut your mound of dough in half for the two loaves. (It's fun to let husband, friend, child, or visitor shape one loaf while you do the other. One teacher has her five-year-old

Begin braiding from the center.

Turn the board and braid the other way.

group help her with Challah: the dough is that easy to handle.) Now, for a three-strand braid, cut the dough for your loaf into three equal lumps. Using your hands and gravity (do not roll on the board), squeeze and roll each of the three lumps of dough into a rope about an inch thick (the length of the loaf depends, of course, on the thickness of the ropes), laying them parallel on the board to be braided. (If you've never braided anything before, take a piece of string and practice.)

Begin braiding in the middle. If you start at one end you are likely to have fat ropes at the beginning and then end with them getting thinner and thinner. By starting your braid in the middle and braiding overhand down to one end, and then turning your board and braiding underhand down to the other end, you stand a much better chance of coming out with a symmetrical loaf.

But lopsided braiding doesn't really matter. This is a beautiful bread—both to eat and to look at—and an unpracticed braiding can't hurt it. In fact, irregularities almost disappear as the loaves expand during rising and baking.

Transfer the braids onto a large greased baking sheet, centering and separating them. Leave room: these loaves will rise and spread a lot.

Rising the Loaves

Cover the loaves and return them to that warm place, and allow to stand for a half hour or more, until the loaves look well-risen. (They will get even bigger as the baking begins.)

Glazing

Break an egg into a cup and beat it with a fork. Using your fingers or a pastry brush smear the egg over all the visible parts of both loaves (smear gently so as not to dent).

Sprinkle **poppy seeds** over the tops of the loaves.

If you've begun to bake the Challah and realize you've forgotten the poppy seeds and feel you can't eat Challah without them, don't despair. Even after a half hour's baking, the loaves can be taken out, smeared with a little more egg, and seeded (but do it quickly—the heat of the hot loaf will soon dry out the new glaze).

Baking

Egg Breads should bake low and slow. This one will go 50 minutes to an hour in the middle of a medium-low oven —about 350°.

If your oven—like mine and like most—gives uneven heat, turn the loaves back to front after about 40 minutes.

Use any of the standard tests for doneness (see pp. 21–23), especially a toothpick through any crack in the top, but bottom color is quite useful here—it should be a rich, almost reddish, brown. If you dripped when applying the glaze, use a metal spatula or a large-bladed knife to unseal the loaves from the baking sheet so you can take a look. (Looking at the color of the top is almost useless—the egg glaze makes the top look beautiful before it's really ready.)

Remove the loaves and stand them on a wire rack to cool. If you want to eat the Challah hot, tear chunks off the loaf. It's a poor slicer when hot—but slices well once it has cooled.

Option

☞ For a healthier loaf, substitute **1 cup** or **1½ cups of raw wheat germ** for an equal amount of flour. With a cup of wheat germ in it your loaf will still be fluffy light and the flavor will be faintly *nuttier*, which most people like better.

Hints

☞ Don't skimp on the kneading just because the dough feels so nice so quickly.

☞ If the day is really damp—if it's raining now or has recently rained long and hard—decrease the water in the recipe by ⅛ cup or so. Otherwise, the loaf will accept extra flour and could come out a bit dry and less sweet.

☞ Make the braids up as soon as you have squeezed out the ropes. Otherwise, the strands tend to dry and come apart in the baking. However, if you do have to answer the phone, for instance, while braiding, and don't want to knead up the whole batch to shape anew when you come back, moisten your fingertips with water and lightly wet the ropes, especially the ends where you seal them together.

CHALLAH—SUMMARY

A. 2 tbsp. active dry yeast
   4 tsp. sea salt
   ¾ cup honey
   1¾ cups hot water

B. 2 cups flour

C. 1¼ cups oil
   3 eggs

D. 5–6 cups flour
   1 egg
   poppy seeds

Measure A into a bowl, and stir.
Mix in B.
Stir in C.
Add enough D to lose stickiness, and begin kneading in bowl.
Dump dough onto board, and work into a silky texture.
Replace in oiled bowl; cover. Rise in a warm spot for about 1 hour.
Finger-test.
Punch down and knead briefly.
Braid into two loaves. Place on greased baking sheet.
Rise, covered, in warm spot for a half hour.
Glaze with whole egg and sprinkle on poppy seeds.
Bake low and slow—50 minutes to an hour at 350°.
Check doneness by bottom color and by toothpick.

BRIOCHES—THE HEAD AND THE CROWN

The word "brioche" describes a dough—made here with eggs, oil, yeast, honey, and flour, much like the Challah just made—but it also describes the various breads made from that dough: *Petites Brioches* (the small Brioche Rolls that are the most popular), *Brioche à Tête* (the head— a large, round loaf with a topknot, the same shape as the Brioche Rolls), and *Brioche Couronne* (the Crown Brioche). They are all made from the same recipe, and vary only in their shaping.

Imagine a bread lighter than Challah, with a pastry-like texture, a crisp crust that literally melts as you chew it, and a taste that has to be experienced to be believed. If the French have Brioches for breakfast every day, it's a wonder that any Frenchman gets to work on time.

There has grown up around Brioches the idea that this is the most advanced kind of bread you can make (and then only after years of practice) and that it requires two days of preparation. Well, don't you believe it! Brioches, in addition to being among the best of breads, are also among the easiest:

—they *don't* take special handling (in fact, the egg and oil make the dough *easier to handle*)

—the dough does *not* have to be refrigerated overnight (though it can be—even over several nights—without losing a bit of its texture)

—the shaping is as simple as making mudpies

—you can do *all* your kneading right in the bowl.

Brioche Rolls cook up perfectly well in muffin trays, though if you have tart molds (the kind with fluted sides), the flutings add character to the shape. If you have neither muffin pan nor tart molds, individual jello molds will do, also. (My husband and I collect agateware and we picked up a tray perfect for Brioche Rolls: shallower than the jello molds, the indentations are fluted and rounded, giving the underside of the rolls a delightful shape while the enameled iron makes for a deliciously crisp crust. The tray holds six—a morning's restrained indulgence.)

The dough keeps refrigerated for several days in a covered bowl, so don't feel you have to make the whole batch at one go. Also, they're so high in calories that a few at a time is plenty.

The texture of Brioche dough is similar to that of Challah, but it is considerably oilier and yellower in color due to the higher proportion of eggs. This oily-egginess leads to a caution: *don't flour your hands when you're handling the dough*—whether it's shaping the rolls or crown or topknot, or working out the air bubbles the next day after refrigeration—the additional flour will coarsen the texture.

This recipe makes enough for 24 Brioche Rolls or two Topknots or one or two Crowns.

You don't have to be French to be *fou* about Brioches.

BRIOCHES

For the Brioche:
  2 tbsp. active dry yeast
  ¼ cup honey
  1 tsp. sea salt
  ½ cup hot water
  ½ cup skim milk powder
  1 cup unbleached white flour (more to come)
  1 cup oil
  4½ large eggs (4 whole eggs plus 1 egg white)
  4 more cups unb'~~ched white flour (approximately)
For the Glaze:
  1 egg yolk
Equipment:
  large bowl, wire whisk or spoon, muffin pan or tart
  molds for Petites Brioches; large baking sheet or molds
  for Brioche à Tête or Couronne

Mixing

Measure the **yeast, honey, salt,** and **water** into the bowl,
and stir.

Mix in the **milk powder** and **1 cup of flour.**

Add the **oil** and **4½ eggs.** (Reserve the odd yolk for
the glaze.) Beat in until smooth. Eggs and oil should be at
room temperature.

Begin to stir in the remaining **4 cups of flour.**

Kneading

When using the whisk becomes too much like work, push
the dough out from the whisk and work with your bare
hands (see p. 23).

At no point is it necessary to flour your hands. Do
not turn out onto a kneading board; the texture of Brioche
dough makes it ideal for kneading in the bowl.

Knead in flour until your kneading hand (or hands)
is cleaned by the dough and the dough shapes readily
into one large ball. *Then add no more flour.* Continue to
knead until the dough wrinkles—about 10 minutes.

First Rise

Brioche is so oily in itself that it would be superfluous to
oil the bowl, so just cover the bowl with a clean towel,

and put in a very warm place to rise for about 1½ hours. This one is the best riser in the book, practically tripling, so don't be fooled by having it apparently "doubled in bulk"; finger-test (see p. 54).

Punch down when done, and knead for a minute— enough to get the dough down to its original size.

Shaping

PETITES BRIOCHES—BRIOCHE ROLLS
This dough will make 24 Brioche Rolls.

Brioche dough is so oily that greasing the muffin tray is unnecessary.

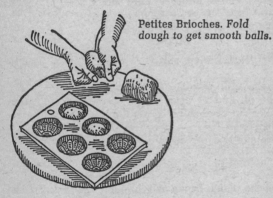

Petites Brioches. *Fold dough to get smooth balls.*

Wet balls with one finger and place little heads with the other hand.

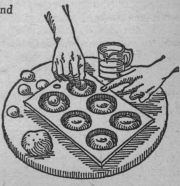

Do not flour your hands. It would be impossible to keep them floured and the oily-egginess prevents your hands from sticking.

Pinch off bits of dough and shape balls about 1½ inches in diameter. The balls are shaped by a stretching and folding or tucking motion (stretch the dough smooth across the top, and then tuck the ends into the bottom), repeated until the ball is smooth to the eye, with the rough ends pinched together at the bottom. Place a ball, smooth side up, into the depressions of your muffin tray or tart molds, and dent the tops with a finger.

Pinch off smaller bits of dough and similarly shape into ¾-inch balls, and place in the dents.

When you have finished the whole tray, wet a finger with water, lift up each smaller ball, and wet the depression—replacing the ball on the wet spot. The wet acts as a glue to keep these little heads on.

BRIOCHE À TÊTE—THE HEAD OR TOPKNOT

Divide the dough in half. (This dough will make two topknots, but I'll describe the making of one with half the dough.)

Reserve about a fifth of the lump, and with the remaining four fifths shape a ball as described for *Petites Brioches* (the topknot and the rolls have exactly the same shape—their only difference is size), stretching the dough across the top and tucking under the bottom. You can get a smooth side to begin with by folding the dough in half. Because this is a much larger dough ball, it will take more stretching and tucking.

Place the ball, smooth side up, on an ungreased baking sheet.

Shape the reserved fifth into a smaller ball, using the same method. Wet two fingers and make a depression in the center of the larger ball. Place the smaller ball into that depression.

BRIOCHE COURONNE—THE CROWN

This dough is enough for one huge crown or for two moderate crowns.

Using the same stretching and tucking method described above, shape a large ball and poke your finger

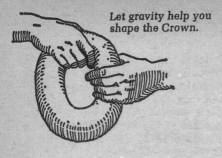

Let gravity help you shape the Crown.

Scissoring the top of the Couronne

through it (the poke goes through from the smooth top to the pinched bottom).

With gravity as a stretching aid, shake the dough and rotate the circle in your hands, forcing in more fingers, to enlarge the hole, until the crown has an outside diameter of about 8 inches, tucking under and pinching together on the bottom as needed.

Place the crown on a baking sheet or in a tube pan (if you are using an angel-food mold, the Brioche should fill it one third or less), and make your final pulls and pokes and tucks to get it into a fairly uniform shape.

With a pair of scissors, clip 8 to 12 slashes evenly into the sides, about a third of the way through. This will encourage the crown to rise out. If you want it to rise up, clip the top.

Final Rising

Cover rolls, topknot, and/or crown and leave in a warm place to rise again for about 40 minutes. You'll see how much they swell—they'll double *before baking*.

Glazing

Break the **egg yolk** and gently spread it over the Brioches with your fingers or with a pastry brush. (If this seems too thick, you can thin the yolk with a teaspoon of water.)

Baking

Bake in a moderate (350°–375°) oven: 30–40 minutes for *Couronne* or *Brioche à Tête*; 20–25 minutes for *Petites Brioches*. The *Couronne* or the *Brioche à Tête* should be deep brown on the bottom when done; the *Petites Brioches* should range from golden to red brown. But test by sticking a toothpick into the neck or a slash.

Cool on a rack or eat them right from the muffin pans.

Although other breads, if refrigerated, would go stale (see Appendix A, pp. 191–195), the oiliness of Brioches makes it possible and in fact desirable (to avoid rancidity) to refrigerate them.

Options

☞ A **half cup of whole milk** can be substituted for the milk powder and water.

☞ Or **2 tablespoons of cream,** and milk to fill ½ cup, can be substituted.

☞ The **grated peel of 1 lemon** gives Brioche dough an even lovelier aroma: the lemon doesn't come out lemony, it makes for a brighter flavor.

(Whenever you finish a lemon, throw the peel—pulp and all, but no seeds—into the freezer; they are so much easier to grate while still frozen.)

☞ For a healthier Brioche, you can substitute up to **1 cup of raw wheat germ** for an equal amount of flour. But in this case you do need to grease the pans, molds, or sheets before baking: the flecks of wheat germ tend to stick.

Hints

☞ For a crustier bottom use some heavier material than lightweight aluminum for baking the rolls.

☞ The *Petites Brioches* can also be baked on a baking sheet—but they will spread and won't rise as high.

☞ When eggs are dear, you can make a good Brioche with as few as 3 eggs (and then glaze with melted butter).

☞ When you break the eggs, do use your fingers to scoop out the white that clings to the shell. It is the white of the egg that has the rising power. If you leave a quarter of the white in the shell, you won't get as high results.

☞ If you are planning to refrigerate your entire batch of Brioche dough overnight, use only 1 tablespoon of yeast. Even in the fridge the yeast plants are increasing and the overnight rise in the fridge becomes equivalent to the second tablespoon of yeast. If you begin with two yeasts, your bowl of dough may push its cover off.

☞ You can do a large topknot in a mold, but let it be a high-sided mold—this one really expands. Let your dough fill less than half the mold. (If you have nothing better, try a 2-pound coffee can.)

☞ And, yes, of course you can braid it, bake it in shaped pans, or put it on a sheet in *whatever new shape you wish to invent.*

BRIOCHES—SUMMARY

A. 2 tbsp. active dry yeast
   ¼ cup honey
   1 tsp. sea salt
   ½ cup hot water

B. ½ cup skim milk powder
   1 cup flour (more to come)

C. 1 cup oil
   4½ eggs (4 whole eggs plus 1 white)

D. 4 more cups flour (approximately)
   1 egg yolk

Measure A into the bowl, and stir.
Mix in B.
Add C, reserving the odd yolk for the glaze, and beat till smooth.

Gradually add in D until dough is cohesive.

Knead for about 10 minutes in the bowl.

Rise for about 1½ hours in a very warm place. Finger-test.

Punch down and knead down to original size.

Shape Brioches as given on pp. 157–159.

Rise again for about 40 minutes.

Glaze with egg yolk.

Bake *Couronne* or *Brioche à Tête* 30–40 minutes at 350°–375°; bake *Petites Brioches* 20–25 minutes at the same temperature.

Toothpick-test for doneness.

9

Pizza, Pitta, and Nan

Pizza, Pitta, and Nan—as marvelous a trio as you'll meet anywhere.

This is an international group of breads covering almost half the globe.

Pizza, of course, is the most western of the three, native to Italy but quite at home all over the United States.

Pitta is Middle Eastern, and can be found (with various spellings) in many countries of the Arabic world, and in Greece and Armenia, though its popularity here is growing.

Nan is pretty much of a newcomer in the States (though very popular in India, its home), but delicious and different.

All three are easier to make than you'd ever think, and all three are guaranteed to elicit the warmest compliments.

There is one trait they all share which may be a bit of a drawback in the warmer months (though more likely with Pitta and Nan than with Pizza)—they like to work in hot ovens: around 450°. Pizza takes only about 20–25 minutes and you open the oven once—to put on the filling. But the other two demand that you stay by the oven, putting in and taking out—and that can be warm work.

These are the only breads in the book for which you must preheat your oven—with Pizza, Pitta, and Nan you just don't want the slow rise that a cold oven gives.

PIZZA

The Pizza we know in America isn't *the* Pizza, but *a* Pizza, because *pizza* is an Italian word for anything that is flat and round and baked—like a pie. So, anything you want to bake flat and round—and anything you want to put on top of it—*that's* Pizza.

After saying which I have to laugh, because the Pizza we'll make together here looks very different from what you'll find in a pizza parlor. We can't duplicate the evenly heated stone linings of the commercial ovens, nor the 600°–650° temperatures. Can you imagine that heat in your kitchen? And, since I can't get large, round baking pans to fit my oven, our Pizza isn't round at all, but rectangular, and baked on everyday baking sheets.

Also, our crust will be thinner and crisper. And the fillings my husband makes for Pizza never see a canned tomato sauce. He makes the topping while I roll the dough—so much of baking is more fun with a friend.

(By the way, if you're tempted to spin your Pizza dough into the air like the professional Pizza twirlers, go right ahead—but it's not likely to do you, or your floor, much good. Commercial Pizza is made from a softer wheat —also a bleached *and* brominated wheat—which makes for a dough that's easier to flip, and one that's nutritionally poorer.)

My favorite Pizza topping is made of zucchini (green summer squash) and onions. I'll give you my husband's recipe after I've described making the crust. And for those of you who are more traditionally minded, his recipe for a tomato topping, too.

As for Pizza dough, I won't give you a recipe simply because *I don't use any particular recipe for the dough.* What I do is set aside a half or a third of whatever kneaded dough I'm making, and put that in the fridge to use for Pizza when I want it: Spiral Bread dough, French or Italian Bread dough, the Pitta dough in the following recipe—even Rich Whole Wheat dough.

And if I'm using a basically white dough, I always make sure I've used wheat germ in the recipe, so we're bound to get, between a healthful topping and the wheat germ, some good nutrition as well as the great goodness of the taste.

PIZZA

For the Dough:
    half of any kneaded bread recipe in the book (except
    Nan—which is too wet)
    3 tablespoons vegetable oil
Equipment:
    kneading board, rolling pin, 2 baking sheets

Mixing

A half of any of the recipes in this book (using 6 to 9
cups of flour) should give you two Pizzas in 11″ × 16″
baking sheets.

That means that, for instance, half of the French
Bread recipe, put aside in the refrigerator and taken out
in a week (or even later), will give you two 11″ × 16″
Pizzas. (Of course, you don't have to make up both Pizzas
at once.)

Although you can make your Pizza as soon as you
rise the dough, I'll assume you've been keeping the dough
in the refrigerator (in a plastic-covered bowl, naturally)
since you last baked (a week or so ago).

First, dig out baking sheets and rolling pin. Your
hands are going to be oily, and you won't want to have to
search. Also, it helps with the rolling-out if you have the
baking sheet in front of you to check for size.

Take the bowl of dough out of the fridge and remove
the plastic or wax paper cover. In the bowl, give a gentle
kneading to get rid of any big air bubbles—just a minute
or so.

Cut the dough in half, in the bowl.

(If you are making one Pizza, return half the dough
to the fridge, and decrease the oil to 1½ tablespoons.)

Light your oven for preheating to as near 450° as it
will get while you prepare the dough.

Pour 3 **tablespoons of vegetable oil** (perhaps olive oil)
over the two halves.

Shaping

Take one well-oiled half from the bowl and place it on
your kneading board. With stiff fingers, poke it flat into
a rectangle. (Notice that instead of flouring the board, we

are oiling it, which has a similar slippery effect.) Now, with your rolling pin, roll the dough flat to the general shape of your baking sheet, with the dough very thin—about ⅛ inch.

When you think you have it large enough, place the inverted baking sheet over the dough, and cut out the dough a bit larger than the dimensions of the sheet (the dough will tend to shrink). Do what patching is necessary. Notice with the oiled dough how easily it handles and how readily any mends blend together.

Your dough should be so oily that you don't need to grease the baking sheet.

Transfer the rectangle to the baking sheet, folding over at the edges to fit the dough in, creating a raised edge.

Repeat the process for the second Pizza.

If there is any oil left in the bowl, smear it over the top of the dough with your fingers.

Baking

Put onto the oven racks to bake for about 15 minutes, or until the pizza shell is crisp.

Pour your favorite topping (or my favorite topping, which follows) over the baking dough, and sprinkle a **couple of tablespoons of grated Parmesan cheese** or **¼ cup of grated mozzarella** over each Pizza.

The topping should be hot, and so all you're waiting for now is for the cheese to heat. (If you've made your topping ahead of time, be sure to heat it before putting it on.)

Bake for another few minutes to melt the cheese.

A Pizza wheel (cutter) is handy for cutting, but a knife, judiciously handled, will do very well.

Eat it hot—sprinkled with ground red peppers if you like hot stuff.

ZUCCHINI TOPPING

    1 large onion
    2 cloves garlic
    2–3 tbsp. vegetable oil
    2–2½ pounds green squash
    1 tbsp. dried oregano
    2 tbsp. dried basil
    1 tbsp. fennel seed
    ½ tsp. sea salt

Cut **1 large onion** and **2 cloves of garlic** (large) into small bits.

Pour **2–3 tablespoons vegetable oil** into a large skillet (enough to cover the bottom without excess), and put the onion and garlic to sautée over a medium flame.

Wash and trim the ends of **2–2½ pounds of zucchini** and cut into ¼-inch slices. (Don't peel it!)

When the onions and garlic are browned, add the **zucchini,** the **oregano, basil, fennel seed,** and **salt,** and stir.

Cover and cook over a medium flame for about 20 minutes, stirring occasionally. (The exact cooking time will depend on the size of your skillet. If it is large enough not to pile the squash high, it will cook faster—if it's small, the zucchini will take longer. If it's too small, it won't hold all that zucchini, and you'll have to cook up your topping in two batches.)

QUICK TOMATO TOPPING

    10 large, juicy tomatoes
    2 tbsp. vegetable oil
    1 tbsp. dried basil
    2 tsp. fennel seed
    ½ tsp. sea salt
    garlic powder

Wash the **tomatoes** and cut them into small pieces. (A hint: These don't by any means have to be hothouse or beefsteak or any other kind of expensive tomatoes. The cheapest you can get are as good as the best. Just make sure they are ripe, not green. They can even be overripe—the taste isn't noticeable after cooking.)

Pour **2 tablespoons of vegetable oil** into a large skillet, and dump the cut-up tomatoes in along with the **herbs** and **salt**. Sprinkle with **garlic powder** to taste. Stir and cover.

Cook over a *high* flame for 6 minutes (yes, that's all), lifting the cover only to mash the tomatoes into a mush after 4 or 5 minutes.

When topping the Pizza, spoon out with a slotted spoon to allow the water which has formed to stay in the skillet. This tomato water makes a great drink or a marvelous liquid for your next baking.

Either of these two Pizza toppings may be varied or combined in any way you please. So be sure to taste during the cooking—you may want to add a little salt or pepper, or your own special Italian trick.

PITTA

The word *pitta* is Greek for—you guessed it—pie!

On the streets of New York, you can buy Middle Eastern sandwiches; they consist of Middle Eastern bread (Pitta or Pita or Peda, etc.) with a few cubes of hot lamb and some cold salad.

The last time I made this bread in class, one of my students brought in falafel and houmis (the one like small vegetarian meatballs, the other a chick pea paste), the time before that a student brought Baba Ganouj (an eggplant puree) and Middle East salad.

But you don't have to eat Middle Eastern to make and enjoy Pitta. It's great just as it is, hot (and I do mean hot) from the oven, or as the bread for any sandwich—it even makes great hamburger rolls.

The greatest thing about Pitta isn't what you put into it, but the bread itself. It is tasty, crisp, with a delicious aroma.

If you've never seen Pitta, ours is a round, flat bread, about 5 inches across, that forms an internal pouch in the baking. (It's this that makes it such a natural for fillings —you just slit it open and there's a ready-made pouch waiting for *something*.) The surface should come out a golden-to-dark brown that is very attractive.

Commercial Pitta is often larger than what we bake (ours is an easy size to handle), thinner, too, but nowhere near as light or tasty.

There are certain things to watch for in making this specialty. The dough is first formed into balls and then flattened into rounds ¼ inch thick. If you leave creases in the dough as you shape the rounds, or if you pinch the dough as you shape them, these creases or pinches tend to stay, and the Pitta won't rise there. You've lost your chance of a pouch along that pinch.

You may have to flour your hands lightly when handling the dough balls for shaping—and you'll certainly have to lightly flour the kneading board where you put them to rest (the balls get a 10-minute rest before flattening).

The dough is medium-stiff: neither very stiff, like Italian Bread, nor almost wet, like French Bread.

The recipe will make a dozen Pitta, each weighing about 4 ounces before baking, if you want to check the dough balls for size.

Greeks or Armenians of the older generation make this bread directly on the bottom of the oven (understand that I don't mean the bottom rack, or under the broiler, but the metal shelf just over the flame). They will pat the balls out, and flip them onto the bottom of the oven (without any greasing) and then pull them out with a long spatula or a baker's peel.

In my city apartment, with my ancient oven, I can't bring myself to bake directly on the bottom, so we'll use a baking sheet (greased only once, before the baking) large enough to hold two Pitta at a time, and then put the sheet onto the bottom. I hope the Greeks will forgive me. If you want to try the bottom of your oven directly, and it's clean enough, there's no reason why you shouldn't.

Bottom color is the indicator for this bread. It has a tendency to go dark on the bottom, and to be completely baked, while the top is still pale. No difficulty. If the bottom shows dark, put the baking sheet under the broiler flame for half a minute or less (I do it for a counted 20 seconds!) until brown on top.

I preheat my oven only for the 10 minutes that the balls require to rest, which means the first pair takes a little longer than subsequent pairs (I bake them two at a time). The first pair bakes in about 7 minutes, the second in about 6 minutes, the subsequent ones in about 5 minutes each.

PITTA

For the Dough:
1 tbsp. active dry yeast
2 tbsp. honey
1 tbsp. sea salt
2 cups hot water
5–6 cups unbleached white flour
For Greasing:
melted butter or margarine
Equipment:
large mixing bowl, mixing spoon or whisk, kneading board, baking sheet

Mixing

(If you've never made a kneaded bread before, read pp. 52–53.)

Into your mixing bowl, combine **1 tablespoon of yeast, 2 tablespoons of honey, 1 tablespoon of salt, and 2 cups of hot tap water,** and stir.

Add the first **4 cups of flour,** 2 cups at a time, mixing in well.

Spread **1 cup of flour** over your kneading board, scrape the dough onto the board, and knead in.

Add as much of the **remaining cup of flour** as required to make up a medium-stiff dough.

Knead for a few more minutes.

First Rise

Drip a few drops of oil into the scraped-out bowl and drop the dough ball back in, turning it to oil the surface.

Cover with a clean towel, and put in a very warm, draft-free place to rise for about an hour.

When the finger test (see p. 54) shows the dough is risen, punch down and knead gently for a moment to get rid of any big bubbles.

Shaping

Dump the dough out onto your lightly floured board. Cut it into 12 roughly equal pieces. Don't try to make all the Pitta exactly the same size. If some are larger and some smaller, no harm. But if you take little bits from one and stick them onto another, the seam or crease that's left will keep the Pitta from rising along that line.

Roll the 12 pieces into 12 balls. Put each ball on the floured board. Cover the dozen with a clean towel and let rest for 10 minutes.

Preheat your oven by setting it on high. You want to bake these at about 450°, but the opening and putting in and taking out tends to keep the temperature down a bit. If yours will go to 450° and stay there, great. If your oven is like mine, set it for high, and let it stay there. If your thermometer shows your oven going much over 500°, level it off.

After 10 minutes, uncover the balls of dough and begin to shape. Pull one gently from the board, lay it on the palm of your hand, and press and pat until it begins to flatten. (If the ball wants to stick to you, flour your hands.)

Now, because the balls have rested for that 10 minutes, the tops have dried out slightly, giving them a dry side and a wet side. Lay the dry side on the board, and, with the palm of your hand, pat, press, and pound (but don't poke) until the ball is flattened into a round of dough, about ⅜ inch thick and 5 inches across.

Gently lift this round of dough from the board, and lay it on the baking sheet, leaving room for another. Flatten it a little more after you've transferred it—it tends to thicken up.

Repeat for the next ball. Don't pinch or squeeze the dough too thin. It won't rise where it's pinched.

Flatten only two at a time—and only when you're ready to put them on the sheet. Made even a few minutes in advance, the rounds will begin to rise and be difficult to handle.

Baking

Put the baking sheet on the bottom of the oven, and bake for 5–7 minutes, or until the bottom color shows dark brown (lift the "pie" with a spatula or pancake turner, and peek).

If the top color is pale, put under the broiler for a few seconds, until brown.

Dump the finished Pitta onto a plate for serving straight from the oven, and begin to flatten your next pair. I told you that you'd be busy at the oven!

If wanted for sandwiches, slit one side and insert the filling.

PITTA—SUMMARY

A. 1 tbsp. active dry yeast   B. 5–6 cups flour
   2 tbsp. honey
   1 tbsp. sea salt
   2 cups hot water

Combine A into a bowl and stir.

Add the first 4 cups of B, 2 cups at a time.

Spread another cup (no. 5) over kneading board and scrape dough onto flour. Knead in.

Add as much of another cup as required to knead up a medium-stiff dough.

Drip a few drops of oil into the bowl and drop in dough, oiling all surfaces.

Cover with a clean towel, and set in a warm, draft-free place to rise for about 1 hour.

Finger-test.

Punch down and knead out large air bubbles.

Roll into 12 balls, and place the balls on the lightly floured board.

Light oven, set for 450°.

Cover balls and rest them for 10 minutes.

After 10 minutes, flatten two balls into rounds about ¼" × 5".

Lay rounds on a greased baking sheet (flatten a little more) and bake on the bottom of the oven until bottom of Pitta shows dark brown.

Brown tops under broiler for a few seconds.

Remove from oven and start flattening the next pair.

Serve very hot.

NAN

I don't know any Hindi but I can't help wondering if nan means pie. Nan is by far the tastiest of this trio (at least as far as the dough itself—I make no comparison between any bread and my husband's good Pizza topping). But, like many beautiful creatures, you have to know how to handle her. Nan is worked with a dough that is almost too wet to handle. What happens is that we mix up a dough that never does get enough flour in to stop sticking to your hands while you're kneading, but which, after being left to rise for about an hour, pulls itself together enough to be just handleable—with floured hands and board.

Like Pitta, this dough is separated into small balls before being flattened into shape. Like Pitta and Pizza, it is baked in a preheated oven around 450°.

Unlike Pitta, this flat bread is not expected to make its own pocket or pouch in the baking. Nor is it used like Pitta as a sandwich of sorts (though it can be). Nan is a dinner bread, brought to the table hot and eaten with the meal—but I find it crisp and delicious enough to have with a cup of tea instead of a sweet roll.

I hope all your burns are healing well from our baking of Pitta, for the same cautions apply here. We'll be opening and closing the oven, putting baking sheets in and taking them out, so be sure you have adequate potholders.

We'll knead and rise Nan in its mixing bowl, but we'll have need of the board later, so be sure it's handy.

Nan is not a beginner's first bread—at least I don't think of it as simple. My recommendation would be to get the feel of a couple of other kneaded breads before you tackle Nan.

When kneading, use only the fronts of your fingers—don't dig in as you would with other, drier doughs. And use only one hand to knead. You're going to require the other hand clean and dry to get you out of the sticky dough and add more bits of flour as you knead. Just push the dough around for a while—until you see the sheeting that we spoke of in Method Breads (see p. 31): that elasticity that shows gluten development. Remember, flour your hands as you work—and when you get to the board, flour your hands and the board.

NAN

For the Dough:
  1 tbsp. active dry yeast
  1 tbsp. honey
  2 tsp. sea salt
  ¼ cup vegetable oil
  ¼ cup yogurt or buttermilk
  1 egg
  1 cup hot water
  3½–4 cups unbleached white flour
For Greasing:
  melted margarine or butter
For Glaze:
  melted margarine or butter
  poppy seeds
Equipment:
  mixing bowl, mixing spoon or whisk, kneading board
  or platter, baking sheet, pastry brush

Mixing

Into a mixing bowl measure **1 tablespoon of yeast, 1 tablespoon of honey, 2 teaspoons of salt, ¼ cup of vegetable
oil** (sesame oil gives a nice Oriental touch), and **¼ cup of
yogurt** or buttermilk. Stir together.

Mix in **1 large egg.**

Add **1 cup hot tap water,** and stir everything together.
Mix in the **first 3 cups flour,** a cup at a time.

Flour your hand, and add more flour, a little at a
time, kneading in the bowl, until the dough begins to
show the first signs of not sticking. You should be kneading with only one hand, and not really digging in, but
rather pushing the dough around with the flats of your
fingers.

From time to time clean your hand off with a scraper
or spoon (and re-flour), because dough tends to stick to
dough.

At somewhere past 3¼ cups of flour, you should be
able to just handle the dough—albeit gingerly.

First Rise

Scrape the dough down off the sides of the bowl, onto
the ball at the bottom. Cover with a clean towel, and set
in a warm, draft-free place to rise.

The rise should take about an hour, but even here give it the finger test (see p. 54).

If it passes, flour your hand, punch it down, and knead out the bigger bubbles.

Shaping

Flour your kneading board (or a large platter—you won't be kneading, so all you require is a place big enough to set down balls of dough without their touching each other).

Scrape the dough ball out onto the floured board and cut into 12 roughly equal pieces.

With floured hands, roll each piece into a ball, and place on the floured board to rise for 10 minutes, covered with a clean towel. Don't try to make perfect balls—you're going to change the shape in 10 minutes anyhow.

Set your oven on high for preheating during the 10-minute rest.

You want to bake these little beauties (like the Pitta) at about 450°.

Grease a large baking sheet—this once for the whole batch.

Pick up your first ball (with floured hands) and flatten it between your hands to an oval shape about ¼-inch thick. Do try not to let it be thicker. If you find round loaves more attractive than irregular ovals, then just flatten the ball into a circle, but still ¼-inch thick.

Lay the oval (or circle) on the baking sheet, leaving room for one other (we bake Nan two at a time), and press it a little flatter with the flat of your hand.

Repeat the process with the second ball—flouring your hands, flattening, setting onto the baking sheet, flattening a bit more.

Dip your pastry brush into melted butter or margarine and brush the tops of the flat loaves. Sprinkle with a few poppy seeds.

Baking

As with Pitta, put the baking sheet onto the bottom of the oven (see p. 169).

The first pair can take as much as 8 minutes to bake;

the last may come out in 4½ minutes: you have to keep track of what's happening in the oven.

When the bottom color is dark brown (not golden—dark brown), the Nan is ready to come out. If the top is pale, as it is likely to be, then slip the baking sheet under the broiler for a fraction of a minute—sometimes only 10 or 20 seconds. But check: it's worth the extra effort to keep your loaves from scorching.

And do not cool.

Serve these wonderful Indian loaves as hot as you can get them to the table—two at a time. You'll seldom get bigger compliments.

NAN—SUMMARY

A. 1 tbsp. active dry yeast
   1 tbsp. honey
   2 tsp. sea salt
   ¼ cup vegetable oil
   ¼ cup yogurt or
      buttermilk

B. 1 egg

C. 1 cup hot water

D. 3¼–4 cups flour
   melted butter or
      margarine
   poppy seeds

Mix A into a large bowl.

Stir in B.

Add C and mix well.

Mix in the first three cups of D, 1 cup at a time.

Add as much more of D as required to show the first signs of not sticking, kneading in bowl, gently. (Keep hand floured during the kneading.)

Knead for a few more minutes.

Scrape down the dough, cover with a clean towel, and set in a warm, draft-free place to rise for about 1 hour.

Punch down (with floured hand) and gently press out any large air bubbles.

Shape into 12 equal balls, and place on floured kneading board.

Light oven, set for high.

Cover balls and let rest for 10 minutes.

With floured hand, shape two balls into ovals, ¼ inch thick. Lay them on greased baking sheet.

Brush tops with melted butter or margarine and sprinkle with a few poppy seeds.

Bake with sheet directly on bottom of the oven, for 5–8 minutes. Check bottom color for doneness.

Put under broiler for a few seconds to darken top color.

Serve hot from the oven.

(Repeat until all are baked.)

10

Batter
Breads

It's appropriate that the last recipes in this book should be Batter Breads as the first were Method Breads, which evolved from Batter Breads.

"Batter" is any dough that is too wet to be kneaded. With all batter breads, you could add about 25 percent more flour, and you'd be able to knead them.

Then, just what is the point of Batter Breads?

Well, these moist batters are able to carry many heavy—and delicious—ingredients that would leave any other kind of bread too dense.

Nor can these recipes be made by our much quicker Method Bread technique. We've tried, but the Cottage Casserole collapses; Rye Batter won't rise. So if you want the delicious breads of this chapter, you're going to have to use the full-rise Batter Bread technique.

We'll work through the recipes of three Batter Breads (and one variation) in this chapter. And when I say "work," I mean work.

To me, Batter Breads are more tiring than any kneaded bread—though some of my students disagree. The kneading motion is easy for me—the stirring and hand-squeezing that batters require tire me out.

But there is good reason to bake Batter Breads—if only for their high-rising lightness.

All of these breads require a similar technique: after the liquid (and most of the other ingredients) you add part of the flour, and whip it, either by hand or by mixer, to develop the gluten early. This beating is most important, because now is when the batter is easiest to work, so you get the most gluten development for your labor.

You then add the rest of the flour a bit at a time, stirring after each addition, until you reach the point where stirring by spoon is too much like work. At this point you clean the spoon off into the bowl, then work the batter by squeezing it between your fingers.

Use only one hand for squeezing; you'll want one hand clean for adding more flour (if necessary) and for scraping the batter off the working hand. This is sticky stuff.

After the flour is all in, the batter squeezed between your fingers for a few minutes, and your hand scraped clean, you put these batters to rise, just like most doughs. But don't finger-test—just *look*, as we did with Rye Breads; these too will look doubled when ready.

As for the beating times, these are flexible. If you beat as rapidly, vigorously, and continuously as my husband does, you can reduce the time. If, on the other hand, you're sitting in front of your favorite soap opera, and beating only when you think of it—you'll take much longer. My beating times are for beating, resting a few seconds, then beating again, and so on. You must judge your own batter. If it seems to lack cohesion, work it some more.

When risen, the batter will be easier to handle (though still sticky). Punch it down, and press out the bubbles. You notice that I don't say knead out. If you start kneading this bread you'll just get all over batter again. Dump the batter into a *well-greased* pan. The heavier your container (a casserole, for instance) the crisper your crust will be.

Don't overfill the containers. If you do, your bread will come out heavier than it should. Or the bread will rise too far above the sides of the container to support itself, and it may fall.

The batter should about half-fill the pan. If the recipe calls for a 1½-quart casserole, and yours is only a 1-quart-er, reserve a third of the dough and make drop rolls from it. (The rolls should bake in 20–25 minutes.) You can substitute a soufflé dish of equal size for a casserole.

Once in, poke the batter into any and all corners, level it off, and smooth out its surface. As with Method Breads, the batter will rise and bake in whatever shape you leave it. If you leave corners unfilled, those corners will stay unfilled. If you leave one side high and one side low, the high side will be higher after baking. If you leave the surface looking like no-man's-land with foxholes and bomb craters, you'll wind up with the same uneven terrain (albeit a lovely dark brown).

If the batter still wants to stick during these pokings and proddings, just butter your hand a little, and you'll come clean. And be careful to *grease the pan generously* —Batter Breads like to stick: don't help them.

I can't emphasize too much how different and delicious these three breads are, though don't underestimate the time it takes to make them. These are by no stretch of the imagination "quick breads." They take no more preparation time than any bread (less than some), but they do, as any bread other than a Method Bread does, need their full rise.

Don't skimp on that first rise.

But don't let the second rise go too far! Once these breads are in the pan, ring, or casserole, *let the batter rise only to the lip of your container,* and then bake. (They will rise still higher in the baking—so leave room in the oven.) If you have let them rise beyond the lip, punch down and let them rise again.

If you have an electric mixer, by all means use it on the first flour: after that, the batter is too stiff (though I had a student who swore she was able to make the Cottage Casserole *all the way by mixer*).

Now that I've thoroughly intimidated you, screw your courage to the sticking place—which in this case is right in the bowl with all that batter—and let's begin.

COTTAGE CASSEROLE

This is my favorite Batter Bread, bar none.

The seeds and onion give it an eye-popping flavor, while the cottage cheese makes for unique texture.

I bake it in a 1½-quart casserole and the crust is so crisp and tasty, it's hard to imagine that this is bread and not some exotic fried dish.

You've noticed that I often give different liquids as options for the hot water in a recipe, on the theory that vegetable water or milk can be even better than plain water. Well, in this recipe, the "water" is cottage cheese. If that isn't reaching for "water" I don't know what is.

(If you want to use pot cheese or farmer cheese, which are drier, add ¼ cup of warm milk.)

The cottage cheese makes this bread tremendously high in protein, while the wheat germ adds vitamins and protein of its own. All in all, a very tasty, nutritious, attractive, and satisfying loaf. (Just add a salad and you have a complete, healthful meal.)

COTTAGE CASSEROLE

The Batter:
    1½ cups creamed cottage cheese
    1 tbsp. vegetable oil
    1½ tbsp. active dry yeast
    2 tbsp. honey
    1 tbsp. dry minced onion (or onion flakes)
    1 tbsp. dill seed
    1 tsp. sea salt
    1 large egg
    2 cups unbleached white flour
    ¼ cup raw wheat germ
For Greasing:
    melted butter or margarine
Equipment:
    large mixing bowl, strong mixing spoon, 1½-quart casserole

Mixing

In a small saucepan, heat 1½ cups of creamed cottage cheese with 1 tablespoon of vegetable oil to hot, not boiling. (Test with a finger.)

In your bowl, combine this mixture with 1½ tablespoons of yeast, and mix.

Add 2 tablespoons of honey, 1 tablespoon of dry minced onion, 1 tablespoon of dill seed, 1 teaspoon of salt, and 1 large egg (at room temperature). Stir together until the egg yolk is all worked in.

Add 1 cup of flour and beat in (by mixer for 2 minutes or by hand for 5 minutes).

Mix in ¼ cup of raw wheat germ and stir for a minute by hand.

Add another ½ cup of flour, and stir for a minute.

Add the final ½ cup of flour, clean the batter off your

spoon into the bowl, and, with one bare hand, squeeze the batter between your fingers and stir it, working it as vigorously as you can for another 2 minutes. (If you can't work vigorously, do it gently for several minutes.)

The batter should be very cohesive. My husband made it recently, and came in to show me the batter around his hand like the "Blob," sticky enough to support the weight of the light mixing bowl.

(By the way, I hope you know where your watch and rings are—this batter can pull them right off.)

First Rise

With a spoon or scraper in your clean hand, scrape the batter from your working hand into the bowl, pushing the odd bits into the rest of the batter at the bottom of the bowl.

Set in a very warm, draft-free place to rise, wash your hands clean, then get a towel and cover the bowl.

Rising will take 50 minutes to an hour, and the batter will look doubled.

Filling the Casserole

When risen, punch down and press out the larger bubbles with your hand.

It should be easier to handle now—a rising does that for a batter or a sticky dough—but if you find it still too sticky, spread your fingers with a little melted butter or margarine.

Generously grease a 1½-quart casserole, either oval or round, and scrape the batter in, making sure to press it down into the corners, and to level off the top, and smooth the surface. For all of this, your hand is the best tool, but it could be done with a well-greased spatula.

When the batter is satisfactorily smoothed and evened and poked, re-cover with that clean towel, and set again *to rise to the lip of the casserole*—about half the time of the first rise.

Baking

When the batter has risen to the lip, bake in a moderately slow oven (340°–360°) for about 35–40 minutes.

Test for doneness (see pp. 21–23). Because of the cottage cheese, you're allowed a few faint streaks on the knife, even when the bread is done.

When done (the top crust will have a lovely dark-golden-brown look), turn out of the casserole carefully (that casserole is hot and dangerous), and bring right to the table.

This bread is not easily sliced when hot, but it can be torn apart with delicious results. If you insist on cutting, use a serrated knife and saw slowly and gently.

Options

☞ The **seeds** are of course variable. You might prefer **caraway** or **fennel** or **anise** or **celery seeds.**

☞ For those of you with a taste for adventure, try substituting **dry minced garlic** for the onion. I did it by accident one day, and was pleasantly surprised.

☞ If you want a topping, brush the top with melted butter or margarine as soon as the loaf is taken from the casserole, and **sprinkle** with **caraway seeds** or **dill** and/or **coarse salt.**

☞ You might want to substitute **bran** for the wheat germ.

COTTAGE CASSEROLE—SUMMARY

A. 1½ cups creamed cottage cheese
   1 tbsp. vegetable oil

B. 1½ tbsp. active dry yeast

C. 2 tbsp. honey
   1 tbsp. dry minced onion
   1 tbsp. dill seed
   1 tsp. sea salt
   1 large egg

D. 2 cups flour

E. ¼ cup raw wheat germ

Warm A in a saucepan.
Add to B and mix.
Stir in C until fairly smooth.
Mix in 1 cup of D and beat (with electric mixer for 2 minutes or by hand for 5).

Add E and beat for 1 minute by hand.

Add another ½ cup of D and beat for 1 minute.

Add another ½ cup of D and work with bare hand for 2 minutes.

Cover with a clean towel and rise in a warm, draft-free place until doubled (about 50 minutes to an hour).

Punch down.

Grease well a 1½-quart casserole, and put in the batter, poking into the corners and smoothing the top.

Return to a warm place, covered, and rise only until the batter reaches the lip of the casserole.

Bake at 340°–360° for 35–40 minutes.

Turn out and serve immediately. Tear apart, rather than slicing.

ANADAMA BREAD

What's more American than cornmeal? After all, corn was the one major New World grain, and all cornbreads and cornmeal breads and similar recipes are rooted in the Americas.

This is an adaptation of a very old recipe (don't ask me what Anadama means) and its main claim to fame is that it is delicious, crunchy, and nutritious.

We bake our Anadama Bread in a 9″ × 5½″ × 2¾″ baking pan, and it makes one large, beautiful loaf, all the handsomer for brushing with butter and sprinkling with cornmeal before baking.

In many cornmeal recipes, the meal is added early on, and mixed into boiling or very hot water to soften it. We prefer the crunchiness, and so add it late in the mixing.

The eggs are added after the first 2 cups of flour to give the eggs something to grab onto in the mixing. It makes for a smooth batter.

Do use 100 percent whole stone-ground cornmeal, it's so much better for you than the usual degerminated pap.

ANADAMA BREAD

For the Batter:
1 tbsp. active dry yeast
1 cup hot water
¼ cup skim milk powder
3 tbsp. vegetable oil
3 tbsp. blackstrap molasses
1½ tsp. sea salt
3½ cups unbleached white flour
2 large eggs
¼ cup raw wheat germ
½ cup whole yellow cornmeal
For Greasing:
melted butter or margarine
For the Crust:
melted butter or margarine
more cornmeal
Equipment:
large mixing bowl, strong mixing spoon, baking pan
(9″ × 5½″ × 2¾″)

Mixing

Into a mixing bowl measure and mix **1 tablespoon of yeast,
1 cup of hot tap water,** and **⅛ cup of skim milk powder**
(⅓ cup if non-instant).

Add **3 tablespoons of vegetable oil, 3 tablespoons of
blackstrap molasses,** and **1½ teaspoons of salt.** Mix in.

Add the first **2 cups of flour** and beat (by hand for
5 minutes, or at low speed by mixer for 2 minutes).

Beat in **2 large eggs** (at room temperature) for another
2 minutes by hand (1 by machine).

(All the following beating times are for hand beating
—if you've a machine that will go this far, more power to
you, and it.)

Beat in, for 1 minute, **¼ cup of raw wheat germ.**

Beat in, for 1 minute, **½ cup of yellow cornmeal.**

Beat in, for 2 minutes, **1 more cup of flour.**

Clean your mixing spoon into the bowl, add the last
½ cup of flour, and work with your bare hand for 2 or 3
minutes, as vigorously as you can manage without strain.

First Rise

Scrape the batter from your hand, into the bowl, and
cover with a clean towel, to rise in a warm, draft-free
place for about 1½ hours or until doubled.

Filling the Pan

When risen, punch down, press out the larger bubbles, and dump into a 9" × 5½" × 2¾" baking pan, greased with melted butter or margarine.

Even the batter in the pan, poke it into any and all corners, and smooth the surface.

Brush the top with **melted butter** or **margarine** and sprinkle with additional **cornmeal.**

Set to rise again, covered with a clean towel, in that same warm place, until the batter reaches the lip of the pan (probably less than half the time of the first rise). Make certain it rises no further before baking. If the loaf *does* rise much above the lip, punch it down and start the rise over again, or the bread is likely to sag in the baking and turn out heavy and disappointing.

Baking

When it has reached the lip, set the loaf to bake at 350°–375° for about 35–40 minutes.

The top will be a dark brown.

Test for doneness (see pp. 21–23).

Cool on a wire rack, but serve hot.

Options

☞ Substitute **millet meal** for cornmeal, if you wish. To me the millet gives the loaf more corn flavor than the cornmeal does.

☞ If you find this bread not sweet enough, you could substitute **honey** for the molasses, but I'd never do it.

☞ Just for a change, how about **bran** for the wheat germ?

☞ If you don't want to brush the crust with melted butter or margarine, brush with **milk** as soon as you've evened the batter in the pan, and then sprinkle with cornmeal. If you've used millet meal instead of the corn, sprinkle with **millet meal.**

☞ For even more crunch, try **cornmealing** the baking pan after greasing and before the batter goes in.

ANADAMA BREAD—SUMMARY

A. 1 tbsp. active dry yeast
   1 cup hot water
   ⅓ cup skim milk
   powder

b. 3 tbsp. vegetable oil
   3 tbsp. blackstrap
   molasses
   1½ tsp. sea salt

C. 3½ cups flour

D. 2 large eggs

E. ¼ cup raw wheat germ

F. ½ cup yellow cornmeal
   melted margarine or
   butter
   more cornmeal

Combine A into a large mixing bowl.

Stir in B.

Add 2 cups of C and beat (2 minutes by mixer, 5 by hand).

Beat in D (2 minutes by hand, 1 by mixer).

Beat in E (1 minute by hand).

Beat in F (1 minute by hand).

Beat in 1 more cup of D (2 minutes by hand).

With your bare hand, work in the last ¼ cup of D, for 2 or 3 minutes.

Cover and set in a warm, draft-free place to rise for 1½ hours (until doubled).

Punch down and scrape into a 9″ × 5½″ × 2¾″ baking pan, greased with melted butter or margarine.

Re-rise until batter reaches lip of baking pan.

Bake for 35–40 minutes, 350°–375°.

Knife-test.

Cool on a wire rack.

RYE BATTER BREADS

Here's a bread that combines the flavor of rye with the coarseness of a Batter Bread.

In the development of this recipe I tried it two ways: the two were so close in popularity with my classes that I decided to give you both. I'm not generous, I just couldn't make up my mind.

First, I'll present Light Rye Batter Bread, and go through the bread with you, and then just give the recipe for Dark Rye Batter Bread, the healthier of the two—the technique is the same.

As this recipe employs rye flour, it's even stickier than the other Batter Breads. However, it's a truly hearty bread, and a treat to bring to the table.

This batter calls for a 2-quart casserole. Remember what I said about not overfilling the pans. If you have only a smaller casserole, use some of the excess for drop rolls—but don't fill the pans more than halfway.

And if the batter rises above the lip, punch it down and start the rising again. One of my students brought in a Rye Batter Bread casserole that had risen above the lip before baking, and there in the center was a lovely hole—looking like a mouse had been nibbling.

LIGHT RYE BATTER BREAD

For the Batter:
    2 tbsp. active dry yeast
    2 tbsp. caraway seeds
    2 tsp. sea salt
    ¼ cup vegetable oil
    ¼ cup honey
    1½ cups hot water
    ½ cup skim milk powder
    2 cups unbleached white flour
    2 cups rye flour
For Greasing:
    melted butter or margarine
Equipment:
    large mixing bowl, strong mixing spoon, 2-quart casserole

Mixing

Into a large mixing bowl measure **2 tablespoons of yeast, 2 tablespoons of caraway seeds, 2 teaspoons of salt;** then **¼ cup of vegetable oil** and **¼ cup of honey** (in the same measuring cup), **1½ cups of hot tap water,** and **½ cup of skim milk powder.** Stir until blended.

Mix in **2 cups of white flour,** and beat for about 5 minutes by hand. (At this point, the batter is already too stiff for my mixer.)

Mix in **1 cup of rye flour** and beat for 2 minutes.

Mix in the **last cup of rye flour,** and work with your bare hand for 3 minutes, squeezing between your fingers, and generally agitating the batter.

First Rise

Scrape the batter off your fingers into the bowl, cover with a clean, *hot*, *wet* towel, and set in a very warm, draft-free place to rise until doubled, about 1½ hours.

Filling the Casserole

When risen, punch down and in the bowl press out any big air bubbles.

Grease well a 2-quart casserole (and I do mean *well*) and dump the batter in, poking into all the corners, even the level of the batter and smooth out its surface.

Set to rise again, covered with a clean, *dry* towel until the batter reaches the lip of the casserole (probably about half the time of the first rise).

Baking

When risen to the lip of the casserole, set to bake in a moderate oven, 350°–375°, for about 45–55 minutes.

Test for doneness (see pp. 21–23).

Turn out of the casserole carefully, and serve hot.

DARK RYE BATTER BREAD

For the Batter:
2 tbsp. active dry yeast
2 tbsp. dark caraway
2 tsp. sea salt
¼ cup vegetable oil
¼ cup blackstrap molasses
2 cups hot water
⅔ cup skim milk powder
2½ cups unbleached white flour
½ cup raw wheat germ
2¼ cups whole rye flour
(into a 2½-quart casserole)

Options

☞ Any of the ingredients that differ in the Dark Rye recipe can be substituted in the Light Rye recipe:

dark **caraway** for caraway; **blackstrap** for honey; and
½ **cup of raw wheat germ** for ½ cup of the rye flour.

☞ For a topping, just before you put the loaf to
rise, brush with **melted butter** or **margarine** and sprinkle
on **coarse salt** and **caraway seeds** (or dark caraway).

LIGHT RYE BATTER BREAD—SUMMARY

A. 2 tbsp. active dry yeast	B. 2 cups unbleached white
2 tbsp. caraway seeds	flour
2 tsp. sea salt	
¼ cup vegetable oil	C. 2 cups whole rye flour
¼ cup honey	
1½ cups hot water	
½ cup skim milk powder	

Mix A into a large bowl.

Mix in B and beat for 5 minutes by hand.

Mix in 1 cup of C and beat for 2 minutes.

Mix in last cup of C and work for 3 minutes.

Cover with a clean, hot, wet towel and rise in warm,
draft-free place until doubled (about 1½ hours).

Punch down and press out air bubbles.

Grease 2-quart casserole and put in batter, pressing
into all corners and smoothing.

Rise, covered by dry towel, until batter reaches lip of
casserole.

Bake for 45–55 minutes at 350°–375°.

Test with knife for doneness.

Serve hot.

Appendix A
Keeping
Bread
and
Dough

Between my classes and research, I bake a lot more bread than we can eat or fit in our freezer, so we give some away to neighbors—which makes for some very happy neighbors. People are not surprised that a home-baked bread tastes better than store-bought: they expect that; what does surprise them is *how well these breads keep.*

Actually, it's not so surprising; for one thing, homemade bread is eaten as much as a day sooner than a commercial bread would be. More important, commercial breads are kneaded in machines which force air into them (which is why so many of them seem to have no substance). This allows their bread to dry out faster.

Most important, though, we use fresher, wholesome, unchemicaled ingredients which are less likely to go stale quickly.

If commercial bakers used honey and the ingredients you can at home, there would be little profit, but they would have no need to use chemical preservatives.

So much for commercial bakers. Let's turn our attention to the keeping of your bread.

KEEPING BREAD

The best way, bar none, to keep bread is in the freezer.

Bread is among the easiest and safest of foods to freeze, even for extended periods of time—up to a year, according to the United States Department of Agriculture.

There is virtually no loss of taste, texture, or wholesomeness in the frozen loaf, and, if you put it in the oven to reheat, it will come out tasting like the next best thing to fresh-baked.

To prepare bread for freezing, let it cool to room temperature. By doing this, we let dissipate whatever water vapor is being evaporated from the hot loaf before we wrap it, and minimize the water touching the crust.

I recommend wrapping the loaf tightly in aluminum foil for freezing. Then, on the happy day when you reheat, just put the loaf, foil and all, into the oven, and bake at high for about 10 minutes. It's amazing how good a loaf can be, even after it's been in your freezer for months.

You can use freezer paper, if you prefer, or even a tightly closed plastic bag. But then you must remove the loaf and put it on something to heat: you save a wash-up by using aluminum foil.

One thing about frozen bread: once thawed, it tends to go stale faster than fresh bread.

A bread gets *stale* (hard) as it loses its moisture. The moisture evaporates into the air while the other ingredients stay where they are, getting drier and drier, and harder and harder. A bread gets *moldy* because the microorganisms of this world find moist places (like bread) a good home to live in. These two problems, staleness and mold, are the two big difficulties in keeping bread fresh out of the freezer.

Let's attack the problem of loss of moisture—staleness—first. Believe it or not, bread retains its moisture best if it's quite warm. Again according to the USDA, bread will keep soft "indefinitely" (whatever that means) at 140° F. Now, that is warm. Just how would you do it? And if you could do it, how would you keep the mold away? Because mold absolutely loves temperatures like that.

The USDA also says that bread will keep soft for 100 hours (for those of you without adding machines, about four days) at 110° F. Also a nice breeding temperature for mold.

At 70° F., 40 hours (less than two days!).

How about putting bread into the refrigerator? We all know that's the reason we have refrigerators—to inhibit the growth of microorganisms. At 32° F., you can expect your bread to stay soft (fresh) for all of 10 hours.

That last figure came as a shock to me. I had been taught at my mother's knee (my mother had notoriously misinformed knees) to put unused bread in the fridge to keep it fresh. And now, the federal government was telling me that if I put my bread in the refrigerator I was just hurrying it to staleness.

So, any bread that isn't being frozen is best kept in a bread box. This will keep your breads at room temperature or slightly higher, and free from dust (though it does little for the problem of mold).

Breads vary greatly in keeping power. Those made with water get stale quickest. Honey will help a water bread keep its moisture (honey absorbs moisture from the air—your jar of honey will absorb moisture and thin out if you don't keep it tightly closed), and if you use enough honey you can keep a bread for weeks.

Shortening of any kind will help a bread stay moist (you know the way a drop of oil just won't dry out). The more shortening in a bread, the longer it will stay moist.

Of our breads, Brioches are the richest in oil: so oily that I can keep my treasure trove of Brioches in a plastic bag in the fridge for as long as 2 or 3 weeks without their going dry. At any weak moment I just pop one or two into my ancient top-of-the-stove potato baker, and, *voilà*, almost like fresh-baked.

But with any bread that uses shortening you run into another problem—rancidity.

Never eat anything rancid—if only the slightest bit. Rancid oils will destroy vitamins—they can also make you damn sick. So, if something sniffs *off*, throw it out. The money loss is not to be compared to the health loss.

Breads that are high in oil can be kept longer in the fridge without going hard. But I still recommend the freezer.

As for plastic bags, if still-warm breads are put in them their crusts are softened by their own moisture release. We like our crusts crusty, so if warm bread is to be kept overnight, or to be given to friends, we put it into a brown paper bag, folding the top several times to make it creature-proof, and let it get one day "stale" to protect the crust. Brown paper lets all the moisture out, keeping the bread clean and dust-free.

When does the process of "stale" begin? In one sense, as soon as you put a bread in the oven. The very process of baking involves moisture loss. (If you want proof, weigh your pan before and after baking. The weight loss is water.) Your nose also confirms this. When breads get done, their odor becomes very strong. Well, that odor is the result of evaporation—you smell the bread because of moisture particles.

Reviving stale bread involves trying to retrieve some of the lost moisture. Sprinkle a little water over the stale bread and then place it in the oven or toaster, just until the moisture reaches its original level. Alternatively, place the dry bread in a wet paper bag in the oven.

STORING DOUGH

Unbaked dough is more perishable than bread, but it keeps better in the fridge. Its life in the freezer and its life in the fridge are about the same—2 to 3 weeks. I have kept dough in the refrigerator for over a month, then baked it into rolls, to find myself with a good texture but a very "winey" flavor. I wouldn't recommend it.

Much as I recommend freezing bread, I can't see any point to freezing dough. In the refrigerator, the yeast is still working, though slowly, and you can get an extra rise or so from the dough, which only improves the texture of the bread you bake from it. In fact, many bakers prefer to work with refrigerated dough, finding it easier to handle.

To keep dough in the refrigerator, just cover the bowl of dough with clear plastic. If the dough rises out of the bowl, punch it down and push it back.

If you want to freeze shaped unrisen loaves or rolls, just wrap them in greased plastic film and put them in the freezer. Many doughs with things in them, such as seeds, actually improve in flavor during the freezing.

On baking day, the full-sized loaf will take 5 to 6 hours to thaw and rise, so you can save time by moving it from the freezer to the refrigerator the night before.

Rolls will only take 2 hours to thaw.

Unshaped dough can be frozen, too, but you'll have to thaw it before you can shape it.

BROWN-AND-SERVE ROLLS

These are very popular as convenience rolls, and you can make your own, very simply and inexpensively (not to mention healthily). Bake any recipe at low temperatures (250°–275°) for half an hour, just long enough to make sure all the yeast is killed and the shape is set. They will still be pale in color. These can be stored 2 weeks in the fridge and indefinitely in the freezer. When you want to have them, simply bake in a high (400°) oven until brown. (An egg glaze just before the second baking will give you beautiful results—but don't put that egg glaze on before you stick the rolls in the fridge. Raw egg is very perishable.)

Appendix B
Federal Standards
for Commercial
Bread

The following is excerpted from BAKERY PRODUCTS, DEFINITIONS AND STANDARDS under the FEDERAL FOOD, DRUG, AND COSMETIC ACT. A full copy can be obtained free from the Department of Health, Education, and Welfare local office in your area. It states what may go into commercially prepared bread and in what amounts. To my eye it's a real horror story.

This is not an unbiased view. I have cut out the figures describing amounts, and condensed and left out the less harmful and commonplace ingredients—though what may go into bread as "milk" and "eggs" is also surprising and frightening.

You'll see the word "harmless" occasionally used. I don't think it's out of place for me to remind you that cyclamates were considered "harmless" until subsequent investigation proved otherwise.

Even if the individual chemical names don't mean much to you, read on, remembering that none of the ingredients shown in the following excerpts has to be listed on the label of the bread (except for those ingredients in paragraphs 13 and 14).

PART 17—BAKERY PRODUCTS

Sec. 17.2 Enriched bread and enriched rolls . . .

(a) Each of the foods enriched bread, enriched rolls . . . conforms to the definition and standard of identity . . . prescribed by . . . 17.1 (a) and (c) [see below] except that: . . . [standards of enrichment follow]

(3) . . . may also contain as an optional ingredient added harmless calcium salts . . . [amounts]

(6) . . . As used in this section, the term "flour," unqualified, includes bromated flour and phosphated flour; the term "enriched flour" includes enriched bromated flour . . .
Sec. 17.1

(a) . . . the potassium bromate in any bromated flour used and the monocalcium phosphate in any phosphated flour used shall be deemed to be optional ingredients . . .

(1) (ii) Mono- and diglycerides of fat-forming fatty acids, propylene glycol mono- and diesters of fat-forming fatty acids . . . [amount]

(5) . . . glucose sirup, dried corn sirup, dried glucose sirup, nondiastatic dried malt sirup . . .

(6) (ii) Harmless preparations of enzymes obtained from Aspergillus oryzae or bromelain preparations . . . in a suitable harmless carrier but the quantity of any such carrier shall be no greater than reasonably necessary to effect a uniform mixture of the enzymes with the flour used.

(iii) Harmless preparations of α-amylases, obtained from Bacillus subtilis . . . quantity . . . reasonably necessary . . .

(11) Calcium sulfate, calcium lactate, calcium carbonate, dicalcium phosphate, ammonium phosphate, ammonium sulfate, ammonium chloride, or any combination of two or more . . . [amounts]

(12) (i) Potassium bromate, calcium bromate, potassium iodate, calcium iodate, calcium peroxide, or any combination of two or more . . . [amounts]

(ii) Azodicarbonamide . . . in a carrier consisting of starch . . . tricalcium phosphate may be added as an anticaking agent . . . [amount]

(13) (i) Monocalcium phosphate . . . [amount]

(ii) A vinegar . . . [amount]

(iii) Calcium propionate, sodium propionate, or any mixture of these . . . [amount]

(iv) Sodium diacetate . . . [amount]

(v) Lactic acid, in such quantity that the pH of the finished bread is not less than 4.5.

(14) Spice, with which may be included spice oil and spice extract.

(15) Polysorbate 60, calcium stearoyl-2-lactylate, lactylic stearate, sodium stearyl fumarate, succinylated monoglycerides, ethoxylated mono- and diglycerides, alone or in combination . . . [amounts]

(16) L-Cysteine (which may be added in the form of the hydrochloride salt, including hydrates thereof) . . . [amount]

If you are eating commercially baked bread, you are eating any or many of these ingredients.

☞ **Index** ☜

Note: Recipe pages are indicated by italics.

About the Authors

FLOSS DWORKIN has taught hundreds of women, men, and children—from cooking teachers to absolute beginners—to bake bread, as well as having taught crafts, knitting, dance, and even psychology.

STAN DWORKIN, a short-story writer and a creative health-food cook himself, learned to bake bread during the preparation of *Bake Your Own Bread*, testing out the recipes invented by Floss.

Both the Dworkins are enthusiastic horticulturalists, folk dancers, bicyclists, and campers.

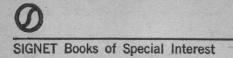

SIGNET Books of Special Interest

☐ **BITE: A New York Restaurant Strategy by Gael Greene.**
This is a very special kind of restaurant guide for those
who delight in being raked over the coals by New York's
expensive, snobbish and sometimes not so good restaurant scene, or those who will stop at no lengths to beat
the system. BITE presents a rare, fascinating and hilari-
ous look at New York's stomachs, egos, and some of its
most expensive little insanities.   (#W5010—$1.50)

☐ **BEWARE OF THE FOOD YOU EAT; The Updated and
Revised Edition of POISONS IN YOUR FOOD by Ruth
Winter.** A book that should be read by anyone concerned
about his health, BEWARE OF THE FOOD YOU EAT
shows what has and what has not been done to correct
the abuses in food processing.   (#Y5061—$1.25)

☐ **THE FOOD GARDEN by Edna Blair.** Revised and updated
by Martin Jezer. A comprehensive easy-to-follow guide
to making your very own food garden, including the lat-
est information in organic gardening. (#Y4967—$1.25)

☐ **THE SIGNET BOOK OF WINE by Alexis Bespaloff.** Everything you need to know about wine from the noblest
vintages to the everyday vins ordinaire. Over 500 wines
from eighteen countries are described. Contains maps,
ratings of recent vintage years, a pronunciation guide, a
comprehensive index and advice on how to start your
own wine cellar.   (#Y4588—$1.25)

THE NEW AMERICAN LIBRARY, INC.,
P.O. Box 999, Bergenfield, New Jersey 07621

Please send me the SIGNET BOOKS I have checked above. I am
enclosing $_____(check or money order—no currency
or C.O.D.'s). Please include the list price plus 25¢ a copy to cover
handling and mailing costs. (Prices and numbers are subject to
change without notice.)

Name_____

Address_____

City_____State_____Zip Code_____
Allow at least 3 weeks for delivery

SIGNET Books You Will Enjoy

☐ **THE I NEVER COOKED BEFORE COOKBOOK by Jo Coudert.** A basic guide in plain English on how to prepare simple, delicious foods with ease . . . and the certainty of success. No experience necessary.
(#Q5303—95¢)

☐ **LET'S COOK IT RIGHT by Adelle Davis.** For the first time in paperback, and completely revised and updated, the celebrated cookbook dedicated to good health, good sense and good eating. Contains 400 easy-to-follow, basic recipes, a table of equivalents and an index.
(#E5378—$1.75)

☐ **THE EASY WAY TO CHINESE COOKING by Beverly Lee.** In this practical, easy-to-follow guide to authentic Chinese cooking, Beverly Lee shows how to make delicious Chinese dishes—from the simplest to the most festive and elaborate. Included is a list of Chinese stores throug' out the U.S. which carry the items listed in the book.
(#Q4813—95¢)

☐ **THE GOURMET'S GUIDE TO MEAT AND POULTRY by William and Chesbrough Rayner.** In a world where meat prices keep getting higher and quality is constantly being questioned, only the person who can judge cuts of meat can afford to buy meat. This book will show you how you can stretch your budget and turn inexpensive cuts of meat into delicious, nutritious meals.
(#Q4783—95¢)

☐ **EVERYDAY FRENCH COOKING by Henri-Paul Pellaprat.** A former Cordon Bleu professor has written an easy-to-use, complete French cookbook.
(#W4118—$1.50)

THE NEW AMERICAN LIBRARY, INC.,
P.O. Box 999, Bergenfield, New Jersey 07621

Please send me the SIGNET BOOKS I have checked above. I am enclosing $_____(check or money order—no currency or C.O.D.'s). Please include the list price plus 25¢ a copy to cover handling and mailing costs. (Prices and numbers are subject to change without notice.)

Name_____

Address_____

City_____State_____Zip Code_____
Allow at least 3 weeks for delivery

COLLECTION FOLIO

Philippe Labro

La traversée

Gallimard

© *Éditions Gallimard, 1996.*

Philippe Labro est né à Montauban. Il part à dix-huit ans pour l'Amérique. Étudiant en Virginie, il voyage à travers tous les États-Unis. À son retour, il devient reporter à Europe n° 1 puis à *France-Soir*. Il fait son service militaire de 1960 à 1962, pendant la guerre d'Algérie. Il reprend ensuite ses activités de journaliste (R.T.L., *Paris-Match*, TF1 et A2) en même temps qu'il écrit et réalise plusieurs films. En 1985, il est nommé directeur général des programmes de R.T.L., et, en 1992, vice-président de cette station.

Il a publié chez Gallimard *Un Américain peu tranquille* (1960), *Des feux mal éteints* (1967), *Des bateaux dans la nuit* (1982). En 1986, *L'étudiant étranger* lui vaut le prix Interallié. En 1988, *Un été dans l'Ouest* obtient le prix Gutenberg des lecteurs.

Après *Le petit garçon*, en 1991, Philippe Labro publie *Quinze ans* en 1993, puis, en 1994, *Un début à Paris*, qui complète le cycle de ses cinq romans d'apprentissage.

À ma mère.

« Au petit matin sur le lac, assis à l'avant de la barque avec son père en train de ramer, il avait l'entière conviction qu'il ne mourrait jamais. »

Ernest Hemingway

« Pour moi, chaque heure de lumière et d'obscurité est un miracle,
Chaque pouce cubique de l'espace est un miracle. »

Walt Whitman

PROLOGUE

1

Les visiteurs

Ils sont debout, en un seul rang serré, en ligne droite, le long du mur blanc (ou bien est-il jaune clair) et ils sourient tous. Leurs regards, leurs gestes, leurs visages expriment un drôle de sourire, comme une invitation. Tout, dans leur attitude bienveillante, semble vouloir me dire :

— Viens !

D'ailleurs, l'un d'entre eux, le plus âgé, finit par ouvrir la bouche et il prononce précisément cette parole que je croyais deviner :

— Viens !

Puis il ajoute :

— Viens nous rejoindre. Nous t'attendons.

Comme s'il s'agissait d'une évidence, une chose acquise. Je regarde le petit groupe aligné devant le mur. Certains sont âgés, certains sont jeunes. Il y a un gros, un maigre, une rousse, une Noire, une blonde, deux jeunes hommes plutôt minces, des vieux. Certains portent des lunettes, l'un d'entre eux un grand chapeau blanc. Je les connais tellement bien !

Les femmes sourient, comme les hommes. Je les aime tous, ces hommes et ces femmes. Ils ne sont pas plus d'une dizaine. Je les ai tous aimés, mais ils sont morts, et je les aime encore, puisqu'ils n'ont jamais quitté ma mémoire. Ce sont les morts de ma vie. Je me demande pourquoi je devrais les rejoindre. Ce n'est pas dans mes projets. Pourtant, ils insistent. On dirait qu'ils ont adopté la même rondeur dans le maintien, dans le sourire, la même gentillesse un peu lourde, un peu répétitive dans le ton. Il y a une douceur, une douceur ferme, lente, doucereuse :

— Viens, mais viens donc ! Mais qu'est-ce que tu attends ?

Une douceur au ralenti, comme leurs gestes, rares et ralentis. Ils savent ce qu'ils font et ce qu'ils veulent, et cela provoque chez moi un soupçon d'irritation. Car j'ai beau les aimer, je n'aime pas leur insistance, leur face de carême réjouie, cette espèce de componction qui les habite, leur certitude que ça va marcher et que je vais leur obéir et traverser la ligne ! Non : ce sont des morts. Je ne veux pas y aller.

Ils sont morts, ai-je dit, mais ils ne sont pas morts puisque je suis vivant et puisqu'ils sont là, bien présents le long du mur blanc-jaune, et puisqu'ils me parlent. Ou alors, est-ce moi qui ne suis plus vivant ?

Ils demeurent presque figés, face à moi, de l'autre côté, pas loin, à un mètre à peine, mais je ne vais pas les rejoindre. Je ne veux pas. Ai-je le choix ? Est-ce un devoir, un ordre ? Que me veulent-ils et quel est ce bruit infernal qui passe à travers moi ? Mes yeux abandonnent ces gens debout et mon regard se déplace de quelques degrés, et voilà que je ne vois plus du tout les gens le long du mur. Soudain, il y a du bleu qui envahit la pièce. Car je suis dans une pièce, je suis sur un lit, et je m'aperçois que j'ai des tubes plein la gueule.

Et voilà que soudain apparaissent des ondes de forêts bleues. Pourquoi ?

2

La Raison
n'a pas toujours raison

Il existe, au pied du pic Dolorès, dans la chaîne des montagnes de l'Uncompaghre, un long et plat promontoire rocheux, entièrement nu, taillé en son centre comme par une hache géante. Les Indiens Ute, qui ont habité la région bien avant l'arrivée de l'homme blanc, l'ont appelé la Faille de l'Aigle. Il n'est pas simple d'accéder à la Faille, mais tous ceux qui y sont parvenus en reviennent différents. Ils ont vu. Ils ont vu une mer d'une consistance et d'une beauté uniques.

C'est une mer de sapins, bleu-vert, vert-bleu. Elle ondule sous les yeux comme un immense, un interminable tapis de velours bleu au sein duquel se mêlent toutes les couleurs, lavande, citron, ocre, noir d'encre, pourpre et carmin, mais que le bleu recouvre et assimile pour imposer son ondoiement à la fois immobile et changeant. Le ciel, au-dessus de cette mer pas comme les autres, est souvent d'un bleu plus clair, pur et délavé, sans addition d'une autre teinte. La combinaison de ces deux bleus — le chatoyant et sombre tapis d'une part, et la limpide et transparente toile du ciel de l'autre — confère à cette vision un pouvoir d'attraction presque magique, et peut-être fatal.

Une légende de la région dit, en effet, que si l'on se penche avec trop d'insistance au-dessus de cette mer, on peut être gagné par la tentation de s'y jeter, de s'y perdre. On dit aussi que certains animaux n'ont pu résister à la tentation et peut-être certains hommes, et que l'on n'a jamais retrouvé trace de leurs corps, même en cherchant pendant plusieurs jours dans les sous-bois, au pied des grands arbres de la forêt de l'Uncompaghre.

Je voudrais vous raconter une histoire qui m'est arrivée il n'y a pas très longtemps et qui ne s'est pas du tout déroulée dans les montagnes du Colorado que je viens d'évoquer, mais plus banalement dans la ville où j'habite, à Paris, et plus précisément dans un minuscule espace entre quelques murs de diverses chambres d'un grand hôpital de cette même ville. C'est une histoire qui a changé ma vie... puisque j'ai failli la perdre ! Par un phénomène qui peut paraître d'abord obscur et compliqué mais qui finira par se révéler très simple, et que je n'ai découvert que le jour où je me suis décidé à raconter mon histoire, je ne peux commencer à le faire sans parler de la Faille de l'Aigle et des milliers de crêtes bleues, des milliers de sapins qui ressemblaient à cet océan dans lequel, avec mes amis, lorsque j'avais dix-huit ans, j'ai, une fois, désiré me fondre.

Cette image est en effet, immédiatement après celle des visiteurs en rang serré dans la pièce, celle que j'ai vue apparaître lorsque je me suis réveillé de la première anesthésie, à l'hôpital, et c'est peut-être celle qui est le plus souvent revenue dans mon esprit, dans mes pensées, tout au long du voyage immobile que j'ai fait sur ce lit d'hôpital, un voyage qui m'a conduit aux portes de la mort.

Tout est lié, tout se tient. Si l'image inoubliable est au cœur même d'un récit qui se passe à des années et des kilomètres de distance de cette chambre d'hôpital, c'est qu'il existe une raison qui n'a rien à voir avec la Raison.

Les grandes personnes, et bien souvent les Français, croient qu'on peut tout expliquer en faisant appel à la Raison. J'ai appris à ne pas juger ainsi. En fait, j'ai appris à ne pas trop juger. Je tente seulement de comprendre. La vie est un mystère, le temps est un mystère, et chacun d'entre nous obéit à des lois différentes, et la Raison ne constitue pas la Loi. J'ai souvent quelque difficulté à dire ces choses-là devant ceux qui s'accrochent avec excès à la Raison, parce qu'ils me regardent alors avec, dans leurs yeux, ce vide qui traduit l'incompréhension, voire la condescendance, de qui se réfère exclusivement à son intelligence pour comprendre la vie et le monde. Je n'ai plus aujourd'hui aucun mal à établir la différence entre la Raison et le reste. Dans l'histoire qui m'est arrivée, ce n'est pas seulement la Raison ou l'intelligence qui ont joué un rôle, mais d'autres éléments bien plus forts : le cœur, la volonté, l'amour, l'imprévisible.

Mon histoire n'est pas imaginaire, il ne s'agit pas de fiction, et je voudrais utiliser des mots simples, authentiques et sincères pour la raconter — mais il me faut d'abord revenir à la Faille.

3

Une mer de sapins bleus

La Faille! L'image revient constamment maintenant que je sors peu à peu des limbes dus à
l'anesthésie. Je ne prends aucune conscience
encore de mon corps ni des entraves et des freins
qu'on lui a mis. Je suis envahi par cette seule
image. Pourquoi?

Nous étions quelques-uns au camp, au pied de
la montagne, à être intrigués par cette Faille. Si on
l'atteignait, nous disait-on, une sensation inconnue vous gagnait, qu'aucun alcool, aucun amour,
aucun rêve, aucune violence, ne pouvait procurer
à un être humain. Un homme nous l'avait dit et
nous le croyions. Nous étions trois ou quatre à vouloir le croire et à vouloir faire connaissance avec la
sensation. Celui qui nous avait initiés nous avait
dit :
— Il faut mériter la Faille.
L'homme était un vieux sang-mêlé, blanc et

indien, il s'appelait Nuage Rouge, un nom emprunté à de glorieux ancêtres. Il ne travaillait pas au camp mais nous apportait une fois par semaine, au volant de son ancien pick-up Ford tout cabossé, le courrier et quelques provisions. Il était si âgé que des rides partaient de ses rides comme les rivières viennent des ruisseaux. Il avait repéré le groupe de jeunes gens dont je faisais partie et qui, le soir venu, au cours de la dernière demi-heure de répit après le repas de six heures — on dînait tôt pour se coucher tôt et se lever tôt —, s'asseyait sur la butte d'herbe le long des tentes au-dessus de la rivière et levait la tête vers le pic Dolorès, vers la Faille. Nuage Rouge nous avait rejoints :

— Vous voulez y monter ?

— Comment le sais-tu ? avait répondu l'un de mes amis.

Il avait souri ou du moins avais-je cru lire un sourire sur ce visage crispé et tanné, craquelé comme l'argile sèche, mais il n'avait pas répondu à cette question, puisque c'était une question idiote : comment sait-on ce qui se passe dans la tête des jeunes gens ? On sait parce qu'on est plus vieux qu'eux.

— Vous devrez partir tôt, avait-il dit, car le chemin est plus long que l'on croit. Prenez des boissons et de la nourriture. Empruntez la piste du Castor, suivez-la jusqu'au pied du pic. Après, il suffit d'escalader, mais attention aux blessures. La roche écorche la peau.

L'un d'entre nous avait suggéré :
— On peut prendre des gants ?

Il avait éclaté de rire.

— Non, pas la peine de porter des gants.

Nous avions suivi son conseil et marché dans le froid de l'avant-aube, dans une nuit noire et glacée, avec le vent venu de la montagne qui agitait les pins Ponderosa au sein desquels nous nous enfoncions et qui nous envoyaient leurs odeurs enivrantes de fruit et de résine. Il faisait bon monter doucement ainsi vers cette frange de terrain où bientôt les arbres disparaîtraient et nous n'aurions plus droit qu'à la caillasse, l'aridité. Les aiguilles et les brindilles craquaient sous nos pieds et l'on sentait, sans les apercevoir, la présence des insectes et des rongeurs, qui laissaient passer les hommes — réfugiés sous la mousse, les fougères, les souches et les troncs des arbres abattus, les cadavres de sapins déracinés par d'anciens orages, d'anciennes foudres, d'anciens ouragans qui avaient tenté de détruire la forêt mais étaient repartis, pulvérisés dans le néant de l'air. La forêt avait été entaillée et blessée, mais elle avait tenu bon. Aucun orage n'était assez fort pour abattre cette forêt-là.

Pourquoi ces détails reviennent-ils avec une telle précision ? Ces couleurs, ces sons, dans la pièce jaune où j'ai vu les visiteurs alignés en rang et me faisant signe de les rejoindre, pourquoi cet acharnement à recomposer notre marche vers la Faille ?

On a fini par arriver dans la zone de la roche. Le soleil commençait à poindre. Un voile de soie rose venait recouvrir et envelopper le noir de la nuit. Très vite, on s'est retrouvés à quatre pattes, courbés, comme le lynx ou le lion de la montagne qui rôdaient pas loin de là. La pente était trop forte pour que l'on puisse encore avancer en restant debout. L'air était sec et poudreux et il fallait respirer en mesurant son souffle. Ça a duré deux heures. Le soleil tapait de tout son plein maintenant, et c'était étonnant parce que l'on sentait en même temps le froid venu des neiges éternelles et le chaud, pas vraiment chaud, venu du soleil. On s'arrêtait fréquemment pour boire à la gourde et humecter la bande de toile intérieure de notre chapeau afin de conserver la nuque fraîche et éviter l'insolation. On savait bien qu'elle était impossible, à cause du froid, mais on la craignait néanmoins. Nuage Rouge avait eu raison : nos mains étaient ensanglantées.

Quand nous fûmes parvenus là-haut, j'eus l'impression d'avoir franchi une invisible barrière qui nous séparait d'un monde chaud et réel et ouvrait sur un monde différent, hors de la réalité quotidienne. La grande dalle fracturée s'est offerte à nous, lisse et nue, légèrement en pointe dans le ciel, si bien qu'il fallait se coucher de tout son long sur elle. Le vent était très violent. Une sensation de vertige ou du moins de déséquilibre constant vous poussait naturellement à vous étendre sur la roche. Une fois couchés, on rampait vers la fracture et vers le vide, anxieux de savoir et de contempler enfin la mer, le tapis.

Il y avait donc ce vide et ce vent qui vous tournait la tête et tout ce bleu ondulant en dessous de nous, cette beauté, cette pureté des choses et du temps, et cette envie troublante qui pouvait poindre — l'envie de plonger dans la mer pour s'y fondre. De rouler sur ce tapis, si c'était un tapis, comme un enfant peut rouler sur des draps ou un bébé sur le ventre de sa mère. Cette envie de se mélanger définitivement à la beauté et à la couleur de cet au-delà, ce monde différent qui semblait vous dire :

— Viens !

Mais je ne suis plus du tout allongé sur la dalle de l'Uncompaghre et je n'ai plus dix-huit ans, et de longues et longues et longues années ont passé et pourtant le bleu est là, sous mes yeux, il ondule. Et pourtant je suis étendu dans une pièce aux murs blancs (ou jaunes) et je peux voir à nouveau un groupe d'hommes ou de femmes. Ce sont les morts de ma vie et ils m'ont dit :

— Viens !

Quel est ce bruit qui me traverse ?

PREMIÈRE PARTIE

LA TRAVERSÉE

4

La « *réa* »

Le bruit provenait d'une machine que l'on appelle un « ventilateur artificiel » qui pompe de l'air et en insuffle à travers un tube de silicone — lequel, rentré dans la trachée du patient, lui permet de respirer.

Le patient — je préfère écrire le malade — ne savait rien de tout cela. Il entendait seulement le bruit de la machine et son propre bruit — celui de sa respiration, saccadée, hoquetante, toussotante, et le tube, aussi ténu qu'un insignifiant petit fil électrique, lui semblait, dans sa bouche, plus volumineux que la patte d'un ours. Il était étendu sur un lit, les deux bras attachés par des bandes velcro aux barres métalliques du lit.

Il sentait qu'on avait, autour de ses lèvres, son nez, ses joues, installé toutes sortes de cordelettes, sparadraps, tampons de coton, un harnachement qui le paralysait autant que le système de perfusion établi sur son avant-bras gauche, ou que les électrodes appliquées sur sa poitrine et reliées à un scope, dont l'écran renvoyait un tracé de couleur verte — celui de son cœur — mais il ne le voyait pas.

De fait, à son réveil, il ne voyait rien. Il émergeait d'une sombre et chaotique rêverie, qui lui avait laissé croire que, accompagné par sa femme, les médecins, les assistantes, on l'avait transporté dans cette pièce dont on lui avait expliqué qu'elle se situait au bout du couloir, la dernière du bâtiment, et il était persuadé qu'on l'avait emmené là en chantant des hymnes et que le cortège portait des bougies, comme pour une veillée funèbre. Il ne parvenait pas à démêler la part de réalité et celle du rêve. Il émergeait, encore pénétré par les produits anesthésiants. Et il ne souffrait pas. Mais s'il avait pu clairement reconstituer ce qui avait précédé son arrivée dans la pièce, il aurait ainsi résumé :

— Depuis longtemps, tu n'étais plus en état de respirer normalement. La toux, chez toi, était devenue une habitude. Bientôt, ton larynx s'est trouvé obstrué. Ta vie quotidienne en a été modifiée. Tu as perdu du poids, le sommeil, tu as dépéri. Tu as essayé trop de médecins, trop de médicaments, et le professeur que tu consultais irrégulièrement a fini par te dire : «Je ne peux plus vous soigner ainsi, faites-vous hospitaliser.» Tu as longtemps refusé — longtemps, deux jours ! — et puis tu as fini par appeler le professeur et lui dire : «Je suis prêt.» C'étaient les seuls mots que tu pouvais encore prononcer, puisque l'œdème qui bouchait l'entrée de ton larynx était sur le point de t'étouffer. Tu es entré à l'hôpital. On t'a endormi pour te faire une fibroscopie et tu te retrouves ici, mais dans quel état ? Et quel est cet ici ?

Ici, c'est le service de la réanimation. La « réa », comme on dit dans le jargon hospitalier. La réa, un univers, un monde avec ses règles, ses codes, son ambiance et ses couleurs, ses sonorités, c'est-à-dire ses bruits, tous reliés à la maladie et au travail réalisé autour des malades.

Le mot définit bien la fonction de l'endroit. Il s'agit de vous ré-animer, c'est-à-dire vous maintenir puis vous redonner de la vie et de l'âme, de l'animation. Tous ceux qui sont passés par la réa savent à quoi correspondent ces trois petites lettres et sans doute sont-ils innombrables à avoir parcouru un chemin plus atroce, plus long que le mien. Sans doute d'autres ont-ils connu une expérience moins cruelle. À chacun son chemin, son « passage en réa ». Il n'empêche : ce passage, pourvu qu'on en sorte, vous donne une petite dose supplémentaire d'expérience, un petit savoir en plus. Oh, rien, léger, à peine aussi palpable qu'une larme de libellule sur une feuille de roseau, mais tout de même, vous n'êtes plus semblable à celui que vous étiez avant la réa. Vous êtes allé de l'autre côté, vous avez franchi le cap Horn.

Il est possible que ces expressions paraissent banales : « Aller de l'autre côté », quel cliché ! « Passer le cap Horn », quelle image facile ! Il faut se moquer de ces remarques. Si l'image paraît facile, c'est qu'elle est l'image vraie. Le problème n'est pas d'écrire : «l'autre côté», mais d'essayer de décrire à quoi cela ressemble. Et d'abord, d'affirmer ceci : il y a un autre côté.

5

Ceci n'est pas un roman

La maladie qui m'a conduit à la réa m'a emmené plus loin que la réa, bien au-delà du cap Horn, au-delà des quarantièmes rugissants et des cinquantièmes hurlants, dans ce que les Anglo-Saxons appellent une NDE — *Near Death Experience* — et qu'il convient de traduire ainsi : expérience de mort approchée. En français, cela donnerait comme initiales EMA, et cela fait non seulement plus français, mais je m'aperçois que c'est le mot « âme » à l'envers. Hasard…

Au cours de cette traversée, j'ai vu et entendu toutes sortes de choses. Des monstres, des anges, des paysages et des visages, du vide et du trop-plein, de la compassion, de l'horreur et de l'amour. Aux prises avec un bouleversement constant du temps et de la durée ; quand les jours et les nuits n'avaient plus aucun sens, aucune construction ; lorsque je perdais tout repère ; lorsque je revoyais des moments de ma vie ancienne et de ma vie à venir. Lorsque deux Moi-même s'affrontaient en un dialogue permanent, quand l'un de ces deux Moi disait :

— Tu vas mourir, laisse aller, c'est foutu, tandis que l'autre Moi répliquait :

— Non, bats-toi, il faut vivre.

De ce combat et de ces dialogues — que personne n'a entendus mais dont je peux réécrire chaque ligne —, de ces instants du vrai passé revécu et de ces instants d'un présent irréel, de mes deux EMA, l'une baignée de lumière, l'autre au bord d'un gouffre noir, de ce qui s'est ensuivi, c'est-à-dire une sorte de deuxième naissance, et de ce qui demeure aujourd'hui, découvertes et convictions, je souhaite tenter de reconstituer le tissu et la trame.

Lorsque je suis sorti de l'hôpital Cochin après six semaines — dix jours en réa et le reste en chambre —, j'étais partagé entre le désir de raconter mon passage et la volonté aussi forte de me taire. C'était l'été. Je naviguais à petite vitesse entre la forêt où je me reposais et quelques incursions à Paris. J'étais volubile ou silencieux, selon les heures et les rencontres. J'avais envie d'embrasser des inconnus, leur parler interminablement et puis j'avais envie de rester seul et ne plus rien dire. Cette ambivalence n'a pas duré longtemps. L'autre jour, B., le radiologue chez qui je me soumettais à un examen de routine, m'a interrogé et nous avons parlé. Il m'a dit d'une voix amicale et chaude :

— Vous devriez raconter tout cela.

B. est grand et massif, cheveux noirs et yeux clairs, lunettes à légère monture quasi transparente. Je l'aime beaucoup, mais sans doute ne le sait-il pas. D'abord, je ne le lui ai jamais dit. Ensuite, je ne l'ai rencontré qu'une douzaine de fois à l'occasion de la douzaine de radios que j'ai subies dans son cabinet. Il est jeune et alerte, limpide dans ses évaluations des radios et il dégage cette chaleur, cette aisance si particulière à certains juifs pieds-noirs avec lesquels je me suis toujours senti en harmonie et dont l'amitié a accompagné mes voyages, des découvertes professionnelles, une guerre. Quand je lui parle, j'ai l'impression de converser avec le frère de tous ces hommes avec qui j'ai assisté à des explosions, des émeutes ou des inondations — avec qui j'ai suivi des procès ou des mariages de princes — avec qui j'ai écrit des scénarios et tourné des films — avec qui, la nuit, quand j'étais jeune, à Paris, New York ou Los Angeles, j'ai fait le fou, j'ai déconné et dérapé. C'est le frère des autres hommes avec lesquels j'échange chaque jour ou presque, quoi qu'il arrive, quelques phrases sur ce que nous avons lu, fait ou vu, ce que deviennent nos proches. B. fait partie d'une famille anonyme et vaste. On entretient ainsi des affinités avec des hommes et des femmes qui ne s'inscrivent pas dans le même univers intime. Il paraît que tout le monde connaît cela. Ce qui m'intéresse c'est d'éprouver cette sensation de façon plus forte depuis que je suis «passé en réa».

Après avoir vérifié son cliché et livré son analyse dans un petit dictaphone, format paquet de cigarettes, après m'avoir dit que tout allait bien, B. m'interroge et puisque je suis en confiance avec lui, j'évoque ce que j'ai découvert sur «l'autre côté» et sur moi-même. Il répète :

— Vous devriez le raconter.

— Tout le monde me dit la même chose. J'ai envie et puis je n'ai pas envie. Ça va faire un an, bientôt. J'hésite. Je ne suis ni le premier ni le dernier à avoir souffert, être passé de l'autre côté et être revenu. Ce n'est pas aussi exceptionnel que cela.

— Ça n'est pas vrai, dit-il. Ce n'est pas votre douleur qui nous intéresse, c'est le reste, cette chose inconnue que vous avez effleurée et abordée et que la plupart des gens ignorent. Racontez-le avec vos mots, tout droit.

Je n'avais pas attendu B., ses yeux clairs et sa voix chaude, pour me dire qu'il était temps d'aborder ce récit. J'avais pris des notes et l'image obsédante des sapins du Colorado mêlée à celles qui m'avaient traversé, ces visions et ces sensations, ces transformations, je pensais qu'elles ne devaient pas demeurer miennes. Je tournais autour du pot, un peu comme en ce moment dans cette page, je tourne autour du vécu récent, je tourne encore quelques lignes autour du livre. C'est que j'avais retrouvé mon enveloppe habituelle, mon métier, mes routines. Pourtant, rien ne gomme l'épreuve, rien ne gomme le passage du cap Horn. Au vrai, peut-on et doit-on gommer une telle épreuve ? Non, bien sûr.

Si l'esprit et le corps se laissent reprendre par le quotidien, et si l'on retrouve ses démons, ses défauts, ses mesquineries, ses égoïsmes, et si l'on retrouve aussi ses passions, ses pulsions, ses intérêts, ses projets, on n'est plus tout à fait le même. Ce grand remuement mérite qu'on le décrive sans fiction, sans imagination, sans transformer, sans mentir.

Le romancier que je me suis efforcé d'être dans mes livres précédents doit s'effacer, cette fois-ci, pour de bon. J'ai toujours brouillé les cartes dans mes écrits et c'était normal : le travail habituel du romancier. Je mettais ma vie au service du roman et j'inventais à partir de ma vie. Beaucoup de lecteurs ont cru que je racontais ma vie telle qu'elle m'était arrivée, à la virgule près. Ce n'était pas le cas. Cette fois-ci, je n'écris pas un roman.

Tu vas raconter ce qui est vrai. Tu l'as vécu. Et même si tu dois raconter ce qui n'a pas eu lieu, toi, tu l'as vécu. Donc, ça a eu lieu.

6

Les femmes
les plus importantes de ma vie

D'abord, il y a les femmes. Je vis dans un univers régi par des femmes, plutôt jeunes. La plupart du temps, quand je les découvre, elles sont deux. Ensuite, elles se sépareront puis se retrouveront et je n'aurai plus droit qu'à une, mais à ma première vision, elles sont deux.

Elles portent des tenues légères de couleur verte, un masque à hauteur de la bouche, elles parlent entre elles, et elles parlent de « lui », c'est-à-dire de moi comme si je n'étais pas dans la pièce. Peut-être estiment-elles que je ne les entends pas. Il est vrai que je ne les entends pas toujours et ce que je crois entendre d'elles n'est pas forcément ce qu'elles ont dit.

Elles sont rapides mais pas expéditives, méticuleuses. Elles ont un travail à accomplir, des actions à mener. Ce sont des femmes qui à aucun instant, sous mes yeux — mi-clos, mi-comateux, mais mes yeux tout de même —, ne se reposent et ne font rien. Je ne les connaîtrai pas autrement qu'en train de s'activer — soigner, sauvegarder, sauver et garder. Elles font toujours, toujours quelque chose. Elles se partagent les tâches après avoir étudié des feuilles de prescriptions, établi le planning des soins à apporter à chaque malade. Elles échangent des mots pour savoir qui va s'occuper de tel ou tel malade, puisqu'il est clair qu'elles ont plusieurs lits à leur charge. Ainsi, quoique habité entièrement par mon seul sort, traversé par mes seules ondes de grand danger, je vais, grâce aux propos des jeunes femmes, comprendre que je ne suis pas le seul habitant de la réa. Il y a d'autres cellules, et les bruits que j'entends ne sont pas toujours ceux de « ma machine » et les sonneries qui alertent les jeunes femmes ne viennent pas toutes de la seule poire à portée de ma main. Je vais finir par sentir qu'il y a quelqu'un d'autre dans la pièce, juste à côté. Je comprendrai qu'il s'appelle Monsieur Picolino ou Picolini et d'après le temps que les jeunes femmes lui consacreront, je prendrai conscience que Monsieur Picolino ou Picolini va très mal et soulève de grandes inquiétudes.

Par brefs instants, en écarquillant les yeux, en faisant un effort pour arracher mon regard à son rideau de larmes, je peux distinguer la pancarte que la jeune femme restée dans la pièce affiche sur le mur au-dessus de son plan de travail. Il y a des cases, cochées par un triangle noir, vert ou rouge. À chaque case correspond une tâche : faire ingurgiter telle potion, vérifier la tension, température, effectuer une prise de sang, nettoyer le tube qui vous relie à la machine et vérifier la machine, la perfusion, le sérum physiologique, les doses et les vitesses.

Les femmes vont changer selon des rythmes de travail — trois équipes de deux filles, qui font trois fois huit heures — et ce seront les surgissements de noms et couples nouveaux, de voix et visages nouveaux qui formeront les seuls repères de l'écoulement du temps. Le temps est un fil qui se brise fréquemment, s'embrouille et s'emberlificote, se perd et ne se retrouve pas. Seules, les infirmières vous permettent de continuer de comprendre qu'il y a des heures, il y a un jour, il y a une nuit. Certes, la lumière qui flotte dans la pièce — à droite là-haut, dans le mur, il y a comme une lucarne ou la petite fenêtre d'une prison avec des barreaux — vous apporte la notion que c'est le jour, et quand, au plafond, les néons s'allumeront, vous comprendrez plus ou moins que ce jour vient de s'achever. Mais si les infirmières ne changeaient pas, nouveaux noms, nouveaux accents et nouveaux visages, vous n'auriez aucune idée qu'il se déroule un temps tel que, jusqu'ici, dans une vie normale, vous l'avez connu. Les infirmières sont donc, entre autres multiples identités, votre horloge, votre unique explication du temps. Mais elles sont plus que cela. Les infirmières de la réa sont devenues les femmes les plus importantes de votre existence.

J'ai besoin de ces femmes comme je n'ai jamais eu besoin de personne. Je dépends entièrement d'elles. Je sens que ma vie repose entre leurs mains, que ma vie dépend de leur vie. Elles seules peuvent et savent me soulager.

Lorsque les effets les plus puissants de l'anesthésie ont commencé de se dissiper après la fibroscopie, après le réveil, après la visite des morts de ma vie et les visions du ciel du Colorado et de ses forêts, lorsque j'ai compris que le bruit infernal provenait de cette machine à laquelle j'étais relié par le tube qui avait pris possession de ma bouche, ma trachée, lorsque j'ai vaguement — mais vaguement seulement ! — retenu les quelques informations qu'est venu me dispenser un homme (tiens ! un homme !) vêtu de blanc et qui est penché vers moi et a insisté pour que je réponde d'un hochement de tête puisque je n'ai plus la capacité de parler, intubation oblige, j'ai assimilé cette réalité : ces infirmières qui vont, viennent, travaillent, se taisent et parlent, sont ton seul recours. Ton seul secours. Tu as l'impression d'être en permanence en train de te noyer. Elles seules peuvent tenir ta tête hors de l'eau. Tu as l'impression, en permanence, d'être dévoré par un incendie, elles seules peuvent l'éteindre. Mais c'est provisoire. Car l'incendie revient, régulièrement, et la noyade recommence, tout aussi régulièrement. Alors tu vas incessamment faire appel à elles, appuyer incessamment de la main gauche sur la petite poire qui te relie au monde — qui va actionner une nouvelle fois une lumière clignotante à hauteur de la porte d'entrée de la pièce et déclencher une nouvelle fois une sonnerie courte, répétitive,

41

un tit tit tit tit tit malgracieux et insupportable, et qui va, une nouvelle fois, conduire une des jeunes femmes à revenir dans la pièce, éteindre le clignotant et la sonnerie, se rapprocher de toi, prisonnier de tes attaches et de ton silence, et te demander, une nouvelle fois :

— Qu'est-ce qu'il y a ? Que voulez-vous ? Qu'est-ce que je peux faire pour vous ?

Alors, tu vas, en agitant faiblement ton poignet, compte tenu du peu d'espace qui lui est alloué pour s'agiter puisqu'il est ligoté aux barres du lit, en oscillant la tête, en tentant de parler avec les yeux, tu vas essayer de faire comprendre que le tube est obstrué, ta respiration plus difficile, que tu crois que tu vas être submergé par ce qui vient du fond de tes bronches et que tu ne parviens plus à unir ton souffle à celui de la machine. Tu n'es plus synchrone avec la machine et elle aussi se met à sonner. Une autre sonnerie plus frénétique, plus odieuse, plus sirène de catastrophe — et la jeune infirmière va comprendre et prononcer les mots que tu attends :

— Bon, je vais vous aspirer, ne vous inquiétez pas.

Elle va t'« aspirer ». C'est le terme qu'elles emploient toutes. Ce n'est pas très joli, ce n'est pas très élégant, mais dans le monde de la réa, le joli langage, ça n'existe pas. Ici, les mots sont clairs, concrets, précis. On appelle un chat un chat, et un tube un tube. Et « aspirer » veut bien dire ce que cela veut dire : à l'aide d'une sorte de pipette, après avoir rapidement et provisoirement déconnecté le tube du ventilateur, l'infirmière aspire, dans toutes les parois de ta gorge, ton palais, ta trachée, cette matière à la fois fluide et épaisse qui était en train de susciter une terrible sensation d'étouffement. La jeune femme t'aspire. Cela fait du bruit, cela fait du mal, mais c'est un mal qui te délivre d'un autre mal et donc cela fait du bien. Elle réinstalle les cordelettes qui maintiennent le tube, et tu te retrouves, un court instant, soulagé. Elle redispose ta tête sur l'oreiller, elle profite de cette occasion pour te resituer sur ta couche. Tu la regardes et tu souhaites que ton propre regard soit suffisamment fort pour qu'elle comprenne à quel point tu désires qu'elle reste là, qu'elle ne reparte pas pour s'occuper de Monsieur Picolino ou Picolini, et à quel point tu admires la rapidité avec laquelle elle t'a aidé, elle t'a permis de continuer.

Alors, comme tu ne peux exprimer un seul de ces sentiments, tu ébauches un signe des deux doigts de la main droite pour signifier que tu veux écrire. L'infirmière comprend vite. Elles comprennent les gestes, elles savent interpréter les signes. Elles ont vécu ces scènes tant de fois. On ne va pas en réa par hasard. En général, on n'y reste pas plus de deux ou trois ans. C'est très dur. Il y a de la casse. Il y a des gens qui meurent. Le stress est constant. Certaines filles ne trouvent, dit-on, leur équilibre que parce qu'elles sont conscientes qu'elles aident, que l'exercice de cette profession sert véritablement à quelque chose. Ce sont des volontaires. On ne va en réa que si l'on a choisi d'y aller et que si l'on vous a choisi. Donc, elles savent ce que tu veux. Elles te tendent un minuscule tableau en matière plastique et un crayon-feutre au moyen duquel tu inscris lentement — c'est drôle comme tu éprouves de telles difficultés à écrire, n'aurais-tu donc plus aucune force dans les doigts ? — les deux mots : « Merci beaucoup. »

La jeune femme lit ton message, murmure un :
— Je vous en prie. J'espère que ça va aller maintenant.

Elle tourne le dos pour quitter la pièce. Dans son regard vers toi, après qu'elle a effacé le message et reposé ardoise et crayon-feutre sur le plan de travail et annoté une remarque sur le cahier d'infirmière, tu as cru deviner une interrogation. Comme si elle s'étonnait : « Pourquoi donc me remercie-t-il ? »

7

Où l'on fait connaissance
avec Karen la Coréenne

Il était incapable de calculer au bout de combien de temps il avait réussi à identifier chaque infirmière par son prénom. Il croyait les connaître presque toutes. Il y avait une Patricia, une Élisabeth, une Chantal, une Catherine, une Fabienne, une Bénédicte, une Nathalie. Et puis dans les équipes de nuit, il y avait une Coréenne qui s'appelait Karen.

Elle était plus belle que les autres. Elle avait des cheveux bruns, découpés à la diable, une peau mate, des lèvres ourlées, des sourcils longs et de hautes pommettes. Elle paraissait coquette, préoccupée d'elle-même, sensible aux flatteries que lui prodiguait sa coéquipière de nuit, une petite jeune femme boulotte aux cheveux courts et à l'accent du Sud-Est, il pensait que c'était un accent de la région de Béziers. Les deux infirmières formaient un couple étrange, exécutant leur travail, certes, mais lui donnant l'impression, au contraire des autres, que ce n'était pas leur motivation première. Elles bavardaient d'abondance, racontant leurs histoires intimes, l'une, celle au physique le plus ingrat, le maillon faible du couple, prêtant une oreille complaisante aux chagrins d'amour de l'autre — Karen la Coréenne — et lui faisant comprendre qu'elle avait tort d'avoir choisi les hommes. Les femmes, c'était mieux.

Il lui semblait que Karen n'était ni très adroite ni très professionnelle. La première fois qu'il l'avait vue pénétrer dans la pièce, la nuit, pour prendre le relais et qu'elle s'était mise à consulter la feuille de prescriptions, il l'avait entendue commenter à haute voix toutes les séquences qu'elle devait observer au long des huit prochaines heures :

— Oh ! là là ! Il y a tout ça à faire ! Oh ! là là ! mais je ne vais jamais y arriver, moi.

Il lui trouvait une voix vulgaire, contrastant avec son physique de mini-star asiatique. La Biterroise intervenait alors :

— Ne t'inquiète pas, Karen, je suis là. Je t'expliquerai et puis je peux t'aider et faire ce qui est le plus difficile. Je vais m'occuper de ça, ça et ça. Après, on trouvera le temps de se reposer un peu toutes les deux et tu me raconteras tes petites amours, et ça se passera très bien, tu verras. On a toute la nuit devant nous. On va bien s'organiser. On va pas se laisser embêter par « lui », hein !

« Lui » écoutait inquiet et stupéfait, aux prises avec sa douleur, son tube, sa machine, ses bruits et ses cadences, ses cycles de toux, et il croyait percevoir à travers le dialogue des deux filles la naissance ou la prolongation d'il ne savait quelle

46

intrigue dans la nuit de la réa. Elles se permettaient de vivre une vie au sein de laquelle il n'était pas le facteur le plus important ! Mais Karen, soudain, se rebellait :

— Je vais me débrouiller. Et puis, dans ma vie, je fais ce que je veux. Je fais mes choix, moi.

La Biterroise semblait déçue et retrouvait le ton sec des courtisans ou des soupirants que l'on délaisse :

— C'est comme tu veux, Karen, c'est comme tu veux.

Karen tournait le dos à la Biterroise. Karen semblait vouloir se préoccuper un peu plus de sa feuille, des doses de médicaments à répartir, des horaires à organiser, des perfusions à renouveler. Mais il l'entendait soliloquer :

— La petite salope, la petite salope, elle ne m'aura pas comme ça, j'ai mieux à faire !

Le malade sentait monter en lui une anxiété plus forte que celle qui l'habitait depuis son réveil en réa. Allait-il être victime des sautes d'humeur de deux infirmières ? Comment pourraient-elles le soigner si ce cirque se mettait en place ? Il s'agita, sentant encore plus le douloureux chambardement dans sa poitrine et son corps. Il pensa qu'il devrait se battre contr e l'endormissement, contre cette sorte de sommeil sporadique, fractionné, qui ponctuait ses nuits. Ce qu'il croyait être du sommeil. Il se dit que ce serait l'une des nuits les plus angoissantes et les plus épuisantes depuis qu'il était arrivé ici.

Mais la vie privée de Karen la Coréenne n'était

pas la seule raison de cette accélération d'angoisse. À la vérité, dans le même espace de temps ou presque, il avait enfin pris conscience qu'il avait de très fortes possibilités de mourir.

8

Premier précepte de la traversée

Vous prenez conscience que vous pouvez mourir lorsque vous comprenez que personne, jusqu'ici, n'a encore précisément découvert de quoi vous souffrez. Et n'a donc trouvé de remède pour vous sortir du trou. Vous prenez conscience du trou.

C'est un trou sans fond et sans repère. Sans comparaison. Ni verbale ni temporelle. Aucune des douleurs que vous avez connues dans votre vie ne peut se mesurer à celle-là. Le trou est bruyant, à cause de la machine dont le rythme s'emballe à chaque fois que votre respiration s'affole et votre quinte de toux dérange son cycle mécanique. Tout sonne. Les portes s'ouvrent, les infirmières arrivent, et parfois l'interne de garde. Il vous dit :

— Mais apprenez donc à travailler avec la machine, monsieur. C'est une excellente machine. Adaptez-vous. Travaillez avec elle.

« Travaillez avec la machine » ! Vous haïssez cette machine. Vous ne comprenez pas que, sans elle, vous auriez déjà étouffé et vous auriez droit à la trachéotomie. Cette machine, ce trou, ces notions de vide, tout indique que ça va mal, très mal, et surtout, d'autres visages interviennent. Ils vous expliquent, ils vous parlent, ils vous disent que l'on cherche à identifier ce que l'on pense être une bactérie anormale, infréquente, qui a gravement entamé votre système respiratoire, et c'est pour cela que l'on vous ponctionne autant de sang. Pour attraper les germes et réaliser des hémocultures, six fois par jour au moins. On vous dit six, mais vous avez l'impression que cela n'arrête pas. Que les heures défilent avec une litanie de ponctions dans vos veines. Que l'on ne cesse de prendre votre sang, que votre temps tout entier n'est consacré qu'à cela : se faire piquer, se faire vider. Le pire, c'est cette expression qui revient :

— On va vous prendre les gaz du sang.

Vous ne comprenez pas. Votre regard indique que vous voulez savoir. Quelqu'un vous explique :

— C'est pour mesurer la pression et la qualité d'oxygène et de gaz carbonique, pour évaluer la sévérité de l'atteinte pulmonaire et contrôler, aussi, que la ventilation est de bonne qualité.

Les «gaz du sang», ça se déroule non pas dans la veine de l'avant-bras, comme une prise de sang normale, mais dans un endroit plus précis et plus minuscule, dans une artère située au poignet. C'est une piqûre beaucoup plus dure, aiguë et profonde. Comme il faut éviter un hématome, une fois la ponction effectuée, l'infirmière appuie très fortement avec son pouce contre cette artère. Et ça fait très mal, les « gaz du sang », ça fait vraiment très mal. Et vous vous interrogez :

— Y aura-t-il une fin à tout cela ?

La fin, mais quelle fin ? Un autre visage de femme m'aide à comprendre qu'il y a peut-être une fin. Jusque-là, embourbé dans les miasmes de la postanesthésie, dans la découverte de ce qui m'emprisonne (tubes, machine, perfusions), la prise de connaissance avec la machine et ses cycles et le bombardement d'images qui s'abat sur moi, je n'ai eu affaire qu'à des visages de femmes, certes, mais de femmes inconnues. Réconfortantes, puisque me démontrant leur capacité de soulager, surveiller et assister. Sécurisantes, certes, puisque répétant les mots les plus simples :

— On s'occupe de vous, ne vous inquiétez pas.

Dans les yeux, les sourires, les mimiques de ces inconnues, je n'ai vu que ces messages rassurants. C'est sur le visage de la femme la plus proche de moi que j'ai lu un autre message.

Car, enfin, surgit le visage espéré de ma femme. C'est sa première apparition. Elle vient me dire ses mots à elle, ses mots à nous. Ses mots empreints d'amour. Elle me parle, parle, parle. Je suis incapable de répondre. Comme je connais ce visage mieux que tous ceux qui se sont penchés au-dessus du mien, je crois lire quelque chose d'autre. Je lis d'abord la douceur et la tendresse, la sollicitude et l'amour. Je lis tout : notre passé entier, les enfants, les étendues de complicité et de compré-hension, toutes choses partagées en toutes saisons. Je réussis, grâce à elle, à ressentir une émotion chaude qui n'est pas la chaleur âcre de l'incendie qui parcourt régulièrement mon corps, mais une chaleur calmante qui, un très court instant, m'a fait retrouver ce qui me manque le plus depuis l'entrée en réa : ce que l'on appelle le bien-être.

Les médecins lui avaient dit :

— Vous pourrez lui parler, mais il ne vous entendra pas. Il n'entend pas grand-chose.

Mais elle n'a pas écouté les médecins. Comme tout être qui aime et se retrouve face à celui ou celle qu'il aime, sur un lit d'hôpital, elle a fait par-ler son cœur. Elle a pensé : «Il va m'entendre. De tout ce que je vais dire, il y aura bien ne serait-ce qu'une infinitésimale sensation qui passera et il saura que je suis là.»

Je l'ai entendue. C'est une femme — c'est ma femme, oui, et c'est une femme. C'est-à-dire que, comme toutes les femmes, depuis la nuit des temps, comme les infirmières et les sœurs — et ce n'était pas tout à fait fortuit si on les appelait les «bonnes sœurs» —, elle sait que la bonté et l'amour peuvent transpercer le rideau chimique, briser la barrière mécanique. Et si elle ne le sait pas, elle le veut.

J'ai reçu cet amour. Brève dose de bien-être, mais si brève fût-elle, l'effet sera presque trop vio-lent. J'ai vite éprouvé une oppression, un trop-plein. J'ai esquissé un geste qui voulait dire que c'était impossible à intégrer, que cet excès d'émotion me submergeait. Je n'étais pas assez fort pour savourer un moment de bonheur. Ce qui me bouleverse, c'est qu'elle a compris ce qui m'arrive. Cela veut-il dire que, au milieu des tubes et des cordelettes, elle a su lire mon oppression ? Elle dit immédiatement :

— Tu veux que je m'en aille, c'est cela ? Tu veux que je te laisse seul ?

J'ai approuvé de la tête. J'aurais voulu crier :

— Ça n'est pas parce que je ne veux pas te voir, c'est parce que te voir est une trop grosse émotion. ça n'est pas parce que je ne t'aime pas, c'est parce que je t'aime trop. Et en ce moment précis, aimer trop m'empêche de respirer. C'est parce que je t'aime qu'il faut éloigner l'image de cet amour et que ta main, tes yeux, ton visage et ton regard, tout cela doit s'en aller, parce que je ne peux simplement pas l'assumer. Je ne veux pas que tu partes, mais tu dois partir.

Mais privé de l'usage de la parole, incapable d'exprimer un tel fatras de mots qui se pressent en moi sans que je puisse les évacuer, je ne peux qu'approuver de la tête. Elle tend une main vers la mienne et j'ai tenté d'imprimer un semblant de mouvement à mes doigts afin qu'elle ressente ma pression. Elle s'est penchée sur ma main, l'a embrassée et elle est partie.

À cet instant de la traversée, il est bon d'énoncer le premier des préceptes que vous apprend ce voyage : il faut parler aux malades. N'écoutez pas les hommes de science et de technique, les hommes d'autorité et de compétence, les hommes de savoir dont la connaissance s'arrête aux portes des sentiments et dont la rationalité limite leur approche de la vie et des êtres. N'écoutez pas ceux qui vous disent que le malade, le comateux — voire le mourant, voire le mort ! — ne vous entendent pas. Il faut parler à ceux dont on croit qu'ils ne sont plus en état de recevoir une parole — parce que, justement, la parole passe. Il suffit qu'elle soit parole d'amour.

9

Le temps ne se mesure pas

Françoise ne m'a pas seulement prodigué des paroles d'amour. Elle m'a répété ce que les médecins étaient déjà venus me dire et me redire à mon premier réveil, puis mon deuxième, puis mon troisième — ce que les infirmières avaient confirmé lorsque je les interrogeais au moyen de la petite ardoise-tableau et du stylo-feutre :

— On n'a pas identifié votre maladie, pas encore. Les prélèvements ont été effectués et envoyés en anatomopathologie — au labo, en bactériologie. On cherche. Dès qu'on aura trouvé, on pourra procéder à une médication qui devrait vous soulager et réduire l'œdème. Si l'on arrive à réduire, au bout de huit jours, peut-être, si l'inflammation s'amenuise, on tentera de vous extuber.

J'ai compris qu'en attendant j'en ai au moins pour huit jours, donc huit nuits, à rester attaché, perfusé et tubé, secoué par les quintes et les fièvres, face à rien d'autre que le temps dont je ne maîtrise pas l'écoulement. Il va falloir tenir au moins huit jours, au moins huit nuits, et il va falloir mettre au point un moyen pour compter ces jours et ces nuits. Si j'arrive à les compter, si, comme le prisonnier inscrit des petits bâtons sur son mur, je parviens à calculer, à mon tour, dans ma propre prison, le moment où j'approcherai de la délivrance, les choses iront peut-être mieux. Quand on est sous l'effet d'une si forte médication et d'une si forte douleur, la notion du temps est coupée, éclatée. Une vision peut durer quelques secondes, on croit qu'elle a duré un jour ou une heure. Le temps ne se mesure plus.

Or, je sens que j'ai besoin de me fabriquer une notion du temps. Je dois trouver un moyen : compter les relais des équipes d'infirmières, leurs changements. Me raccrocher à tout ce qui évolue : la lumière artificielle, la lumière du jour. Les bruits du matin dans le couloir de la réa, le silence de la nuit. Les bruits de mon voisin, Monsieur Picolino, et la sonnerie de sa machine, plus alarmante que la mienne, qui sonne encore plus comme une sirène de guerre, de panique à bord. Tout cela va peut-être m'aider à définir le temps — tout cela, ainsi que visites et entrevues comme celle que je viens de vivre, la première, avec le visage de ma femme, le visage de l'amour.

Mais je n'ai pas seulement vu l'amour sur ce visage. J'y ai vu la peur.

10

La deuxième voix intérieure

J'ai vu la peur, parce que je connais si bien le visage de ma femme que j'ai lu autre chose.

Notre entrevue m'a laissé épuisé, comme à la fin de je ne sais quel long exercice physique, labeur surhumain à effectuer pendant des heures, comme après avoir soulevé des tonnes de plomb sous le soleil. Il fait nuit. Je revois le visage de Françoise et je me dis : « Elle doit avoir très peur. J'ai dû lui faire très peur. »

Jusqu'ici, lorsque je me parlais à moi-même, une seule voix s'exprimait. C'était simple et facile, et cela s'était passé ainsi pendant toute ma vie, depuis ma plus petite enfance : une seule voix intérieure. Or, voici qu'un phénomène nouveau, dérangeant, inattendu, intervient. Voici qu'une deuxième voix se fait entendre et vient répondre à mon habituelle voix intérieure. La deuxième voix ne ressemble en rien à la première. Elle dit :

— Eh bien, si tu lui as fait peur, c'est que tu es peut-être en train de mourir.

Et je réponds :

— Peut-être.

C'est à l'instant où ce dialogue entre Moi et Moi s'est amorcé que j'ai entamé une nouvelle étape de la traversée. Deux voix vont désormais sans cesse se croiser, comme les vagues se rencontrent au milieu de la mer déchaînée. Elles font partie de moi, ces deux voix sont miennes, mais elles vont s'affronter dans un combat dont je suis seul acteur et seul témoin. La voix de la tentation de la mort. La voix de la lutte pour la vie.

11

Il est nécessaire que les enfants
rient de leurs parents

Il fait nuit. J'ai si peur de la nuit que, une fois les soins prodigués, alors que l'infirmière s'apprêtait à éteindre avant de sortir, je me suis agité pour qu'elle comprenne que je tenais à ce que l'on conserve de la lumière dans la pièce. Elle a laissé allumé, et puis elle est partie, et je suis seul, j'ai peur. J'ai peur de tout. Une panique vaste, pleine, s'empare de moi. La panique s'ajoute à la douleur physique et ces deux puissances négatives viennent ouvrir grand la porte à Madame Négation. C'est la voix de la tentation de la mort. Elle s'exprime à nouveau. Elle répète :

— Après tout, tu es peut-être en train de mourir.

Ce coup-ci, mon autre voix, ma voix ordinaire, oserais-je dire, a été incapable de lui répliquer. C'est une défaite, une capitulation, l'acceptation d'une évidence. Si ma première voix, l'habituelle et la familière, n'a pas pu répondre à la deuxième, la nouvelle, c'est que quelque chose s'est mis en route, en même temps que le mal dont je souffre.

La nouvelle voix continue. Elle est plutôt aimable, posée et courtoise. Un peu condescendante, un peu professorale, protectrice — du genre «j'en sais beaucoup plus que toi». Et elle susurre, et elle ronronne :

— Eh bien oui, répète-t-elle, après tout, c'est peut-être ainsi. Ah, bien sûr, tu ne l'avais pas prévu comme ça. Tu pensais avoir encore beaucoup d'années, beaucoup de temps devant toi, mais que veux-tu, même si ce n'était pas programmé, c'est en train de se produire. Tu seras peut-être le premier à t'en aller des quatre frères qui formaient ta famille. Et pourtant, tu n'étais pas l'aîné, ni même le second, mais rien ni personne n'a jamais énoncé que l'on quitte la vie dans l'ordre dans lequel on l'a abordée. Rien ! Il n'y a pas de loi, c'est écrit nulle part. Il va falloir l'accepter. Tu seras le premier à rejoindre ton père.

La nouvelle voix s'est tue. Ses paroles me hantent. Je n'entends plus que ses mots qui se répercutent et se bousculent dans ma poitrine et ma bouche au rythme des douze cycles par minute de la machine qui ventile l'air. Elles font corps avec le bruit de la machine et avec ma douleur. C'est alors que j'ai revu les visiteurs.

Voici les gens dans la pièce. Curieusement, il ne fait plus aussi sombre. Est-ce déjà le matin ? Les gens sont debout, alignés le long du mur, là où, habituellement, les infirmières viennent afficher leurs feuilles de soins et consulter leur « liaison ».

Ils se tiennent en un seul rang, tranquilles, debout dans leurs habits coutumiers, souriants et immobiles. Je me suis demandé comment ils avaient réussi à entrer dans la pièce sans que je m'en aperçoive. Sans doute avais-je fermé les yeux et étais je parti dans une de ces échappées — non chronométrables — dans le trou sans fond du semi-coma. Pourquoi ces gens se trouvaient-ils là, sans blouse, ni gants, ni port obligatoire du petit masque du visiteur et sans l'autorisation de l'aide-soignante ? Tout cela n'avait pas d'importance. Ils étaient gentiment alignés et me regardaient avec ce que j'ai déjà tenté de décrire comme une immense, patiente et indulgente attitude. Comme pour dire : « Il n'a pas l'air très pressé de venir. Il n'a pas l'air d'avoir encore bien compris qu'il n'a plus tellement le choix. Mais ça ne va pas tarder, c'est un garçon raisonnable, il va bien finir par nous rejoindre. Donnons-lui encore un peu de temps. »

Le temps, peut-être, de les identifier ?

Ce n'est pas difficile. Je les reconnais instantanément, puisque je les connais par cœur, les morts de ma vie. Il y a Valdo, qui s'est suicidé à Paris. Dans un de mes livres, il était mort dans sa vingtième année au volant d'une voiture, de façon romanesque. Dans la vie, il s'est pendu, vers les soixante ans, de façon pathétique. Il y a Jean-Pierre Melville, mort dans mes bras, au milieu d'un repas, en plein restaurant, d'une rupture d'anévrisme. Quel mal j'avais eu à accepter cette disparition et avais-je seulement réussi à le remplacer, celui qui était mon ami et mon maître en cinéma? Il y a May, qui s'est suicidée dans le Maryland. Il y a Jean-François, assassiné à Alger. Il y a mon père, mort sous mes yeux, sur son lit, avec ma mère et l'un de mes frères à mes côtés, à Nice. Il y a Jude, elle aussi s'était suicidée, à New York, le jour de ses quarante ans. Elle ne supportait pas l'idée d'avoir atteint la quarantaine. Et le ravage de la drogue, et la solitude. Il y a Dick qui s'est tué en voiture dans le Mississippi. Il y a Boby qui est mort dans un hôpital à Besançon. Courageux, souriant, patient jusqu'au dernier jour, figure d'amour pour ses filles — pour sa fille, ma femme. Il y en a encore quelques autres et, parmi eux, une toute jeune fille et, aussi, un petit homme chauve et rond. Ils doivent être une douzaine, mais comme la nouvelle voix intérieure a prononcé les mots « ton père » (« Tu seras le premier à rejoindre ton père »), c'est vers lui que se concentre d'abord mon regard.

Il porte sa fameuse veste d'intérieur, coupée à mi-cuisses, dans le même tissu qu'une robe de chambre, à carreaux verts et rouges, avec de larges poches et une ceinture ample — veste qu'il mettait toujours lorsqu'il travaillait dans son bureau. Si je dis que la veste était « fameuse », c'est parce que mes frères et moi-même en avions fait, à son insu, un objet de dérision. Nous admirions et craignions notre père et il nous eût été impossible, en sa présence ou celle de notre mère, d'émettre une seule plaisanterie à son encontre. Mais il est nécessaire que les enfants sachent rire de leurs parents — c'est un travail de lente démystification qui commence tôt, dont ne peuvent se priver les enfants, et que les parents doivent accepter. Mus par la nécessité de réduire l'image trop imposante du père, nous cherchions le moindre détail, chez un homme aussi solennel et sérieux, pour échafauder un monument de comique qui servirait de contraste à son monument de solennité. La veste d'intérieur faisait partie du répertoire. C'était si drôle d'imaginer qu'il l'avait coupée dans une robe de chambre, afin d'économiser de l'argent. Qu'il avait l'air d'un vieux gentleman-farmer anglais, qu'il ne lui eût plus manqué que des pantoufles taillées dans le même tissu et pourquoi pas un bonnet de nuit ? Dormait-il avec ? L'emmenait-il en voyage ? Cette veste d'intérieur était d'un ridicule, d'un vieux, d'un démodé, d'un rigide et d'un figé ! Le rire alors se déclenchait, cascadait, nous inondait, à la simple mention de cette veste. La Veste.

En ce moment précis, cependant, la veste d'intérieur ne me fait plus rire. C'est plutôt lui, mon père, qui me sourit à travers la pièce. Sur ses lèvres habituellement sévères, un sourire engageant est apparu. Il s'exprime. Toujours immobile, le long du mur de la chambre d'hôpital, il parle et répète, pour la cinquième ou sixième fois :

— Viens. Mais viens donc. Qu'est-ce que tu attends ?

12

Kennedy :
une conviction intime

Pourquoi la seule image qui s'associe à la présence de mon père dans cette pièce, pourquoi le seul souvenir est-il celui d'une moquerie ? Papa et sa veste d'intérieur ! N'y a-t-il rien d'autre qui remonte en moi que cette insignifiante réminiscence d'un rire collectif d'enfant ? Un rire venu des années quarante, un rire venu de rien, de l'innocence, des jours dorés dans le grand jardin dominé par le bruissement des feuilles de peupliers sous le vent soufflant depuis la vallée du Tescou, depuis le Tarn... Quelle légèreté, quelle superficialité, quelle sensation éphémère et pulvérisée. Rien... Une aile de papillon qui s'effrite et s'épuise sous les doigts du passé.

Il m'a dit :

— Viens.

Or, je me tais et ne bouge pas et refuse de répondre à son invitation. Comment cela ? Mon père qui m'a tant aimé, que j'ai tant aimé, se trouve devant moi en chair et en os. Il est vraiment là. Je ne l'ai pas revu depuis que sur son lit de mort à Nice, dix ans auparavant, ma mère lui a fermé les yeux en murmurant inlassablement des « mon chéri, mon petit chéri », et il me parle, me sourit, et je refuse de lui répondre ? J'entends quelqu'un me dire :

— N'y va pas.

C'est ma voix habituelle, la première, qui s'est enfin décidée à parler. Ce n'est plus la nouvelle voix complaisante et protectrice qui me disait que tout était joué, tout était foutu. Non, c'est l'autre, c'est mon Moi familier, c'est ma vie. La voix de la vie qui parvient à se faire entendre.

— Regarde-les, me dit-elle. Ils se moquent de toi. Tu vois bien que tu les fais rire.

Il est vrai que je les trouve un peu ironiques, tous ces masques en apparence si aimables. Je commence à me méfier d'eux. Pourquoi irais-je les rejoindre ? La voix de la mort interrompt :

— Ne dis pas de bêtises. S'ils te sourient, c'est parce qu'ils t'aiment et qu'ils désirent t'accueillir, ils te demandent simplement d'arrêter de te battre dans un combat inutile et perdu. Regarde ces sourires, y a-t-il quelque chose là-dedans de méchant et d'ironique, qu'y a-t-il qui puisse te déplaire ?

Rien, à la vérité, ne me déplaît dans cette longue rangée d'hommes et de femmes patients, venus si gentiment me rendre visite à une heure pourtant insolite, dans cette réa où l'on n'accueille guère de monde. Rien ne m'offusque. May est toujours aussi belle et Jean-Pierre Melville, avec son chapeau blanc et ses Ray-ban noires qui cachent ses gros yeux dont il n'aimait pas la couleur, est toujours aussi fascinant.

May est toujours aussi belle, avec ses yeux jaunes qui illuminent son visage à la peau noire. Elle porte une robe de toile claire, à boutons serrés à la taille. Ses lèvres semblent vouloir offrir le même cadeau interdit, ce même goût de vin et de fruit lorsque je l'embrassais, timide et fou, à l'arrière de la voiture que m'avait prêtée un étudiant plus riche que moi.

Il n'avait jamais oublié May.

La deuxième année de son séjour, pour tromper un ennui qui le prenait de plus en plus souvent sur le joli petit campus endormi, et pour satisfaire sa curiosité, il s'était amusé à essayer de retrouver sa trace dans la partie «nègre» de la ville. Comme il avait plus d'expérience, comme il savait un peu mieux mentir et truquer, même corrompre, il avait fini par obtenir des renseignements. On lui avait confirmé que May avait quitté sa famille et la région pour reprendre ses études dans le Maryland. Alors, il avait décidé que c'était véritablement quelque chose de perdu et il s'était juré de ne plus y penser, ne fréquentant que des étudiantes convenables, bien blanches, de bonnes petites Américaines dépourvues de sensualité et de mystère. Mais il n'avait jamais oublié cet amour clandestin et la jeune femme qui lui avait révélé le pouvoir de sa sensualité. Qui l'avait fait jouir de plaisir, un autre plaisir que celui que, jusqu'ici, dans son adolescence, lui avaient donné ses propres mains.

Huit ou dix ans plus tard, il se trouvait à Baltimore dans le Maryland, pour les besoins de son interminable quête de la vérité sur la mort de J.-F. Kennedy. Il y avait eu un accord à ce sujet avec le petit homme son patron. Un jour, alors qu'il en était à son quinzième aller-retour à Dallas, le petit homme l'avait invité a le rejoindre dans son bureau, au journal, au deuxième étage de la rue Réaumur, et lui avait dit de sa voix parigote et zézayante :

— Écoutez, coco, cette histoire n'aura jamais de fin. C'est le plus grand et le plus passionnant mystère de la deuxième moitié du vingtième siècle. Ça fascine le public et surtout les Français. Alors, n'ayez aucun scrupule : chaque fois, vous m'entendez bien, chaque fois que vous aurez un tuyau, un indice, un témoignage, quelque chose qui nécessite que vous repartiez aux États-Unis, n'importe où sur le territoire américain, n'hésitez pas et partez. Vous avez carte blanche. Tout ce qui concerne l'assassinat de Kennedy, c'est pour vous.

Il avait dû y consacrer quelque trois années de sa vie de journaliste. Il savait tout de l'affaire, c'est-à-dire rien. Plus on fouille, moins on en sait. Il connaissait par cœur la carte des rues et de la ville,

les horaires et les noms. Il était devenu une ency-
clopédie vivante de tout ce qui se rapportait au
23 novembre 1963 à Dallas. À l'époque, il était
impliqué dans un réseau d'universitaires, biblio-
thécaires, journalistes, chercheurs et détectives,
criminologues et hommes politiques, en majorité
américains, qui ne cessaient d'échanger théories
et pistes, informations et révélations. Son meilleur
correspondant s'appelait Martin Waldron, il cou-
vrait tout le sud des États-Unis pour le *New York
Times*. Grâce à Waldron, il avait obtenu, avant tout
le monde, une info sur un district attorney de La
Nouvelle-Orléans, un inconnu nommé Jim Garrison, qui prétendait avoir entièrement résolu
l'énigme. Une ramification de son enquête sur
Garrison l'avait mené jusqu'à Baltimore, dans le
Maryland.

Son informateur lui avait dit :

— Si vous voulez rencontrer Santos, installez-
vous à l'hôtel et attendez qu'on vous fasse signe.
Ne quittez pas l'hôtel.

L'attente avait duré deux jours. Il savait qu'il se
trouvait dans la ville où May avait achevé ses
études. Y était-elle demeurée ? Pour tromper son
attente, il avait entrepris de lire, nom après nom,
l'annuaire téléphonique de Baltimore et de la
région suburbaine. Il avait retrouvé douze personnes dont le nom de famille correspondait à
celui de May. Il avait composé les numéros les uns
après les autres :

— Bonsoir, pourrais-je parler à May ?

— Il n'y a pas de May, ici, vous faites erreur.

Au huitième appel, il avait cru reconnaître son accent du Sud, cette voix de gorge, ce rauque, ce râpé dans la voix, cette voix qui pouvait se faire murmurante et cajoleuse, mais aussi amère. Elle avait dit :

— Qui parle ? Qui veut parler à May ?

Le simple son de la voix l'avait tendu à l'extrême. Il avait eu l'impression que le même désir et la même faim reprenaient possession de lui, comme lors de ses dix-huit ans, lors de leurs courtes rencontres charnelles à l'arrière de la Buick.

— Qui parle ? avait-elle répété.

— Un ami, avait-il dit, un ami d'autrefois, un Français.

Il se voulait discret et prudent. Vivait-elle seule ? Y avait-il un homme, des enfants, des parents autour d'elle ? Silence au bout de la ligne. Il avait insisté :

— May ? Allô ?

Elle avait parlé doucement, avec lenteur. Elle avait chuchoté :

— Qui êtes-vous ?

Son « who are you » lui avait paru chargé de toutes sortes d'intentions. Étonnement et incrédulité, mais une touche d'invitation aussi, et un je-ne-sais-quoi de méchant, de presque vulgaire. Alors, il s'était aperçu qu'il était en train de se méprendre. Il avait cru reconnaître la voix de son amour perdu parce qu'il avait souhaité que ce soit elle — mais quelque chose, désormais, dans le prononcé du « who are you » lui disait qu'il s'était trompé. Soudain, la fille avait ri au téléphone. Un rire triste et sec. Il avait senti retomber la bouffée de désir sexuel. La fille avait dit :

— Vous cherchez May, mais elle n'est plus là. Je suis une cousine. May est partie. Elle a pris sa vie l'an dernier, si vous voulez tout savoir.

« *She took her life.* » Les Américains utilisent des formules formidables pour éviter de prononcer les mots qui leur font le plus peur et plutôt que de dire « *she killed herself* » — elle s'est tuée — ou « *she is dead* » — elle est morte —, ils préfèrent cette phrase sibylline, poétique et profonde : « elle a pris sa vie ».

Il avait bredouillé des mots d'excuse, incapable d'avancer une seule question, ce que, plus tard, il regretterait. Il avait raccroché. Le sentiment aigre de sa méprise, de la tromperie de cette voix dans la nuit, resterait longtemps en lui, bien après qu'il eut quitté Baltimore, bien après qu'il eut rencontré le parrain mafieux, Santos T. Et que celui-ci lui eut confirmé avoir effectivement dit, devant témoins, quelques mois avant l'attentat de Dallas :

— Kennedy est un caillou dans ma chaussure.

De toute façon, sur Dallas, il possédait une conviction intime.

Comme il aimait voyager, comme, à cet âge de sa vie, il était un fana de séries noires, il se disait que chercher la vérité sur l'affaire lui permettait de jouer, dans la vie, un rôle dans une réelle série noire ; comme il aimait la chasse aux scoops, la poursuite d'un secret, et la découverte bout par bout, tel l'archéologue, des menus morceaux d'un puzzle impossible à reconstituer, il avait accepté de feindre, de simuler. Il avait accepté de jouer, comme tous les autres enquêteurs, avec la thèse non pas d'un complot, mais des complots. Néanmoins, à chaque fois qu'il se penchait sérieusement sur sa documentation et qu'il scrutait sa mémoire, l'intime conviction revenait à la surface. À l'époque, il était presque seul à penser ainsi. C'était presque comme un blasphème, mais il ne le disait pas à haute voix, il ne l'écrivait pas. Il lui suffisait de penser à la grimace souriante de Lee Harvey Oswald dans le couloir du quatrième étage de la « police-station » de Dallas, grimace dont il avait été le témoin, au visage rapproché, à un mètre près, il lui suffisait de penser à cette grimace et l'intime conviction revenait.

Son enquête avait un peu avancé à Baltimore. Mais de ce séjour dans le port du Maryland, aux nuits hantées par la plainte des sirènes de bateaux se mêlant aux appels des voitures patrouilleuses, aux matinées quand le cri des mouettes venait s'ajouter aux concerts du port, de ce séjour, il n'avait retenu que l'annonce de la mort de May, la jeune femme noire qu'il avait aimée quand il était encore un novice :

— Elle a pris sa vie.

Alors, maintenant, voici May devant moi, dans la pièce de la réa, au milieu des autres visiteurs. May qui me parait frêle et forte, avec ses avant-bras croisés l'un sur l'autre devant sa poitrine. Elle aussi, elle sourit. Ce n'est pas le même sourire que celui de mon père. Il n'y a plus la trace de cette provocation amusée que je lisais dans ses yeux lorsque nous nous rencontrions clandestinement dans la Buick, dans le froid de l'hiver du Sud, en Virginie, quarante ans auparavant, quand nous aimions autant parler que faire l'amour et parler à nouveau et faire l'amour à nouveau, quand le Sud était sudiste, c'est-à-dire mortel pour qui osait transgresser les coutumes et la barrière des races. Dans le sourire de May, aujourd'hui, je ne vois plus que de l'indulgence et presque de la miséricorde. Je me dis que, si elle est venue me rendre visite, c'est pour que je puisse enfin obtenir une réponse à la question que je n'avais pas osé poser à sa soi-disant cousine, un soir, à Baltimore :

— Dis-moi, May, pourquoi as-tu pris ta vie ?

Mais elle disparaît de mon regard tandis que mes yeux veulent se porter vers un troisième visiteur. Et j'entends ma voix familière me dire :

— Oublie ces gens-là. Lâche-les. Laisse-les tomber. Ne les regarde plus. Oublie la mort. Fais l'effort considérable de déplacer ton regard vers un autre coin de la pièce. Fais-le, putain de Dieu, sinon tu ne vas pas t'en sortir. Ne te laisse pas aspirer par eux. Regarde ailleurs !

J'ai accompli cet effort. Il m'a semblé gigantesque. Mes yeux sont parvenus à se détourner de la rangée de gens le long du mur et ont pu découvrir un espace dans la pièce, vide et dépourvu de visiteurs. Et dans cet espace, les ondes des sapins bleus du Colorado ont dévalé en rafales. Le bleu m'a envahi et submergé.

Je vois les étendues de cette pureté bleue, verte, jaune et noire qui m'attiraient tellement lorsque j'avais dix-huit ans et ne connaissais rien de la vie. Couché sur la pierre, le vent soufflant le long de mon corps et pénétrant mes vêtements, je peux à peine tourner la tête pour savoir si mes amis allongés comme moi, à même la Faille, sont autant possédés par ce spectacle. Ce qui est étrange, c'est que nous en parlerons peu lorsque nous serons redescendus au camp tout à l'heure. Dans la tente que nous partageons, autour du poêle, nous n'échangerons que quelques phrases à propos de notre escalade vers la Faille et des images que nous avons contemplées. Peut-être ne possédions-nous pas les mots pour commenter ce que nous avions vu. Mes compagnons étaient incultes, et moi j'étais inculte aussi, à ma manière — inculte de la vie.

13

Popa, où il est popa ?

Lorsque les gens vous racontent que l'on « revoit sa vie se dérouler devant soi », au cours d'un accident, une noyade, une opération ou au cours d'un voyage aux marges de la mort, il faudrait leur demander d'être un peu plus précis ou plus honnêtes. Il est vrai que toute expérience étant, par définition, unique, ce que vous disent les gens est peut-être exact. Mais je n'y crois pas.

Je n'y crois plus. Je crois — parce que je le sais — que l'on voit sa vie, certes, mais qu'on ne la voit pas se « dérouler » comme une suite chronologique d'événements. On ne voit que des morceaux, des lambeaux, un chaos de vie. C'est le désordre, le charivari, le maelström, c'est un kaléidoscope qui s'agite furieusement et qu'aucune main ne repose afin que l'image se stabilise. C'est du fragmenté, de l'éclaté, de l'atomisé, comme si vous vous retrouviez dans un chaudron, un tuyau qui se retournerait dans tous les sens et charrierait des débris de vie. Ou de rêve. Vous êtes à l'épicentre d'une sorte de séisme. Vous êtes le séisme.

Et le plus étonnant est que les morceaux de vie, l'éparpillé de vie que vous revoyez, ne sont pas forcément les plus importants.

Tremblement d'images. Tremblement de mémoire. Un petit avion décolle de l'aéroport d'Amman. Poussière de sable ocre, visages fermés et moustachus, masses blanches qui s'effacent à mesure que nous prenons de l'altitude. L'appareil est rempli de types sans foi ni loi. Vêtus de treillis, porteurs d'armes. Tueurs et mercenaires, déserteurs, agents doubles. Une cargaison d'irréguliers, de fauteurs de troubles. Je ne sais plus comment on nous a permis de monter à bord, mais c'était le dernier zinc pour Beyrouth avant que le petit roi décide de mettre toute la presse occidentale en quarantaine. Nous sommes à la fin des années cinquante. Arrivés au-dessus des montagnes qui séparent la Jordanie du Liban, un violent trou d'air, des turbulences extrêmes, l'avion perd l'équilibre. Tout valse à bord. Ce sont les montagnes russes. Le cœur et l'estomac sursautent. Les durs à cuire deviennent livides. Tout le monde dégueule. On entend des gémissements d'enfants, des couinements de chats. Il n'y a pourtant aucun enfant, aucun animal à bord. Ce sont les «hommes de guerre» qui geignent et gémissent. Des matières curieuses coulent en rigoles le long de la petite allée. Le ciel est noir. Sommes-nous absorbés par une tempête de sable? À genoux, un porteur de mitraillette sanglote et psalmodie. J'entends à mes côtés Pradas, le coriace photographe qui m'accompagne partout, qui crie :

— Le trou du cul du diable ! On va voir le trou du cul du diable !

On dirait que cette perspective l'exalte. L'appareil semble devoir partir en vrille. Révulsé, je vois passer mon sac devant mes yeux, mes papiers et mes carnets de notes. Nous faisons des loopings. Dans les oreilles, une pression nous assourdit. Et puis, la clarté soudaine, le calme, l'appareil se stabilise. On est déjà en train d'atterrir. Dans la carlingue, les hommes ont l'air pitoyable, essuyant leur vomi au moyen de leur keffieh à carreaux rouges et blancs. Pradas, hagard, dit à regret :

— On l'a pas vu, on l'a pas vu. On est passé près, mais on l'a pas vu.

Dehors, Beyrouth, le vent frais, nos pieds touchent le sol et je me dis que je n'ai pas un instant pensé à la mort. J'ai vingt et un ans. Ça ne m'a pas effleuré. C'était trop tôt. Ce n'était pas pour moi.

Tremblement d'images et de mémoire.

La bonté dans les yeux de l'Abbé, enfin retrouvé à la sortie d'une chapelle à Buenos Aires. Cette bonté amusée dans le regard quand je lui dis avoir parcouru dix mille kilomètres pour qu'il me raconte comment il a sauvé vingt vies dans le naufrage d'un ferry-boat, dans les eaux glacées du

Mar del Plata. L'Abbé qui refuse de commenter son héroïsme et me dit seulement :

— Je n'avais pas peur, j'attendais la délivrance, j'attendais que Dieu me reprenne par la main.

Images et mémoire — petite image, petite musique.

Les frères sur leurs vélos descendent la grande rue vers le lycée de Montauban. Tout est limpide, joyeux, calme et clair. L'enfance se résume à cette musique des roues à rayons qui s'amplifie à mesure que la pente augmente...

Le rire de dérision des défoncés de Californie, fin des années soixante, dans les nuits sur les collines de Topanga, leurs yeux orangés, leurs cheveux fous, l'arrogance et le vide absolu de leur brouillon théologique, leurs balbutiements. Et comment, pour échapper à leur volonté de me faire partager leur vision du monde, je suis obligé de fuir en rampant le long d'une piscine, pour me retrouver à quatre pattes dans les buissons et les épines de ce qui est l'amorce d'un désert. Cette nuit-là, j'avais marché pendant huit heures avant qu'une voiture daigne s'arrêter pour me recueillir, tellement, sans doute, mon aspect faisait peur. J'avais l'impression d'être un chien. Ca m'avait définitivement guéri de la fascination hippie : «*peace*», «*love*», et tout le détournement de ce qui, à l'origine, procédait d'un mouvement innocent.

Morcellement d'images.

Noël dans la grande maison et la voix de maman qui chante « Il est né le divin enfant ».

L'Alfa Romeo fait trois tonneaux sur une route de montagne entre la frontière suisse et l'Italie. Je suis seul à bord et je m'en sors sans une blessure. Des paysans me contemplent, ahuris :

— Eh bien, vous auriez pu y rester !

Les nuits blanches du divorce. Des couloirs d'hôpitaux. Les pavés de la rue Gay-Lussac. L'odeur de pomme pourrie des grenades. Les larmes silencieuses d'une petite fille dans une voiture, à l'arrêt sur le terre-plein d'une station à essence sur l'autoroute, à quarante kilomètres de Paris : « Je ne veux pas rentrer chez moi. »

Les tirs de mortiers au-dessus de la Casbah. Les femmes égorgées dans le quartier d'Hydra. La colère capricieuse d'une star de cinéma qui casse un décor à coups de pied et de poing et se retourne vers moi et l'équipe qui n'a pas bougé : « Les gros plans sur moi et sur moi tout seul ! » Et je me dis sans répondre : « Est-ce donc bien cela, mettre en scène ? »

Les pieds nus des enfants, à Vazerac, dans les cuves des vendanges, pour écraser le muscat sous le soleil des Causses. Des trains que j'essaye de rattraper à la course ; un oreiller que je ne retrouve plus ; une peur indicible après un coup de téléphone anonyme dans un hôtel de Dallas, et une voix texane au bout de la ligne : « Quittez la ville et n'insistez plus » ; un vol de corneilles noires au-dessus des jardins de l'hôpital psychiatrique de Vienne.

Un souvenir des Pyrénées. Font-Romeu. Un lac froid, bleu et glacé, impassible. Une barque. J'ai huit ans. J'avais mal à la poitrine, alors on m'a envoyé là pour me fortifier. Il y a un lac tout près d'un grand chalet habité par des enfants aussi ché-tifs que moi. J'entends la voix du poète qui chante :

> *Mes jeunes années*
> *Courent dans la montagne.*

Et je me demande alors, revenu dans ma chambre d'hôpital en réa, aujourd'hui, si tout ce que je vis, ou plutôt tout ce que je meurs, n'est pas lié à cet épisode de mon enfance, si tout n'avait pas commencé là-bas. Tout tremble.

Le séisme continue, puisque je saute de mon enfance à celle de mes enfants. J'entends le petit Jean, en Sierra Leone, en dehors de la hutte en paille où je suis en train d'écrire *Un été dans l'Ouest*. Il a vu un gros lézard traverser le sentier et il crie :

— Popa, où il est popa ?

Pendant quelques instants, son cri rond et drôle va courir en moi : « POPAOUILÉPOPA », et je vois les petites mains de sa sœur Clarisse qui tapent à l'unisson contre les siennes. Cette fois, ils sont ailleurs, au Kenya, assis dans la brousse, au bord d'une piste d'herbe et de terre, en attendant un petit avion. Ils jouent à des jeux incompréhen-sibles avec des chansons qui leur appartiennent :

Pépito, c'est le capitaine
Le capitaine du navire,
Pépito c'est le capitaine,
Capitaine du bateau.

Et je me retourne alors pour voir le visage illuminé de tendresse de leur mère, ses yeux gris-vert noisette sous le chapeau de toile kaki. Elle sourit en silence. Tout tremble.

Le tremblement de la mémoire n'est pas forcément douloureux. Bien sûr, la souffrance est toujours présente, celle du corps. Mais je vais vous épargner le récit de la douleur. La douleur ne se raconte pas. Il me semble, en tout cas, que je n'en ai ni le talent ni la capacité. C'est horriblement répétitif, la douleur. Horriblement semblable. Ça n'arrête pas, c'est tout, c'est tout ce qu'il faut dire. Ça n'arrête pas de vous tenir la poitrine, la gorge, l'ensemble de votre système, et vous en voulez au monde entier, aux infirmières, aux tubes et à la machine, à votre propre faiblesse, de souffrir autant — mais vous finissez par si bien connaître la douleur que vous l'acceptez. On accepte tout, même l'inacceptable. Il faut bien. On n'a pas le choix. Il paraît, je crois que c'est Dostoïevski qui a dit cela, que la meilleure définition de l'homme est celle-ci : « Un être qui s'habitue à tout. » Je suis donc un homme, puisque je m'habitue à cette douleur?

Je ne cesse de me répéter : « Capitale de la douleur. » Était-ce le titre d'un poème ou d'un recueil d'Eluard? Peu importe, l'image me convient, elle est appropriée : tu habites dans la Capitale de la Douleur, boulevard des Allongés, rue des Tubulés, impasse des Quasi-comateux, carrefour du Larynx Bouché, à l'étage de la Bactérie Inconnue et Non Identifiée, dans l'appartement des Perfusés, dans la pièce des Réanimés. Dans le quartier des Angoissés.

Si je supporte la douleur, c'est que, contrairement à ce que je crois, elle n'est pas toujours continue. Les produits que l'on m'administre me permettent certainement de connaître des petits répits, des plages de quasi-coma, des glissements dans un faux sommeil. Dans un autre état. Est-ce dans cet état que je retrouve le tapis bleu? Est-ce au cours de cette étape que s'entrechoquent et se croisent mes débris de vie, les éléments du séisme? Certains passent vite, comme les météores, d'autres reviennent de façon régulière et obsessionnelle. Ainsi, je n'arrête pas de voir ces images qui chassent toutes les autres : la Faille de l'Aigle, la forêt Uncompaghre.

C'est beau, comme de la mer ou de la soie, cela m'attire et me submerge, et j'en oublie les gens alignés devant le mur, j'oublie la machine, le tube et la perfusion, je n'éprouve même plus le lancinant besoin d'appuyer sur la poire d'appel à l'aide. Et le petit bout du caoutchouc quadrillé, serti de métal, qu'on appelle l'oxymètre et qui enregistre en permanence, au bout de l'index gauche, la saturation d'oxygène dans le sang, n'a plus l'importance que je lui accorde.

L'oxymètre, pourtant, joue un rôle primordial dans la vision que j'arrive à obtenir des quelques éléments de mon corps. Il est là, ce corps, droit, sans forces, étendu devant moi. Au bout de mon doigt gauche, l'oxymètre diffuse une petite lumière orange. C'est un objet sécurisant, je l'ai vite compris. Il me ferait penser à l'extrémité du doigt de l'extraterrestre du cinéma, E.T., si j'avais la force d'établir cette comparaison. Lorsque les aides-soignantes font ma toilette, me retournent, me manipulent, renversent mon corps qui n'a plus de muscles ni de poids (combien de kilos ai-je perdus ?), je vois bien l'importance de l'oxymètre à la façon dont elles s'arrangent pour ne pas l'ôter trop longtemps de mon doigt. J'ai noté que c'est le premier geste qu'elles accomplissent dès qu'elles ont achevé de me nettoyer — elles s'empressent de fixer l'oxymètre à nouveau au bout de mon index. Et puisqu'elles le font, j'ai compris que j'avais besoin de cette présence et j'y ai pris goût. Tant que je sentirai le petit objet caoutchouté gainant mon doigt, je me dirai que je ne suis pas irrémédiablement perdu.

Eh bien, maintenant que le bleu a investi mes yeux, ma tête et la pièce elle-même, l'oxymètre ne compte plus. Je ne forme qu'un avec cette inlassable ondulation de sapins. C'est le présent : je suis couché sur la Faille et il fait froid mais cela ne me gêne guère. Je ne sais pas ce que pensent mes compagnons, mais l'océan d'arbres bleus devient, en effet, la tentation dont parlait la légende. Je me dis que si je plonge dans cette mer, je passerai sans histoire de l'autre côté et je découvrirai quelque chose dont j'ignore tout.

Mais j'avais dix-huit ans, mes compagnons aussi, et nous n'avons pas sauté dans le vide pour nous écraser sur le sommet des pins Ponderosa. Nous sommes redescendus vers le camp et nous n'avons pas parlé des tentations que nous avions ressenties. Il est vrai que mes compagnons n'étaient pas loquaces. Pachéco, Branch, Donald, le Suédois n'étaient pas de grands intellectuels ou des discoureurs. Mais pourquoi, maintenant, aujourd'hui, dans cette pièce de la réa, l'océan de sapins fait-il à nouveau signe ? Quel est le sens de cet appel ?

À peine ai-je eu le temps de contempler les sapins bleus que la voix de la mort a repris possession de moi. Dans la pièce, tout d'un coup, il n'y a plus de sapins, ni de gens alignés. Les visiteurs ont quitté la réa. Sont-ils partis manger quelque chose à la cantine et reviendront-ils ? La voix de la mort s'empresse de me répondre. Elle est toujours aussi aimable, la voix de la mort, toujours prête à vous rendre service. Elle dit :

— Rassure-toi. Ils ont promis qu'ils reviendraient te voir. Ils seront là dans très peu de temps.

Je hais cette voix. J'aime tellement mieux la mienne. Qui va l'emporter, des deux voix qui se croisent en moi ? Un duel s'engage.

14

La force du rire et de la poésie

C'est une autre nuit, et j'ai toujours aussi peur.
Et je me sens faiblir. La voix de la mort est omni-
présente :

— Laisse-toi aller, me dit-elle. Les médecins
n'ont toujours rien trouvé, sinon ils seraient venus
te le dire. Ils te laissent bien seul, tu ne trouves
pas ? Elle est très calme, ce soir, la réa. Aucun bruit
dans le couloir — à part les sonneries activées par
le pauvre Monsieur Picolino. Tu dois en être arrivé
à la troisième ou quatrième nuit. Tes forces s'ame-
nuisent. Crois-tu vraiment que tu vas être capable
de traverser une nouvelle nuit ? Ça commence à
être long, tu ne trouves pas ?

Je n'arrive pas à chasser la voix.

— Tiens, continue-t-elle, voici Karen la Coréenne. Elle va encore te faire mal lorsqu'elle
s'emploiera dans un instant à changer tes cordelettes, renouveler ta perfusion, prendre ta température et surtout te prendre les gaz du sang, l'horrible épreuve ! Son pouce sur ton artère va être dur
comme de la pierre. Elle va te prévenir : «Je vais

vous faire un peu mal », de sa voix aiguë et vulgaire. Et elle te fera mal. Elle n'a pas envie que tu guérisses. Karen est trop préoccupée par son père qu'elle n'a pas réussi à obtenir au téléphone, là-bas, à Séoul. Elle a passé la moitié de sa journée à tenter de le joindre pour lui souhaiter sa fête — c'est aujourd'hui la fête des Pères. Elle s'entend de plus en plus mal avec l'amant de sa mère. Ils ont encore eu une scène, hier, avant qu'elle revienne à l'hôpital prendre son service. Elle a raconté tout cela à sa consœur, la petite Biterroise à la voix mauvaise. Ça va être encore un enfer, cette nuit, avec ces deux filles, tu ne crois pas ?

J'ai besoin de trouver une arme, des armes, pour lutter contre la perversité de cette voix de la mort. Je n'ai pas d'autre arme que celle qu'emploie la voix : des mots. J'ai besoin d'aller chercher au fond de moi les mots les plus simples, les phrases les plus évidentes, les répliques les plus énormes. Alors je me dis, avec ma voix à moi, la voix de ma vie :

— Arrête de délirer, reprends-toi. Ressaisis-toi, ricane. Ricane-lui à la gueule à cette mort de merde. Tu ne veux pas d'elle et ce n'est pas le moment, ce n'est pas l'heure. Il suffit de lui dire. Tu lui dis : Salut ! Va-t'en ! Casse-toi ! Ce n'est pas l'heure ! Tu ne vas quand même pas te laisser avoir par cette ordure, tu es quand même un peu plus costaud que ça, non ? Tu en as vu d'autres !

C'est faux, je n'en ai pas « vu d'autres ». Je n'étais pas préparé à cela. Qui est préparé à cela ? Mais j'ai trouvé le fil conducteur et je m'admoneste. Je me secoue, je me fouette, je me fustige, je m'injurie, je m'insulte, je me tance et me discipline. Je m'astreins à des injonctions autoritaires et orgueilleuses. Je décide, enfin, de rire dans ma tête. Un rire vachard, le rire du mec qui sait qu'il est plus fort que le connard en face de lui qui essaye de lui bousiller la tronche sur un ring de boxe. Le rire du soldat, au front, dans sa tranchée de terre, et qui a déjà subi deux heures de tirs d'artillerie de l'adversaire. Tout autour de lui, le sol n'est plus qu'une suite de cratères et d'arbres calcinés, mais il est resté recroquevillé sous son casque, l'arme au travers du bras, à genoux sous la poussière, la cendre, la boue, la fumée et le vacarme, il a gardé l'esprit lucide et il se dit :

— Tiens bon. Tiens bon. Ça va se calmer. Alors tu vas pouvoir te défendre. Et tu vas même pouvoir attaquer. Allez, mon vieux, encore un effort. Allez, mon vieux, tout n'est pas perdu.

Je ne m'étonne pas d'avoir recours à des phrases et à des idées aussi élémentaires. Ce ne sont pas des idées, tout juste des mots. Des pauvres mots, des mots de tous les jours. Et puis, je n'en suis pas là, je ne peux pas me permettre de juger la valeur et l'originalité de mon discours. Mes amis, les intelligents, diraient que «je fais dans le premier degré absolu», le comble du «premier degré», le primaire intégral. Ils diraient : «C'est du basique, tout cela ! » Mais de quels amis parlons-nous ? Où sont-ils ? Aucun d'entre eux n'est à côté de moi pour m'aider. Je suis tout seul. Seul au monde. Alors je rigole intérieurement et je ne cesse de me répéter :

— Rigole, ricane-lui au nez. Tu vas t'en tirer. Tu vas baiser la mort. Tu vas la niquer. Il y a un groupe de chanteurs qui s'appelle Nique Ta Mère. Toi, tu vas t'appeler Nique Ta Mort.

J'ai découvert que l'injure à la mort me procure un semblant de vigueur. L'usage de ces mots grossiers me stimule, comme à l'armée, comme au front, comme en sport de compétition. Le recours à l'insulte raffermit mon hostilité, ma capacité de survie, empêche mon corps de céder à la résignation.

— Tu vas niquer cette connasse. Tu vas baiser tous ces cons. Elle va fermer sa gueule, cette ordure.

Et je m'assène cette vérité crue à plusieurs reprises pour étouffer l'autre voix, pour ne pas m'abandonner au vide.

Tout mon effort, maintenant, va consister à empêcher la voix de la mort de revenir en moi, de chevaucher mon autre voix. Je dois lui interdire l'entrée de la porte de mon corps, ne lui laisser aucune chance de venir se glisser dans ma gorge pour reprendre son discours insinueux. Alors, va se déclencher un nouveau réflexe d'autodéfense, tout aussi inconnu de moi, puisque je suis en train de traverser l'inconnu. Je me mets à répéter sans fin, sans une fraction de seconde de silence dans ma tête, une suite de mots et de phrases. Si je parvenais à analyser froidement ce que je suis en train de mettre au point, je pourrais dire qu'il s'agit d'une sorte d'équivalence au « mantra » des bouddhistes.

Au premier stade du contrôle de soi, la répétition attentive d'une ou de plusieurs formules peut arrêter le flot des images qui détruisent l'esprit et le portent vers le néant. Sans m'en rendre compte, je suis en train de me construire un rituel de formules répétitives qui vont aider à endiguer la résignation et la faiblesse, la tentation du vide, le spectacle du rien, le saut dans le néant. Le néant, ça aussi je suis en train de l'apprendre, il ne faut jamais lui laisser plus de quarante secondes d'avantage.

Alors, dans mon « mantra », tout passe, tout arrive, tout ce qui relève de l'absurde inconscient et dans mon cas, cette nuit-là, cela donne une abondance de bouts de poèmes, des vers, des bribes de textes sortis d'autrefois, les déchets de ma petite culture à moi, mon bagage intérieur, ouvert en vrac, dans le désordre, comme les valises éventrées lors des déraillements de chemin de fer. Et puis, avec ces extraits, interviennent des noms propres, venus de je ne sais où, je ne sais pourquoi.

Cela procède par cycles, et je vais aller d'un nom répété une centaine de fois à un autre — ou d'un fragment de poème à un autre. Cela sans raison. Il n'existe, en effet, aucune raison pour que surgisse le nom propre d'un homme que je n'ai jamais rencontré : Christophe de Ponfily. Pourquoi ce nom a-t-il émergé ? Je le scande à l'infini, de façon presque musicale, en observant un bref arrêt entre les sonorités :

— Chris - tophe (j'insiste sur le *e*) de Ponfily.

Aucune raison pour que ce « Chris-tophe *e e e* de Ponfily » me serve de bouclier contre la tentation du néant. Mais pourquoi y aurait-il une raison ? Y a-t-il aussi, et encore, une raison pour que, au bout de je ne sais combien de centaines, voire de mille « Ponfily », j'enchaîne sur le titre d'un livre que je n'ai jamais lu, dont je ne suis pas certain qu'il soit le titre authentique : *La Volte des Vertugadins* ? Le même phénomène s'empare de ma voix intérieure, investit le peu qui me reste de facultés, et avec la même manie de découper les mots et d'en faire un chant rituel, une incantation :

— La Vol - te - des - Ver - tugadins.

Là encore, cela va se reproduire des centaines de fois. Et puis l'esprit se lasse et il dérive vers des phrases plutôt que des mots, et viennent des douzaines et des douzaines d'extraits de poèmes. Mais je suis incapable d'aller plus loin que deux ou trois vers par poème.

En fait, cela ressemble à des épluchures de poésies, des miettes, des copeaux de menuisier.

Il faut laisser maisons et vergers et jardins
Vaisselles et vaisseaux que l'artisan burine.

Ou bien encore :

Puisque les jours ne t'ont laissé
Qu'un peu de cendres dans la bouche.

Et encore :

Soirs de Paris ivres du gin, flambants de l'électricité.

Et encore :

Mes amis m'ont enfin avoué leur mépris.

Et encore :

Mon automne éternel Oh ma saison mentale
Les mains des amantes d'antan jonchent ton sol
Les fleurs ne laissent plus tomber aucun pétale
Les colombes ce soir prennent leur dernier vol.

Et encore :

Un frais parfum sortait des touffes d'asphodèle
Les souffles de la nuit flottaient sur Galgala.

Et encore :

J'ai plus de souvenirs que si j'avais mille ans.

Et encore :

J'aime de vos longs yeux la lumière verdâtre.

Et encore :

Nous aurons des lits pleins d'odeurs légères
Des divans profonds comme des tombeaux.

Et encore :

Il va neiger dans quelques jours.
Je me souviens de l'an dernier
Je me souviens de mes tristesses.

Ah ! Je me trouve plutôt éclectique, quoiqu'un peu banal, dans ma sélection. Je vais aussi chercher Verlaine :

Je fais souvent ce rêve étrange et pénétrant
D'une femme inconnue et que j'aime et qui m'aime.

Et puis voici que Hugo revient :

Nous ne voyons jamais qu'un seul côté des choses.
L'autre plonge en la nuit d'un mystère effrayant.
L'homme subit le joug sans connaître les causes.
Tout ce qu'il voit est court, inutile et fuyant.

Et là, et c'est moins surprenant, un poème que je peux presque réciter en entier. Il est d'Aragon :

Suffit-il donc que tu paraisses
De l'air que te fait attachant
Tes cheveux ce geste touchant
Que je renaisse et reconnaisse
Un monde habité par le chant
Elsa mon amour ma jeunesse.

C'est miracle que d'être ensemble
Que la lumière sur ta joue
Qu'autour de toi le vent se joue
Toujours si je te vois je tremble
Comme à son premier rendez-vous
Un jeune homme qui me ressemble.

Je ne suis pas surpris que ces lignes d'Aragon soient plus longues que les autres fragments éclatés de poèmes, puisque c'est le dernier poème que j'ai appris, tout récemment, pour l'anniversaire de Françoise à Venise. Je me souviens que je l'avais récité devant des amis, c'était le soir, il faisait beau, et je sentais la maladie grimper dans ma poitrine, et quelques jours plus tard, je serais hospitalisé.

Il me semble que si j'avais eu la possibilité de trier ce flot désordonné de poésie, j'y aurais vu assez clair. D'abord, tout tournait autour du passage du temps. Il y avait de la mélancolie et de la nostalgie. Ensuite, ce que j'avais appris tôt, dans mes années d'écolier ou de lycéen, revenait le plus aisément à la surface. Cela signifie-t-il, alors, que lorsque vous déambulez sur les marges de la mort, l'enfance revient en premier ? Ainsi que la jeunesse ? Et cela explique-t-il l'obsession du Colorado ? Cela veut-il dire que vous revenez à votre état d'enfance ?

Oui, je suis de plus en plus un enfant. Je cherche mon enfance, toutes les images du passé qui m'ont assailli le prouvent. Et je suis réduit, aussi, à cet état d'impuissance de l'enfant, du bébé entre les mains des mamans. Les mamans sont les infirmières. Je les attends, comme le bébé attend son biberon. Et de même qu'il crie parce qu'il a faim, peur ou mal, je crie à ma manière, en actionnant la petite poire d'appel qui sonne au secours et les fera revenir auprès de moi.

Cela pourrait me désespérer de n'avoir conservé dans ma mémoire que quelques premières lignes de poésie. Mais je me ris de tout cela, continuant de dévider mes litanies, et me disant que cela va me permettre de tenir. Je me ris aussi de moi :

— Si l'on t'ouvrait le cerveau, si l'on voulait définir qui tu étais, on ne trouverait à dire que ceci : « C'était un homme qui n'avait pour toute connaissance que des vers dispersés de certains poèmes de la poésie française, la poésie la plus banale et la plus facile à retenir. Il était incapable d'aller plus loin. Voilà ce qu'il était. »

Car une autre question vient s'insérer dans le cours de mon délire, mon « mantra ». Elle ne m'est pas posée par la voix de la négation, la voix de la mort que j'ai réussi à juguler grâce à mes poésies. Je ne l'entends plus depuis quelque temps. Mais il semble que c'est d'elle que pourrait venir cette interrogation :

— Que voudrais-tu que l'on dise de toi, si tu dois ne pas revenir ?

Je ne livre pas ma propre réponse. Une seule fois, peut-être, je me suis dit :

— J'aimerais que l'on dise : c'était quelqu'un de bien.

Ainsi donc, la famille ; les enfants ; l'amour de ta femme et puis, par ailleurs, les livres et les films ; l'agitation et la création ; la réussite et les échecs ; le bruit de la gloriole ; la poussière des étoiles ; ce qu'ils appellent aujourd'hui la « communication » ; le poids que tu as cru avoir dans l'influence que tu as cru avoir sur certains hommes et certaines femmes ; la direction des équipes ; les maîtres et les disciples ; ton rôle au sein d'une entreprise ; ta notoriété acquise ou perdue et l'illusion d'y avoir gagné quelque chose ; ainsi, rien de tout cela ne devrait compter si tu t'en allais ? Tout ce que tu souhaites, c'est que l'on puisse dire : C'était un type bien ? Mais si cette question te vient à l'esprit, c'est sans doute que tu ne te considères pas comme un « type bien ».

15

Le menteur à la noix de coco

C'était quoi, un « type bien » ? Une expression que l'on ne prononçait plus aujourd'hui. Une définition d'autrefois, du temps de son père.

Il se souvenait d'une journée d'automne, sur ce que l'on appelait « les Grands Boulevards », à Paris. Son père, coiffé de son éternel chapeau, les yeux calmes et impérieux derrière ses lunettes à monture épaisse, lui tenait la main. Il marchait. Petit provincial, à peine déniaisé, il regardait autour de lui, ébahi, émerveillé.

> *J'aime flâner sur les Grands Boulevards*
> *Il y a tant de choses, tant de choses à voir.*

Ainsi chantait, à peu près à la même époque, un jeune homme vêtu de marron, qui ressemblait à un cow-boy et que, bientôt, il applaudirait, lui, petit garçon, au théâtre de l'Étoile, avenue de Wagram en compagnie de son frère aîné — le grand Yves Montand dont il ne pouvait imaginer que, vingt ans plus tard, il l'installerait devant une caméra et lui dirait : «Action!»

Ils flânaient donc, le père et l'enfant. C'était un cadeau, une récréation : le simple spectacle de la foule, du va-et-vient des passants, constituait, selon le père, une récompense aux premières bonnes notes obtenues dans le grand lycée Janson, au préau immense, aux élèves moqueurs et avertis, pleins de sarcasme à l'égard du «paysan» à l'accent du Midi qu'il était demeuré. Les notes ayant été convenables — adjectif volontairement restreint dans la voix du père qui procédait selon le principe que l'on ne doit pas étouffer un enfant sous les compliments, pas plus que sous la critique — la récompense avait été annoncée :

— Je t'emmènerai demain sur les Grands Boulevards.

Ils avaient marché du théâtre de la Porte-Saint-Martin au carrefour Haussmann, s'arrêtant pour consommer un café liégeois, debout derrière une table haute et ronde, dans un établissement d'un nouveau genre : une Maison du Café. Il avait observé les femmes en tailleur, les hommes en costume, les moustachus et les rousses, les maigres et les cossus, les coquettes et les discrètes. Il avait si peu connu la foule dans le grand jardin de province de son enfance, que la vision de ces spécimens d'humanité l'intriguait. Il cherchait, derrière ces visages, autre chose que l'apparence. Il lui semblait que certains jouaient une comédie, d'autres pas. Son père, sans qu'ils se fussent parlé, avait-il pressenti l'interrogation du petit garçon ? Il se pencha vers lui :

— Viens, je vais te montrer ce que c'est qu'un menteur.

Ils s'étaient alors attardés sur la partie du boulevard, entre le cinéma Rex et la bouche du métro, où s'alignaient les marchands à la sauvette, les camelots. Certains vendaient des ustensiles de cuisine, des savonnettes, des pralines, le tout sur des planches disposées sur deux tréteaux. D'autres, moins fortunés, n'avaient, pour étaler leur marchandise, qu'un large parapluie qu'ils ouvraient et posaient à l'envers sur le bitume. Ainsi pourraient-ils vite le refermer si un agent de police, animé par je ne sais quel zèle, venait leur réclamer une autorisation qu'ils ne possédaient évidemment pas.

— Regarde, lui dit son père, regarde un menteur. Regarde une représentation de la vie.

Trois camelots vendaient la même chose : de misérables morceaux de noix de coco coupés en triangle. Il n'y avait personne ou presque devant les deux premiers. Tout le monde s'était regroupé autour du troisième. Or, celui-ci vendait exactement le même produit que les deux autres.

Le troisième camelot avait le cheveu noir et épais, un cou de taureau, des sourcils mobiles et des lèvres gonflées. Un visage large et sensuel. Il parlait vite et bien, donnant l'impression de n'avoir aucun besoin de reprendre son souffle, souriant en parlant. Il agitait ses deux mains carrées aux doigts lourds et forts, ayant recours à un geste que le petit garçon n'avait pas encore vu faire, une manière de réajuster les boutons qui retenaient les manchettes de sa chemise aux poignets en faisant virevolter les manches — un geste que, plus tard, le petit garçon, devenu homme, reconnaîtrait comme l'infaillible traduction d'une vulgarité certaine, l'assurance, le culot et la gouaille, un sens catégorique de sa supériorité sur les concurrents voisins. Avec un accent irrésistible de Parigot, gras et complaisant, envoyé avec force et éclat, qui ne manquait pas de révulser mais aussi de séduire, l'artiste s'exprimait. Il avait du bagout, un charme populacier. Il était intarissable et personne, sur le grand boulevard, ne songeait à l'arrêter. Son discours montait, descendait, s'élevait au-dessus de celui des deux autres camelots :

— Approchez, approchez messieurs dames si vous voulez savoir pourquoi ma noix de coco est meilleure que celle que mes collègues pas loin de moi, je vais vous le dire. Voulez-vous que je vous dise pourquoi ma noix de coco est meilleure ? Eh bien, je vais vous le dire, c'est une révélation, parce que c'est la meilleure, voilà pourquoi ! Il y en a qui vous diront qu'ils vendent de la bonne noix de coco, de la savoureuse noix de coco, de l'authentique noix de coco, bien africaine venue de nos bonnes colonies de nos bons négros, il y en a qui vous diront qu'ils vendent pas cher de l'excellente noix de coco et je ne les contredirai pas. Mais pas du tout, loin de moi cette idée de faire du tort à ces braves garçons qui ont commis l'erreur de venir vendre leur camelote sur mon territoire. Je ne leur veux pas de mal et je suis sûr qu'ils ont raison mais aucun d'entre eux n'a osé et n'osera vous dire que leur noix de coco est la meilleure du lot et je suis le seul à pouvoir vous l'affirmer et je vous l'affirme : si vous l'achetez, vous constaterez que ma noix de coco est meilleure que toutes les autres. Voulez-vous savoir pourquoi elle est meilleure ? Je vais vous le dire sans attendre : c'est tout simplement qu'elle est meilleure. Ma noix de coco, la tranche à dix centimes, est la meilleure noix de coco, parce que c'est la meilleure.

Le père avait repris la main du petit garçon dans la sienne et l'avait éloigné du camelot qui continuait de dévider le fil sans fin de son argument.

— On comprend vite le discours d'un menteur. C'est toujours attirant mais on comprend, parce que c'est toujours le même discours. Et l'on finit par comprendre que le menteur lui-même y croit. C'est ce que l'on appelle un menteur de bonne foi. Ce sont les plus dangereux. Eh bien vois-tu, cet homme n'est pas un type bien. Un type bien, c'est le contraire de ce que tu viens de voir et d'entendre.

Les phrases du père datent de loin. Elles reviennent à la surface dans mon esprit habité par la maladie, hanté par la mort, sur ce lit. Suis-je un menteur moi-même ? Ai-je beaucoup menti dans ma vie ? Ai-je toujours été de « bonne foi » ? Et plus profondément : ai-je été à la hauteur de ce que j'aurais voulu être, de ce que j'aurais souhaité que mon père et ma mère, et ceux que j'aime, puissent penser ? Ai-je beaucoup blessé ? Ai-je si peu donné ?

100

Ces questions surgissent et disparaissent vite. Je n'ai pas la force ni le temps de m'y attarder. Mais elles me ramènent à cet état d'enfance dont je parlais, il y a un instant : le bébé qui attend son biberon. J'appuie sur la poire d'appel pour faire revenir les « mamans », c'est-à-dire les infirmières, auprès de moi.

Car, comme tous les bébés, j'ai des cauchemars.

16

Voici l'indéfinissable

Je croyais avoir fait taire la deuxième voix et gagné une sorte de bataille, grâce à mes poèmes éparpillés et à mes jeux de mots. Mais voici qu'au moment où je pourrais estimer avoir droit à une sorte d'entracte, à un répit, voici qu'une nouvelle porte s'ouvre vers la mort. Voici des choses indéfinissables.

17

Les hommes-toupies
et le tunnel noir

J'ai voulu fermer les yeux. Karen la Coréenne est dans la pièce, s'activant autour de son plan de travail, vérifiant sa feuille de liaison. Elle me tourne le dos. La machine et moi « travaillons » à peu près en harmonie. J'ai cru enfin pouvoir dormir un peu. Or, à peine ai-je clos mes paupières, que je vois apparaître des choses molles, fondantes, orangées et jaunâtres. Elles pendent du plafond que j'aperçois au-dessus de moi, elles s'apprêtent à me submerger.

Je me trouve dans une pièce décorée à la façon de ces chambres d'hôtel américaines comme il s'est mis à en proliférer au milieu des années soixante-dix, quand le monde entier a commencé à ressembler à une chambre à coucher d'un motel Californie-Floride, avec des plantes artificielles, des faux feux de cheminée, de la moquette épaisse aux teintes fluo, de la pâtisserie sur les murs et les portes, du rococo et des moulures partout. Le comble du mauvais goût, de la standardisation du vulgaire. Tout est étudié pour que ce décor et cette ambiance procurent à l'occupant de l'hôtel une sensation d'évasion et de vacances, de fin de stress et de relâchement. Dans mon cas, le décor va se transformer.

Objets, meubles et peintures commencent à se ramollir et à se muer en une sorte de pâte orangeasse qui coule inexorablement dans ma direction, comme pour me recouvrir et m'étouffer. Des stalactites de guimauve qui pendraient d'une voûte pour enlacer votre corps. C'est oppressant, effrayant, parce que, paralysé sur mon lit, je ne peux m'échapper. Simultanément, voici que se présentent de drôles de créatures.

Au début, ils sont plutôt drôles en effet. Ce sont des petits hommes ronds, comme des toupies, sans hanches ni taille. Ils sont nombreux, hilares, coiffés de casquettes de joueurs de cricket britanniques — ce qui leur donne un air plutôt distingué et élégant — mais porteurs, en même temps, de pantalons laids et amples, à carreaux multicolores avec des bretelles larges, façon clowns de cirque. D'ailleurs, ils ont des billes de clowns : des nez rouges et épatés, des oreilles difformes. Ils sont hilares — c'est la seule définition exacte que je puisse leur attribuer — et ils gigotent sur leurs deux grosses et courtes pattes comme pour danser une sorte de ronde. Une musique de carnaval se fait entendre : zim boum boum. Cymbales et tambours, trompettes bouchées, et la plainte d'une sorte de mélodie d'un piano bastringue. Ce rythme tient à la fois de la musique de foire, de parade, style majorette, mais avec, aussi, des accents tropicaux, une tonalité afro-cubaine, caribéenne. C'est la foire tropicale. Le junkanoo jamaïquain. RATA-TAM — BOUM-BOUM — ZINGA — ZINGA-BOUM. C'est abrutissant, et bête, mais au bout d'un moment, c'est effrayant.

Les types ne cessent de me regarder en rigolant. Ils ont l'air de trouver que je suis un objet de comique irrésistible. Ce qui m'arrive est, pour eux, une vaste blague. Comme pour souligner à quel point ils se foutent de moi, ils soulèvent leur casquette et la reposent sur leur crâne d'œuf, à mon intention. Je vois apparaître, autour d'eux, des plages, des parasols, des matelas pneumatiques à rayures, des jetées de bois avec des pavillons ringards, style années vingt, style station balnéaire des bords de Manche. Les plages sont occupées par des hordes de ces mêmes bonshommes, touristes étranges, amuseurs suspects. Le tout dans le vacarme de cette musique de foire, une confusion assourdissante, dont je n'arrive pas à identifier l'origine ou l'explication. Jusqu'ici, tout ce que j'ai vu et entendu dans ma tête avait un rapport avec ma vie, avec mes vies, avec ma mémoire et mes expériences. Mais ces clowns en casquette, ces paysages et cette musique n'appartiennent à rien. Ce n'est pas moi, ça ! Ça n'a aucun sens. Mais si cela m'épouvante, c'est que l'apparition des hommes-toupies en casquette coïncide avec la lente et inexorable coulée orange qui, descendue des murs et des plafonds, est en train de m'encercler. La menace est double : il y a cette matière qui dégouline et ces bonshommes qui se trémoussent en se tapotant le ventre.

Qui sont ces nains rigolards? Que me veulent-ils? Ils s'appellent la Mort. Leur hilarité forcenée prend des allures de grimaces menaçantes. Ils ne rigolent plus du tout. Ils s'avancent. Leur visage et leur corps se sont décomposés et ils sont devenus des monstres. Ils se mélangent les uns dans les autres, à l'image de la coulée de lave, en une sorte de festin copulatoire, difforme et cauchemardesque. Ils sont nus. Je vais perdre la raison. Un hurlement silencieux prend possession de mon esprit.

Alors, au prix d'un effort désespéré, j'ouvre les yeux. Je crois que, si je parviens à garder les yeux ouverts, ils s'en iront. Karen la Coréenne n'est pas là. Je scrute et reconnais le couloir de la réa sur ma gauche, les faibles lumières du plan de travail sur ma droite, l'oxymètre au bout de mon doigt. Je sens la perf sur mon avant-bras gauche, les tubes et la machine. Tout est là. Garde les yeux ouverts, les monstres ne reviendront pas, me dis je, surtout ne glisse pas! Et je m'interroge :

— Pourquoi dois je subir cet assaut? C'est donc ça, la mort? Non seulement ton corps souffre et l'on t'attache, et l'on te met des tubes dans la gorge, et tu t'affaiblis et tu as l'impression de t'en aller, mais en plus tu deviens fou? C'est donc ça, mourir? C'est perdre la raison, c'est devenir fou? Mais alors, quand je vais m'engouffrer dans le tunnel noir qui s'ouvre devant moi, je deviendrai définitivement dément? Et je mourrai fou?

106

Car il y a un tunnel, béant et charbonneux. Ai-je refermé les yeux, ou bien le tunnel vient-il tout juste de s'ouvrir devant moi, au centre du mur de la pièce de la réa ? Il semble obscur et sans fin et j'y tombe. Je m'y vois tomber. Je glisse et je glisse et je perds toute accroche, toute ancre, je suis en chute libre, en chute noire. Tout est noir et il n'y a rien que ce noir et ce vide noir et je ne cesse de tomber, dans l'effroi total, dans la réalisation que ma vie n'a été qu'une sombre farce inutile saluée par des crétins qui vont me dévorer aux sons de rythmes tropicaux.

Le noir. Cette couleur dans laquelle je plonge ne m'étonne guère puisque c'est la couleur de ma maladie. J'ai dit plus haut que la douleur ne se décrivait pas. Il faut pourtant, à cet instant, que je la cerne, cette douleur : c'est comme un feu noir qui habite une poitrine. Il vous ravage. Il est épais et fait du bruit. Un bruit inhumain, qui n'appartient pas au monde des vivants. On m'a dit que traverser le cap Horn ressemble à cela : vous êtes sur un océan qui explose à chaque vague, dans le haut de la vague, puis dans le trou, le trou noir. Et vous perdez toute notion d'horizon, d'équilibre et d'harmonie, et vous ignorez comment tout cela va finir.

Le bruit des vagues, c'est la machine. Le noir, c'est le liquide qui a envahi mes poumons et bouché mon larynx, et c'est dans cette noirceur bruyante que je plonge et que je tombe, tombe, tombe vers ma tombe. Je tombe dans la mort. Elle est en train de m'ouvrir ses portes.

Mais puisqu'il me reste encore de quoi parler à moi-même, je m'entends dire pendant ma chute :

— Si tu ouvres encore les yeux, tu vas revenir. Il suffit de rien pour que tu reviennes du tunnel. Freine, fais marche arrière, tiens-toi, tiens ! Tiens bon !

Est-ce le salut ? J'ai l'impression que je reviens. Là encore, le cap Horn. On dit aussi qu'au sortir de l'enfer des rugissants, on a l'impression d'être sauvé, secouru, guidé. Je n'en suis pas là, mais je sens que je tiens et que je reviens. Et si je tiens, c'est parce que quelque chose m'a sauvé. Je crois savoir ce qui m'a sauvé et peut me sauver.

D'abord, je sais que je ne peux pas mourir fou, puisque je sais que je ne suis pas fou. Quelqu'un a écrit un jour de la folie que c'était « quand on ne peut plus travailler ni aimer ». Que je ne puisse plus travailler, c'est une évidence ! Peut-être même ne pourrai-je plus écrire des livres, réaliser des films, diriger les équipes d'une station de radio, les aimer, les écouter, leur accorder ma confiance et espérer qu'ils me rendent cette confiance. Tout cela, je le comprends, puisque je peux à peine bouger et respirer, puisque je suis un invalide, une petite chose ligotée sur un lit, retenue à la vie par une machine qui fait BOUM et BOUM et RATATAM en permanence et sonne Tiiiiiitt Tiiiiiitt dès qu'elle trouve que je ne suis plus à son diapason. Machine de merde, machine que je hais, dont je n'arrive pas à comprendre qu'elle m'est indispensable. Ne pas pouvoir travailler, ça, c'est sûr ! Mais aimer ? Je peux encore aimer.

Que je ne puisse plus aimer et donc que je sois fou est un mensonge. Je veux aimer et j'aime. Au cours de ma chute dans le tunnel noir, c'est, je crois, ce qui a dû freiner mon aspiration vers la mort. C'est cela qui m'a tenu.

18

Quelques petits mots pour un grand voyage

Dix-huit mois plus tard, grâce à l'amitié de ceux qui m'avaient soigné et guéri, j'ai pu avoir accès à quelques lignes du cahier des infirmières de la réa. J'ai essayé, pour les besoins de ce livre, afin de ne pas abandonner mon souci d'authenticité, de reconstituer la différence entre la façon dont j'avais plongé dans le tunnel, dont j'avais entrevu toutes ces choses, ces êtres et ces visions, et le rapport qu'en avaient fait celles qui me soignaient. Pour ces nuits d'effroi et de lutte, pour cette chute sans fin dans une béance noire, pour ces nuits qui restent celles du grand voyage noir, la grande traversée, quel rapport fut fait par une observatrice professionnelle et objective?

Quelques mots seulement. Sur le cahier d'infirmerie de la réa, il est noté :

« Patient éveillé toute la nuit. N'a pu dormir malgré quinze gouttes de Tercian. »

La nuit d'après :

« Très anxieux. Le rassurer. »

La jeune femme avait rajouté trois fois, le signe +,

après le verbe «rassurer» à l'intention de celle qui lui succéderait. La nuit d'après, l'une d'entre elles avait écrit :

«Patient très angoissé. Paniquant quelquefois. Se fatigue vite.»

Si peu de mots pour un si grand voyage…

C'est donc au cours de ces trois nuits que j'ai connu ma première EMA — mon expérience de mort approchée, c'est-à-dire le tunnel noir. Et puis la seconde, dont je vais bientôt parler, radicalement contraire. C'est aussi au cours de ces nuits que j'ai découvert ce qui pouvait me sauver.

19

La mort est juste derrière, à gauche

À la première force, la première source d'énergie positive que je m'étais fabriquée au moyen de mots idiots, des bribes de poèmes répétées à l'infini, et du rire contre la mort, est venue s'ajouter une autre force. Peu à peu, une prise de conscience :

— Pense à ce que tu as, me suis-je dit. Pense à ce que tu pourrais perdre.

Qu'avais-je ? Les paroles, les gestes, les êtres et le visage de l'amour.

J'avais d'abord connu une sensation de solitude absolue, la conviction que je luttais seul et l'impression de ne voir que moi et mon passé, les morts dans ma vie, mes angoisses. Je me disais que j'étais parvenu à réduire au silence la voix de la tentation de la mort grâce à mes insultes, mon acharnement orgueilleux et mes inventions verbales pour rester éveillé. Mais cela ne suffirait pas.

Je pensais que la mort était beaucoup plus forte que cela, qu'elle n'avait pas abandonné son combat. Elle était présente dans la pièce, la mort, et moi, j'étais immobile. Elle avait tous les avantages. J'avais tous les handicaps.

La mort n'a aucun visage. Proust, sur son lit de mort, dit à Céleste :

« Vous savez, elle est venue, elle est grosse, très grosse, très grosse et très noire. Elle est tout en noir. Elle est affreuse et elle me fait peur. »

Ces phrases me touchent au plus profond. J'y reconnais l'enfance, celle qu'on retrouve quand on est aux portes de la mort, que l'on s'appelle Proust ou n'importe qui. Mais je ne partage pas cette représentation de la mort. À chacun sa manière de la voir. Pour moi, c'est un vide. Mais un vide que l'on peut presque toucher. Dans mes moments de calme, je la situais plutôt derrière la partie gauche de mon corps, en deçà d'une ligne, derrière les scopes et les appareils de mesure de tension et de rythmes cardiaques — un endroit que, naturellement, je ne pouvais voir puisqu'il m'était impossible de bouger. Mais j'étais persuadé qu'elle se trouvait là. Car ce point me semblait le plus silencieux de toute la pièce. Sur la droite, il y avait le bruit de la machine. En face de moi, le va-et-vient des infirmières et le bruit de leurs actions. Au bout et toujours en face, à gauche, la porte ouvrant sur le couloir et les bruits venus du couloir, ceux de la chambre de M. Picolino. J'avais posé cette question sur la petite ardoise :

— Dites-moi ce qu'il y a derrière moi, à gauche.

Ça avait été long à écrire, pénible, et peut-être illisible pour l'infirmière de service. Je crois qu'il s'agissait de Bénédicte, grande, forte, rassurante, sachant me parler et me toucher, sachant transmettre un sentiment de certitude, de sécurité, de savoir-faire. Bénédicte, dont j'aimais les bras musclés, la densité, la limpidité directe dans le regard, une sorte de jovialité dans la voix. Bénédicte, efficace jusqu'à une certaine dureté, mais faisant les choses avec dextérité. Quand elle prenait le service, je sentais revenir l'espoir. Lorsqu'elle me quittait, je retrouvais l'inquiétude.

Elle avait déchiffré mon interrogation et l'avait lue à haute voix, avait secoué la tête en un geste d'incompréhension et avait répondu vite, comme toujours, comme tout ce qu'elle faisait — vite et bien, clair et net :

— Je ne comprends pas votre question. Il n'y a rien derrière vous, à gauche, rien !

Cela m'avait confirmé dans mon intuition. Si Bénédicte, infirmière idéale, celle qui ne commet aucune erreur, me dit qu'il n'y a rien, c'est qu'il y a la mort — puisque la mort, c'est le rien. Et je suis prisonnier de ce rien. Le rien est installé dans la pièce avec moi et je ne peux pas quitter cette pièce. Je ne peux pas jouer avec ce rien.

20

Une route à Alger
et quatre vers de saint Bernard

Jusqu'ici, lorsqu'il avait joué avec la mort, il avait toujours été mobile. Il avait de la ressource, et les moyens de bouger, esquiver, contre-attaquer.

Dans les quartiers du haut Alger ; sur une route en ligne droite entre Norwood et Montrose dans le Colorado ; sur les plages du Liban ; derrière les sacs de sable de Cam Ranh Bay ; sur le trottoir d'une rue du Bronx. À chaque fois, il avait disposé d'espace et de son corps pour se déplacer dans cet espace. Tant que l'on n'est pas enfermé dans la même pièce avec la mort, on peut toujours la tromper.

À Alger, il avait joué plusieurs fois avec elle. La fois la plus aiguë, ça avait été dans le dernier virage montant vers le boulevard Bru, au volant d'une

404 bleu-noir. Il avait vu une représentation de la mort. Elle était incarnée par deux types vêtus de pantalon de toile et d'un battle-dress camouflé. Ils portaient des lunettes noires. L'un des deux était agenouillé derrière un fusil-mitrailleur dont il était en train de monter les pièces. Il était 13 h 50. Sa chance, c'est qu'il avait de l'avance sur l'horaire habituel. En règle générale, en règle stricte, il leur avait été recommandé de ne plus rouler dans la ville basse après 14 heures.

— Vous voulez aller vous baigner, vous bronzer pendant l'heure du déjeuner ? leur avaient dit les responsables de la sécurité de l'immeuble. Vous êtes cinglés, mais libre à vous. Seulement, ne revenez pas après 14 heures parce que, après… les flingueurs, ils font comme vous, ils sont aussi cons que vous : ils se baignent à l'heure du déjeuner mais, dès 14 heures, ils reprennent du service. Ils remettent leur barrage en place, pas plus tôt, mais jamais plus tard.

Ils étaient trois ou quatre dans l'immeuble à aimer pratiquer ce sport. On partait en voiture — deux voitures, ne jamais rouler avec un seul véhicule. On allait se jeter dans l'eau pure et salée de toutes ces plages désertées, avec les fantômes des baigneurs, le souvenir de leur joie de vivre, la musique fantomatique des accents pieds-noirs disparus — ils avaient tous pris des cargos et des avions, et les plages n'appartenaient plus qu'au passé. On savait que l'on disposait de peu de temps, et s'il n'y avait personne sur les plages, on se sentait surveillé et épié. Alors on allait se jeter

116

dans l'eau, vite, et puis l'on revenait, vite, à travers les terrasses de bistrots vides aux rideaux de fer baissés, aux chaises abandonnées, avec l'impression d'un univers vidé, aux horloges arrêtées, on ne s'attardait pas pour se sécher. On mordait dans une tomate et un sandwich à la sardine qu'on avait emporté dans du papier. On mangeait debout, adossé à la portière ouverte de la voiture — il faut toujours laisser les portes ouvertes pour gagner une minute au moment du départ. On se partageait une canette de Kro et on repartait en arrachant les vitesses, en faisant hurler les moteurs. Les 404 étaient cassables à merci, et on se croyait invincibles.

Il fallait rentrer à l'heure. On savait très bien qu'on ne pouvait courir le risque de tomber sur un barrage. Il aurait fallu décliner notre identité et nos noms étaient inscrits sur les listes des Delta, puisque nous travaillions dans l'immeuble de la radio, là-haut, à Bru, et que tous ceux qui travaillaient à Bru avaient été condamnés à mort par les Delta. Savoir cela, quand on rentrait à fond la caisse par les rues vides, avec le goût de la tomate, de la sardine et de la bière dans la bouche, avec les vitres grandes ouvertes par lesquelles s'engouffrait le vent chaud venu de la mer, sous le soleil plombé de la mi-journée, en embrayant, débrayant et double-débrayant, en faisant gémir les pneus dans les virages sur le bitume fondant sous la chaleur, savoir et sentir tout cela, avec le copain assis à sa droite qui annonçait les rues, les carrefours, les dos-d'âne, la présence de rails de tramway comme dans un rallye, le rallye le plus excitant du monde, ça l'exaltait, ça faisait monter et battre le rythme de son cœur, cogner ce que les Indiens appellent le tambour de la vie dans ses veines. Suprême excitation, comble de ce sentiment de jouer un grand jeu de piste, un grand jeu de mort. Il sentait aussi, calée sous sa cuisse droite, sur le siège de cuir déchiré, la crosse du petit pistolet Beretta que les gorilles chargés de la sécurité de l'immeuble lui avaient exceptionnellement donné, en cas de « vrai pépin ». Aucun de ses camarades n'y avait eu droit, et il était fier d'être le seul à porter un pétard à la ceinture. Ça aussi, c'était excitant.

Ils étaient arrivés dans le dernier virage avant la montée qui passerait devant l'hôtel Saint-Georges pour ensuite déboucher sur l'immeuble Bru, et il avait vu les deux types en train d'installer leur fusil-mitrailleur, leur FM. Il avait crié à l'attention du copain qui, une seconde après lui, venait de découvrir les silhouettes en pantalon de toile et en veste de treillis, accroupis autour de leur arme, et des chevaux de frise qu'ils déploieraient pour barrer la route :

— Qu'est-ce qu'on fait ?

L'autre avait répondu en criant, lui aussi :

— T'as pas le choix. On accélère et on passe. Tu ralentis pas, tu vas tout droit puis tout à gauche. Débraye ! Rétrograde en 4 puis en 3 et pousse les feux ! Vite, vite, fissa !

Il avait cru entendre son copain émettre un glapissement pointu comme un cri de guerre ou de peur. Il avait ressenti tout son être répondre aux directives imposées par l'urgence de l'instant : les pieds sur la pédale, les mains sur le volant et le levier de vitesse, les abdominaux tendus, sa vision englobant à la fois les corps des deux types qui se rapprochaient, l'amorce de la ligne puis du virage, un coup d'œil dans le rétro, un autre sur le tableau de bord. Il s'était senti maître de tous ses réflexes. Il avait foncé vers les tueurs, puis viré sec en accélérant. Les types avaient dû s'écarter, le trépied du FM avait valsé sur le bord de la route dans un nuage de poussière et de graviers. Un des deux hommes avait fait le geste de dégainer un pistolet de l'intérieur de son battle-dress, mais il était trop tard. Il pouvait voir sa silhouette diminuer à vive allure dans le rétroviseur.

Ils avaient passé la ligne. Ils avaient traversé. L'excitation qui avait gagné toute sa personne avait duré bien longtemps après qu'ils eurent réintégré l'immeuble Bru. Il lui avait fallu une journée entière pour que ses nerfs se calment. Il en avait gardé un goût inconnu au bord des lèvres et dans les narines. Il se disait qu'il avait joué avec la mort et qu'il avait gagné. D'ailleurs, il n'avait jamais envisagé qu'il puisse mourir. Si les types représentaient la mort, il avait pensé que sa mort à lui n'était pas pensable. Il avait trouvé cela presque facile. Forcément : à l'époque, il était mobile. Il n'était pas le prisonnier du rien, attaché sur un lit d'hôpital. Le jeu n'était pas le même.

Ici, dans la chambre 29, en réa, il n'est plus question de jeu, mais d'une lutte. Je dois me battre mais je ne peux le faire avec mes mains, ou le volant d'une 404, ou l'inconscience de mes vingt-trois ans. Je dois avoir recours à d'autres forces qui ne sont pas physiques, nerveuses, ne se puisent pas dans la sève de l'adrénaline, dans l'action pure. J'en ai découvert deux.

L'une m'a été procurée par le rire. De façon intermittente, certes, mais cela m'a aidé. J'ai ri intérieurement plusieurs fois pour combattre la résignation. Je me suis moqué de moi : mes répétitions obsessionnelles, mon incapacité de réfléchir, l'éparpillement d'images, les papillonnements de ma vie, superficielle et vulnérable. Je me suis dit :

— Mais tu es nul, mon pauvre vieux, nul ! Te voilà au milieu d'une épreuve ultime et tu ne trouves rien d'autre en toi que des images désordonnées, les ânonnements de quelques mots, les amorces de quelques poèmes. Tu n'as aucune pensée cohérente. Tu devrais te préparer au mieux pour la confrontation et la rencontre avec — avec Qui et Quoi ? Et tu ne fais que bêtifier et gâtifier dans ta tête. À quoi t'ont servi tes lectures ? Tes voyages, tes travaux, tes expériences, tes amours, tes échecs et tes réussites ? Tu me fais rire. Tu es risible.

Cette moquerie de soi m'a autant aidé que la capacité de ricaner de la mort en l'insultant et en la traitant d'ordure. Deuxième précepte de la traversée en réa : nous possédons un rire intérieur qui peut nous permettre de tout diminuer, tout réduire. Nous devons nous référer aux quatre vers de saint Bernard :

Spernere Mundeum — Se moquer du monde
Spernere Ipsum — Se moquer de soi-même
Spernere Neminem — Ne se moquer de personne
Spernere Se Sperni — Se moquer du fait que l'on se moque

Ces vers de saint Bernard m'avaient été cités neuf ans auparavant, dans la lumière rose et brumeuse d'un paysage de fin de jour au cœur des Landes, par un ami que je ne voyais pas assez souvent, mais dont j'aimais la recherche de spiritualité, le don de charité qui émanait de chacune de ses actions qu'il tenait secrètes. Ils ont pris tout leur sens et ils sont revenus, cette fois sans difficulté.

Mais la force du rire ne vous suffira pas. Il vous faudra une autre force pour que, immobile et impuissant, vous parveniez à chasser le rien de cette chambre d'hôpital, à le chasser de votre corps et de votre esprit. Car vous avez compris cette règle fondamentale : si votre esprit cède, le corps cédera. Il cédera car il est indissociable de votre esprit.

21

D'une Harley Davidson,
d'Yves Montand,
et de « l'autre côté »

C'est le troisième précepte essentiel que m'a révélé la traversée de l'autre côté. Les Occidentaux, lorsqu'ils parlent de leur corps, disent souvent :

— Le corps que l'on a.

Les Orientaux, lorsqu'ils parlent de leur corps, disent :

— Le corps que l'on est.

Ils sont plus proches de la vérité. Je suis mon corps. Il n'y a pas de différence et de division entre ce que je pense et ce que je ressens, entre mon esprit et les battements de mon pouls. Mais c'est mon esprit, néanmoins, mon vouloir qui peuvent réguler mon pouls. Si mon vouloir lâche, je crois que mon corps et mon cœur me lâcheront aussi. Soudain, nouvelle vision : une piste sèche et droite dans un ciel clair.

— Tu arrêteras quand tu voudras. Ce sera ta décision, pas la mienne.

C'était une longue piste plutôt qu'une route. Une longue ligne à une seule voie, parallèle à la vraie route bitumée qui menait de Montrose à Norwood, la US 29 dans le sud-ouest du Colorado. Une piste de graviers et de caillasses concassés, posés par-dessus la terre dure et jaunâtre.

Le jeu était dangereux et absurde. Il s'agissait de monter à l'arrière de la Harley conduite par Bill. On vous tendait un bandana rouge et blanc, le mouchoir porté par tous les gens de l'Ouest. Large en son milieu, étroit aux pointes, un bandeau serré que vous aviez pour consigne d'appliquer sur les yeux de Bill lorsqu'il conduirait, lorsqu'il serait lancé en ligne droite. C'était un jeu compliqué et pervers, un jeu fou. C'était vous, à l'arrière, qui alliez guider Bill, lequel serait aveuglé momentanément par le bandeau que vous aviez posé sur ses yeux. Il démarrait la Harley, passait ses vitesses et s'engageait dans la longue ligne droite. Une fois qu'il était bien engagé, vous lui bandiez les yeux et c'était à vous à décider, le regard sur la ligne, à quel instant il faudrait arracher le bandeau avant que la moto ne s'éclate, et vous avec, dans le décor ou dans le virage au bout de la ligne. Avant la mort.

— C'est toi qui décides. C'est ton vouloir qui te guidera, pas le mien. Je garde la ligne. Si tu sens qu'on dévie ou qu'on approche trop près de la courbe, tu me redonnes la vue. Moi, je suis prêt à aller le plus loin possible à l'aveugle, si tu sais me conduire. Tu seras mes yeux.

123

Il s'était demandé pourquoi il avait accepté de jouer à ce jeu imbécile, tordu. Quel en était le but ?

— On voit combien de temps on tient avant d'avoir peur et que la peur vous dicte qu'il faut redonner la vue. On chronomètre comme ça la durée de ton parcours de la peur.

Bill était à l'aise, heureux d'expliquer le pourquoi et le comment de ce jeu mortel mis au point dans le chapitre d'Oakland des Hell's Angels, en Californie — jeu auquel ceux-ci s'étaient livrés sur une plage droite, au sable dur comme du ciment, du côté de Carmel. C'était un rite de passage. Si le type avait tenu plus de quelques secondes sans perdre ses nerfs, il était admis, intronisé en tant que frère dans le chapitre.

— De toute façon, on ne peut pas tenir longtemps parce que j'ai beau connaître ma bécane, savoir que j'ai de quoi rouler tout droit pendant plus de trente secondes, moi aussi à un moment je perds mes équilibres, mais ça n'est pas moi qui gueulerai « éclaire-moi », parce que si je gueule en premier, je ne serai pas digne du chapitre. T'as compris ou t'as pas compris ?

Et Bill ajoutait :

— Et puis comme ça, c'est la preuve qu'on est une équipe. Tu comprends, c'est un rite de solidarité.

Bien sûr, pensait-il, oui, bien sûr, toutes ces conneries bien sûr, je suis d'accord, mais à quoi ça me sert tout ça et pourquoi me suis-je embarqué dans ce piège ?

Il était 18 heures, une bonne heure selon Bill,

car le soleil était dans votre dos, de l'autre côté de la piste derrière Durango et parce que, à cette heure-là, toujours selon Bill, on était certain de ne pas voir arriver la seule voiture-patrouille de la police d'État. On savait qu'à cette heure-là, les deux flics de la voiture-patrouille buvaient leur bière dominicale, à cinquante miles plus au sud, dans l'unique saloon de Norwood. On connaissait leurs occupations et leurs horaires, à la minute près. On avait le champ libre, mais cela ne lui expliquait pas pourquoi il avait accepté de participer à ce jeu de fous. Peut-être parce que le soir à la cantine, sous la tente du « mess », à la table des durs à cuire, où il s'était trop intéressé à leur description de ce jeu, il avait été « enrôlé » sans s'en rendre compte. Et maintenant les gars (Steeve, Dick et Longue Figure) lui faisaient répéter les opérations, après l'avoir assis à l'arrière de la Harley immobilisée.

— Bon, on répète une dernière fois, OK ?

Un sentiment d'exaltation venait de céder la place à son interrogation inquiète. Soudain, il trouva ça formidable. C'était le jeu le plus dangereux auquel il avait jamais joué et il pensa qu'il n'y participait pas pour épater les durs du camp, ni parce que, plus tard, quand il rentrerait en France, dans le douillet appartement familial à Paris, il pourrait se vanter et raconter ça à ses frères aînés. Ils ne le croiraient même pas, tellement c'était absurde. Non, s'il allait y participer, c'était pour lui seul et pour savoir, en effet, quelle différence il y avait entre son corps et sa peur, son corps et son vouloir. Sa capacité de prendre ou non une décision. Ça, au moins, c'était une épreuve, et autrement plus redoutable que toutes celles auxquelles il avait été initié depuis son arrivée au camp, fin juin, il y avait deux mois de cela, deux mois qui lui semblaient une vie. Longue Figure, avec ses deux rides verticales le long de ses joues, ses rouflaquettes noires, son allure de lanceur de couteaux, d'assassin potentiel, ses quenottes de chien de chasse, incisives longues et aiguës lorsqu'il souriait, lui refit le décompte de la manœuvre :

— C'est ta volonté contre ta peur. D'accord ?

Le temps était beau et sec mais un peu moins chaud qu'au début de l'été. Une brise venue des montagnes soufflait entre leurs jambes et leurs bottes noires Acme, à boucles d'acier, agitait le col de leurs blousons Schott qu'ils avaient relevé sur les côtés, comme c'était la coutume chez les voyous et les motards de la côte nord-ouest de Californie. Il sentait leurs odeurs mélangées de tabac et de graisse à cuire, leur after-shave bon marché, et ces odeurs étaient parfois submergées par le parfum plus violent des bouleaux et des pins, des herbes sauvages autour d'eux. La piste était située au cœur d'une étroite vallée, entre deux caissons de montagne, une piste ignorée de tous.

Son cœur battait lorsqu'il enfourcha le siège arrière de la Harley, il pensait que ce n'était pas la peur, mais l'excitation avant l'épreuve. Bill démarra. La Harley s'engagea sur la piste, prit sa vitesse. Il pouvait voir, en se penchant du côté du flanc gauche de Bill, que l'aiguille du compteur atteignait rapidement quatre-vingts miles. Il sentit le dos de Bill se cabrer et il l'entendit crier :

— Quand tu veux !

Il commença d'exécuter le geste au rythme et selon les conseils indiqués par Longue Figure, mais il ne put passer le bandana sur les yeux du motard et il cria :

— J'peux pas, Bill, j'peux pas, on va s'écraser dans le décor ! J'y arrive pas !

Bill lui répondit :

— C'est ta décision.

L'expérience s'arrêta là. Bill ralentit et fit demi-tour sur la piste. Steeve, Dick et Longue Figure vinrent jusqu'à eux.

— Qu'est-ce qui s'est passé ? demanda Longue Figure.

Bill devança sa réponse :

— C'est sa décision. Il a décidé de ne pas le faire.

Les hommes le regardèrent en silence. Il avait redouté qu'ils sourient, le traitent de poule mouillée et l'excluent de leur conversation, de leurs sorties et de leurs travaux. Mais cela ne se passa pas ainsi. Ils demeurèrent silencieux, visages impassibles, désireux de recevoir son explication. Au moment d'aveugler Bill, il avait éprouvé une sensation violente et irrésistible de refus. Il voulut le dire en peu de mots, car dans l'Ouest, on ne parlait pas, et on mentait peu :

— Non seulement j'ai eu peur, mais j'ai voulu. Vous aviez dit que c'était ma volonté contre ma peur. Eh bien, c'était une volonté, tout simplement. J'ai décidé que ça ne valait pas le coup de le faire.

Il crut lire la compréhension sur les visages. Seul, Longue Figure commenta sans ironie, mais avec une sorte de lourdeur sentencieuse :

— Tu as décidé, d'accord, mais tu as eu peur. Tu as eu peur de voir comment c'était de l'autre côté.

Il regarda Longue Figure. L'homme devait être âgé de quatre ou cinq ans de plus que lui, mais il lui semblait déjà un vieillard revenu des choses, ayant traversé assez de combats et reçu assez de coups ou de blessures pour se situer à des années-lumière du jeune Français et de son inexpérience.

— Ça doit être ça, avait-il répondu.

Quand le camp ferma ses portes, les quatre hommes décidèrent de continuer à ramer ensemble à travers l'Ouest, vagabonder de job en job, de provisoire en provisoire, et ils ne lui proposèrent pas de les suivre. Pour eux, il était évident qu'il allait retourner sur son campus. Ils lui dirent, sans agressivité :

— Naturellement, tu rentres chez toi.

Il les regarda. N'oublie pas ces visages, se dit-il, tu ne reverras jamais un seul d'entre eux. Au moment des adieux, il comprit que les hommes l'avaient depuis longtemps écarté de leur cercle. Il n'appartenait pas à la même race qu'eux. Il avait une vie devant lui, des projets et une ambition. Eux n'avaient pour autre perspective que la route et la nuit, la poussière, la violence, une vision réaliste du peu que pouvait encore leur offrir l'existence. Il n'avait pas regretté ses choix. Il était heureux d'avoir eu peur sur la moto de Bill. Il était fier d'avoir accepté sa peur. Ainsi, il avait maîtrisé son corps. La peur lui avait permis de contrôler l'absurdité dans laquelle les longues figures, les longs visages avaient voulu le plonger.

Je revois Longue Figure, visage perdu dans ma vie, anonyme, inculte, sauvage. Longue Figure me semble soudain plus présent que les douzaines de visages qui ont repassé devant moi, dans l'incessant va-et-vient de la mémoire, dans le chaos dont je suis irrégulièrement le réceptacle depuis mon entrée en réa. Pourquoi lui ? Parce qu'il avait prononcé une expression qui, aujourd'hui, prend une autre dimension que celle du simple jeu de la moto, du rite imbécile des Anges de l'Enfer. Longue Figure avait dit : « *The other side.* » L'autre côté.

J'avais pris, à l'époque, ce mot pour un cliché, une façon superstitieuse de parler des approches de la mort. « L'autre côté » revient à toute allure dans mon inconscient, avec l'accent de l'Ouest de Longue Figure : « *The other side.* » Et je comprends que rien de ce qui surgit de mon passé, de ma mémoire, depuis mon entrée en réa, n'est insignifiant. J'ai cru que c'était un chaos, mais il n'y a pas de hasard dans les images qui ont décidé de revenir me voir.

C'est parce qu'il avait prononcé les mots de « l'autre côté » que le visage anonyme et crapulard d'un vagabond primitif de l'Ouest américain l'emporte sur tous les autres visages : des plus célèbres au plus inconnus.

Longue Figure, au hit-parade de ma mémoire morcelée, se retrouve en tête de liste. Il devance les rides, l'amour de la vie et le sourire de Lazareff ; les yeux violets et désespérés de Jude, qui avant de finir seule dans une chambre d'hôtel, entre Madison et la Soixante-Cinquième, personnifia la vie de New York ; il devance le géant du cinéma, devenu mon maître, mort dans mes bras en plein restaurant dans Paris. Il devance les joues creuses de Valdo, le modèle de mes vingt ans quand je débutai à Paris, Valdo qui chercha toute sa vie à rattraper la grâce ayant fait de lui le petit prodige de la presse. Comme il ne la retrouva jamais, il finit par se pendre. Il devance Gainsbourg, Serge, aux côtés de qui j'avais vécu trois mois de complicité totale ; cigarettes ; Peppermint Get ; chansons composées d'une seule traite, derrière son piano noir ; nuits blanches allant jusqu'au bout du dérisoire et parfois de la dépravation. Il devance la barbe en forme de collier sur les longues mâchoires de Boby, le père de Françoise, le grand-père de mes enfants, dont la tendresse et la drôlerie, l'humilité et le sens de la précarité des choses ont profondément marqué la vie de la famille. Il devance Malraux, que j'ai la chance de rencontrer plusieurs fois et qui, en un après-midi, auprès d'un feu à Verrières, me raconte comment il imagine la rencontre que Nixon va avoir avec Mao — Malraux, dont le verbe transforme le visage, pourtant déjà gonflé, épuisé, mais que la seule puissance de ses phrases transfigure et dont je me dis en le quittant : « Me voilà un peu moins sot qu'il y a quelques heures. » Il devance les cheveux blancs, magistralement plantés sur la tête carrée et rude de Jacoto, l'Homme Sombre, figure mythique de mon enfance, et qui venait parler la nuit avec mon père, dans la villa, parler de sentiments que je ne comprenais pas. Il devance Montand, Yves, larmes aux yeux, la veille du tournage d'une scène d'amour, m'ayant convoqué dans sa chambre d'hôtel pour m'expliquer devant le miroir de la chambre, en me montrant son visage, qu'il est trop vieux, désormais, pour jouer les séducteurs et que personne n'y croira :

— Regarde, mais regarde donc, petit ! Ce n'est plus de mon âge. Regarde ces poches, regarde ces bajoues, regarde ces rides, comment veux-tu faire croire qu'elle va tomber amoureuse de moi ?

Et d'un seul coup j'ai la prémonition que nous n'y arriverons peut-être pas, en effet, et que le film, quels que soient le talent et le travail qu'il y mettra et que nous y mettrons tous, sera un échec. Mais je sens aussi que le problème ne s'arrête pas à Yves. Le problème, c'est moi, et l'erreur commise sur le scénario même de ce film. Mon péché d'orgueil, ma prétention.

Toutes ces têtes défilent à vitesse accélérée,

depuis celle, angélique, d'une petite fille étouffée par un torrent de boue et que sa mère vient revêtir d'un linge blanc, jusqu'à ceux des jeunes appelés fauchés à la mitrailleuse à l'arrière des camions blindés dans les rues de Bab el-Oued et comment, lorsque nous les retrouvâmes, ils nous parurent stupéfiés, les yeux écarquillés devant la découverte de la mort...

Aucun de ces visages ne savait à quoi ressemblerait « l'autre côté » dont avait parlé Longue Figure et qu'ils ont tous déjà rejoint. Si une force ou une volonté que je ne maîtrise pas a décidé, dans mon état présent, de faire réapparaître Longue Figure et ses trois petits mots et de faire que ces mots, cette image, comptent autant que tout ce que j'ai pu assimiler, observer et comprendre depuis, c'est sans doute qu'il l'avait dit mieux que personne, ce cliché, cet « autre côté ». Sa voix venue de nulle part parlait plus vrai que tout ce qui a suivi...

Je suis déjà passé une fois de « l'autre côté », pendant le tunnel noir. Était-ce cette nuit ou la nuit dernière ? je ne sais plus. Pendant les petits hommes à casquette, que je ne veux pas revoir. Quant aux peurs diverses, celles du Colorado ou de l'Algérie, ou les enquêtes policières à Dallas, elles n'ont aucune mesure avec celle qui m'a possédé et me possède encore sur ce lit, dans cette pièce aux murs jaunes, dans ce combat, cette perte de toute attache avec les heures et les gens, les rendez-vous et le travail, les enfants et la vie, «simple et tranquille». C'est qu'il y a peu de points communs entre le jeune homme que j'ai été et l'homme que je suis. Le jeune homme ne savait pas ce qu'il pouvait perdre lorsqu'il défiait la mort. Même si une certaine raison l'avait empêché d'aller plus loin dans un jeu absurde, il n'avait pas assez à perdre pour avoir peur de perdre. Tandis que sur son lit, dans sa maladie, l'homme que je suis sait comment peser le poids de ce qu'il pourrait perdre, le poids de la vie. Et cela explique son angoisse. Elle gagne son cœur.

Alors, ça y est, maintenant, c'est le cœur?

J'ai appuyé sur la poire. Il m'a semblé que non seulement la machine et moi ne respirions plus ensemble, mais que mon cœur faiblissait, avec une sorte de petite pointe aiguë entre mes côtes, près du thorax. L'interne, alerté par la machine et par l'infirmière, a tenté de rétablir une meilleure respiration. Le dialogue s'est passé comme d'habitude, entre l'ardoise et ceux qui peuvent parler. J'ai écrit :

— Ça ne va pas ce soir. Mon cœur va céder.

L'interne m'a dit posément :

— Votre cœur n'est pas le problème. Il va très bien. C'est votre respiration qui compte. Vous n'êtes pas ici pour un problème de cœur mais pour un problème respiratoire. Travaillez en harmonie avec la machine.

Moi, par écrit :

— Oui, mais, angoisse.

Lui, par sa parole :

— Vous n'avez aucune raison de vous angoisser.

Il s'est retourné vers le mur pour me montrer une petite lettre manuscrite que l'infirmière avait scotchée.

— Pouvez-vous lire d'ici ?

Je fais non de la tête.

— C'est votre femme qui vous l'a apportée. Vous vous souvenez de la dernière visite de votre femme ?

Je fais oui de la tête.

— Voulez-vous que je vous la relise ?

Je fais oui de la tête et il lit :

— «Bonne fête, papa. Tes enfants qui t'aiment.»

Alors revient comme un contre-courant, la parole, le geste, le visage de l'amour. Alors revient la troisième force. Première force : la volonté et la résistance, transformées en un combat verbal entre les deux voix (la négative et la positive). Deuxième force : le rire. Troisième force : l'amour, les autres.

DEUXIÈME PARTIE

LA TROISIÈME FORCE

22

Il est très difficile de se mettre à la place des autres

Les autres sont ceux que j'aime et qui m'aiment.

Il y a d'abord ma femme. Elle vient régulièrement me rendre visite. Je ne suis pas sûr de pouvoir faire le compte de ses visites : une, deux, trois fois par jour ? Je ne peux pas compter les jours, comment compter les visites ? Je sens peu à peu qu'elles sont des injections de lumière dans le noir. Autant à la première fois, le trop-plein d'émotion m'avait oppressé et provoqué son départ, autant par la suite, je vais attendre et souhaiter, prier pour ses visites.

Bien souvent, je croirai l'entendre parler dans le couloir alors qu'elle n'y est pas — entendre le bruit que je suis seul à reconnaître de sa démarche — et bien souvent, pourtant, elle ne poussera pas la porte. Mais si j'ai cru qu'elle était là, c'est que j'en avais besoin, et la notion même de ce besoin m'a aidé. Je ne parviens pas à distinguer quels vêtements elle porte, d'autant qu'elle doit se soumettre à l'obligatoire blouse de toile bleue ou verte. Mais je suis convaincu qu'elle s'est habillée de façon nette, ni mode ni démodé, comme ça lui va. De même, bien que je ne puisse apercevoir qu'une partie de son visage, car elle porte le masque facial comme les infirmières et les internes, je l'imagine coiffée et maquillée sans ostentation, mais avec ce soin, cette recherche du mieux qui fait partie de sa personnalité. Et quelle que soit l'heure de sa visite, le matin avant de partir à son travail, ou le soir au retour de ce même travail, je suis persuadé qu'elle est, je cherche le mot juste : impeccable. J'en suis persuadé parce que je sais qu'elle a été élevée ainsi — dans le refus de l'à-peu-près, le respect de soi, dans le principe que l'on n'exhibe pas les peines, les soucis, les douleurs, les chagrins et que l'on doit présenter à la face du monde et d'autrui, une apparence et un visage composés et maîtrisés.

Il ne s'agit pas pour elle de jouer une comédie. Mais d'une approche de la vie, des échecs et des réussites, des drames et des bonheurs. Elle s'est faite ainsi, elle n'a pas seulement été élevée ainsi. Elle s'est construit son tableau de valeurs, ses règles et ses contrôles, ses croyances, ses appétits spirituels et artistiques. Elle arrive portant cette éthique avec elle : claire, déterminée à ce que la vie gagne, tout entière ramassée sur elle-même pour me transmettre cette foi. Elle vient armée de son expérience de femme, son amour, les décisions prises dès l'instant où j'ai basculé dans l'inconnu de la maladie. Elle vient me voir en réa avec sa volonté de transmettre sa force de vie. Un sourire dans les yeux, la tonicité dans la voix, du calme, certes — une voix posée, douce et ferme, pleine d'intonations qui tendent à me faire comprendre que je ne dois pas céder, que je ne suis pas seul. Elle sait que l'homme qu'elle aime est un abîme d'angoisses contradictoires, de sensibilités exacerbées. Je suis celui qui a « besoin de savoir », qui a toujours voulu être « au cœur des choses », de l'information de la ville et du village, au cœur de son époque. Celui qui ne cesse de poser la question : « Quoi de neuf ? », qui ne cesse de dire : « Racontez-moi », « Dites-moi ». Je suis celui qui ne peut vivre sans téléphone, sans échanges. Elle sait que je ne supporte pas la profonde ignorance dans laquelle je me trouve de mon propre état, et que cette ignorance doit décupler mes inquiétudes. Je le sens à sa voix, à ses paroles. Et de même que j'ai été traversé par des ondes de grands dangers, lorsqu'elle est à mes côtés, je suis traversé par des ondes de lucidité. Je me dis :

— Si elle vient vers toi dans cet état d'esprit, quelle que soit l'image que tu peux présenter à cet instant, avec tes tubes et ta machine, fais en sorte de répondre à son geste.

Alors, soit au moyen du tableau en plastique et du crayon-feutre, soit par pressions des mains ou mouvements de la tête, je tente de faire comprendre que je suis avec elle, que je reçois son langage et que je l'entends.

Je n'entends vraiment bien qu'elle. Elle m'a d'abord informé de mon état — de ce que les médecins lui ont dit et qui indique que l'on a identifié le mal, que l'on commence donc à pouvoir et savoir médiquer de façon plus précise et plus efficace mais qu'il faut encore attendre avant de m'ôter les tubes. Tout cela m'avait été dit dans la journée, mais je ne l'avais pas assimilé. Maintenant qu'elle le dit, je retiens l'information et je la crois. Il y a un objectif. Cinq jours, cinq nuits ? Huit jours, huit nuits ? J'ai, au moins, maintenant, des certitudes et un projet. J'intègre les choses une à une, lentement. Puis, elle va me relater comment cela se passe avec les enfants, les amis, les cercles d'affection, de solidarité ou de sympathie qui l'entourent. L'état dans lequel se trouvent «les autres». Je me dis : «Si tu crois que tu souffres et que tu vas encore souffrir, demande-toi seulement quelle épreuve cela doit être pour elle et pour les enfants. Essaye de te mettre à sa place, à leur place.»

La belle expression ! Si coutumière, donc vidée de son plein sens parce que utilisée à tout propos, en toute circonstance par les hommes et les femmes. La belle et impossible proposition :

— Essaye de te mettre à ma place.

Combien d'entre nous procèdent réellement et sincèrement à cette inversion de rôles ? Je n'en ai pas la vigueur, mais je comprends ceci : la visite de cet être que j'aime et qui m'aime m'aura permis, pour la première fois depuis le début de la traversée en réa, de penser à un autre vivant qu'à moi-même. Depuis qu'elle est là, j'ai cessé de me préoccuper de moi, m'apitoyer sur moi-même, m'angoisser sur moi-même, me complaire dans mon indifférence à tout sauf à moi-même. Jusqu'ici, les seuls êtres dont les images ou les paroles ont habité mes pensées étaient des êtres morts. Voilà que je pense aux vivants, aux plus proches vivants. À ceux que je pourrais perdre.

23

Le quatrième précepte

S'il est difficile, voire impossible, de « se mettre à la place » de quiconque lorsqu'on est soi-même aux prises avec cette stupéfaction que provoque la grande maladie, l'aller et retour dans l'inconscient, la lutte contre l'abandon de sa volonté, le voyage dans le fleuve noir, il faut tenter d'y parvenir.

J'y parviens avec peine et à petite dose. Mais je m'y efforce, et chaque fois que j'y parviens, cela prend un sens. Cela va créer, peu à peu, comme une entaille, une encoche dans les vagues de fièvre et d'angoisse, dans le flux désordonné de la mémoire, une victoire contre la mort. Je ne pense qu'à des petits gestes, des petites choses. Elles tournent essentiellement autour du cercle familial, les enfants et ma femme. Ma femme et les enfants. Le rite du petit déjeuner. La disposition des bols et des tasses aux quatre coins de la table en bois clair, les serviettes dans leur rond, l'appartement qui se réveille et comment la vie commence là, dans cette cuisine de taille moyenne, avec l'arrivée successive

des deux enfants aux visages endormis, légèrement boudeurs, avec cette saveur jamais épuisée,
toujours nécessaire, des premières petites caresses,
du baiser du matin, la main sur les cheveux, le
corps encore chaud de sommeil qui vient se blot-
tir contre le vôtre.

Parfois, l'enfant — qui n'est plus une enfant
mais déjà une jeune fille, mais qui demeure l'enfant — vous écarte sans hostilité, avec cette sorte
de refus du corps encore embourbé de sommeil,
cette volonté d'autonomie, ce qui ne se dit pas,
mais se ressent : «Laisse-moi sortir de ma nuit, de
mes rêves, de ma gêne d'être qui je suis, laisse-moi
me recomposer avant de te dire un mot, fût-il un
mot d'amour, et un geste, fût-il un geste de tendresse.»

Les départs du matin, les retours du soir. Je les
imagine, maintenant, parmi leurs amis, filles et
garçons, en classe et hors de la classe. J'essaye de
«me mettre à leur place». Quelle importance
accordent-ils à tout ce qu'ils savent ou ce qu'ils
ignorent? Que leur a dit leur mère? Quel rapport
leur fait-elle de l'état de leur père et de la façon
dont cela avance, ou cela stagne ou cela recule?
Comment supportent-ils ce que je n'imagine pas
mais qui a lieu — les téléphones qui sonnent, sonnent jusque très tard dans la nuit. Les phrases
déguisées, les mots couverts. Leur a-t-elle tout
expliqué? Conserve-t-elle, pour elle seule, l'angoisse majeure puisqu'il y a un mystère que n'ont
pu encore dissiper les médecins? Il faut bien
qu'elle se confie à une ou deux de ses meilleures

amies, et je sais où se trouvent les téléphones, dans quelles pièces, et comment les enfants peuvent tout entendre.

Avoir pu imaginer l'univers familier du foyer un court instant m'a aidé un moment dans ma nuit. Je n'ai pas pensé à moi, je n'ai pas pleuré sur moi-même, je ne me suis pas abandonné à cette envahissante complaisance que procurent douleur et peur. Face à cette découverte, je vais redoubler d'efforts pour évoquer «les autres», ceux que j'aime et qui m'aiment, ceux dont les noms viennent cogner contre la vitre de mon apparente opacité lorsque ma femme les mentionne à chacune de ses visites :

— J. et S. ont invité les enfants à dîner hier pour me soulager. P. et G. t'embrassent et appellent tous les jours. Alexandra est formidable, elle a laissé tomber un voyage pour rester avec moi. Elle t'embrasse. Valérie aussi. Tous tes frères ont téléphoné.

À cette litanie de prénoms du cercle intime, viennent s'ajouter d'autres prénoms, moins intimes, représentant celles et ceux avec qui je travaille ou que je fréquente dans les univers croisés de ma vie et qui envoient des signaux par l'intermédiaire du seul relais possible, ma femme. A-t-elle compris ou décidé que cela pourrait m'aider d'entendre ces noms qui font le tissu d'une vie et que, depuis quelques jours et quelques nuits, j'avais totalement occultés? Je ne savais même plus, en effet, que j'étais entouré de plusieurs cercles d'amis, collaborateurs, confrères, amis lointains vus ou entendus depuis longtemps qui soudain, parce qu'ils apprennent ce qui arrive, se manifestent. Je les avais oubliés, parce qu'ils étaient vivants et je ne m'étais occupé que des morts, si proches de moi. J'avais été habité par les morts de ma vie : ils étaient dans la pièce, pas les autres.

Mais ils ont quitté la pièce. Les visiteurs souriants et affables semblent n'être jamais revenus de la cantine où j'avais cru les voir partir pour se nourrir avant de réapparaître pour me prier à nouveau de les rejoindre, de «l'autre côté». Ils ont été remplacés par les noms de tous ces vivants que ma femme décline, en m'offrant une sorte de rapport de ce qui se dit et se fait du côté de la vie et cela me pousse et me force à réfléchir à eux, à vouloir les garder, les retrouver. Des noms, cela signifie des visages, des regards, des sourires, des complicités. J'enregistre le rappel de tout ce qui me rattache à la vie : mon travail, mes projets, mes espoirs.

— J. a reçu S. et O. et ils ont tout mis en place pour que tout marche bien en ton absence. J. m'a bien dit de te dire de ne t'inquiéter de rien. Tout se passe pour le mieux et se passera pour le mieux.

Je ne me suis inquiété de rien. Dans un premier temps, tout ce qui constitue la trame de ma vie professionnelle avait disparu et seul était revenu à la surface le reste de ma vie, le passé. Et la peur de la mort. Mais maintenant, c'est comme une petite goutte de la vie quotidienne qui revient avec les goutte-à-goutte de la perfusion.

Quatrième précepte : lorsque vous êtes en face d'un malade en proie à l'incertitude sur sa propre vie, et à la solitude provoquée par cette incertitude, ne lui dites pas seulement que vous l'aimez. Dites-lui aussi que les autres l'aiment, parlez-lui de ces « autres ». Parlez-lui de ce qui fait une des beautés de la vie : parlez-lui des vivants. Car s'il passe ce seuil mystérieux au-delà duquel il devient étranger à vous et aux autres, alors le monde des vivants lui paraîtra une pure absurdité. Empêchez-le de tomber dans cette absurdité et poussez-le doucement à recenser tout ce qu'il doit à ceux qui l'aiment et qu'il aime. Poussez-le à comprendre que votre amour, comme celui des autres, ou celui qu'il a pour les autres, vaut qu'il lutte pour vivre.

24

Le souhait de Florence

L'amour qui sauve, c'est aussi celui que vous donnent ceux pour qui vous êtes un inconnu. Celui des femmes qui vous soignent.

Aides-soignantes, assistantes, ou infirmières — des IDE, pour être précis et réglementaire : Infirmières Diplômées d'État.

Il y a celles qui ne vous prodiguent que des soins strictement pratiques : entretien et toilette. Elles assistent les autres, celles qui président à la bonne marche des choses et assurent le vrai suivi, le plus délicat et le plus sensible. Mais je ne fais aucune différence dans la hiérarchie, les grades, l'ancienneté ou le pouvoir. Pour moi, elles sont toutes égales, c'est-à-dire qu'elles sont toutes supérieures. Je ne sais rien, elles savent tout. Elles sont supérieures à toutes les autres femmes qui se déplacent et s'activent au même instant dehors, dans la ville, la rue, les bureaux, les magasins, les ateliers, dans cette ville dont j'ai tout oublié, à laquelle je ne pense pas.

Y a-t-il une ville ? Y a-t-il un ciel ? A-t-il une cou-

leur? Y a-t-il des sons — et quels sons? J'ai tout
oublié de la vie quotidienne de la ville : le bour-
donnement sur les boulevards, le bruissement aux
carrefours, le flot des objets métalliques et le flux
des hommes et des femmes sur les surfaces de
ciment, de goudron, sur les planchers des appar-
tements, sur les sols dallés de caoutchouc des aéro-
ports, sur la moquette des chambres d'hôtel, les
carreaux des cuisines, les parvis des églises. Quant
à la nature elle-même, je n'y pense pas plus. Y a-t-il
des arbres? Y a-t-il des oiseaux et des rivières? Le
monde extérieur m'est plus qu'indifférent. Il est
mort. Là où j'habite, il n'y a pas de monde extérieur. Il y a autre chose, il y a cet autre côté dans
lequel un pouvoir inconnu m'a plongé, réquisi-
tionné, emprisonné. Il n'y a qu'une pièce jaune ou
blanche dont les dimensions semblent se déformer
ou se reformer selon mes peurs et mes douleurs
avec, traversant cette pièce, des femmes dont l'apparition ou la disparition rythment le peu de sens
que j'arrive à donner au temps ou aux heures. Des
jeunes femmes aux prénoms de tous les jours, aux
visages de tous les jours, mais qui sont devenus les
visages les plus importants de cette matière fragile,
impermanente, qu'est le déroulement, seconde
par seconde, de la vie.

Je les vois parfois surdimensionnées, grandes,
gigantesques, avec des mains vigoureuses, capables
de me déplacer, de me retourner, de me manipuler comme le mitron palpe le morceau de pâte en
voie de devenir du pain. Je les entends parfois, tels

des indicatrices, des conductrices, des contrô-
leurs :

— Respirez plus lentement. Reprenez votre
rythme. Ne vous agitez pas.

L'une d'entre elles s'évertue à badigeonner le
fond de ma bouche et mes lèvres afin d'atténuer
les multiples aphtes qui, boursouflant le système
buccal, s'ajoutent aux autres effets secondaires
provoqués par le mal qui me traverse. Quelque
chose en moi résiste. D'abord, je ne comprends
pas ses intentions. Ensuite, j'ai peur de trop ouvrir
la mâchoire car je pourrais perdre ce tube qui
m'est indispensable. Mon corps se crispe à toute
occasion, sous tout prétexte. Je serre les dents et
j'oppose une résistance au minutieux travail que
la jeune femme essaye d'effectuer. Elle s'y reprend
à plusieurs fois, avec une ferme douceur et cette
obstination de l'artisan qui ne sera satisfait que
lorsqu'il aura accompli son œuvre, quelle qu'elle
soit, et où qu'il se trouve. La jeune femme pourrait renoncer, s'énerver, forcer le geste, quitte à
me faire souffrir. Au lieu de quoi, je l'entends dire
cette phrase d'une précision et d'une politesse
rares :

— Je souhaite atteindre votre palais.

Je ne l'avais pas encore vue jusqu'ici. Une de ses
consœurs l'a peut-être appelée tout à l'heure Florence. Elle semble avoir la peau mate et les cheveux courts. La délicatesse et le choix de ses mots

ne m'ont pas frappé sur l'instant, mais plus tard, les mots vont revenir comme un des plus beaux exemples de cette intelligence de la vie que possèdent ces femmes. Une phrase juste, prononcée sur un ton pédagogique, persuasif et néanmoins tolérant, qui va momentanément me décrisper. Je coopère mieux. Je desserre largement les dents, j'entrouvre la bouche, pas longtemps mais assez pour que le « souhait » de Florence soit exaucé : elle a « atteint mon palais ».

Alors, je l'ai aimée parce que sa paisible et subtile parole m'a autant secouru que le médicament lui-même. Dans ce moment de répit, lorsque la machine et moi étions en train de bien travailler, sans les accès de toux qui engorgent les tubes, sans les secousses qui affolent le corps, lequel affolement se transmet à la machine, qui se met à sonner — lorsqu'on peut dire que, au milieu de ce mal, « tout allait bien » —, j'ai ressenti un amour sans retenue pour ces femmes. Je voulais le leur faire savoir. Exprimer ma gratitude pour leur endurance, la netteté de leurs gestes, leur économie d'action, leur souci de respecter les consignes et ce malgré la lassitude, la probable exaspération ou la connaissance résignée de la répétitivité de leurs existences.

Comment transmettre que l'on comprend leur labeur, la condition de leurs jours : arrivant tôt le matin ou tard le soir pour prendre la suite de l'équipe en place ; débarquant du RER, encombrées de leur propre vie, soucis ou problèmes. Enfants, mari. Pas d'enfants, pas de mari. Argent, pas d'argent. Solitude, pas de solitude. Amour ou pas. Parents difficiles ou parents absents ou parents trop présents; inconfort matériel, difficultés administratives; peu de satisfactions, beaucoup d'efforts, peu de lumière, beaucoup de grisaille. Le planning les attend avec l'organigramme des soins à prodiguer à chaque malade, une planification longue et minutieuse, compliquée, même quand elles savent, même quand elles sont là depuis longtemps. C'est toujours compliqué puisqu'on ne doit commettre aucune erreur, aucune inattention, aucune négligence. Et il y a ce patient échoué dans son lit, heurté et heurtant, incapable de s'exprimer, mi-être humain, mi-objet, qui vous retient par le poignet, vous supplie du regard comme si vous pouviez tout résoudre. Ce malade qui dépend entièrement de vous, qu'il faut traiter comme un bébé et comme un blessé, comme les autres patients, ceux qui étaient là avant lui et ceux qui le suivront. Cet inconnu.

L'inconnu n'est pas en état de se livrer à une réflexion du genre : ça n'est pas qu'elles t'aiment, c'est simplement qu'elles exécutent un travail. Pour l'inconnu, leur travail n'est pas du « travail ». Je veux croire qu'elles y mettent une manière de dévotion qui équivaut à une manière d'amour et même si je fais erreur, même si l'on peut me rétorquer qu'elles ne font que leur métier, le sens que j'attribue à leurs gestes est la seule chose qui compte. Je les reçois comme le signe que je ne suis pas abandonné, pas perdu. Comme on reçoit l'amour, le vrai, celui qui se prouve. Pour le leur dire, j'agite ma main droite afin d'écrire sur l'ardoise :

— Merci.

Elles lisent et répondent avec une infime irritation dans la voix :

— Vous nous avez déjà remerciées, hier, à la même heure.

Elles tournent le dos. Elles m'ont répondu d'une telle manière que, brutalement, je change d'avis. Un cycle nouveau, aussi violent et inattendu que l'accès d'amour que j'ai éprouvé pour ces femmes, se met en marche. À peine ont-elles quitté la pièce, je ne sais quel démon vient me dire :

— Elles ne t'aiment pas. Elles ne te veulent aucun bien. Elles veulent même te tuer.

25

Il est arrivé quelque chose
à Monsieur Picolino

Je connais ce démon. Je peux l'identifier. C'est la voix de la peur, la paranoïa. C'est la voix qui vous entraîne vers le contraire de la vie. Il y a déjà quelque temps que je n'ai pas entendu cette voix. Je croyais l'avoir jugulée, lui avoir fermé sa vilaine gueule. Elle est revenue, aussi persuasive et douceâtre que les premières fois. Elle dit une chose terrible :

— Ces filles se foutent de toi. Elles veulent ta mort.

Le retour de cette voix me désespère. Je ne suis pas assez costaud pour m'opposer à son retour. Je crois à ce que dit la voix. Avec la même brusquerie, le même éclatement du temps, la même absence de transition, je me retrouve prisonnier de mes peurs.

J'ai d'autant plus peur que j'entends un silence différent autour de la pièce. Des portes s'ouvrent. Agitation dans le couloir de la réa, puis un autre silence. Les filles vont et viennent à un autre rythme. Elles murmurent et s'affairent, on dirait qu'elles se consultent. Je trouve cela suspect. Que se passe-t-il ? Est-ce qu'on complote ? Jusqu'ici, elles ne s'étaient jamais gênées pour parler à haute voix entre elles, comme si j'étais incapable de les entendre. Or, voici qu'elles chuchotent. Que veut-on me cacher ? Je saisis des mots :

— Dialyse… C'est fini… Il faut prévenir… Mais il n'y a personne… Personne ne venait le voir…

J'entends un nom qui me rappelle soudain que le monde ne tourne pas exclusivement autour de ma petite personne :

— Monsieur Picolino.

Les infirmières parlent de mon voisin, cet homme que je n'ai jamais vu, que je ne verrai jamais, et dont je comprends en un bref instant de clairvoyance qu'il lui est arrivé quelque chose de fatal. Il y a une effervescence feutrée dans la pièce voisine et dans le couloir. Je le sens plus que je ne le vois, puisque je ne vois pratiquement rien, mais il me semble que je possède des moyens de capter ce qui se passe sans avoir besoin de voir. Comme tout est clair, soudain ! Je comprends tout : mais non, l'infirmière ne m'avait pas rabroué lorsque je lui avais écrit « merci », elle était simplement plus préoccupée par son autre malade que par moi. Elle ne voulait pas me « tuer », mais si la notion de mort revient ainsi à la surface pour bousculer mes élans d'amour, c'est parce que au moment même où la voix de la négation prononçait le mot (« Elles veulent ta mort »), eh bien, cet événement se déroulait à un mètre de moi, de l'autre côté du mur qui sépare nos deux pièces. Je suis persuadé que cela s'est passé ainsi : au moment précis où Monsieur Picolino a rendu son dernier soupir — événement qui se préparait depuis déjà longtemps mais que, noyé dans mon propre voyage, j'avais été incapable de deviner —, au même moment, cette mort a traversé l'espace qui me sépare de la chambre de Picolino pour venir, au moyen d'une phrase intérieure, me rappeler qu'elle existe.

La mort se promène dans la région. Elle rôde dans le silence du couloir. Oui, j'en suis maintenant sûr, il est tard, c'est le creux de la nuit, et le couloir de la réa fait entendre un de ces silences secs, insondables, au milieu desquels on n'éprouve plus un seul sentiment d'appartenir à l'humanité. Un silence comme la nature n'en fabrique pas, puisqu'il n'y a jamais de véritable silence. Et je réussis à entendre et à comprendre la blancheur et la noirceur de ce silence, même si la porte de la pièce que j'occupe est fermée. Cela ne m'étonne pas. Rien ne m'étonne. Je suis au-delà de l'étonnement.

Personne ne venait voir Monsieur Picolino. Tu as bien retenu cette phrase : il était tout seul et tu ne sauras jamais à qui il ressemblait. Son nom avait une sonorité risible et pathétique, quand sa machine à lui émettait une sonnerie différente de la tienne, tu avais pendant quelques secondes la fugace capacité de l'imaginer petit, «picolo», brun et vieux, souriant peut-être dans son malheur. Pourquoi l'imaginais-tu en train de sourire? Monsieur Picolino n'avait aucune raison de sourire puisque «personne ne venait le voir». Toi, on vient te voir. Le mot « personne » n'a jamais été prononcé par les infirmières à ton sujet. Il y a tout un mouvement d'amour autour de toi. Tu l'as compris. Dans les profondeurs opaques des vagues que tu traverses, tu as fini par t'assurer de ce fait tangible : tu n'es pas seul. Le départ de Monsieur Picolino ne va pas te bouleverser. Il va même peut-être, de façon cruelle, te faire du bien. Car tu ne vas plus cesser de te dire :

— Moi, je ne suis pas comme Monsieur Picolino. J'ai du monde. Je n'ai pas « personne ». Ça va aller.

26

Apparition d'un verbe étrange

C'est le matin, je crois. Il fait clair dans la pièce. Plusieurs hommes en blanc sont penchés au-dessus de moi, plusieurs hommes en vert aussi. Ils insistent pour me dire « bonjour » et je comprends qu'ils le font afin que je leur réponde : « bonjour », au moins d'un mouvement de la tête. Pour bien leur montrer que j'ai entendu ce qu'ils sont venus me dire. Je m'exécute et je fais « bonjour ».

Je reconnais quelques-uns de ces hommes. L'un d'entre eux est l'interne qui est souvent venu dans mes nuits d'angoisse et m'a expliqué que mon cœur allait bien et n'a pas cessé d'employer l'expression détestable :

— Travaillez avec la machine.

L'autre, qui porte des lunettes, était déjà apparu au-dessus de mon visage lorsque j'avais émergé de l'anesthésie après la fibro, à mon premier réveil en réa. C'est lui qui a présidé à mon entrée, ou plutôt ma rentrée, dans l'atmosphère. Il parle sur un ton lent, posé, articulant les mots comme on s'adresse aux enfants :

— Les produits que nous vous donnons depuis que nous avons identifié la bactérie semblent commencer à faire leur effet. Et l'œdème de votre larynx paraît se résorber. La respiration a l'air de s'améliorer. Nous allons essayer de vous extuber d'ici deux jours.

« Extuber » : verbe étrange que j'entendrai souvent dans les heures qui vont suivre. Parfois, le mot sera déformé. Certaines filles prononceront « extubuler ». Cela veut simplement dire que l'on va tenter de m'ôter le tube de silicone qui me relie à la machine qui me ventile. L'« extubulation » va devenir le mot clé des prochains jours et prochaines heures que je ne saurais compter, puisque ma notion du temps n'est plus celle de tout le monde. Cela devrait m'encourager. Curieusement, et simultanément, je reçois cette information avec scepticisme : rien de tout cela n'est sûr, rien n'est fait. Comme si je refusais la solution qui se présente à l'horizon des médecins.

Ça n'est pas que je n'ai pas confiance dans l'homme qui me parle. Mais je le sens prudent, désireux de ne dire que la vérité, et de me faire comprendre que cette vérité est évolutive, fragmentaire. J'ai surtout retenu qu'il a dit : « On va essayer. » J'ai aussi entendu :

— Nature de votre germe... De quoi faire régresser l'inflammation... On ne peut plus ventiler très longtemps... Risques de lésions...

Je les quitte. Les hommes en blanc et vert sont en train de parler entre eux et ne s'adressent plus à moi. Leurs visages se dissipent, se dispersent, et je me retrouve ailleurs, plus au fond de moi que je ne l'ai été, en cet état de semi-coma qui m'a sans doute permis de moins souffrir mais m'a régulièrement amené aux portes du cauchemar, et de tout ce que je ne veux plus revoir.

Or, c'est à ce moment, et dans cet état, lorsque ma prochaine extubation m'a été annoncée, que je vais connaître une nouvelle étape de la traversée de l'autre côté, la plus invraisemblable.

Ce n'est peut-être pas racontable. Mais je vais essayer de la raconter.

27

Un tunnel de lumière

Je me sens sortir de mon corps. J'ai l'impression que je me vois sur le lit, entouré des hommes en blanc et en vert, avec, derrière ce rideau d'hommes, les assistantes et les infirmières. Je vois toute la pièce, les objets, les murs, la machine et les écrans. Je peux les décrire avec une précision de laser : cheveux — ailes du nez — manchettes de chemises sous les blouses — boucles blondes — gants en plastique — masques et tissu piqueté des masques.

Et puis, je me vois étendu sur le lit : je suis très maigre, très jaune, les tubes et les bandelettes de coton encombrent mon visage et le dessinent comme en plusieurs morceaux. Je ne suis pas rasé. Il y a beaucoup de gris sur mes joues. Du gris et de la cendre. La vérité, c'est que je ne suis pas très beau à voir. Je prends un peu d'altitude et je flotte au-dessus de la pièce et au-dessus de mon corps et j'entends, plus précisément que tout à l'heure, tout ce qui se dit, les consignes données, les questions posées sur la suite du traitement, les rendez-vous pour l'extubulation — ce sera le matin, dans quarante-huit heures. Dans le vocabulaire du cinéma, on pourrait dire que j'ai une vue en « plongée » de toute la scène.

J'ai exercé le métier de cinéaste, j'ai mis sept films en scène, je sais comment l'on peut montrer à un spectateur la même scène ou les mêmes personnages de mille manières différentes. Il existe des objectifs qui permettent d'isoler un détail, de grossir un visage ou, au contraire, d'embrasser l'ensemble d'une scène. Il existe aussi toutes sortes de mouvements — avant, arrière, latéral, parallèle — qui, d'une autre façon encore, vous donnent la possibilité de reproduire les gestes et les positions de chacun, et cela peut vous conférer, lorsque vous exercez le métier de cinéaste, la sensation de créer le monde, de le dominer. Cela peut expliquer la tentation mégalomaniaque dont sont victimes les « metteurs en scène » qui croient que le monde tourne autour d'eux, puisqu'ils font tourner le monde — « Silence ! On tourne ! ». Eh bien, c'est précisément ce que je suis en train de faire lorsque je flotte au-dessus des médecins, de mon lit, des infirmières, de la pièce, et surtout au-dessus de moi-même. Je suis devenu une caméra qui se promène autour de moi-même. Je suis une caméra, l'expression est un peu trop facile — mais que recouvre-t-elle ? Ce ne sont pas mes yeux qui ont vu mon corps sur le lit, entouré des médecins.

C'est mon esprit, c'est ce qu'il y a dans mon cerveau — ou bien est-ce autre chose, à quoi aucun d'entre nous ne peut trouver de nom ?

Ce phénomène ne dure pas. Sans aucune liaison, je perds cette position de spectateur et me retrouve dans l'enveloppe de mon corps. Et voilà que ce corps et cet esprit, qui ne font qu'un, sont entraînés dans le même trou en forme de tunnel qui m'avait fait si peur la première fois.

Or, le tunnel n'a plus rien d'effrayant. Non seulement il n'est pas en pente, il ne descend pas, mais il semble monter doucement, dans une ascension bienveillante. En outre, il est clair, de plus en plus clair, il devient même tellement lumineux que je suis aveuglé par cette lumière et je ne vois plus que cela : de la lumière. Comme lorsque, petit enfant, je voulais regarder le soleil en face, suffisamment longtemps pour que ma rétine ne soit baignée que de blanc, de doré, d'illumination. Lorsque je jouais à ce jeu imbécile, solitaire et dangereux, qui me laissait pendant parfois plus d'une heure incapable de lire, de voir ou de fixer mon regard sur la vie réelle, je payais le prix de ce jeu. Je souffrais. Mes yeux pleuraient, des barres noires entravaient ma vision des gens et des choses, une irritation des muqueuses m'obligeait à me frotter, en vain, les paupières. Et plus je les frottais, plus je payais le prix de mon choix destructeur : vouloir voir la lumière en face.

Ici, maintenant, il n'y a aucune souffrance. La lumière vient m'apporter une sensation de paix comme je n'en ai pas connu depuis mon entrée en réa, depuis que je me suis retrouvé subissant la machine et les prises de sang, les étouffements et le chaos. Je n'éprouve qu'une consolante et surprenante sensation de paix et encore plus d'amour que je n'en ai ressenti récemment, à l'intention des miens ou des autres. Cet amour est indéfinissable. Je voudrais pouvoir le donner et l'offrir autour de moi comme du miel, mais je ne suis entouré que de lumière. Comme des voiles de lumière, des passages et des courants de blancheur, quelque chose de diaphane, quelque chose de cristallin. Il n'y a personne vers qui je puisse dispenser l'abondance d'amour qui me submerge. Il n'y a personne, jusqu'à ce que, fugacement, apparaissent des formes.

Je crois entrevoir, sinon des visages, du moins des esquisses de visages. Elles ne me rappellent aucun des êtres qui comptent dans ma vie ou dans mon passé. Au vrai, ce sont à peine des contours, des suggestions, rien de net, et si j'essayais de les toucher, je n'y parviendrais pas et ils reculeraient devant ma main. Ils n'ont aucun trait, ni bouches, ni nez, ni yeux, ni mâchoires. Ces esquisses sont traversées comme par des suggestions de sourires. Telles des lignes dessinées. Ces faces sans aspérités me semblent pénétrées par l'essence du sourire. Non pas le sourire lui-même, mais son essence, et contrairement au ricanement narquois des bonshommes-toupies de mon voyage dans le noir, mon arrivée dans ce blanc me fait découvrir des étendues horizontales, et j'évolue à travers des rubans de compassion, de tendresse, de compréhension.

C'est comme si je vivais ma première traversée à l'envers. Au cours du premier voyage, je m'étais trouvé de façon vertigineuse dans un trou noir au bout duquel je ne devinais que l'horreur et dont il fallait que je m'échappe. Au cours de ce voyage-ci, aucune voix ne me pousse à quitter cet espace blanc, illuminé, doux et fraternel. J'aurais même la tentation de vouloir m'installer dans cette nébuleuse de lumière, de pousser plus loin mon voyage, tant il est bienfaisant.

Mais cela ne dure pas.

Cela a eu lieu

Cela ne dure pas plus longtemps qu'avait duré la phase pendant laquelle j'étais devenu une caméra. Il n'y a eu aucune transition. Aucun temps réel n'est passé entre l'instant où j'ai été projeté dans cette lumière, au sein d'un immense sentiment d'amour, et l'instant du retour, c'est-à-dire le lit, les tubes, la machine dont j'entends le bruit, le monde cruel et fermé de la réa. Il me semble que je reviens d'un saut dans quelque chose d'autre, d'ineffable, et que je retrouve la douloureuse, épuisée, inquiète, exténuée et comateuse condition qui était la mienne.

À reconnaître toutes les gênes, et les maux, les barrières, les multiples punitions qui assaillent mon corps, je pourrais même croire que ce saut dans la lumière n'a pas eu lieu.

Mais cela a eu lieu. Ça m'est arrivé. J'y suis allé et je suis revenu.

Romain Gary avait raison

À mesure que s'approche l'heure de l'extubation, je suis gagné par de nombreuses émotions.

D'abord, l'espoir. La voix de l'espoir a le même timbre, le même ton que celle de la volonté qui n'avait cessé de m'aider et de me parler, qui avait fait taire la voix de la tristesse et de la tentation de la mort et cette voix dit des choses simples et répétitives, aussi répétitives que ce mot ex-tu-ba-tion qui joue à ricochet, qui joue au billard à multiples bandes dans ma tête :

— Tiens bon, il ne te reste que deux jours. Tu tombes moins souvent dans l'inconscient. Tu reconnais mieux les gens et les choses. Tu peux même procéder à des déductions faciles sur les heures, les changements d'équipe des aides-soignantes, les visites de ta femme. Tu travailles plus calmement avec la machine. Tiens bon, dans deux jours, extubation, et tu passeras à une autre étape.

— Laquelle ?

— Peu importe. Tu seras moins prisonnier et moins ligoté, moins dépendant.

Ensuite et contradictoirement, j'éprouve une immense et une incommensurable fatigue. Ma volonté a beau me dire : « Tiens bon », je ne tiens plus rien — rien d'autre que la poire sur laquelle je continue d'appuyer afin qu'on vienne « m'aspirer ». Je ne sens plus mes pieds, mes jambes, mes bras, mes avant-bras bleuis par les piqûres. Je ne sens que ma poitrine et mon larynx, les deux lieux de ma douleur. Je ne sens que mes côtes et mon dos qui ont tant supporté les soubresauts provoqués par les quintes. Les côtes ont tenu. Le corps a tenu. Nous sommes d'une fragilité inouïe et à la fois nous possédons une résistance tout aussi insoupçonnable. Ces deux vérités contraires racontent tout le voyage : la fragilité m'a mené de l'autre côté du miroir. La résistance m'en a fait revenir. J'ai tenu, j'ai tenu, mais j'arrive épuisé au bout du terme, de la traversée, avant l'acte majeur que l'on va effectuer sur moi. Alors, à cette fatigue, viennent se greffer toutes sortes d'interrogations :

— Et s'ils n'arrivent pas à t'extuber ? Tu as entendu Karen la Coréenne, cette garce qui parlait de toi cette nuit avec sa copine, la petite Biterroise. Tu as entendu ce qu'elles disaient : « Mais c'est pas du tout sûr qu'ils arrivent à l'extuber, hein ? Ça marche pas à tous les coups ! » Imagine un peu que Karen ait raison et qu'ils n'y arrivent pas. Tu as entendu le mot « trachéotomie » l'autre jour, quand les toubibs penchés sur toi ne savaient pas que tu les entendais. Que se passera-t-il alors ?

Dans quelle autre dimension va-t-on entraîner ton corps ? Et le supportera-t-il ?

Il s'était toujours posé trop de questions.

Il avait toujours envisagé sa vie comme une aventure, un voyage vers l'inconnu, pour satisfaire son immense curiosité du monde. Mais il avait toujours dissimulé que cette curiosité était la sœur jumelle d'une forme constante d'inquiétude. Petit garçon ; jeune adolescent ; étudiant perdu au milieu d'une Amérique inconnue ; journaliste débutant puis chevronné ; cinéaste débutant puis aguerri ; romancier débutant puis plus maître de sa plume ; mari blessé et blessant, puis ayant eu la chance de refaire sa vie et de tirer un trait sur les blessures ; père de famille aveugle parce que trop jeune, trop narcissique et maladroit ; puis père de famille à nouveau, enfin plus altruiste et devenu conscient du rire et du cadeau de l'enfance ; pour chaque réussite, une erreur de jugement ; pour chaque aller, un retour ; pour chaque succès, un échec. Une négation, une affirmation. Toute chose appelant son contraire. Dans presque chacune des circonstances de sa vie, il avait toujours été accompagné par l'inquiétude et l'interrogation, par le doute. Pour masquer cette perpétuelle tendance, il avait très bien façonné sa comédie.

Il avait su jouer l'arrogance et l'insolence, l'audace, la sûreté du geste et du propos. Très jeune,

168

il avait su se fabriquer un deuxième personnage à l'inverse de l'autre : à l'aise dans la vie, séduisant, nonchalant, souriant, au-dessus des mesquineries et des jalousies, impavide devant l'hypocrisie, la discourtoisie, la vulgarité d'âme. Les deux pieds sur la table, mais avec un souci d'élégance, la désinvolture d'un prince. Et pour faire taire les questions, il s'était jeté dans l'action, le voyage, la création sous toutes ses formes, l'éclectisme échevelé. Romain Gary lui avait dit un jour :

— Tu sais pourquoi tu multiplies autant les travaux, les défis et les performances ? Tu sais pourquoi ? Parce que tu refuses de vieillir et de réfléchir à la mort.

L'action lui avait toujours permis de chasser la réflexion. Le travail lui avait servi de protection. Et le deuxième personnage éclipsait parfaitement le premier. L'un et l'autre, au fond, s'entraidaient et se complétaient. Plus il avait été anxieux, dévasté par le doute, plus il avait usiné, fourni, produit, labouré et labeuré, plus il avait poussé les feux de son énergie. Plus il avait été curieux du monde, voyageant, aimant, œuvrant pour être disponible, différent et reconnu.

Ça le faisait parfois rire intérieurement de suivre, dans le regard des autres, l'image de celui qu'il n'était pas. Tant d'étiquettes, tant de clichés ! On les lui avait tous attribués. Il avait eu droit à tout le catalogue : tour à tour arriviste, ambitieux, jeune loup, jeune homme pressé, le plus américain de nos romanciers, de nos cinéastes, de nos journalistes... Une ribambelle de banalités :

— Si seulement ils savaient, pensait-il alors.

Mais « ils » ne savaient pas, et comme lui ne voulait pas qu'« ils » sachent, il ne cessait de leur lancer des défis et de s'en lancer à lui-même.

30

Tirer sur la corde

Maintenant, il se souvenait d'un défi — huit jours et huit nuits passés dans la banlieue de Londres avec Lee, Tom, Micky, Johnny et les autres. Johnny l'avait appelé à Paris un jour :

— J'enregistre un album entier. On a des ébauches de musique, mais pas plus. On aura tous les musiciens des Beatles. Pas longtemps. Il faut en profiter. Je n'ai aucun texte. Tu veux les faire ? Tu es prêt à venir passer dix jours avec nous, en studio, sans débander ? Écrire douze titres en dix jours ?

Il n'avait pas hésité. Ils avaient vécu comme des reclus. Fumant, mangeant, buvant, dormant peu, dormant mal, allant de l'hôtel au studio et du studio à l'hôtel, sans jamais voir la lumière du jour. Lee, avec ses rouflaquettes rousses et son accent de l'Oklahoma. Tom et Micky, les compositeurs, les complices, l'un frisé blond et l'autre brun vif, écrivant des mélodies simples et faciles à retenir, habitées par un tempo, une pulsion, le rythme de leur époque. Il tapait ses textes sur une Olivetti portative, la machine à écrire de ses années de grand reportage, sous enveloppe de cuir bleu. Il tapait fort dans le silence creux de la chambre d'hôtel. On frappait à la porte. C'était Johnny, l'œil allumé, rigolard, une guitare Wilson au bout de la main :

— Montre, disait-il, montre-moi. Où en es-tu ? Tu as déjà fait *Sarah* ?

Johnny. Avec ses jambes arquées, son dos voûté, son sourire mi-canaille, mi-innocent, ses yeux pleins de bleu, pleins de nuits blanches, sa carcasse d'exception qui lui permettait de passer à travers tout (accidents de voiture, défonces à l'alcool ou à d'autres produits, à l'époque on l'appelait La Bête), avec cette voix surprenante de douceur, cette vulnérabilité dès qu'il évoquait les souvenirs de son enfance détruite — il était, à cette heure avancée de la nuit, dans l'embrasure de la porte, comme l'apparition de ces primitifs américains dont, autrefois, en Virginie, au Texas ou au Colorado, il avait été l'ami. S'il avait l'allure d'un cowboy, la dégaine d'un routard, sa voix et sa vérité étaient autres. C'était un artiste.

Il possédait une manière de saisir la phrase forte, la formule clé et de la recadrer dans la musique que lui proposaient les autres. Il savait discerner la lacune dans une liaison de mots, le pied qui manque, la mauvaise rime. Il était un interprète, mais aussi un stimulateur. Sa personne même, la vie qu'il avait déjà menée, sa popularité encourageaient l'inspiration. On écrivait sans peine pour lui. Quand il avançait dans la chambre, à 3 heures du matin, pour essayer sur sa guitare les mots qu'on venait de lui proposer, Johnny se transformait. La délicatesse de sa recherche pour le son juste, son instinct pour récupérer ce qu'il fallait gommer, suggérer ce qu'il fallait rajouter, rendaient tout plus facile. Sur le papier enroulé dans l'Olivetti, on corrigeait à la main dans un état d'euphorie et d'amusement. D'ébriété aussi : bières, tabac, privation de sommeil et autres outils. On repartait en studio. Les instrumentistes avaient enregistré de nouveaux fonds, de nouvelles bases musicales. La Bête se tenait debout derrière le micro pour une première tentative sur son nouveau texte :

> *Les hommes qui aiment chasser*
> *Ont découvert un nouveau gibier.*

Ou bien aussi :

> *Car tout passe et tout casse et tout lasse*
> *Le désir, le plaisir se diluent dans l'espace*
> *Et je n'y suis pour rien.*

Ce n'étaient jamais que quelques mots, quelques lignes et cela devenait une chanson. Le marathon avait duré des jours et des nuits au bout desquels, exténué, il était rentré à Paris. Laissant Lee, les musiciens et La Bête parachever le travail. Il s'était alité le soir même : quarante de fièvre, une infection bronchique.

— Vous avez trop tiré sur la corde, avait dit le généraliste barbu à l'accent russe.

Vingt ans plus tard — c'est-à-dire hier — ai-je aussi trop « tiré sur la corde » ? Lorsque j'ai voulu remettre à temps le manuscrit de mon dernier roman : des nuits à dicter, à corriger. Et au bout de ces nuits, une sensation d'étouffement, la fièvre, et la chute dans la maladie.

Je repense à ce manuscrit : son écriture a-t-elle contribué à m'emmener jusqu'au seuil de la mort ? En ce moment même, on compose le livre chez mon éditeur. Un ami écrivain, précieux et solidaire, veillera à ce qu'il se fabrique sans moi. Je l'ai appris par ma femme. Il corrigera les épreuves à ma place. Cela s'appelle *Un début à Paris*. Il m'a semblé, à mesure que j'avançais dans son écriture, que j'y tenais plus qu'à tout autre des livres qui l'avaient précédé. Peut-être parce que, dans deux personnages qui m'importaient, Vence — un ami prématurément disparu — et Lumière, une jeune fille aux dons prémonitoires, j'avais décrit des indices sur la précarité de la vie, la fragilité de l'existence. C'était un livre sur la jeunesse, sur ce sentiment trompeur, fou et fallacieux, qui poussait le héros narrateur (c'est-à-dire moi-même) vers les risques et l'amour, vers le travail et la passion, avec la conviction que l'on peut, à cet âge, triompher de tout. Que l'on dure longtemps, toujours, que la durée n'est pas un obstacle. Plus tard, lorsque le livre paraîtra, après ma traversée en réa, Sollers, qui le lira, me dira :

— Qui est-ce qui t'a dicté ce passage ?

Il me citait des lignes à travers lesquelles le narrateur sent et voit sa vie basculer vers un destin inconnu. Qui donc, en effet, m'avait soufflé ces courts paragraphes, où, à 4 heures du matin sur le boulevard du Montparnasse, le narrateur voit partir des jeunes gens dans des voitures décapotables avec la soudaine certitude qu'ils ne seront bientôt plus rien que vanité, ombre et poussière. « Qui est-ce qui t'a dicté ça ? » Quand j'avais écrit ce passage, on était à la fin du printemps, ma santé commençait à se détériorer. Quelque chose en moi, dans mon corps, avait entamé un travail souterrain, un travail de sape, quelque chose qui me minait. Ce quelque chose — aujourd'hui en réa, on l'appelle la « bactérie inconnue » — m'avait-il distribué les mots, les scènes et les phrases qui sentaient si fort la mort ? J'avais dicté le manuscrit à haute voix sur un petit magnétophone, afin de le faire retranscrire. Les enregistrements avaient duré une semaine de nuits blanches. Les huit nuits m'avaient amené à une extinction de voix, à l'œdème du larynx, à la sensation d'étouffement, à des fièvres récurrentes, à la perte de mes défenses immunitaires. J'avais la sensation d'être arrivé au bout d'une série de murs qui s'étaient écroulés les uns après les autres. Et puis, cette toux ininterrompue, et au bout, le professeur qui me dit :

— Je ne peux vous soigner que si vous acceptez enfin de vous faire hospitaliser.

31

Quatre moins un égale trois

Se faire hospitaliser ! J'avais d'abord refusé.

Tout en moi disait non à l'hôpital, non seulement à l'idée de cesser mes activités et de céder à
la maladie, mais surtout de m'abandonner à un
univers que je n'avais connu que comme visiteur :
amis ou parents malades ; visites à tous les suicidés
manqués, ou mort brutale comme celle de Melville
et sa rupture d'anévrisme dans la nuit, son transport à l'hôpital et moi, sur le carreau du couloir,
suppliant les toubibs de le « réveiller » et eux me
disant, en montrant l'immense corps de mon
immense ami, déjà blanchâtre, vidé de sa vie :

— On ne peut plus rien faire pour lui, on a tout
essayé.

Je détestais la perspective de l'hôpital.

Ma fille et ma femme m'avaient dit :

— Il faut y aller.

Devant elles, étendu sur mon lit, j'avais pleuré
comme un enfant :

— Non, je ne suis pas prêt.

Il y avait eu un semblant de querelle. Les deux

femmes, la mère et l'adolescente, m'avaient joué
la comédie :

— Si tu n'y vas pas, on ne te parle plus. On te
laisse seul.

Quelques heures plus tard, à bout de forces,
paniqué par le vide du corps, la fièvre des
membres, et l'étouffement qui gagnait, j'avais
appelé le professeur :

— Je suis prêt.

Elles m'avaient accompagné. Je me souviens de
cette dernière course en voiture. C'était un
samedi. Il faisait beau et chaud, fin mai, début juin.
Je n'avais plus la force de parler. Le lendemain
matin, en fibroscopie, on avait mesuré l'étendue
du désastre et j'avais été transporté en réa.

Je songe à ces séquences dans leur ordre. Ça y
est, je suis enfin parvenu à reconstituer la chrono-
logie. Je m'interroge alors :

— Et si ce manuscrit était ton dernier livre ? Si
tu n'en sors pas, le laisseras-tu comme livre posthume et sera-t-il à la hauteur, justement, de cette
identité ? Prendra-t-il l'allure d'un livre posthume ?
Le jugera-t-on autrement ? Y lira-t-on ce que tu
ignores toi-même avoir voulu mettre ?

Mais aussi rapidement :

— Quelle importance cela a-t-il ? Aucune. Si tu
ne te réveilles pas, l'important n'est pas ce que tu
laisses, ou pas, de ta petite œuvre littéraire, mais
plutôt ce qui arrivera à celles et à ceux que tu
aimes et qui t'aiment.

Interrogation :

Que deviendront les enfants? Quel effet pourrait avoir sur eux, à leur âge encore si frêle, la perte d'un parent?

Comment leurs goûts, leurs rires, leurs amitiés, leur vocation, leurs amours, leur enseignement, leur grâce, leur physique seront-ils affectés par ce départ inattendu? Tout, chez un être jeune, peut être radicalement bouleversé par cette sorte de fracture. Le deuil inopiné transforme tout, jusqu'aux rides, jusqu'aux mouvements des mains, jusqu'au langage des yeux et du corps. J'ai eu la chance d'atteindre l'âge que l'on dit adulte avec un père vivant, une mère vivante. Mon père est mort à l'âge de quatre-vingt-dix ans et cela ne pouvait pas constituer une surprise, un choc. Mon chagrin a été à la mesure de ma préparation. Ce chagrin, et l'idée que je m'étais faite de l'inévitable déclin de l'homme que j'avais aimé, craint et respecté. Le temps m'avait laissé tout le temps nécessaire pour m'accoutumer à l'événement. Je le regrette toujours, mais la peine a été douce, d'une certaine façon. Or, s'il devait, tout à l'heure, se passer quelque chose de fatal, comment les enfants subiraient-ils et vivraient-ils cet inattendu? Ce à quoi rien ne les a préparés?

Leur mère n'a pas connu ma chance. Elle a perdu sa propre mère, tôt dans sa jeunesse, trop tôt pour elle comme pour ses sœurs. À l'écouter, à la suivre, à l'observer, j'ai incomplètement, superficiellement, mesuré le sens et les conséquences d'une disparition prématurée. Pourra-t-elle et saura-t-elle trouver les forces nécessaires, malgré le rappel de cette première expérience fondatrice de sa vie ? Savoir est une chose, pouvoir une autre : qu'elle sache faire face à cette douleur ne me préoccupe pas. Plus que moi, elle a été accoutumée au malheur. Mais qu'elle puisse... qu'elle entretienne assez d'énergie chaque jour pour aider ses enfants à vivre le manque d'un père ? Bizarrement, la même image de la scène du petit déjeuner rituel dans la cuisine revient, alors, avec la précision d'une photo grand-angle : des recoins de la fenêtre jusqu'au bord du meuble blanc où l'on découpe le pain, mes yeux peuvent parcourir la pièce. Murs blancs, carreaux blancs, objets de cuisine bleus, reproductions de vieilles couvertures dessinées du *New Yorker* : couleurs bleu et émeraude. Je peux reconstituer, sans qu'aucune brume de délire ou de douleur déforme cette image, les trois silhouettes, la mère, la fille et le garçon, chacun assis devant le bol de céréales ou la tasse de thé.

Je suis parti. Ils ne sont plus que trois. J'imagine que cette scène peut devenir définitive, qu'ils ne seront plus jamais quatre. J'ai peur pour eux. J'ai peur pour les yeux clairs de Clarisse, pour le sourire illuminé de Jean, et pour cet air spirituel et mutin de Françoise que j'ai constamment lu sur les hautes pommettes de son visage, quelles que soient les circonstances. J'ai toujours vu, derrière toute autre expression de ses sentiments, une réserve de gaieté. Une faculté de surmonter le désespoir de la vie et de le transformer en une approche enjouée de cette même vie.

Ils ne se parlent pas. Écoutent-ils la radio? Où est la chienne? Je la vois, sur les genoux de ma fille, la tête sous la table.

Je me dis que si je parviens à recomposer de telles séquences, à m'interroger sur mes interrogations, c'est que mes pensées sont devenues plus claires. C'est que je vais pouvoir aborder l'ex-tu-bation dans un état d'extrême fatigue, certes, mais aussi dans une sorte de quiétude.

À quoi doit-on cette tranquillité inusitée, cette pacification de l'esprit? Je devrais être saisi par l'angoisse. Je me sens vidé de toute crainte.

32

« *On va vous envoyer très profond* »

C'est peut-être mon passage à travers le tunnel blanc et vers la lumière qui m'a préparé.

Tandis que je vois la porte s'ouvrir, que le docteur C. entre, donne des ordres, installe ses appareils, sur ce ton posé et expert qui m'avait déjà frappé lors de ses précédentes visites, je ne ressens plus aucune peur. Ma paranoïa habituelle semble s'être évanouie, avoir quitté mon esprit et mon corps.

C'est le matin. Deux aides-soignantes venues très tôt m'avaient lavé, soupesé, tourné et retourné, avaient contrôlé la perfusion, pris la température, contrôlé la tension, changé la literie. Je crois bien même que l'on m'avait lavé le visage et que l'on m'avait rasé. L'une des aides m'avait dit :

— Vous savez qu'on vous extube à 10 heures ? On vous l'avait déjà dit hier, n'est-ce pas ?

Ne disposant d'aucun repère horaire, j'ai acquiescé de la tête. Comme chaque fois que l'on s'adresse à moi depuis ce qui doit être une pleine semaine de ma traversée de la réa, j'aurais souhaité dire «bonjour», «merci», poser des questions. L'impossibilité de m'exprimer a pesé et m'a rendu plus conscient de mes limites. Quand pourrai-je à nouveau parler? Tout simplement parler! Aux autres, aux inconnus, à ceux que j'aime. La privation de la parole est une autre forme de privation de liberté. La réa est une prison.

J'ai attendu. Il m'a semblé que je n'avais pas aussi mal qu'auparavant. Était-ce l'effet de ce que l'on m'avait donné pour préparer l'extubation? Je n'ai pas cessé de repenser à cette lumière blanche, à l'émotion, à l'émanation d'un sourire d'amour qui m'avaient fugacement atteint. Je ne parvenais pas à reconstituer la lumière et les notions de sourire en termes concrets, en images ou en mots — mais il me restait cette impression, cette vision. Je me suis dit que si cela ne se passait pas bien, si le tube se cassait, s'il fallait opérer, si ce qui s'ensuivrait fatalement, c'est-à-dire la trachéotomie, devait m'emmener définitivement de «l'autre côté», il me resterait toujours la probabilité d'y retrouver le tunnel blanc et la lumière. Par conséquent, je devais attendre sans peur et en paix. C'était le seul moyen, le meilleur moyen de faire face à ce tournant majeur, le dernier avant la mort. Et puis j'ai à nouveau pensé à mon fils, le petit garçon qui, ce matin, allait partir pour l'école en sachant qu'on allait «extuber» son père. Et à ma fille, l'adolescente à qui la mère avait sans doute fait la même confidence :

— Ce matin, ils vont délivrer papa.

Sans doute leur avait-elle dit à eux deux la même

chose, à la même heure, devant les céréales au chocolat du matin. J'ai deviné sa volonté de ne laisser paraître aucun signe d'anxiété. Avait-elle réellement prononcé les mots que j'avais imaginés :

— On va délivrer papa.

Le mot « papa » m'a fait penser à mon père et au groupe de mes visiteurs. Finalement, ils n'étaient plus jamais revenus dans la pièce pour dire :

— Viens ! Qu'attends-tu pour nous rejoindre ?

Ils m'avaient laissé tomber. Ils avaient abandonné leur invitation. J'ai pensé que c'était un signe. Le docteur C. est entré dans la pièce. Il devait donc être 10 heures du matin.

Il est très coordonné, le docteur C.

Je suis chacun de ses mouvements, j'entends chacune de ses paroles, comme au spectacle. À la façon dont il distribue les rôles aux aides-soignantes qui l'écoutent avec respect, je me dis que j'ai affaire à un excellent professionnel. Ça se reconnaît, un pro. À la tête d'une équipe ou au volant d'une machine, dans les sous-sols de l'imprimerie d'un journal ou derrière un micro ou une caméra, vous identifiez le pro à l'économie de ses gestes, l'impression que tout a déjà été répété, digéré, expérimenté. Et il y a cette espèce de douceur ferme dans les ordres donnés — l'autorité qui n'a pas besoin d'être autoritaire pour se faire comprendre. Ça vous rassure. Ça vous ôte réticence et agressivité. Le pro fait son boulot, comme le menuisier de Charles Péguy faisait sa chaise.

Moi qui ai perdu toute mémoire, hormis une fragmentaire, moi qui ne puis depuis jour et nuit ne réciter, pour survivre, que quelques strophes de poèmes, soudain, à la vision du docteur C. qui travaille, j'entends, lu par la voix de mon père, un texte de Charles Péguy, qu'il nous offrait pendant mon enfance :

«... Il fallait qu'un bâton de chaise fût bien fait. C'était entendu. C'était un primat. Il ne fallait pas qu'il fût bien fait pour le salaire... pour le patron ni pour les connaisseurs, ni pour les clients du patron. Il fallait qu'il fût bien fait pour lui-même, en lui-même, pour lui-même, en son être même. Une tradition venue, montée du plus profond de la race, une histoire, un absolu, un honneur voulait que ce bâton de chaise fût bien fait. Toute partie dans la chaise qui ne se voyait pas était tout aussi parfaitement faite que ce qu'on voyait. C'est le principe même des cathédrales. »

Je me souviens du ton un peu incantatoire avec lequel mon père nous disait ce texte, tout en arpentant de long en large la grande salle à manger familiale. Et comment le lyrisme répétitif de Péguy nous assénait cette vérité, cette volonté de sacerdoce : il fallait que le bâton de chaise fût bien fait. Eh bien, étendu, les bras ligotés, intubé et cortisoné, antibiotiqué et amoindri, ayant traversé le noir puis la lumière, j'observe le docteur C. en train de préparer l'acte le plus important de ma

184

vie avec cette sensation qu'il s'agit d'un ouvrier qui se conforme à l'honneur et au respect de soi qu'invoquait Charles Péguy. Dans ce que j'ai essayé d'accomplir, dans l'exercice de toutes les professions auxquelles, «par peur de vieillir», comme me disait Romain Gary, je me suis attaqué, j'ai été en grande partie influencé par ce texte venu du fond de mon enfance. Et je regarde le docteur C., patient, méthodique, concentré sur son travail artisanal, avec la certitude qu'il appartient à la race d'hommes dont parlait Péguy et je me dis qu'il existe une liaison secrète entre ce docteur C., que je ne connais pas, et mon père, qui n'est plus là depuis longtemps et qui venait déjà d'un monde ancien. Le lien entre le docteur C. et mon père porte un nom que plus personne n'ose prononcer de nos jours — cela s'appelle «une valeur».

Le docteur C. dispose, sur une tablette située au bout de mon lit, une sorte de petite caisse métallique d'où il extrait des objets que je ne peux reconnaître. Il est accompagné d'une jeune femme dont je me dis que je l'ai déjà vue, ici, à l'hôpital. Son prénom me revient alors que personne dans la pièce ne l'a prononcé : Lisyane. C'est cela, elle s'appelle bien Lisyane, c'est une rousse, elle a des yeux vert clair, et j'ai déjà vu ces deux couleurs — le roux et le vert clair — se pencher vers moi.

— Vous me reconnaissez ? me dit-elle. C'est moi

qui vous ai anesthésié pour votre première fibroscopie.

Elle était donc présente à la première étape et
je la retrouve maintenant, pour ce qui devrait entamer le processus de départ de la réa — si tout va
bien. Les yeux ressortent d'autant mieux lorsqu'on
porte un masque. Les yeux de Lisyane accompa-
gnent ses paroles :

— Je vais vous donner de quoi vous endormir
peu de temps, car l'extubation est d'une durée très
courte, mais de façon profonde. On va vous
envoyer très profond.

Cette dernière phrase a pour effet de me faire
sourire intérieurement. Peut-on « m'envoyer plus
profond » que ce que vers quoi, par plusieurs fois,
je suis allé ? Va pour la profondeur ! Je connais. Je
sais comment c'est.

Bientôt, le visage du docteur C. et celui de
Lisyane s'évanouissent, et, cette fois, je n'en suis
pas conscient. Ça s'est passé très vite et j'ai dû aller
si « profond » que je n'ai, à ce jour, aucun souvenir de la profondeur dans quoi, avec son savoir-
faire, l'anesthésiste aux yeux vert clair m'avait
envoyé. Alors que j'écris ces lignes et que je me
souviens exactement de ce que j'ai traversé, cette
profondeur-là ne suscite aucune image, aucun
effroi, aucune obscurité, aucune lumière. Totale
oblitération de tout.

Je ne me souviens que du réveil et de ce qu'il a
signifié.

TROISIÈME PARTIE

NAÎTRE
UNE DEUXIÈME FOIS

33

Comme un parchemin vierge

Le silence. Et des petits bruits, sans malignité, sans intention de nuire, des bruits quotidiens. Il n'y a plus de BOUM-ET-BOUM-ET-RATATAM TATA-BOUM.

Il n'y a plus de machine. Il n'y a plus de sonnerie. Il n'y a plus de souffle rauque.

Il n'y a plus de tube. Il n'y a plus cette menace permanente que je sentais peser dans la pièce, autour et au-dessus de moi.

Il n'y a plus ce fleuve épais, chaud et noir, qui dévorait mes poumons. Il y a un air frais, aussi surprenant et vif que celui d'un matin, dans la rosée d'un sous-bois. J'aspire cet air de mes narines libres, de ma poitrine dégagée, de ma gorge dénouée, désopacifiée. Je n'étouffe plus. Je ne crache plus. La force étrangère qui m'avait possédé a quitté mon territoire. Je ne suis plus occupé par les puissances ennemies.

L'air que je respire, de ma bouche libre, je l'expire. Je respire et j'expire. Je me sens revivre.

La pièce dans laquelle je me trouve, le lit sur lequel je repose, le plafond que je vois au-dessus de moi sont les mêmes que ceux que j'ai quittés une demi-heure auparavant. Néanmoins, tout a changé. Les proportions sont normales, réelles. J'ai perdu cette impression de surdimension et de déformation, ce qui me semblait démesuré, fantastiquement vide et obscur parfois, et d'autres fois terriblement étroit et contraignant. Je sens que je suis en état de pouvoir parler. Je n'ose encore le faire, mais je devine les mots qui attendent au bout de ma gorge, de mon palais. Une lente et profonde satisfaction m'envahit. Je ne suis plus prisonnier ! Ça veut dire qu'ils ont réussi, que je suis extubé, que je suis repassé de l'autre côté, vers ce côté-ci. Que je reviens chez les autres. Mon esprit et mon corps sont parcourus alors par une onde de soulagement et de clarté. Faiblesse totale des membres, certes, mais lucidité et transparence. Bien-être. Comme une odeur vert et jaune, une odeur de fleurs et de feuilles. Odeurs et parfums ! Je n'avais plus la notion d'un parfum. Je ne sentais plus rien depuis si longtemps.

Je suis éveillé, un aérosol sur mon visage. Je connais ce système. Un petit objet de plastique au-dessus du nez qui vous envoie, par un tube relié à un petit flacon, des émanations et une sorte de fumée, d'un mélange de Soludécadron que vous aspirez et qui vous fait du bien. Je me rendors une ou deux fois, puis je vais me réveiller définitivement et il va alors se passer toutes sortes de choses sans précédent. Dans ces heures qui vont suivre l'extubation, je vais voir devant moi comme un parchemin vierge qui se déroule et sur lequel viennent s'imprimer des messages. Je vais voir ce que je dois faire, dire, écrire, projeter et fabriquer. Comment je dois aborder la vie, telle que je la retrouve.

Je vais, en un laps de temps que je ne peux évaluer, sentir que le chaos que j'ai connu se désembrouille, que les parcelles de ma pensée et de ma mémoire se remettent en place. C'est une remise en ordre, un reclassement, une redistribution des idées et des sentiments. Mes premières pensées sont :

— Je vais bien. Je suis faible, mais je suis vivant. Je suis vivant !

Et puis, aussitôt après, dans un déferlement qui n'a rien de chaotique, mais à la vitesse d'un ordinateur, les tâches à accomplir me sont données : il faudra que je dise à tous ceux à qui je ne l'ai pas assez dit que je les aime et pourquoi ; il faudra que je m'excuse et que je m'explique pour avoir fait, récemment, telle et telle chose qui ont pu blesser ou troubler tel et tel être humain ; il faudra que j'écrive et que je construise tel livre, telle émission, tel texte. Je vois apparaître sur le parchemin les objectifs de mon travail. Je vois défiler des scénarios et des titres — des personnages et des thèmes. Puis je vois s'esquisser, sur une durée de une à cinq années à venir, la construction de mon activité. Mais je vois aussi, en même temps, s'inscrire les actes et les paroles, les gestes, tout ce que je n'ai pas assez fait. Tout ce que, s'il m'était arrivé le grand malheur, j'aurais, à la seconde même précédant ma mort, regretté de n'avoir ni fait ni dit. On dit : «Je l'ai regretté toute ma vie. » Il faut corriger l'expression : «Je l'aurais regretté toute ma mort ! »

Il faudra que ce que j'ai dit et fait par orgueil, narcissisme, égoïsme, impatience, négativité, je le défasse puis je le refasse en chassant toutes les manifestations de mon ego. Et que je substitue à l'orgueil un peu de modestie ; au narcissisme un peu de recul sur moi ; à l'égoïsme un peu de générosité ; à l'impatience un peu de sérénité ; à la négativité un peu d'optimisme. Et je pense que ce sera facile. Ce sera même enfantin !

Dès que mes forces le permettront, il faudra que je voie ceux avec qui je travaille depuis presque dix ans dans la même entreprise et que je leur parle, non pas de ce qu'ils ont décidé en mon absence, et comment ça s'est passé, et qui a fait quoi, ou qui a dit quoi, mais ce que je pense d'eux, et combien j'apprécie ce qu'ils sont, qui ils sont, et que je les interroge sur eux-mêmes, leur santé, leur famille, les soucis de leur vie. Il faudra surtout que je me préoccupe de Françoise, qui a dû passer par des affres, ni dormir, ni se nourrir, ni se reposer, qui a sans doute dû tout subir, faire face et faire front, qui a porté la maison, les enfants, sa vie professionnelle en même temps, et qui a sans doute organisé et distribué les attitudes et les tâches de chacun. Je commence seulement à pouvoir imaginer qu'il lui a fallu organiser et filtrer, distiller et distribuer visites et appels, relais — et comment elle aura été, au milieu des interrogations de toute ma famille, le pivot central de cette pièce dont la fin n'était pas écrite. Il faudra que je fasse attention à elle et pour elle : au bout d'une expérience aussi singulière, il peut arriver que le fil se brise, le cristal se fêle.

Enfin, il faudra que je parle mieux et plus à mes enfants, comme à mes amis. Moi qui ai cru savoir parler, savoir démontrer, savoir montrer et savoir écrire, savoir « communiquer », expression lourde et moderne, que je rejette au moment où elle me vient à l'esprit, je découvre que je n'ai pas tout à fait su exprimer la vérité, choisir la sincérité, que je n'ai pas assez affirmé des choses évidentes. Je me dis ceci :

— Imagine seulement que tu ne t'en sois pas sorti, et que tu sois resté dans le trou noir. Tu n'aurais laissé que de l'inachevé, de l'approximatif. Tu viens de recevoir une seconde chance d'être un peu mieux que ce que tu as été. D'être un peu plus clair, sincère, aimant.

Puis, j'ai cette autre pensée :

— Il te faut mieux vivre la vie que tu retrouves.

Et je m'endors sans avoir encore pu parler. Je m'endors en me souhaitant d'être véritablement tiré d'affaire.

34

Savoir re-la-ti-vi-ser

C'est que l'on n'y croit pas complètement.

Le sommeil joue des tours. On a beau ne plus être prisonnier de la machine, les séquelles des sédatifs font leur effet. La mer ne se retire pas en une seule vague, l'horreur non plus.

Ainsi, le grand cauchemar noir, les petits hommes-toupies en casquette de cricket et les formes orange qui dégoulinaient vers vous, tout cela apparaît encore, par fragments, par secousses. Alors, vous cherchez la lumière et vous ouvrez les yeux.

Le réel chasse tout. Ce qui apparaît, vivant et bougeant autour du lit dans la pièce, dans le couloir au-delà des vitres, tout vous rassure et confirme la sensation du réveil : tout respire. Ce véritable mystère, qui consiste à ce que l'air voyage normalement en vous, vous n'en prenez conscience que parce qu'il a failli vous être retiré. Les premières manifestations naturelles sans l'aide de l'aérosol, dont on vous débarrasse pour vous réhabituer à la norme, ressemblent à la découverte d'un pays nouveau où tout serait différent, accueillant, agréable. C'est frais, vierge, beau, initiatique. C'est le vent au milieu des arbres bleus du Colorado. Je comprends pourquoi j'y ai autant pensé : c'était la privation d'air, de vent, de ciel, de liberté, qui me faisait tant rêver à ces espaces.

C'est une sensation première. Cela dépasse l'expérience la plus enivrante du premier amour, la première symphonie, la première émotion poétique ou artistique, la première victoire créatrice que vous avez remportée, la première fierté d'avoir bien fait quelque chose. Cela dépasse la définition même du dépassement. Vous êtes en train de vivre un moment unique et à la fois, pour compenser l'exaltation qui irradie votre esprit, une autre impression surgit, aussi forte, celle d'une grande humilité, celle de la relativisation :

— Ce n'est rien. Essaye de comparer et de mettre en perspective. Imagine-toi ce qu'ont été, ce que doivent être et ce que seront les épreuves, les souffrances, les calvaires et les labeurs des grands cancéreux, des sidéens, des cœurs qui flanchent et que l'on triple-ponte ou quadruple-ponte, les paralysies, les atteintes au cerveau, aux glandes, au sang. Imagine les autres. Tu n'as rien vécu de tellement dramatique, au fond.

Ce lit, cette pièce dont je peux détailler la banalité, je sais maintenant que d'autres hommes ou femmes les ont occupés et y ont connu un plus terrible voyage. Une traversée sans retour. Je l'imagine sans difficulté, avec cette clarté exclusive que donne la connaissance. Le regard que je jette sans angoisse sur le plafond en face de moi, combien de frères et de sœurs en douleur l'ont posé pour la dernière fois avant de s'éteindre ? Alors, l'humble conscience d'avoir approché le néant, de n'être qu'un cas perdu parmi l'incessante et universelle population de ceux qui souffrent, apporte une sorte de calme à l'exaltation du retour. Un nouveau refus de l'ego — le grand Moi n'est plus rien désormais qu'un petit « je ».

Et puis, et simultanément, vient l'envie irrésistible de voir, de toucher, d'entendre les autres. C'est une faim, une soif, un désir. Au fil des heures et des journées qui vont suivre, dans cette même pièce où vous avez vu l'invisible, et connu l'inconnu, ceux que vous connaissez vont se succéder et vous les redécouvrez avec d'autres yeux.

35

La chanson du petit clampin

La première visite, c'est Françoise, très tôt après l'extubation. Elle porte l'habituel et obligatoire masque de gaze mais je vois le sourire derrière le masque. Comme je ne peux encore parler, j'écris sur la petite ardoise.

J'écris comme un fou, ma main va à une allure excessive. J'essaye de livrer le soulagement et la gratitude que j'éprouve à la revoir. Mes mots sont pour elle et nos enfants. Je vois pétiller dans le fond vert noisette de ses iris une lueur de bonheur. La crainte a disparu de ce beau visage rayonnant.

Je travaille activement : j'écris, j'écris. L'ardoise est pleine, recto verso. Je la lui tends. Elle lit, elle répond par des gestes de tendresse, le masque de gaze atténue en partie la force pudique de ses réponses, mais je comprends la moindre de ses intonations. On dirait que le grand bouleversement dont j'ai été l'objet m'a donné la singulière faculté de mieux lire mouvements et regards, mieux peser, apprécier et comprendre les silences. Sur l'ardoise dont elle a effacé les phrases puisque j'ai fait signe que je n'avais pas terminé et que j'avais encore tant de choses à exprimer, je demande qu'elle me parle d'elle — qu'on cesse de se préoccuper de moi —, qu'elle me dise si elle va bien. Je prie que l'on m'oublie une fraction de seconde. Elle réagit avec peu de mots, soucieuse de me laisser déverser le trop-plein de sentiments, de laisser passer ce défoulement indispensable, inévitable.

Elle me tend un carnet à couverture noire que l'on peut mettre en poche avec, sur la tranche du papier, dans une mince gaine de feutre, un petit crayon pour noter, et un élastique qui entoure la couverture afin de fermer le tout.

— Tu auras beaucoup de choses à noter dans les jours qui vont venir.

J'essaye d'écrire ce que je souhaite être une vraie phrase d'amour qu'un homme peut dire à une femme, une femme à un homme :

— Je t'aime pour ce que tu es. Parce que tu es.

J'insiste et j'écris encore :

— Tu m'es nécessaire.

J'insiste et j'écris encore :

— Parle-moi de toi.

Elle répond sobrement que « ça va ». Et que les enfants vont venir très vite.

En réalité, mais je ne l'appris qu'un peu plus tard, ils étaient déjà venus.

Mais dans mon délire-douleur, ma douleur-délire, je ne m'en étais pas aperçu. J'avais bien cru, ouvrant les yeux pour m'arracher aux grimaces ricanantes des petits hommes-toupies, voir une fois la silhouette de ma fille, ses longs cheveux, cette démarche si familière pour un père, devant la porte vitrée, et j'avais cru aussi voir son corps reculer dans un mouvement de refus et de peur. Je m'étais dit : « Ce qu'elle voit de moi l'a horrifiée, elle s'en va. » Naturellement, cela ne s'était pas passé ainsi — et il nous faudra peu à peu apprendre que rien de ce que j'ai pu voir ne s'est « passé ainsi ».

Mais elle était venue en effet, puisqu'elle était en âge d'avoir le droit de visite en réa. Elle avait vu un homme bardé de tubes, sur un lit. Et elle ne m'a jamais dit ce qu'elle en avait pensé. Pour le petit garçon, cela s'était avéré plus difficile. Il était trop jeune. Grâce à la compréhension du médecin, on l'avait fait passer par une courette intérieure, à la hauteur de la fenêtre de la pièce dans laquelle se trouvait son père. Je ne m'en étais pas aperçu mais il avait été utile qu'on le lui fasse faire, important qu'il constate que son père était bien là.

Maintenant que je suis en état de lui donner de véritables signes de vie, il est revenu dans la même courette. Sa mère a tout agencé pour qu'il vérifie que l'on m'a « délivré » :

— Papa est sorti d'affaire.

Je distingue son visage et je peux détailler sa silhouette à travers la fenêtre. Une sorte d'hygiaphone lui permet de parler, mais il préfère se taire. Sa pudeur l'empêche-t-elle de s'exprimer ? Il y a des gens autour de lui. Une infirmière, sa mère. Il penche sa tête en avant et il sourit. Je vais faire alors toutes sortes de gestes et de signes. De frénétiques V de la victoire, de mes deux mains, comme autrefois lorsque, encore plus petit garçon, il utilisait ce geste universel qui signifie « on a ga-gné ». Le pouce levé, ensuite, pour indiquer que j'ai maîtrisé la bête, tout va bien. Puis je mime une série de gestes de la main : poings fermés, ouverts, les doigts qui donnent des chiffres : c'est la « chanson du clampin ». Il est seul à la connaître avec moi. Elle fait partie des innombrables secrets que partagent un père et un fils. C'est lui, le « petit clampin », et la chanson que nous avons concoctée ensemble n'est que l'énumération des coups que l'on se porte lorsque l'on fait semblant de se battre : « une beigne (traduit par un doigt de la main), quatre parpaings » (quatre doigts de la main), « trois marrons », (trois doigts de la main), « et vingt-cinq boulins » (les cinq doigts des deux mains bien ouverts fermés vite, deux fois de suite, puis une seule main, ce qui fait en tout vingt-cinq). La suite du rituel ne peut pas se traduire par des gestes.

> *Ça fait beaucoup de petits pains*
> *Pour un gentil petit clampin.*

Mais je me débrouille pour imiter également la fin de cette comptine et tendre vers lui mon index, lui, mon « clampin ».

Il réagit à ce simulacre et sourit. Peut-il, à travers

la fenêtre, déchiffrer que je souris aussi ? Nous sommes deux Indiens qui se sont reconnus dans l'obscurité et dans la savane, et nous avons échangé nos codes gestuels. Complicité, tendresse, jubilation intérieure. Après de multiples signes d'au revoir de la main, le petit garçon quitte sa station d'observation.

— Tu as de la chance, tu as de la chance, tu as de la chance.

Comme les roues d'une locomotive, comme les pistons d'une machine qui monte et descend à un rythme régulier, ces mots s'inscrivent en une musique répétitive et martèlent mon inconscient. Car l'effet retard de l'anesthésie me remet, par intervalles, dans des états de brève perte de conscience.

36

Quatre étapes
pour aborder la douleur

Cela ne dure pas : très vite, je retrouve mon état d'extrême lucidité, avec la pièce et les infirmières, les objets et la lumière du jour et une pensée qui revient en spirale : les autres. Ceux qui ont occupé cette pièce, ceux qui l'occuperont.

Tu n'as pas subi grand-chose. Il y a des hommes et des femmes qui ont subi des douzaines d'anesthésies, d'interventions, de séjours répétés en réa. On a labouré, charcuté, examiné, retourné, manipulé, enlevé, remis, remplacé, déplacé leur foie, leur cœur, leurs poumons, leur vessie, leur pancréas. Ils connaissent mieux que personne ces murs vides, cette bouche d'aération, ces plafonds bleus ou jaunes, ce mobilier d'hôpital, cet univers nu, et leurs bras sont presque, comment dire ? accoutumés à s'offrir au goutte-à-goutte de la perf et à la seringue pour la prise de sang. Ils ont emmagasiné plus de douleur et d'acceptation de cette douleur, plus de connaissance de cette douleur que tu n'en auras accumulé dans ton aller et retour.

Parce que, après tout, la traversée a été courte — et tu n'as pas à te plaindre.

D'ailleurs, je ne me plains pas.

C'est une autre surprise du retour à la vie : pas de plainte. Aucune envie, aucun besoin de prendre le monde à témoin de ce que l'on a vu et traversé. Moi qui frémissais au moindre mal, l'hypersensible, l'hypocondriaque qui se complaisait dans ses «bobos» autant qu'un enfant fragile — qui n'avait en réalité jamais joué d'autre rôle, dans la maladie la plus banale, que celui d'un bambin douillet et dorloté appelant soins et réclamant attention —, j'ai cessé de me plaindre.

Rentre en toi-même, Octave, et cesse de te plaindre.

Et puis :

Sois sage ô ma douleur et tiens-toi plus tranquille.

Nouveau précepte à ajouter à ma liste : il existe quatre étapes pour aborder la douleur. Premièrement, il faut la reconnaître. Deuxième étape, si tu l'as reconnue, il faut l'accepter. Troisième étape, puisque tu l'as acceptée, tu peux essayer d'en sortir. Quatrième et dernière étape, tu es donc capable de la dépasser, puisque tu la connais.

Je possède désormais un mètre étalon de la douleur comme le «radar à merde» dont Ernest Hemingway disait qu'il lui servait pour démasquer les imposteurs et les bidons, la fraude. Pour moi, ce mètre étalon, cette boussole interne permettant au voyageur de ne pas perdre le cap, m'aide à relativiser toute autre douleur. Chaque fois que l'on viendra (il faut bien continuer de vérifier si je vais mieux) ponctionner un peu de mon sang, me manipuler, ou lorsqu'on m'ôtera la sonde et quand, la sonde ôtée, je pisserai des lames de rasoir pendant des semaines parce que, au passage (avatar classique d'un séjour en réa), j'aurai développé une violente et durable infection, il suffira que, juste avant l'irruption de la douleur, mon corps me dise :

— Ce n'est rien. Pense à ce que tu as connu, et dis-toi que ce que tu traverses n'est rien. C'est une toute petite chose par rapport aux coups que tu as reçus.

Quand on a autant souffert, on ne souffre plus. J'accueille les aides-soignantes avec le sourire de celui qui sait. Je ferme les yeux, on me pique une veine, je n'ai rien senti. Ce n'est pas important. Quand on a autant eu peur, on ne peut plus avoir peur. Ainsi, à partir de ce réveil, s'installe une certitude : si j'ai frôlé la mort et si elle m'a fait peur, si je l'ai regardée, si elle m'a palpé, si je l'ai récusée, maintenant que je sais, je n'aurai plus peur. Ce n'est pas que j'avais peur de la mort *avant* — mais je voulais l'ignorer bien que l'ayant côtoyée autant que d'autres hommes. Chaque fois qu'elle

intervenait autour ou près de moi — guerre ; accident ; deuil ; hôpitaux ; amis, parents ou inconnus —, chaque fois que j'en étais spectateur,
témoin, ou même accompagnateur, je la rejetais
entièrement. Je refusais d'entendre son message
d'avertissement :

— Je suis là : je peux arriver à tout moment.
N'oublie pas que je suis à toi, que tu es à moi. Nous
nous appartenons. Ne l'oublie pas.

Je ne l'oublierai jamais plus — mais cela ne me
fait pas peur.

37

Où est passée Karen ?

Les infirmières savent que je sais. Nous n'en parlons pas, mais je le vois dans leur regard, dans leur
démarche. Je ne connais rien d'elles : j'ai eu
besoin d'elles, je les ai aimées et parfois haïes, mais
je ne sais rien d'elles et j'éprouve un grand besoin
de leur parler.

Car, ça y est, je peux parler. Mes lèvres, ma
bouche, ma gorge et mon palais sont libérés. On
ne vous administre en effet l'aérosol qu'à certaines
heures. Le reste du temps, j'ai le visage libre.
Certes, les bras sont encore encombrés de
quelques fils, l'index de son oxymètre, mais on a
détaché les bandes velcro des rebords métalliques
du lit puisqu'il n'y a aucune raison que j'essaye
d'arracher des tubes qui ont disparu. Je sens
encore, cependant, leur présence autour de ma
bouche et de mon palais, la trace du tube, des cordelettes, et je crois encore m'abrutir du bruit de la
machine avec laquelle j'étais censé « travailler ».

Aussi bien, les premiers mots que je vais m'entendre prononcer à voix haute seront :

— La machine et les tubes. Les tubes et la machine.

Comme pour les exorciser, les chasser de la mémoire de mon corps. Je me croyais seul dans la pièce, mais une voix m'a répondu :

— Qu'est-ce que vous dites ?

C'est une des infirmières, Bénédicte, celle dont j'attendais tant dans mes moments de plus grand désespoir, celle qui personnifiait l'aide, la main tendue de la vie. Je prononce son nom comme un remerciement et un compliment, à plusieurs reprises. Elle vient auprès de moi.

— Alors, dit-elle en me tapotant l'avant-bras, ça va aller maintenant ? On n'aura pas beaucoup le temps de se parler, vous savez, avant que vous quittiez la réa, j'ai d'autres malades qui ne vont pas bien du tout.

— Je n'ai pas dû être très facile, lui dis-je. J'ai dû vous embêter toutes les nuits et j'ai beaucoup trop appuyé sur la poire pour que vous veniez « m'aspirer ».

Elle secoue la tête, geste qui m'est devenu si familier, mélange de bonhomie expéditive, expression de bon sens, mais aussi façon de traduire sa grande expérience de la maladie, de la douleur et de la mort, qui lui confère cette supériorité sur beaucoup d'autres et qu'il n'est pas nécessaire de déclarer, cette évidence de celle qui sait et n'a même plus envie, besoin, ou le temps d'en parler. Son hochement de tête équivaut à la vieille phrase orientale : «Celui qui sait ne parle pas, celui qui parle ne sait pas. »

— Mais non, finit-elle par répondre, tout en continuant de s'activer, vous n'avez pas plus souvent appuyé sur la poire qu'un autre.

Il y a plus de deux ans qu'elle est en service, ici, à la réa. C'est la plus forte, la plus écoutée, la plus cabocharde, aussi, de toutes les infirmières. Une des plus anciennes de l'équipe. Elle sait bien qu'elle va finir par « avoir sa dose de la réa » et, en même temps, elle n'est satisfaite que dans cette atmosphère, cette tension constante, dans ces conditions limites, aux portes de l'essentiel, aux prises avec le danger et le besoin qu'« ils » ou « elles » ont de sa compétence. Elle est célibataire, elle vient en RER à son service depuis le fin fond des Yvelines ; ses parents sont natifs de la Touraine, je ne sais pas pourquoi je croyais qu'elle était d'origine corse. Elle envisage avec une autre fille du service, qui vient à peine d'intégrer la réa, de partir en Afrique, au Rwanda, dans un de ces camps d'extrême urgence où l'on est encore au plus près des souffrances, où il faut encore plus « aller au bout », dit-elle. Comme si son expérience de la réa dans un grand hôpital parisien, loin de la lasser du combat contre la mort, lui donnait un élan supplémentaire pour ces choses qu'elle ne nomme pas — pudeur, orgueil, ou simple refus de mots qu'elle ne peut ignorer ? —, ces choses que nous baptisons charité, communion, amour, dépassement de soi.

Son amie vient d'entrer dans la pièce. Elles vont

208

former équipe pour les huit prochaines heures. La jeune femme est une Guadeloupéenne au teint clair, aux cheveux courts, au parler calme et au visage serein, au choix de mots judicieux. Lorsqu'elle s'approche pour nettoyer ma bouche, je la reconnais. Il n'y aucun doute : je lui raconte alors à quel point j'avais été touché par son expression courtoise, sa patience, lorsque, me débattant contre l'incapacité de suivre ses consignes, en proie à la toux, prisonnier des tubes, je ne parvenais pas à répondre à sa phrase répétée avec une douce insistance :

— Je souhaite atteindre votre palais.

Elle en sourit. On parle. Je tente de l'interroger sur son parcours. Sa vie. Elle est mère d'une petite fille, le père n'est plus au foyer. Elle vient de faire un long passage d'infirmière dans un service psychiatrique. Quand je pousse mes questions un peu vite ou trop loin, la jeune femme fait tomber un mince et poli rideau de silence et de discrétion, sans doute parce que, ayant retrouvé l'usage de la parole, je fais preuve d'une trop grande volubilité, d'une curiosité maladroite et d'un excès de rapidité dans mon désir de me familiariser avec l'une de ces femmes qui ont tant compté pour moi. Son silence a la même signification que le hochement de tête de Bénédicte tout à l'heure :

— Oui, oui, bien sûr, vous nous aimez et vous vous intéressez passionnément à nous et c'est très bien, et c'est aimable, et c'est même très agréable parce que ça n'est pas aussi fréquent que cela — mais cela ne durera pas. Vous allez être vite

« démédicalisé », d'ici quarante-huit heures à peine, et l'on vous transférera dans une chambre normale, en étage, dans le pavillon de pneumologie, et vous serez pris en charge par d'autres aides-soignantes, d'autres infirmières, et vous nous oublierez. Oui, oui, bien sûr, pendant votre traversée de la Nuit, vous avez eu besoin de nous, un tel besoin que vous vous êtes attaché à nous de façon anormale, et nous avons tout fait pour vous aider, mais vous allez nous quitter et nous resterons ici, agents de circulation au carrefour de la capitale de la douleur, dans cette réa qui est à la fois une prison dont nous sommes les gardes-chiourme, un centre de sauvetage dont nous sommes les anges. Votre lit sera occupé par un homme ou une femme auxquels nous devrons donner la même attention extrême, la même vigilance, le même zéro faute, la même compassion, les mêmes mots autoritaires et adoucissants. Et nous n'allons pas, tout de même, dès lors, vous ouvrir le secret de nos vies, nos amours, nos échecs et nos espoirs, nos faiblesses, sous prétexte que, affamé de curiosité humaine, vous nous interrogez avec cette indiscrétion que nous savons reconnaître chez ceux qui reviennent d'aussi loin, d'une aussi grande solitude.

J'ai bien compris ce discours, qu'elles n'ont jamais prononcé. Je sais mieux, aujourd'hui, respecter un silence et un hochement de tête. Il me semble que je sais mieux faire et mieux être avec les autres, quels qu'ils soient. Je sais mieux écouter, par exemple, lorsque Florence, la Guadeloupéenne, me parle de mes filles aînées, de ma femme. Et comment elle voyait que l'une entrait presque inconsciemment «en prière», tandis que l'autre était toute volonté et toute énergie déployées, et la troisième tout dévouement et toute pudeur.

Bénédicte et Florence me laissent seul. Je regarde le plan de travail momentanément vide. Je m'interroge : Vais-je aussi revoir Karen la Coréenne ? Karen la vénéneuse ? Karen qui me faisait si peur dans sa blouse verte, quand je la voyais de dos, la nuit, alors qu'elle préparait les doses de médication tout en racontant ses amours contrariées, avec sa voix de garce, à sa petite copine, et dont je craignais qu'à elles deux, elles ne m'assassinent ? Où est passée Karen ?

38

De la crétinisation du monde

Le professeur D. semble satisfait et soulagé de me voir sur le « bon chemin ».

Il m'explique de sa voix un peu voilée les futures étapes de ma « démédicalisation » : encore quelque temps en réa, puis plusieurs semaines ici à l'hôpital, en chambre, afin de me laisser retrouver mes forces, mon poids, mais aussi et surtout afin de s'assurer que le traitement choisi prend tout son effet.

— Vous nous avez fait peur, me dit-il. Nous avons été assez paumés, je dois vous l'avouer, pendant quelques jours. Mais on a cherché. Vous savez, c'est la seule vérité en médecine : on cherche. On croit savoir, mais on se trompe souvent et l'on cherche. C'est le labo qui nous a donné la réponse. Je vous avoue que j'ai même consulté plusieurs collègues. Ça ne me gêne pas de vous dire ça. On a beaucoup cherché : ne vous faites pas raconter de blagues sur la médecine, on sait tout et on ne sait rien.

Puis :

— Je ne vous lâche pas avant d'être sûr que tout

est en place. Ça peut prendre du temps et il va falloir encore nous donner ce temps-là, dit-il.

Il y a sur son visage comme une expression d'excuse — c'est à lui que je refusais d'entrer dans cet hôpital, ce qu'il me réclamait pourtant, parce que je lui disais que je n'avais pas « le temps ». À lui que j'expliquais, quelques semaines auparavant, ma vie, la radio et la télé, les livres, les responsabilités, les choses, les engagements, les déplacements, les rendez-vous, le calendrier — et lui qui écoutait, respectueux de l'« importance » de mes « fonctions ». J'en éprouve aujourd'hui comme une honte, une envie d'en rire :

— Je vous donnerai tout le temps que vous voudrez, lui dis-je. Ce n'est pas grave, j'ai tout mon temps. Je n'ai plus du tout la même notion du temps qu'auparavant. Je ne suis pas du tout pressé.

Il me regarde avec un sourire incrédule.

— Écoutez, lui dis-je, croyez-moi, cette comédie est terminée.

La « comédie du temps ». Je l'avais jouée, comme tout un chacun, peut-être un peu mieux et plus intensément que d'autres garçons de ma génération. La comédie de l'« homme pressé », le frère aîné de celui qui avait été étiqueté comme un « jeune homme pressé ». En une seule phrase, une seule respiration sans aérosol, dans la pièce vide de la réa, sous le regard d'abord amusé, puis incrédule, puis convaincu du professeur D. —

convaincu puisqu'il sait qu'on ne ment pas, lorsqu'on sort de l'épreuve et que l'on a, en face de soi, un homme conscient de ce que vous avez traversé et d'où vous revenez —, cette comédie se détruit sans difficulté, l'une de mes comédies. Je me sens nu, vrai, plus naturel que j'aie jamais pu l'être. Les obstacles tombent d'eux-mêmes.

À la notion de la comédie que j'ai pu jouer vient s'ajouter une sensation de clairvoyance, comme un peu plus tôt, lorsque j'avais cru voir s'inscrire devant moi ce que je devrais faire dans l'avenir, ce que je devrais dire et à qui.

Clairvoyance et légèreté : c'est avec légèreté que j'abandonne en ce même instant certaines défroques, certains habits. Les discours et les bruits des hommes, le bla-bla éphémère, ça veut dire quoi ? Ce n'est rien — Montaigne l'avait dit mais je n'avais pas toujours écouté : « Le plus haut prince du monde n'est jamais assis que sur son cul. » Je n'avais jamais prétendu être un prince, mais j'ai souvent cru que j'étais un peu plus haut que sur mon cul. Je me revois, décontracté et faisant semblant d'en sourire, mais, à l'intérieur de moi, très satisfait, recevant décorations et médailles, récompenses et prix. On me parle de moi, en public. Je parle de celui qui parle de moi. Il y a des flashes, il y a des lustres bien éclairés, des micros et des caméras, des ministres et des stars. Tout le monde applaudit. Le plancher du grand salon du cercle de l'avenue Franklin-Roosevelt ne porte plus mes pieds, je vole, je souris, je serre des mains, j'embrasse et l'on m'embrasse — ah, mon Dieu, comme je suis important !

Ah, mon Dieu, comme ça n'est pas important !

— D'habitude, me dit D., compte tenu des médicaments que vous avez pris, on ne se retrouve pas dans l'état dans lequel je vous vois.

— Quels médicaments ?

— On vous a donné beaucoup de sédatifs, des produits pour atténuer vos douleurs. N'oubliez pas que vous avez été anesthésié deux fois en huit jours. Certains produits condensent et coupent de toute définition du temps. Ce qui peut durer quelques secondes réelles, on croit que ça a duré des heures.

Je repense aux deux tunnels : le noir, puis le blanc. Je repense aux hommes-toupies en casquette de cricket. À ce concert de sons tropicaux et crétinisants qui venaient envahir mon esprit, et rythmaient le bruit de la machine.

— D'habitude, continue-t-il, on sort de là dans un véritable potage, mais certainement pas avec la clarté que je vois chez vous. Vous avez été l'objet d'un grand, un très grand remuement. On dirait que cela vous a amené là, maintenant, à une belle faculté de lucidité. C'est assez rare.

Il a dit : certains produits. Sont-ils l'explication de quelques-unes de mes visions ? Avaient-ils libéré quelque chose qui se trouvait dans mon subconscient — ou bien créé quelque chose qui n'était simplement pas moi ? Je ne l'interroge pas. Je suis plutôt gagné par le besoin de lui prendre la main et de la serrer longuement. Ces pulsions d'affec-

215

tion, de contact charnel, je les ressentirai à l'égard de toutes celles et ceux que je vais revoir dans les jours qui suivront. Quelques phrases m'échappent :

— Vous faites un métier extraordinaire, vous faites dans le concret. Nous, ce qu'on appelle les gens de média, nous travaillons dans la représentation de la vie, de ce concret. Et pour certains même, dans la présentation. Ce terme de « présentateur » est impropre, il réduit à peu de chose. Ainsi, on ne ferait que présenter la vie, comme à un étalage, comme dans une vitrine ? Petit programme ! Vous la vivez, vous, la vie. Vous la touchez, vous la sauvez, vous la surveillez à longueur d'exercice. Vous êtes au cœur du cœur des choses. Et quand je dis vous, j'englobe aussi bien le spécialiste que vous êtes, vos anesthésistes, vos ORL, vos infirmières. Oh, notre métier n'est pas plus léger ni plus vain que d'autres activités, mais au regard du vôtre, on se sent inutile, superflu. Et je me dis parfois que je n'ai fait que brasser des mots, assembler des images. Vous, vous touchez le corps, le sang, le cœur et les poumons, vous au contact de ce qu'il y a de plus mystérieux. Pas étonnant que ceux qui écrivent parmi vous aient débouché sur la spiritualité, la question de la foi.

Impossible de m'arrêter :

— Il y a tellement de clowns dans les mondes que je traverse, d'impostures, de nullités. Il est vrai aussi qu'il y a du talent, de la création, de la passion, de la grâce. Et du rire ! Mais nous rencontrons parfois trop d'approximatif. Vous êtes au centre de la preuve, du vrai. Vous êtes dans la vie.

— Peut-être, répond D. Mais sans doute vous faites-vous quelques illusions. Notre univers aussi connaît le faux, l'hypocrisie, les apparences, les vanités, les mégalomanies. Il est vrai que nous sommes ceux qui guérissent. Il est vrai que, parfois, nous réussissons à guérir. Peut-être savons-nous comment nous le faisons, mais je ne suis pas sûr que nous sachions pourquoi. Il y a un mystère dans la guérison.

— Les crétins intelligents diraient que vous êtes, face à ce mystère, en pleine « déconstruction du rationnel ».

Il éclate de rire :

— Les crétins intelligents ?

— Oui, il peut exister une crétinerie dans l'intelligence — celle qui ne veut se fier qu'au rationnel. Et puis, ce que je viens de connaître me fait entrevoir, je ne sais trop pourquoi, la crétinisation du monde actuel. Ce mot revient tout le temps à mes lèvres depuis l'extubation. Est-ce cela que j'ai entrevu dans ma traversée ? C'était ca, les hommes-toupies ? Nous vivons une civilisation bombardée d'images et de sons crétinisants. Le monde se crétinise à vitesse accélérée, à la vitesse de l'image. C'est ce que je ressens en ce moment même, pendant que je vous parle. Je me dis que je devrai être plus attentif à préserver mes enfants de la communication de masse, de l'insuffisance de la culture vers eux. Est-ce que nous les élevons correctement, est-ce que nous n'avons pas abandonné

217

notre devoir d'explication, de nourriture esthé-
tique à leur égard ? Donnons-nous à l'éducation
toute l'importance qu'elle devrait avoir ?

D. regarde le carnet de comptable posé sur la
tablette roulante que l'on installe au-dessus du lit.

— Je vois que vous prenez déjà des notes, me
dit-il. Il faut dormir, aussi. Le cahier des infirmières semble indiquer que vous dormez très peu.

C'est vrai, j'ai du mal à dormir longtemps. Je suis
trop exalté. Je fais ça par courtes phases. Un sommeil sans rêves, un sommeil abyssal.

Et lorsque je me réveille, je découvre un visage
nouveau.

39

Où l'on fait connaissance
avec le docteur T.

C'est un inconnu, vêtu d'une blouse blanche, comme les internes ou les autres médecins. Qui est-il? Que fait-il auprès de moi?

Il doit avoir la quarantaine, un visage de pilote d'hélicoptère ou de premier de cordée, ou de navigateur solitaire. Ou d'un soldat sans arme. Le faciès d'un homme qui aime le plein air, avec des rides d'effort autour des yeux, brillants, un sourire franc et fréquent, une voix sans apprêt, douce et chuchotante comme celle d'un ami. Mais un ami que je n'ai encore jamais rencontré. Pourtant, d'emblée, un mouvement d'amitié me relie à lui.

— Je suis le docteur T. Jean-Pierre T., me dit-il. J'ai été amené jusqu'à votre femme par des amis communs, et elle m'a amené à vous. Je n'ai rien fait dans cet hôpital mais j'y connais du monde, et j'ai pu me renseigner au fil des jours, suffisamment pour aider les vôtres, leur parler, les écouter et les rassurer. Je vois que vous allez bien. Je vous embrasse de la part de Sergio, dont je m'étais aussi occupé lorsqu'il avait, comme vous venez de le faire, passé le cap Horn.

Il se penche et embrasse mon front.

Pendant les semaines qui suivront, il viendra dans ma chambre, à l'improviste, pour évaluer et enregistrer mon «retour du cap Horn» et échanger, avec moi, ses impressions sur la douleur — un phénomène qui semble le passionner. J'apprendrai ainsi à le connaître, car je n'ai pas eu besoin d'apprendre à l'aimer — je l'ai aimé dès notre première rencontre, dès ses premiers mots auprès de mon lit. Et je me suis dit que je connaissais déjà cet homme, que c'était un ami de longue date.

Il possède une faculté de vous pacifier, une totale disponibilité. Plus tard, quelques mois plus tard, il mettra son temps et son savoir au service d'un célèbre homme d'État gravement malade. Mais en ce moment, T. se rapproche d'une définition possible de l'ange gardien. De l'ange, il possède la douceur protectrice, une nature constamment prête à répondre à votre appel. Du gardien, il a l'expérience, la sûreté, la fiabilité. On irait sans hésitation à la guerre avec lui.

Son allusion à Sergio et au «passage du cap Horn» m'avait intrigué sur-le-champ. J'ai obtenu que Sergio vienne me voir, le jour même. En dehors des membres de ma famille, il sera celui que je désirais voir en premier. Pourquoi Sergio, qui n'appartient pas tout à fait au cercle le plus rapproché de ceux ou de celles que je côtoie quotidiennement ? Parce qu'il avait, un an auparavant, failli perdre son visage, ses membres, et jusqu'à sa vie même dans un accident de voiture. Il avait lutté des semaines contre la mort. On l'avait patiemment et talentueusement recomposé. À chacune de nos rencontres (un déjeuner tous les deux mois), je m'intéressais à cela : le passage, le franchissement, l'aller et le retour. Mais je ne parvenais pas à obtenir des phrases ou des mots suffisamment explicites. Il préférait se résoudre à un :

— Parlons d'autre chose.

Ou encore :

— Tu ne peux pas comprendre si tu n'y es pas allé toi-même.

Maintenant, il était là devant moi, souriant et amical. Nous avions dorénavant cette expérience en commun. Certes, elle était différente en durée, en degré, en douleur, et j'ai imaginé que c'était lui qui, de nous deux, avait le plus souffert même si, une fois toutes choses confrontées, il reconnut que j'avais sans doute plus « dégusté » psychiquement. Il n'avait vu ni gouffre noir ni tunnel blanc. Peu importait — nous pouvions, complices, initiés, évoquer nos deux voyages. Il n'avait pas vu « l'autre côté », parce qu'il avait été trop occupé, trop mentalement acharné à la seule idée fixe de survivre. Mais les voyages se ressemblaient au moins en ceci : nous étions de retour. Et nous pouvions en rire. Je n'étais pas sûr qu'il ne se mêlait pas, à notre tête-à-tête, une sorte de fierté simpliste, cette manière de vanité sans vice de ceux qui possèdent le privilège d'avoir vécu un événement hors norme. On peut aussi appeler cela de la fraternité.

Il me rapporta des nouvelles du «village» auquel nous appartenions tous les deux. C'est Paris : chaque profession évolue dans un village qui bruit de toutes sortes d'histoires, anecdotes, transformations et révélations. Notre village journalistique se compose de myriades de réseaux, politique ou spectacle, affaires ou économie — et ce que l'on raconte sur les hommes et les femmes n'est ni plus ni moins salace, étonnant, banal, que dans les autres villages qui forment la ville. Tandis que Sergio m'annonçait les débuts de la vraie chute d'un imposteur notoire au parcours jusqu'ici sans fautes, ou me révélait les amours dangereuses d'une jeune et insolente nouvelle venue dans notre métier, ou pesait pour moi les chances d'un candidat non encore déclaré à la présidence de la République, et comment tout le monde, désormais, le donnait gagnant, je sentis la fatigue me gagner. Il s'arrêta :

— Ce que je te raconte n'a aucun intérêt, n'est-ce pas ?

— Aucun, dis-je, tu as vu juste.

Il prit congé :

— Je t'embrasse. Tout ce que tu vas vivre, maintenant, tout, c'est une chance, c'est du bonus. Tu as passé le Horn, réjouis-toi. Et prends ton temps avant de recommencer à t'intéresser au village.

J'ai répondu :

— Si ça doit encore m'intéresser un jour…

J'ai regardé son visage une dernière fois. Je ne

222

l'ai pas vu de la même manière. Avant, lorsque je regardais Sergio, je voyais le séducteur, l'homme d'influence, l'homme de talent, le pro un peu cynique autant que l'ami. Il me semble que je ne vois plus tout à fait les gens comme autrefois. Nous portons tous plus ou moins des masques. Ma traversée semble m'avoir donné, peut-être provisoirement, la faculté de mieux lire au-delà du masque. Je vois les gens tout nus. Sans doute parce que je suis nu moi-même. Chez Sergio, à l'instant où il me quitte, je vois l'enfant qui reste en lui. Je vois les éléments de bonté et de gentillesse qui l'emportent sur les pulsions d'ambition et de pouvoir ; je vois sa vulnérabilité plus que sa force. Je vois même le mort qu'il aurait pu être.

40

« *Je ne sais quelle puissance* »

Le passage du cap Horn.

Cette comparaison est revenue assez souvent pour que, lorsque je me suis retrouvé au milieu de l'écriture de ce récit, j'aie eu envie d'interroger un marin qui a fait la grande traversée. Quand je relis les notes prises pendant notre conversation au téléphone, je me dis qu'elles peuvent très bien s'appliquer à mon propre voyage en réa.

— D'abord, me dit le marin, là-bas, près du pôle Sud, le cap Horn, tu sais que lorsque tu pars, tu n'es pas sûr de revenir. Tu es tout seul. Personne ne peut venir t'aider. Tu es seul au monde. Tu es le premier homme. En vingt-neuf jours de mer, j'ai dû voir le soleil une seule fois. Les vagues se croisaient comme des trains qui se rentreraient dedans : des trains de vagues à gauche qui rencontrent des trains de vagues venus de droite. C'était infernal. Tu ne peux pas naviguer. Tu connais les peurs de l'enfance, les frayeurs d'un homme mûr, mais ce sont celles d'un enfant de huit ans. En fait, tu as huit ans. Tu es en danger permanent pendant un mois, c'est-à-dire que le moindre incident devient un accident et le moindre accident devient la mort. Parce que tout est augmenté, surdimensionné, magnifié. Personne ne circule là où tu es, personne ne peut venir à ton secours et, pour t'en sortir, il ne suffit pas que tu aies les ressources de ton corps, ton énergie, et la sûreté de ton bateau, il ne suffit pas de ce que tu peux et de ce que tu sais faire, il faut aussi un peu de poudre de perlimpinpin.

— Tu veux dire, de la chance?

— Bien sûr. Et quand tu remontes du Horn, tu revis. Tu quittes le monde de la mort, tu es content. Tu as élargi ta gamme. Cela t'amène à grimper à une autre échelle de la vie. Tu as envie et besoin de plus aimer les gens que tu aimes. Tu es aussi envahi par des besoins : voir des gens que tu n'as pas vus depuis longtemps, modifier les choses, corriger le tir, traiter une partie de toi que tu n'as jamais pris le temps de traiter. Parce que ç'a été un moment capital.

— Merci, Olivier, ça correspond assez bien. C'est presque pareil. Merci.

— Je t'en prie, salut.

— Salut.

Une différence, tout de même, quand je relis mes notes. Lorsque Olivier me dit : «Tu es tout seul», il faut apporter un sérieux bémol : je n'ai pas été seul. J'ai cru l'être, mais je ne l'étais pas. Si j'ai passé le cap Horn, si je suis revenu vers le soleil, si je navigue dans l'océan Pacifique, ce n'est pas seulement parce que ce n'était pas l'heure, pas seulement parce que mon corps et mon esprit ont résisté, c'est aussi parce qu'il y a eu des hommes et des femmes qui m'ont aidé à traverser ce «moment capital». J'ai eu de la chance, j'ai eu un peu de force en moi, j'ai eu, surtout, le personnel tout entier d'un grand service d'un grand hôpital. J'étais le corps. Ils étaient le bateau.

On ne choisit pas son «moment capital». Il vous est distribué par une force inconnue, et cela surprend de s'apercevoir qu'au milieu de ce moment ce n'est pas ce que vous aviez cru être les choses importantes qui a pris de l'importance : une route poussiéreuse du Colorado ; une promenade avec un père sur un boulevard au milieu des camelots ; les petits déjeuners du matin avec les enfants dans une cuisine ; un virage en voiture dans une route sur le haut Alger ; un studio d'enregistrement enfumé dans la banlieue de Londres. Qu'y avait-il de «capital» qui puisse justifier qu'au cours de mon «moment capital» cela soit revenu à la surface ? Que dire, alors, des forêts bleues qui, elles, déferlaient sans cesse ? Je finirai par trouver la réponse d'ici quelque temps.

Je viens d'écrire : «une force inconnue». Qu'est-ce que cela veut dire ? En relisant certains passages dans Balzac, j'ai fait une petite découverte bien intéressante. À plusieurs reprises, lorsque l'écrivain ne veut pas ou plutôt ne peut pas expliquer ce qui est à l'origine de certaines actions ou de certains sentiments, il emploie le même terme : «je ne sais quelle puissance». Lisez ces trois extraits :

«Dans la vie des ambitieux […] *il se rencontre un cruel moment où* je ne sais quelle puissance *les soumet à de rudes épreuves. »*

Ou alors :

«Il se passe chez les poètes ou les écrivains philosophes un phénomène moral, inexplicable, inouï, dont la science peut difficilement rendre compte. C'est une sorte de seconde vie qui leur permet de deviner la vérité… Ou mieux encore, je ne sais quelle puissance *qui les transporte là où ils doivent et veulent être. »*

Enfin, le plus intéressant extrait que je vous livre, cette fois, en intégralité :

« Quel nom donner à cette puissance inconnue *qui fait hâter le pas des voyageurs sans que l'orage se soit encore manifesté, qui fait resplendir de vie et de beauté le mourant quelques jours avant sa mort et lui inspire les plus riants projets, qui conseille au savant de hausser sa lampe nocturne au moment où elle éclaire parfaitement, qui fait craindre à la mère le regard trop profond jeté sur son enfant par un homme perspicace ? »*

Et Balzac ajoute :

«Nous subissons tous ces grandes influences dans les grandes catastrophes de notre vie, et nous ne l'avons

encore ni nommée ni étudiée ; c'est plus que le pressenti-
ment, et ce n'est pas encore la vision. »

Comme beaucoup de gens, je tiens Balzac pour un écrivain considérable. Ça n'est pas une opinion très originale. « Il n'a pas de style », couinent les imbéciles. Que m'importe ! Il a un univers, c'est un démiurge, un génie qui n'a pas eu le temps de se préoccuper du « style », tout absorbé qu'il était à son immense tâche, son œuvre sans égale : recréer un monde, embrasser la comédie humaine. S'il n'a pas de « style », Balzac possède la maîtrise des mots. Or, voici un homme qui, chaque fois qu'il se trouve aux prises avec l'énigme de la vie, avec l'ir-rationnel ou l'irraisonnable, va chercher l'expres-sion : *« je ne sais quelle puissance »*. On remarquera qu'il évite soigneusement de parler de Dieu. Il en parle, par ailleurs, au long de son œuvre. Mais il ne va pas chercher Dieu lorsqu'il souhaite aborder l'inexplicable — ce qui dépasse notre intelligence. Ce qui modifie le cours de nos vies.

Alors, plutôt que d'employer des termes spiri-tualistes — plutôt que de vouloir définir ce qui n'est pas définissable, ce « pourquoi » que le pro-fesseur D. et ses collègues ne sont pas plus à même que vous ou moi de comprendre —, Balzac a recours à cette expression pratique et passe-par-tout, qui me convient à moi aussi parfaitement, et que je vais rencontrer à plusieurs reprises dans la chambre 29, troisième étage, à gauche dans le cou-loir : *« je ne sais quelle puissance »*.

QUATRIÈME PARTIE

MATINS ET NUITS
DE JUIN

41

Rien n'est grave

J'ai quitté la réa pour la chambre 29.

Des murs clairs et nus. Une chambre minuscule, impersonnelle, propre. Fraîchement peinte, des couleurs blanc et gris, comme l'étage, le pavillon, tout le bâtiment récemment rénové. La chambre a été désinfectée pour effacer tout risque de germes laissés par l'occupant précédent. Au cours des premières quarante-huit heures, la forte odeur pique les yeux, brouille la vue, déclenche des migraines. Ce n'est pas grave.

Il y a tout juste place pour mon lit, un fauteuil pour moi si je parviens à me lever, une chaise pour un visiteur; un mince espace entre le lit et le mur permet d'installer une tablette pour lire, écrire, se nourrir. Un cabinet de toilette, aussi exigu mais aussi commode et fonctionnel que l'ensemble de la chambre. Je l'atteins au prix d'un grand effort, en me tenant aux meubles et aux murs, et je reste de très longues minutes devant le miroir à regarder un visage méconnaissable : hâve, amaigri. Ce n'est pas grave.

Une étroite fenêtre donne sur la cour du pavillon de pneumologie. Depuis mon lit, par les carreaux, je peux à peine voir un simple bout de ciel, mordu par la pente du toit en brique de l'aile perpendiculaire au bâtiment. Ce n'est pas une perspective ni un paysage très riche. Mais ce n'est pas grave.

On dort très peu et très mal à l'hôpital, c'est bien connu. Les jours sont longs et débutent avant le jour. Il y a toujours une lumière au néon dans le couloir si proche de la porte ; il y a toujours des poires sur lesquelles des patients ont appuyé et qui font twaat-twaat dans la nuit ; il y a toujours un appel faiblard, une voix de vieux ou de vieille qui répète « s'il vous plaît, s'il vous plaît » ; il y a toujours le bruit des chariots qui transportent soins et médicaments, plateaux-repas ; il y a toujours ce lit dur, ces draps jaunes sertis de vert en une matière qui ressemble à du papier. Il y a qu'on me réveille très tôt puisque je dois avaler, coup sur coup, quatorze gélules différentes deux heures avant d'avoir droit au petit déjeuner. Il y a un défilé parfois ininterrompu de gens venus pour des tâches précises : température, sang, poids, radio, séance d'aérosol, visite des internes et du patron, ça n'arrête pas

Ça n'arrête pas, mais ce n'est pas grave.

Ce n'est pas grave parce que je sais que je suis sorti du fleuve noir pour atteindre les berges et que je sens, doucement et lentement, un rythme inédit mais auquel mon corps et mes sens vont se plier — je sens que je réapprends tout. Les fonctions les plus élémentaires : manger, boire, marcher, pisser, se laver, se raser, faire les choses tout seul, se servir de ses mains et de ses bras, lire. C'est lent, c'est très fatigant, mais ce n'est pas grave. J'ai compris, dès les premiers jours et les premières nuits dans la chambre 29, que ce n'est pas grave, parce que je sais que je vais partir d'ici. Je sais que la chambre 29 n'est qu'un lieu de transition.

42

Accepter et refuser l'hôpital

Du bon usage de l'hôpital : quelques nouveaux préceptes.

J'ai vite compris qu'il fallait adopter une double attitude vis-à-vis de la vie à l'hôpital : l'accepter, et de la façon la plus disciplinée, organisée, la plus disponible, se soumettre aux contraintes et aux consignes. Écouter les conseils, les interdictions, les préventions. Suivre à la lettre ce que vous disent docteurs, aides-soignantes ou surveillantes. Respecter les horaires, les durées et les limites. Se rapprocher le plus possible du comportement du « patient idéal ». Sourire et être aimable, c'est-à-dire digne d'être aimé. Remercier chacune et chacun pour son geste le plus quotidien, son service, même le plus répété, son effort, même le plus banal. La vie à l'hôpital ne serait pas vivable autrement. Il faut toujours conserver en tête que l'on a en face de soi des gens à qui il est beaucoup

demandé et peu donné. Et qui méritent considération.

Le malade est un égoïste, un enfant gâté qui
attend tout, un «assisté» à 100 %. Or, la jeune
femme qui, à 6 heures du matin, vient lui porter
ses premières gélules ; la jeune femme qui, à
8 heures, vient lui servir son thé chaud et ses tar-
tines ; la jeune femme qui, à 9 heures, vient
balayer et nettoyer le sol de sa chambre, la cuvette
de ses toilettes, les cloisons de ses placards ; le
jeune homme qui, à 10 heures, vient lui poser son
aérosol ou prendre sa température ou son sang ;
les femmes qui, à 11 heures, viennent changer les
draps de son lit et son alaise ; les ouvriers et les
ouvrières de cette incessante manufacture de la
vie qu'est un hôpital méritent toutes et tous votre
considération et votre compassion. Cette considération et cette compassion vous viennent d'autant plus aisément que vous sortez de la réa. Il est
important de conserver ce sentiment et de l'entretenir sans artifice. Infirmières et infirmiers,
kinés, femmes de ménage, surveillantes et internes, assistantes : ils sont comme vous et moi. ils
se posent la même question : qu'est-ce qu'on fait
là, dans cette vie, qu'est-ce que je fais avec ce
corps-là ? Ils savent même un peu mieux que vous
et moi qu'ils doivent mourir, et que ce savoir nous
rend différents de toutes les espèces et créatures
vivantes sur cette terre. Un peu mieux que vous
et moi, ils savent, même s'ils ne l'ont jamais lue,
la vérité du sanskrit : «La vie est instable comme
une goutte d'eau tombée sur une feuille de

lotus. » Et comme ils côtoient à longueur d'année ce fait inévitable, ils l'ont sans doute un peu mieux accepté que vous et moi. Cela ne veut pas dire qu'ils ne soient pas des frères humains fragiles et vulnérables, et que, à fouiller, touiller, plonger en permanence dans vos draps, vos cœurs, vos gestes, vos caprices et vos frayeurs, vos récriminations et vos exigences, ils n'aient pas droit, eux aussi, à un peu de respect, de gentillesse, de curiosité.

Qui sont-ils? Qui sont-elles? Que font-ils quand ils ont quitté la grande manufacture? Que lisent-ils, s'ils lisent? Que voient-elles à la télé? Que font leurs enfants? Où iront-ils en vacances — mais ont-ils assez d'argent pour partir en vacances? Qu'ont-elles vu au cinéma — mais avaient-elles assez d'argent pour aller au cinéma? Qui sont ces anonymes sous-payés que leur nation ignore et qui, pourtant, ont pour profession de soigner cette nation? Qui sont ces ouvriers que leur nation méprise? Une nation qui ignore, méprise et sous-paye ses infirmières, ses policiers, ses chercheurs et ses enseignants est une nation en danger.

Et en même temps que vous devez accepter la vie à l'hôpital, et aimer ses habitants — premier principe —, vous devez la refuser de toutes vos forces, cette vie — deuxième principe.

Vous devez vous « déshôpitaliser », vous « démédicaliser », vous désinfantiliser. Dès les premiers jours, vous devez entamer le chemin du retour vers l'autonomie. Vous devez évaluer vos forces et vos faiblesses afin que, à l'amorce de tel geste d'aide, vous puissiez dire à celle qui, en blouse blanche, vous offre son soutien :

— Merci, mais je le ferai moi-même. Merci beaucoup, mais ça, je crois que je peux le faire tout seul.

Car il n'y a rien de plus dangereux et de plus tentant, de plus avilissant que de succomber à l'installation douillette dans la routine hospitalière. Il faut refuser de devenir un patient professionnel, refuser la grande perversion française : être un assisté. De même que vous vous êtes battu contre la mort et les démons, la perte de la raison, il faut vous battre de même, contre quelque chose de plus insidieux, de plus facile et de plus quotidien : le refuge dans le cocon. La prise en charge. Il y a des patients trop patients. Il y a des « accros » de l'hosto. Il faut mettre, dans le réapprentissage de vos fonctions élémentaires, l'énergie et la volonté des grands explorateurs qui avancent dans les jungles vierges et ne regardent pas en arrière. Chaque minute de chaque jour doit constituer un combat contre la molle dépendance. De même que le prisonnier construit tous les jours en lui son espoir d'évasion et de libération, le patient de l'hôpital doit construire chaque jour le plan de sa sortie, de son échappée belle.

Une nuance, néanmoins : la comparaison est

trop simpliste puisque l'hôpital n'est pas une prison. Et la chambre 29 n'est pas une cellule. C'est là que j'ai connu plusieurs formes de bonheurs absolus.

43

Une carte postale de Californie

Le premier bonheur, c'est celui de la deuxième naissance. La re-naissance.

Vous découvrez tout ce à quoi vous vous étiez tellement habitué que vous ne pouviez imaginer que cela constituait un bonheur. Il en est ainsi du bonheur de pouvoir parler. Quand on a été privé de l'usage de la parole, quand on a cru que le larynx, le palais, les poumons, le système respiratoire entier étaient tellement détériorés que l'on ne pourrait plus parler, cet acte si naturel étonne et remplit de joie.

Alors je parle, je parle. C'est excessif. Le professeur D. m'a ordonné de ne pas « trop en faire » — et je l'écoute, certes, mais je n'y peux rien : il faut que je parle. On m'a installé un téléphone à la gauche du lit, sur la tablette qui me sert de mini-bureau. Sur une série de fiches cartonnées, il y a les noms de celles et de ceux qui ont appelé en mon absence, se sont inquiétés de mon état, aussi bien auprès de ma famille que de mon lieu de travail. Je reprends langue avec le monde extérieur, mon petit monde.

Les mots viennent du fond de moi, du centre de mon corps, je les sens monter et passer à travers ma gorge, atteindre mes lèvres, ma langue, et je les déroule avec stupéfaction. S'entendre dire les mots les plus simples, s'entendre raconter, remercier (pour les lettres, les encouragements, les souhaits de rétablissement), interroger (sur l'état des autres : Et toi ? Et les tiens ? Et ta vie ?), c'est autant de bonheur et d'accomplissement.

Parler, c'est écouter les autres qui parlent.

Ma mère au bout de la ligne, à Nice, à qui, pendant les jours difficiles, mes frères avaient dissimulé la gravité de mon état. Avec sa voix qui me décrit son visage, sa curiosité perpétuelle, cette voix frêle qui me permet de reconstituer son sourire, ses yeux, le déplacement de son corps sur le balcon qui domine la baie des Anges, cette voix grâce à laquelle je reçois son amour et sa bonté, cette voix dans laquelle je retrouve les mots et les sons de notre enfance et il me semble que sa voix n'a pas changé depuis les soirs où elle nous lisait du Victor Hugo, nous récitait de l'Albert Samain, ou nous chantait ses petits cantiques de Noël...

Au répondeur téléphonique, ensuite, une autre voix, celle d'un de mes plus vieux amis. Nous ne nous voyons pas assez souvent mais je le connais et l'aime depuis nos vingt ans, depuis nos « débuts à Paris », et j'éprouve envers lui ce que le marin qui a traversé le cap Horn me confirma plus tard : «Une envie irraisonnée de parler avec des gens que tu n'as pas vus depuis très longtemps.» Mon ami n'est pas chez lui. Je souhaite laisser trace de mon appel, et je chante, dans une très mauvaise imitation d'Yves Montand :

> *La voilà qui revient*
> *La chansonnette...*

Et je suis «content», comme disait le navigateur. Je sais que ce soir, lorsque Pierre rentrera de sa partie de poker ou de son dîner chez la Vieille, il entendra ma chanson et sera soulagé.

Chanter. Parler. Émettre des sons, et puis toucher. Toucher la peau de mes enfants, la joue, les cheveux et les mains de ma femme, caresser la naissance de son cou. Je n'ai toujours pas le droit d'embrasser et lorsqu'on me rend visite, on doit encore porter le masque de gaze blanche qui permet de se protéger de l'éventuel effet retard des bactéries. Mais je peux redécouvrir la peau de ceux que j'aime, effleurer leur chair, être au contact de leur vie. Bientôt, je redécouvrirai aussi les parfums et les odeurs, et le moindre bouquet de fleurs dans la minuscule chambre m'apportera une autre forme d'étonnement devant les multiples trésors que contiennent pétales, tiges et feuilles. La moindre tige, la moindre feuille prendront de l'importance. Et dans la nuit chaude de juin, il faudra retirer le bouquet afin que je puisse dormir.

Mais je ne dormais pas. Et c'était une autre manière de bonheur.

C'était un bonheur de solitude et de silence.

On était en juin, les jours les plus longs de l'année. La lumière ne disparaissait qu'aux alentours de 10 heures du soir. Il faisait très chaud à Paris et je ne pouvais ouvrir ma fenêtre qu'à une heure tardive, précisément au moment où les traces rouges, orange et violacées du soleil couchant venaient se fondre dans l'apparition de l'indigo de la nuit.

Un peu de fraîcheur pénétrait enfin dans la chambre. À cette heure-là, le standard de l'hôpital ne transmet plus d'appels. Je pouvais téléphoner, mais on ne pouvait plus me joindre. J'avais une dernière conversation avec ma femme et mes enfants, et puis, je savais que la nuit était à moi jusqu'aux premiers bruits dans les couloirs du matin, avant les premiers médicaments, avant que surgisse l'aurore.

Je marchais alors à pas prudents jusqu'à la fenêtre ouverte. Je me penchais, pour entendre au-delà du bâtiment d'entrée, venus de la rue Saint-Jacques, les sons des autos déchirant de la soie dans la nuit. J'imaginais les terrasses de café envahies, sur le boulevard du Montparnasse, tout près de moi ; le jardin du Luxembourg aux arbres chargés, gorgés de feuilles ; et Saint-Germain, pas loin non plus, avec cette douce et insouciante effervescence des femmes et des hommes acceptant l'éphémère, l'impalpable fuite des instants. J'entendais la ville et sa « paisible rumeur lasse », et je levais les yeux vers un ciel fort peu pollué, bleu foncé, criblé d'étoiles, un de ces beaux ciels d'été, et malgré l'exiguïté de la fenêtre et la banalité du bâtiment qui bouchait une partie de ma vue, j'avais l'impression que je m'envolais jusqu'au milieu de la toile bleue, au milieu du monde. Je repensais alors à une carte que je venais de recevoir de Californie.

C'était un message de la femme de mon ami Guy A. Elle avait été surprise avec sa fille Sasha, dans leur grande maison de Sherman Oaks, par le récent tremblement de terre de Los Angeles. La femme et l'enfant avaient vu passer meubles et murs, toits et façades, ustensiles et tableaux, lampes et appareils devant elles. Les escaliers qu'elles empruntaient pour déguerpir s'écroulaient derrière elles. Tout craquait, se disloquait, se pulvérisait en une cadence chaotique et elles s'étaient retrouvées au milieu de la nuit, en pleine rue, en pyjama, sauvées par leur rapidité, leur décision immédiate de ne pas emporter quoi que ce fût, puisque, devant l'urgence et l'importance du cataclysme, elles avaient eu la présence d'esprit de fuir sans hésiter. Fuir vers le seul endroit sûr : dehors !

Guy, qui travaillait à deux heures de là, dans le désert de Palm Springs, avait foncé sur l'autoroute et avait fini par les découvrir, assises à même le goudron de l'avenue, entre les rangées de palmiers pulvérisés. Sasha lovée dans les bras de sa mère, dans ce quartier autrefois riant et cossu qui avait eu l'aspect d'un paradis de cinéma, bien composé, bien ordonnancé, vert et tranquille — et qui ressemblait désormais à un décor renversé.

« Nous avons triché avec la mort, me disait le message sur la carte postale. J'ai appris par Guy ce qui vous est arrivé. Je suis reconnaissante d'avoir vu passer ma vie devant moi un court instant. Il faut capturer cet instant et le mesurer. » La carte postale était ornée d'une inscription en anglais : « Ma grange ayant brûlé jusqu'au sol, je peux désormais voir la lune. »

Par la fenêtre, je regardais la lune et je songeais à une autre phrase, prononcée par une autre femme, au cours d'un dîner. Elle nous racontait comment elle avait essayé de faire la leçon à un de ses amis, un des hommes les plus puissants du pays, homme fortuné et qui était incapable de s'arrêter, faire, fabriquer, voyager, vendre ou acheter. Elle lui avait dit cette phrase simple et banale :

— Apprends à compter les étoiles.

Par la petite fenêtre, je continuais de regarder la lune, et je commençais à savoir compter les étoiles.

44

Les larmes du petit matin

Les bruits de la ville s'adoucissent encore. Trafic atténué. Fraîcheur accrue.

Délaissant la fenêtre, assis sur mon lit, je lis d'autres messages reçus dans la journée. On m'a aussi apporté des journaux, je les ai ouverts, j'en ai parcouru les titres et les ai aussitôt abandonnés. Je ne parviens pas à lire. Dans la chambre, il y a une télévision, je ne la regarde pas. Ainsi, tout ce qui m'avait captivé : la marche des choses; les affaires de la veille, du jour et du lendemain; ce grouillement des hommes et des femmes aux prises avec l'agitation du monde, avec l'immense futilité du monde moderne, meurtres et guerres, victoires et compétitions, tout ce qui avait, chaque jour de ma vie de journaliste, de «responsable de média», autant absorbé mon attention et ma réflexion, glisse sur moi et se perd dans l'indifférence d'une nuit fraîche de juin.

Quand, le premier jour dans la chambre 29, ma femme m'a demandé de quoi j'avais besoin, j'ai répondu :

— De musique et de poésie.

Muni de mon petit walkman — lecteur de CD, dans lequel j'introduis, à peine les ai-je reçus, les *Impromptus* de Schubert par Brendel, je passe des instants, dont je ne peux mesurer la durée, à laisser les notes pénétrer et descendre dans mon corps. Il me semble que je n'ai jamais pu, jusqu'ici, écouter la musique aussi intensément. Au concert ou ailleurs, toujours quelque chose venait me distraire : une pensée, un souci, une incidente, et je ne réussissais pas entièrement à absorber la musique, quelle qu'en fût la qualité ou celle de l'interprète. J'estimais que c'était une forme d'impuissance, une incapacité de m'abandonner entièrement à la beauté. Et voici que dans la nuit de juin, les deux écouteurs fichés dans mes oreilles, je suis, pour la première fois, livré à la musique, enveloppé par les sons.

Je connais le même phénomène lorsque j'entame la lecture d'un poème : les mots et les vers, leur cadence et leur structure traversent plus intensément qu'autrefois les filtres de mon esprit et les images qu'ils évoquent s'inscrivent plus fermement en moi. Comme si j'avais acquis de nouvelles dispositions pour distinguer, retenir et goûter ce qui est beau. Ne plus être perturbé, diverti, être capable de ne se délecter de rien d'autre que de ce que l'on goûte, au moment où on le goûte. Je me souviens de cette étrange façon dont, en plein délire de la maladie, quand je luttais contre la tentation de la résignation, l'invasion de la mort en réa, j'avais égrené dans ma tête des fragments éclatés de poèmes. Je me dis :

— Si, avant toute chose, tu as demandé que l'on t'apporte de la musique et de la poésie et si tu t'en nourris avec une telle avidité, c'est que tu as voulu retrouver ce qui t'aurait manqué le plus, en dehors de ceux que tu aimes, ce que tu craignais de perdre et que tu sentais t'échapper, en même temps que le souffle de la vie — c'est-à-dire un besoin de beauté et d'harmonie.

Et je m'endors. Et lorsque je me réveillerai dans quelques courtes heures, je connaîtrai un bonheur encore plus fort.

Ce sera l'ultime forme de bonheur dans la chambre 29.

Il n'est pas 6 heures du matin. Par la fenêtre entrouverte, j'entends un oiseau qui pépie. Qu'est-ce ? Un moineau ? Un petit piaf parisien ? J'ouvre les yeux. Je vois le ciel, le morceau de mouchoir de ciel rongé par l'arête du toit de brique dans l'étroite fenêtre, et je le vois passer doucement du bleu-noir à un bleu moins fort, plus atténué, et qui va peu à peu devenir clair et luminescent. Et je connais un long, un bienfaisant état de grâce qu'il m'est difficile de définir autrement que comme une sorte d'extase. Oui, je suis extasié, et je pleure.

Je pleure de lentes, tendres et abondantes larmes, sans retenue, sans secousses. C'est le simple et pur spectacle de cette harmonieuse arrivée du jour qui ouvre délicatement l'écluse de mes larmes. Je n'ai aucune pensée, aucune réflexion, aucune interrogation. Rien d'autre ne se passe en moi. Je me sens comme un bébé lavé par l'eau de la vie.

«Je ne sais quelle puissance» m'a transporté dans cet état. Les larmes de joie muette, cette sensation de renaître à tout, c'est-à-dire à tout ce qu'il y a de plus simple et de plus renouvelé qu'est l'arrivée du jour par un matin d'été, je vais les connaître plusieurs matins de suite. Comme un rite. Ce sera comme une prière de remerciement, la célébration solitaire et silencieuse de mes retrouvailles avec cette triple évidence : le jour se lève ; le ciel est bleu ; c'est beau, la vie.

Il est tout à fait normal que je ne sois pas mort, dix ou quinze jours auparavant, en réa, puisque je n'avais pas été au bout de cette triple évidence. Jusqu'ici, dans ma vie, je n'avais pas encore accompli ce geste d'humilité, cet acte de reconnaissance : pleurer devant le mystère de la lumière qui apparaît. Et il m'était dès lors impossible de faire face à l'autre mystère : celui de la lumière qui disparaît. Je n'étais pas prêt.

Je ne le suis pas davantage aujourd'hui, puisque je vis et revis et retrouve mes forces, puisque j'ai la chance d'avoir mieux compris l'importance et le prix de chaque instant et que je ne vais pas, pour l'heure, regarder derrière moi. Mais je me dis que si cela doit se reproduire — et je sais bien que cela se reproduira —, alors sans doute serai-je un peu plus prêt, mieux armé, plus capable de chasser la peur et de faire face au moment de la traversée sans retour. Mais ce matin-là, ces six ou cinq matins qui suivaient la belle et douce nuit de juin, les matins de la belle extase, j'ai seulement pensé :

— Tu ne pouvais pas mourir puisque tu n'avais pas vécu cela.

45

Demander pardon
à cinq adolescentes

Maintenant, il était capable de marcher longuement et beaucoup. Il faisait cela tous les jours, et de plus en plus longuement. Il s'habilla d'un pantalon de toile, d'une chemisette, mettant ses pieds nus dans une paire de docksiders usés, aux lacets jaunis. Il dit aux infirmières qu'il allait faire un tour et ne reviendrait pas avant une heure, puis il descendit par les escaliers jusque dans la cour pour parcourir l'hôpital dans tous les sens, comme chaque après-midi.

Il partit d'abord vers les bâtiments de radiologie. Il fit le tour des jardinets, s'attarda devant la petite Maison de la Presse près des guichets d'entrée de la rue Saint-Jacques ; il s'assit sur un banc de pierre au soleil et regarda passer les visiteurs, les patients, le personnel en blouse blanche, les Blacks, les Beurs, les Blancs, les femmes et les enfants, faisant aisément la différence entre ceux qui n'appartenaient pas à l'hôpital et ceux qui, comme lui, dans quelque temps, rejoindraient leur chambre. Puis il se leva et reprit son tour des allées, comme on fait le tour d'un village. Il en connaissait les rues, les places, les carrefours, et même les souterrains au moyen desquels on pouvait se déplacer de service en service sans voir le jour.

Il finit par arriver devant la pente en ciment, bordée d'une rampe de métal, qui amenait vers l'entrée, en contrebas, du bâtiment au-dessus duquel étaient inscrites les lettres blanches sur fond rouge : Réanimation Polyvalente. Il pensa :

— C'est là. Il y a déjà trois semaines que j'attends d'être assez costaud pour y revenir.

Il n'avait cessé d'y penser depuis qu'il occupait la chambre 29. Il était passé et repassé plusieurs fois devant, mais il ne s'était pas encore senti capable de pénétrer dans cet endroit où il s'était tenu «à l'entrée de la mort», le «gouffre illimité» dont parle Victor Hugo. Quelques jours auparavant, le docteur N. T., qui le raccompagnait depuis le service d'urologie vers sa chambre à pas lents sous le soleil éclatant de juin, lui avait montré la rampe métallique et l'enseigne de la réa :

— Vous y êtes revenu ? Vous êtes allé revoir les infirmières ? Vous savez que cela fait parfois plaisir.

— Je sais, avait-il dit, j'en ai très envie. Mais je n'ai pas récupéré encore toutes mes forces.

— C'est là que vous avez connu la détresse, lui avait dit N. T. C'est le terme médical exact que vous devez utiliser et comprendre : vous avez été plongé dans un état de détresse, il faut de très longs mois pour s'en remettre.

— C'est un terme médical ?

— Oui, c'est cela qui vous est arrivé et ça s'est passé là, à cet endroit — et il avait à nouveau indiqué les murs, les rampes et la porte d'entrée vitrée de la réa.

Mais il avait fallu quelques jours pour qu'il se sente apte à sonner à la porte de la réa. Aujourd'hui, il savait que le jour était arrivé. Car il allait bien, il allait de mieux en mieux. Il avait repris quelques kilos, il sentait ses muscles, ses jambes, il respirait clairement et profondément. Le matin même, on lui avait dit :

— Cette fois, vous pouvez envisager de sortir à la fin de la semaine.

Ça l'avait réjoui. Il considérait qu'il était grand temps de quitter la chambre 29.

Il y avait reçu toutes sortes de visiteurs. Il avait passé des matinées à répondre à chacune des dizaines de lettres que ses collaborateurs à la radio lui avaient envoyées. Il avait revu ses frères, quelques amis intimes. Il avait beaucoup embrassé, remercié, souri et parlé. Il avait écouté. Il avait réussi à appliquer le plan qui s'était déroulé de façon surnaturelle sous ses yeux à sa sortie de l'anesthésie, lorsqu'on l'avait extubé, ce plan qui lui dictait les choses à dire, à qui les dire. Ce qu'il fallait corriger et modifier. Une sorte de « dernières volontés » à l'envers.

Ainsi, il accordait une grande importance à une rencontre qu'il avait provoquée. Il avait demandé à sa fille de quinze ans de venir à la fin de ses cours, avec ses cinq meilleures amies. Il faisait plus beau et chaud que les autres jours, les filles étaient en tee-shirt, en chemise ou en jeans. Il s'était assis sur la banquette de pierre située dans la cour, sous la fenêtre de sa chambre, car elle aurait été trop exiguë pour y recevoir le groupe des adolescentes.

Les cours étaient pratiquement terminés, les salles utilisées pour les examens et les professeurs, de plus en plus laxistes, de moins en moins présents. Les filles passaient leur temps entre l'école et de longues stations à boire du Coca aux terrasses, ou à se raccompagner les unes chez les autres. Elles arrivaient du jardin du Luxembourg où elles avaient déjeuné au soleil, sur les chaises, autour du bassin, et il y avait dans leur démarche, leur sourire, la trace récente de ce moment d'insouciance, à laquelle venait s'ajouter la grâce envoûtante de leurs quinze ans. Elles formaient une petite tribu d'amies, toujours reliées les unes aux autres par leurs interminables appels téléphoniques quotidiens, vivant en bande, phénomène qu'il n'avait pas connu à leur âge. Il avait commencé par les interroger sur leurs vacances prochaines, le film qu'elles iraient voir ce soir. Au milieu du groupe, il regardait les yeux de sa fille et il lisait une légère interrogation muette : « Pourquoi papa a-t-il tenu à nous rencontrer toutes ensemble ? » Les autres semblaient attendre une

réponse. Aimables, plutôt silencieuses, sinon inti-
midées, en tout cas sur la réserve.

— J'ai voulu vous voir parce que je vous dois des
excuses, avait-il fini par leur dire. Je n'ai pas été
agréable avec vous cet hiver quand vous appeliez
ma fille au téléphone et que c'était moi qui décro-
chais. J'étais froid et brusque, j'avais une voix
rauque et je vous ai donné l'impression que vous
n'étiez pas les bienvenues, que vous dérangiez, et
que je ne supportais pas que vous appeliez aussi
souvent votre amie. Je crains que cela n'ait fini par
inspirer un sentiment déplaisant, comme si je ne
vous aimais pas et surtout comme si je vous jugeais,
comme si je ne vous considérais pas assez bien
pour ma fille, comme si je vous rejetais, et j'ai peur
que cela ne vous ait blessées, vous et elle. C'est
pourquoi j'ai souhaité vous voir, afin de vous
demander pardon. Je voudrais vous donner
quelques explications et des excuses : j'étais déjà
très malade, mais je ne le savais pas. Pas vraiment.
J'ignorais que quelque chose de destructeur s'était
installé dans mon corps et sapait mes forces, s'at-
taquant à ma vie et, par la même occasion, trans-
formant mon caractère. Le père acariâtre et dérou-
tant que vous aviez au téléphone, ce n'était pas
vraiment moi.

Elles l'écoutaient en souriant sans bouger et il
éprouvait la même impression qu'il avait connue
en réa — celle de pouvoir se dédoubler, de planer
au-dessus de lui-même et d'assister à ce qu'il était
en train de vivre. Il pensait que cela faisait une jolie
scène, les cinq filles dans leurs habits et bonheur

d'été, entourant un homme assis sur la pierre rêche de la murette du petit jardin, un homme en train de demander pardon. En train d'essayer de rectifier une image.

— Alors voilà, je voulais simplement vous dire que je vous aime et que je souhaite vous voir le plus souvent chez nous. Vous entendre autant que vous voudrez. Je vous aime telles que vous êtes, chacune d'entre vous, pour vos différences et vos similitudes. Toi, Rapha, avec tes yeux vifs et ta perception si intelligente des adultes ; toi, Natacha, que j'ai vue courageuse dans un accident de vélo, impassible face à ce qui avait été une vraie souffrance ; et toi, Sibylle, avec ta gaieté, et toi, Émilie, avec ton air un peu mélancolique, et toi, Katia, malicieuse, qui inventes des mots et des expressions qui nous font rire le soir lorsque notre fille nous les répète. Je vous remercie d'être venues. Je vais vous embrasser et vous allez partir car vous avez beaucoup mieux à faire par une aussi belle journée.

Elles l'avaient donc embrassé sans commentaire, sous le regard tranquille de sa fille qui avait été la dernière à le faire, mais sans prononcer un mot. Elles avaient tourné le dos, partant vers le soleil et les tilleuls du Luxembourg, vers la saveur des instants inédits qui s'annonçaient à elles et faisaient imperceptiblement frémir leurs silhouettes.

46

La mort n'est pas une ennemie

Il avait eu bien d'autres conversations avec des grandes personnes : évocation de projets, la vie politique et littéraire, la maladie, images et sensations qu'il n'osait pas trop raconter, voulant les garder pour lui seul, tentant d'abord de les comprendre. Mais il ne savait trop pourquoi, sa rencontre avec les adolescentes lui avait apporté plus de satisfaction. Il n'avait rien dit de très original et il n'était pas convaincu qu'elles aient donné à son maigre discours l'importance qu'il voulait y mettre. Mais cet instant lui avait donné l'impression d'avoir déclenché ce mouvement de compréhension et de tolérance qui, dorénavant, espérait-il, l'habiterait dans son rapport avec autrui. Plus largement, plus solidement qu'autrefois.

Et puis il y avait eu quelque chose de plus impalpable : l'image de ces jeunes filles ensoleillées et la belle gravité tendre de leur écoute. Ç'avait été un instant aussi fragile et « éparpillé » que ceux que sa mémoire désordonnée avait fait réappa-

raître à la surface de la douleur, en pleine traversée de la réa — mais peut-être aussi chargé de sens.

De même, pour chaque visite de son fils, douze
ans et demi.

Il avait fini par apprendre ce qui s'était passé dès
le premier jour de sa chute dans la maladie.
L'école n'était pas située très loin de l'hôpital.
Sans prévenir personne, à la fin des cours, le petit
garçon avait traversé le carrefour Montparnasse-
Port-Royal-Saint-Michel et pénétré dans les grands
bâtiments. Un enfant aussi jeune ne peut, en principe, entrer seul dans l'enceinte d'un hôpital, mais
le garçon avait esquivé tous les interdits, évité les
regards inquisiteurs, et il s'était adressé au comptoir de l'étage où son père était censé demeurer.
Une infirmière lui avait dit :

— Votre père n'est pas là, il est en réanimation.

L'enfant, en suivant les fléchages, avait trouvé
le service en question. Il avait sonné. Il avait
demandé à voir son père, on lui avait répondu que
c'était impossible. Il était retourné à l'école, mais
après les classes, après avoir regagné son domicile
et attendu sa mère, il lui avait déclaré calmement :

— Réanimation, ça veut dire qu'on n'est plus
vivant et qu'on essaye de vous animer, de vous faire
revivre. Alors, maintenant, je voudrais bien que tu
m'expliques exactement ce qu'il a, papa.

Le garçon était malin et efficace. Il avait découvert un élève avec lequel, jusqu'ici, il n'avait entre-

tenu aucune relation d'amitié suivie mais dont il s'était aperçu que la mère exerçait des fonctions administratives au sein de l'hôpital. Du jour au lendemain, le petit garçon s'était pris d'un vif intérêt pour ce camarade, dont il apprit bientôt qu'il habitait dans des locaux situés à l'intérieur même de l'hôpital. Dès lors, l'enfant ne cessa de raccompagner son nouvel et grand ami chez lui. Dès que son père avait été réinstallé dans la chambre 29, le petit garçon, sous le prétexte de jouer avec son copain, passait ensuite, dans une semi-illégalité, quelques moments auprès de son papa. Les infirmières ne le voyaient pas se faufiler sous leur comptoir et il venait, à l'heure du repas de midi, entre deux cours. Il pénétrait doucement dans la pièce, apportant avec lui pudeur et tendresse, s'asseyant dans le fauteuil des visiteurs, faisant face à son père. Ils parlaient de petites choses : la classe, les copains, les premiers résultats de la Coupe du monde de football aux États-Unis. L'enfant scrutait les moindres gestes de son père, ses moindres respirations, la fréquence de ses toux (en voie rapide de disparition). Lorsque le petit lui serrait l'avantbras de sa main, en guise de bonjour ou d'au revoir, le père comprenait que ce n'était pas seulement pour que l'enfant le touche, le sente, lui fasse passer par ce geste furtif le message de son amour, le garçon pouvait ainsi jauger, tâter l'état des muscles du père, et juger s'il était en train de regagner du poids et des forces.

— Ça va ? lui disait-il en riant. Tu m'as bien tâté ? Tu es rassuré ?

Il y aurait toujours entre eux ces jeux d'ironie et de fausse brusquerie, cette façon de ne pas afficher leur entente. Fièrement, l'enfant répondait :

— Mais je n'ai pas peur. Je n'ai pas eu peur. J'ai toujours eu confiance et j'ai toujours su que tu t'en sortirais.

— Pourquoi ?

— Parce que je t'envoyais en secret des vibrations.

L'enfant ne lui en avait pas dit plus sur les « vibrations ». S'était-il agi, lorsqu'il se retirait seul dans sa chambre, devoirs faits et leçons apprises, dîner expédié, d'une sorte de prière, d'une petite méditation ? Alors qu'il n'avait pas sept ans, et qu'ils marchaient ensemble, pieds nus, de rocher en rocher, sur la pointe de la Castagne, au sud de Portigliolo, en Corse, le père lui avait recommandé de « faire attention » aux dangers possibles. Le petit avait répondu :

— Ne t'en fais pas, je regarde d'abord, je réfléchis et j'agis ensuite. Mais il y a des fois où je ne réfléchis pas, ça vient tout seul, ça vibre.

« Vibration » ! Pendant toute une décennie, combien de fois les babas cool l'avaient-ils décliné, ce mot passe-partout ? Partie du langage de la pop music, du rock and roll façon surf californien, passée à travers les modes du mouvement hippie, pour être ensuite récupérée le long des décennies à venir par tous les gogos à sectes, les pigeons à gourous, les victimes de la mode du New Age, les bidonneurs du psy bon marché, les charlatans de la philosophie grande surface, les adeptes du bouddhisme en deux leçons ou du zen en vingt-quatre heures, les harmonisateurs assassins, la « vibration » avait été servie à toutes les sauces et comme tant de mots, tant d'images, elle avait été vidée de son sens. Il s'en était méfié, se faisant une règle de ne pas utiliser l'expression, de la même manière que, plus tard, au soudain surgissement de l'adjectif « magnifique », venu du monde du cinéma et de la chanson et utilisé à tire-larigot par n'importe qui en manque d'épithètes, il avait essayé de le bannir de son vocabulaire. Il n'y était pas tout le temps parvenu. Maintenant que son petit garçon avait dit lui « envoyer des vibrations », et qu'il se souvenait des ondes de danger qu'il avait traversées en réa, ondes d'amour qui avaient contribué à sa résistance et soutenu le combat pour sortir du fleuve noir, ondes de vie qui, désormais, le parcouraient au lever du jour, au piaillement d'un moineau, à la minuscule pousse d'herbe qu'il voyait se plier lorsque, dans les jardinets du pavillon, la brise du soir de juin venait enfin souffler sur l'univers apparemment apaisé de l'hôpital et quand, faisant une dernière ronde à pied, le long des bâtiments silencieux, il observait la subtile transformation des formes et des couleurs, il acceptait volontiers le mot vibration. Et il se disait que lorsque Balzac était allé chercher son « je ne sais quelle puissance », c'était parce qu'à l'époque la « vibration » n'était pas encore sortie de la gangue du dictionnaire.

Le petit garçon l'avait quitté pour rejoindre l'école, laissant derrière lui dans la chambre sa petite vibration personnelle, comme celle qui demeure dans l'air après qu'une cloche s'est tue.

Parmi les autres êtres venus apporter leur « vibration », il y avait l'énigmatique et pourtant limpide docteur T.

Il arrivait à l'improviste, à n'importe quelle heure de la journée, son casque de motard sous le bras, expliquant qu'il ne faisait que passer. Mais pétillant d'intérêt, sa personne tout entière concentrée sur l'homme couché en face de lui. Il s'asseyait, constatait :

— C'est bien, tu as l'air détendu, visage calme, ça va. Tu as de bons yeux aujourd'hui, un bon regard.

Ils s'étaient très vite tutoyés, dès leur deuxième entrevue. T. vérifiait, scotchées au mur, les diverses feuilles de soins et de température, les indications du passage des infirmières.

— Tout est impeccable.

— Oui, mais est-ce derrière moi ?

— Certainement pas. Il y a encore beaucoup de remous en toi, il te faudra du temps pour t'en débarrasser, mais tu avances. Maintenant, il faut sortir d'ici pour te réhabituer aux choses et aux gestes normaux.

— Est-ce que les choses peuvent être normales après un passage pareil ? Je ne vois plus le monde avec les mêmes yeux, je ne m'intéresse plus à ce qui faisait, jusque-là, une grande partie de mes préoccupations quotidiennes.

— Ça reviendra, doucement, mais ça reviendra. Il faut savoir retrouver tes routines, ton quotidien, tes tâches les plus banales, les métiers et les gens, mais on ne doit pas se forcer. Tout reviendra, mais tu as combattu quelque chose d'important, de très près, et ça fera toujours au plus intime de toi, au plus serré, une différence.

Il expliquait à T. qu'il n'envisageait plus, désormais, la mort entièrement comme une ennemie. Elle avait d'abord été une inconnue, une énigme totale. Puis elle était vite devenue une saloperie, une ennemie mortelle. Il racontait à T. qu'il l'avait haïe, insultée, brocardée, engueulée, détestée. Refusant de se laisser séduire insidieusement par son appel, par la deuxième voix qui voulait le convaincre que tout était fichu, il l'avait injuriée : « Nique Ta Mort ! »

— C'est parce que tu n'y étais pas prêt, répondait T. C'était ta manière de résister mais c'est aussi parce que tu n'étais pas prêt.

L'ennemie était ensuite devenue, sinon une amie, du moins une notion plus familière, alors que, une fois traversés les tunnels noir et blanc, il avait, quelques heures avant d'être extubé, senti comme une tranquillité gagner toute son âme. Il pensait que ce n'était pas de la résignation, car il n'était jamais tombé dans le piège, celui de la tentation d'abandonner le combat, mais il avait connu un semblant d'acceptation. La fin d'un conflit. Il avait en partie résolu la question.

— Si j'étais passé de l'autre côté, je ne sais pas ce que j'aurais trouvé.

— Personne ne sait, mon vieux ! Je dis parfois à ceux que l'on accompagne dans une douleur plus longue et surtout plus définitive, sans issue, que ce que tu as pu connaître : ce n'est rien, vous allez vous endormir tranquillement. Après, on entre dans le mystère.

T. se levait, consultait son alphapage par quoi il était relié à tous ses réseaux, amis et patients.

— Ne pense pas à tout cela, dorénavant. La vie. Tu n'as plus qu'à penser à la vie, et à ceux qui t'aiment.

— Je n'y pense pas trop. Je vis, c'est encore mieux, je vis tout le temps. C'est merveilleux.

Alors le visage de T. s'ouvrait, et les rides de son visage devenaient des rayons de lumière :

— Ben voilà, tu vois !

Il repartait, casque de motard sous le bras, messager d'amitié et de réconfort, génie de l'« écoute ».

47

Il n'y a pas de Coréenne
au service de réanimation

À présent, il était assis à l'intérieur du bâtiment de la réa.

Il s'était installé auprès de la large table, au centre du couloir, autour de laquelle il avait vu, dans ses moments de lucidité, que se regroupaient internes et infirmières. Deux d'entre elles l'avaient rejoint, buvant un café, et la surveillante les avait suivies. Il reconnaissait à peine les visages.

— Comment allez-vous ? disaient-elles.

— Bien, bien, et vous ? répondait-il. J'ai voulu vous voir et vous remercier, vous dire au revoir aussi. Je pars dans quelques jours mais je reviendrai vous voir, lorsque je viendrai faire des examens à l'hôpital.

Elles avaient peu de temps à lui consacrer. Elles semblaient contentes de sa visite, mais il y avait des patients avec des soins, et les appels, les poires et les machines qui sonnaient. Il avait demandé des nouvelles de Bénédicte, Florence, Patricia. Elles étaient « de repos », on leur transmettrait son bonjour.

— Et Karen, avait-il demandé, la belle Coréenne?

Son interlocutrice, Élisabeth, l'avait regardé avec quelque étonnement.

— Quelle Coréenne?

— Mais oui, avait-il dit, celle qui faisait équipe de nuit avec une autre jeune femme qui avait l'accent de Béziers.

Les infirmières et la surveillante s'étaient figées, l'air incrédule, un sourire poli et gêné naissant sur leurs lèvres.

— De quoi parlez-vous, monsieur? Il n'y a aucune Coréenne à la réa.

Il eut un rire. Il décida de s'adresser directement à la responsable du service :

— Attendez, attendez, dit-il, je n'ai pas rêvé. Elle m'a même fait très peur, Karen, figurez-vous. Je peux vous l'avouer aujourd'hui, je vous ai toutes trouvées formidables. Toutes vos filles, madame, sont formidables, mais elle, il y avait quelque chose qui n'était pas très fiable, elle m'angoissait. Remarquez, ça s'est bien passé. Je n'ai aucun reproche à lui faire. C'est certainement une aussi bonne infirmière que les autres. Mais je ne sais pas pourquoi, chaque fois qu'elle est venue s'occuper de moi, j'étais beaucoup plus agité, paniqué.

La surveillante se mit de nouveau à rire mais elle adopta un ton ferme, voulant couper court à toute équivoque :

— Écoutez, monsieur, je vous répète qu'il n'y a pas de Karen ici. Il n'y en a jamais eu, jamais.

Il insista :

— Je ne suis pas fou. C'était une grande brune aux cheveux longs, la voix un peu perchée comme l'ont les Asiatiques, et sa copine était une Biterroise, je crois. Elles formaient un drôle de couple.

La surveillante l'interrompit une nouvelle fois, avec plus d'autorité dans la voix :

— Il n'y a pas plus de Biterroise que de Coréenne dans le service. Nous avons une fille de Montpellier, Nathalie, qui faisait souvent équipe avec une Bretonne : Catherine. Elles ont fait, effectivement, partie des équipes de nuit quand vous étiez là. Je peux vous montrer le cahier, si vous ne me croyez pas.

Il sentit que les femmes s'impatientaient.

— Si si, dit-il, bien sûr, je vous crois tout à fait.

Il avait pourtant beaucoup de mal à accepter la vérité de la surveillante. Avait-il à ce point déliré ? Et toutes les scènes, tous les dialogues, toutes les images de Karen la Coréenne n'étaient donc que des chimères, des hallucinations ? Étaient-elles dues aux produits qui atténuaient sa douleur, au semi-coma ? Mais alors, pourquoi aurait-il rêvé ces scènes-là, et pas d'autres ? Pourquoi cette représentation de cette femme, ces dialogues, et pas d'autres ? Il ne parvenait pas à interpréter cette partie de ses nuits. Si encore la vision n'était intervenue qu'une seule fois ! Mais il l'avait souvent vue, Karen, souvent entendue, elle avait littéralement fait partie de son existence en réa, il avait rendez-vous avec elle un soir sur deux. Maintenant qu'il y repensait, il la revoyait se penchant sur son visage pour remettre les cordelettes en place ou pour

266

« l'aspirer », moment horrible, moment sordide. Et il avait beau faire confiance à la tranquille fermeté de la surveillante et des autres infirmières, il avait beau lire dans leurs yeux un semblant d'embarras, il ne pouvait pas croire que Karen n'ait pas traversé sa vie — et son approche de la mort.

— Est-ce que je peux voir la pièce où j'étais soigné ? demanda-t-il alors — par curiosité, mais aussi pour faire diversion.

— Elle est inoccupée. Allez-y, c'est là, juste en face de vous.

Il traversa le couloir et poussa la porte. C'était une pièce rectangulaire, sans trop de profondeur, un lit en son milieu, les appareils de perfusion vides, sur le côté. C'était donc dans ce décor modeste qu'il avait traversé le cap. Dans ce rectangle sans histoires qu'il avait reçu les « visiteurs » — les morts de sa vie. Dans ce lieu impersonnel qu'il avait, à plusieurs reprises, senti partir la vie, senti la chute dans le trou sans fond, senti la patte despotique de la mort lui filer plusieurs coups répétés afin de l'abattre.

Il s'approcha du lit, s'étendit et repensa au coin, sur sa gauche, derrière lui, à cet endroit qu'il ne parvenait jamais à voir, là où l'attendait, patiente, sûre d'elle-même, la mort, prête à l'envelopper. Maintenant qu'il était libre de ses mouvements, il pivota vers le coin gauche, vers l'angle formé par le mur du fond et la cloison le long du couloir. Il ne fut guère surpris de n'y voir que le vide du sol, le vide de l'espace entre les murs, l'immatériel et impalpable vide. Le rien. Le rien et son silence.

267

Sortant de la réa, en retrouvant le ciel, l'activité, les allées dans l'hôpital, le mouvement des hommes et des femmes en blanc ou en vert, le tremblement de toutes les choses, il continuait de se poser la question : Qui était donc Karen ?

CONCLUSION

48

Une hypothèse valable
sur Karen

On est en juillet, maintenant, mi-juillet, et le temps est toujours aussi radieux. La France entière est plongée dans une lourde canicule, on n'arrête pas de m'en parler au téléphone (« C'est insupportable ») mais ici, je ne la sens pas. Je vis dans la fraîcheur.

J'habite dans une maison de bois, en pleine forêt normande. Il y fait très bon. Convalescence. J'écoute de la musique et je lis la poésie que l'on m'avait apportée à Cochin. Quand je ne lis pas, quand je ne fais pas du vélo pour sentir chaque jour muscles et abdominaux revenir à la normale, quand je ne mange pas ou que je ne dors pas, je reste étendu au soleil, les yeux fixés sur les arbres, les sous-bois, les chênes et les bouleaux, les pins, le ginkgo biloba japonais et l'érable canadien qui ont été plantés là par ma femme.

Regarder ces arbres me fait naturellement penser à la vision forte, fréquente, que j'avais à Cochin : le tapis de sapins bleus. Je crois mieux comprendre aujourd'hui pourquoi, sur mon lit en réa, je revoyais aussi fréquemment, de tous les décors que j'avais connus, celui que me semblait le plus pur, celui des forêts de l'Uncompaghre. Celui que je voulais rejoindre, auquel je me raccrochais désespérément. Je crois que cette étendue de sapins bleus était la plus belle représentation de la vie, du vrai, du vent et du ciel, du vide et du plein, des couleurs et des formes. Et puis c'était aussi ma jeunesse — et, au moment d'être happé par la mort, je m'accrochais à cette jeunesse. À dix-huit ans, dans le Colorado, innocent et inexpérimenté, couché sur la Faille de l'Aigle, j'étais, sans le comprendre, parvenu au plus près du point d'équilibre du monde et, comme tous les jeunes gens, je me croyais immortel. Toute ma vie, depuis ces heures d'inconscience et d'innocence, j'avais recherché, parfois trouvé, parfois perdu, puis parfois retrouvé le point d'équilibre. Et j'avais continué de me croire immortel. À l'hôpital, dans l'approche et dans l'aller et retour vers la mort, dans cette traversée vers la vie, j'ai, pour la première fois, cessé de me croire immortel. Avoir failli perdre le monde m'a donné un autre point d'équilibre, et si je m'accrochais autant à l'image des sapins bleus, c'était parce que mon amour du monde et de la vie se concentrait, se résumait à cette vision, cette sensation et cette beauté. Si mon esprit se concentrait autant autour de cette image, c'était pour ne pas perdre le désir de la beauté, l'amour de la vie. Et si mon corps réclamait autant la pureté du ciel et de l'air, c'est parce qu'il était au bord de l'étouffement et du dessèchement. Enfin, quand nous la regardions, cette « mer » de sapins nous indiquait l'étroite et infime limite qu'il y a entre la vie et la mort, et cela voulait dire que la mort (la chute possible dans les arbres) fait partie de la vie (le tapis de velours bleu qui se déroule).

Les sapins bleus, c'était la vie, l'instinct de vie, le désir de vie, qui donnait à mon esprit ainsi qu'à mon corps la force de lutter.

Mais la mort, c'était quoi ? C'était qui ? Ce n'était pas seulement ce coin vide, à gauche, derrière moi, à l'angle de la pièce de la réa. C'était peut-être Karen…

Avant mon départ définitif de l'hôpital, j'ai fait une dernière visite en réa.

Revoici l'univers de ma traversée : les tableaux lumineux sur quoi on étudie les radios, les pendules électriques au mur, les casiers pleins de fiches, les feuilles de route, les tasses de café, les boîtes de médicaments, les flacons, les bocaux de plasma.

Pourquoi cet endroit m'attire-t-il autant ? Les filles sont là, toujours actives, dans leur blouse verte posée à même la peau, avec les stylos-billes ou feutres accrochés au centre du corsage. Le stylo, l'objet le plus rare de la réa (« On en manque

tout le temps, vous nous en enverrez? Ça vaut
beaucoup mieux que des fleurs ou des bonbons»).
Elles sont là, avec leur juvénilité affleurant sous la
gravité de la tâche; leurs boucles d'oreilles et leurs
bracelets modestes; le badge d'identification sur la
poitrine. Avec leur visage affairé, consciencieux,
avec cet air limpide qu'ont les familiers de la douleur avec leurs confidences attrapées au vol:

— Bien sûr, c'est difficile. C'est l'endroit le plus
difficile de l'hôpital, mais pourquoi croyez-vous
qu'on l'a choisi?

Avec les téléphones qui sonnent, auxquels
elles répondent avec patience, amabilité: «Oui,
madame, il va bien, il se repose, non, madame, pas
avant ce soir.» Avec cette électricité dans l'air,
cette nervosité dans les gestes et le langage
puisque, ici, tout va vite et tout est important, tout
compte, rien n'est pardonné. Parce qu'on vit dans
une agression permanente — celle qu'imposent
l'urgence et l'imprévisibilité du danger. La réa,
carrefour des décisions — carrefour des sentiments extrêmes.

— Vous nous avez beaucoup aimées, mais vous
nous avez un peu haïes, non?

— Comment le savez-vous? dis-je.

Elles rient:

— Parce que c'est toujours comme ça.

J'insiste pour revoir Catherine, la jeune infirmière de Bretagne dont la surveillante m'avait
affirmé à plusieurs reprises que c'était elle qui,
durant les nuits, m'avait soigné et assisté — elle, et
personne d'autre.

274

— Vous n'allez pas encore nous parler de votre Coréenne, m'a dit la surveillante, sur un ton faussement sévère.

Catherine est arrivée, son visage, sa silhouette me sont familiers. C'est une Française aux joues un peu plus creuses que ses contemporaines, elle n'a pas de bagues aux doigts, elle est jeune et active, jolie et pressée :

— Alors, monsieur, ça va bien ? Alors ça y est, vous sortez demain ?

De taille moyenne, elle a les cheveux coupés court et bruns. Karen les avait longs et elle était grande. Catherine parle bas, Karen parlait haut. Elle est à peine maquillée, Karen portait un rouge à lèvres vif et toutes sortes de breloques. Il n'y a rien de commun entre les deux jeunes femmes — la réelle, et l'autre, celle que j'ai cru voir et entendre plusieurs nuits de suite. Karen était-elle l'incarnation de la mort qui avait, comme les profanateurs de sépultures, envahi le corps de Catherine et la pièce pour tenter de s'emparer de moi ? Pour me séduire ? Je n'ai pas longtemps retenu cette hypothèse, mais je joue avec. Il n'est pas interdit de jouer avec cette hypothèse : la Mort se prénomme Karen. Même si, sous l'effet des calmants, je sais que j'ai été sujet à des séquences d'hallucinations, elles ont toutes un sens. Tout ce que j'ai vu a un sens puisque je l'ai vu — même si c'était du domaine de l'invisible. Ces produits-là, on en donne à tout patient qui traverse ce que j'ai dû traverser. Or, les patients n'ont pas tous les mêmes visions, images, rencontres. Et je me doute bien, aussi, qu'ils ne sont pas tous tombés dans les tunnels, de même que j'accepte que certains d'entre eux soient allés encore plus loin que moi de « l'autre côté ».

C'est un des nombreux autres préceptes de la traversée : ne recherchez pas l'explication de votre rencontre avec la mort dans le simple énoncé des produits, médicaments, hypnotiques ou morphiniques. Ce serait trop facile, trop « raisonnable ».

49

La vie n'est pas un mot

Pas loin de la forêt où je me repose, il y a la mer. J'y fais une première promenade à pied. C'est le matin, il y a peu de monde. C'est une longue, très longue plage vide.

La marée est basse et l'on peut marcher loin. À chacun des pas que je fais, quand je pose la plante de mes pieds sur le sol, j'enregistre tout. Les différences entre le grain le plus épais de certaines portions de sable depuis le plus friable, entre la matière la plus souple après la plus volatile, entre l'humidité et la sécheresse. Chaque mètre qui me rapproche de l'eau renouvelle le plaisir sensuel d'avancer sur cette surface que la mer a recouverte quelques heures auparavant et qu'elle va, à nouveau, posséder dans quelques heures.

L'air est salé et clair. Je respire profondément, avec une volonté d'absorber en une seule de mes respirations tout ce qui vit autour de moi et qui est immatériel, et je pense à cette tendre phrase poétique de Marguerite Yourcenar : « Et dans tes poumons, l'air, ce bel étranger sans qui tu ne peux pas vivre. »

Comme elle avait raison d'accoler ainsi l'adjectif « bel » au mot « étranger » ! Car l'air n'est pas un mot. Pas plus que la vie. La vie n'est pas un mot : il a bien fallu que les hommes donnent des mots à ces étrangetés, mais avoir enfermé le mystère dans des mots n'a jamais suffi pour le résoudre. Quelqu'un peut-il simplement m'expliquer le mécanisme même de la pensée ?

Au moment où j'atteins enfin la mer, je perçois de plus en plus sous la peau de mes pieds les coquillages et les cailloux, les innombrables et indéfinissables débris jaunes, orangés, gris, noirs, couleur de thé, laissés par la marée. Je m'arrête, et la frange de l'eau, l'écume blanche et mouvante, lèche mes chevilles. Un coquillage plus ferme que les autres se fait sentir sous mon pied. J'ai l'impression que je pourrais le conserver incrusté en moi et qu'il me relierait ainsi au reste de la terre, au reste du monde. Cette présence du coquillage sous le pied, alors que, face à l'océan, je ne cesse d'avaler des gorgées d'air qui viennent de nulle part, tandis que les mouettes, conduites par une puissance que je ne connais pas, empruntent un chemin que je ne connais pas, cette présence ne relève même plus du mystère, mais du miracle. Et je pense alors brusquement à un poème de Walt Whitman. C'est un poème que nous avions étudié près de quarante ans auparavant, sur les bancs de l'université, en Virginie, et que nous avait fait découvrir un professeur aux cheveux roux, aux bras et au visage déformés par une poliomyélite qui datait de son enfance.

50

La leçon de poésie
du professeur Turner

Il s'appelait M. Turner. Nous l'adorions. Son corps tout entier n'était qu'une vivante et permanente douleur.

Il avait les membres atrophiés, un visage aux lèvres tordues, aux yeux trop fixes. Il marchait en boitillant à travers le campus, à peine capable de porter ses livres et ses cahiers lui-même, et il se trouvait toujours un étudiant pour venir en aide à cette silhouette pathétique qui se dandinait tant bien que mal vers la salle de cours, pantin cassé par les infortunes de l'existence.

Mais lorsqu'un peu plus tard le professeur Turner entamait à haute voix, avec lenteur et amour, la lecture du poème de Walt Whitman, l'acte même de lire ce poème faisait oublier toutes les infirmités, les handicaps et les tics du malheureux. La vision du professeur Turner, illuminé par la force et l'évidence de ce poème, nous laissait stupéfiés, nous rendait presque honteux. Stupéfiés par la beauté de ce texte, et honteux, parce qu'un bref instant, certes, mais un instant tout de même, au début de l'année, lorsque nous avions rencontré Turner pour la première fois, nous avions, avec la cruauté de notre jeune âge, esquissé la caricature des gestes et grimaces de l'infirme.

Or, maintenant, le professeur Turner nous récitait, avec la conviction et la ferveur de celui qui sait reconnaître et accepter la souffrance, qui sait aussi en sortir et la dépasser, un texte qui était comme un hymne d'amour à ce miracle qu'est la vie. La leçon qu'il nous donna me revient violemment et entièrement en mémoire à ce moment précis où, quarante ans plus tard — c'est-à-dire une seconde plus tard —, mon pied nu a délicieusement mordu un coquillage sur une plage de Normandie et que je rends grâce (à qui?) d'être guéri, sauvé, d'avoir été instruit et d'avoir côtoyé ce qui n'appartient à personne — d'avoir eu la chance d'emprunter un chemin dont on n'est pas censé revenir. Et d'en être revenu. Voici le poème. Je tiens à vous le proposer tout entier :

Eh quoi — fait-on si grande affaire d'un miracle ?
Quant à moi, je ne connais rien d'autre que des miracles,
Quand je me promène dans les rues de Manhattan,
Ou que je darde mon regard par-dessus les toits dans le
*   ciel,*
Ou que je patauge pieds nus le long de la plage dans la
*   marge même de l'eau,*
Ou que je me tiens sous les arbres dans les bois.

À les réciter, à les redécouvrir dans ma mémoire, on dirait que ces lignes écrites il y a un siècle l'ont été pour l'instant que je vis, les instants que j'ai vécus. Le regard vers le ciel par-dessus les toits, c'est la chambre 29. Les pieds nus dans la marge de l'eau, c'est ce que je connais en ce moment même, en Normandie. La situation sous les arbres, c'est ma convalescence. Le professeur Turner les détaillait avec une jouissance dans l'articulé de ces mots si simples, et chaque syllabe résonnait en nous qui l'écoutions, subjugués :

Ou que je parle le jour avec n'importe qui que j'aime,
Ou que je dorme la nuit avec n'importe qui que j'aime,
Ou que je suis à table en train de dîner avec les autres,
Ou que je regarde les étrangers assis en face de moi dans l'omnibus,
Ou que j'observe les abeilles qui s'affairent autour de la ruche un matin d'été,
Ou les bêtes qui paissent dans les champs,
Ou les oiseaux ou la merveille des insectes dans l'air,
Ou la merveille du couchant ou celle des étoiles qui brillent si tranquilles, si lumineuses,
Ou l'exquise, la mince et délicate courbure de la lune au printemps,
Tout cela et le reste, toutes ces choses et chacune sont pour moi des miracles,
Chacune se rapportant au tout, quoique distincte et à sa place.

Il s'arrêtait souvent sur ces deux dernières lignes. Il nous les répétait, les inscrivait à la craie au tableau noir, du mieux qu'il pouvait, de ses doigts atrophiés au bout de ce moignon, qui était sa seule main valide, et il insistait pour que nous en saisissions l'entière signification :

Tout cela et le reste, toutes ces choses et chacune sont pour moi des miracles,
Chacune se rapportant au tout, quoique distincte et à sa place.

Il émit vêtu d'une veste de couleur verte, un vert cru, et il portait souvent des habits d'une teinte criarde, qui jurait avec ses cheveux roux et faisait de sa silhouette déjà difficilement acceptable une image grotesque, mais en même temps émouvante. Car je suppose, aujourd'hui, que le choix de ces couleurs tapageuses était un pied de nez à la mort, une autre manière à lui de souligner le jouissif et l'extraordinaire de la vie. Il se retournait pour nous livrer la conclusion du poème :

Pour moi, chaque heure de lumière et d'obscurité est un miracle,
Chaque pouce cubique de l'espace est un miracle,
Chaque yard carré de la surface de la terre est jonché de miracles,
Chaque pied de l'intérieur pullule de miracles.

Turner marquait une courte pause avant la chute, debout, devant nous, son regard exalté. Je crois bien me souvenir qu'il y avait des larmes qui perlaient dans ses yeux :

Pour moi la mer est un continuel miracle,
Les poissons qui nagent — les rochers — les mouve-
ments des vagues — les navires avec les hommes
qu'ils portent,
Y a-t-il plus étrange miracle* ?

Turner se taisait enfin, observait un silence, puis il ajoutait :

— Avant que nous nous mettions à l'étude de ce texte, de ses mots, de son rythme et du choix de ses épithètes, je voudrais que vous vous demandiez pour qui ont été écrites ces lignes.

À l'époque, j'étais incapable d'apporter une réponse convenable à la question du professeur Turner. J'avais dix-huit ans, et il m'était impossible de comprendre pourquoi cet homme handicapé, laid, solitaire, avait des larmes de joie dans les yeux lorsqu'il récitait ce poème. Il est intéressant de noter que Walt Whitman, né en 1819, a publié ce poème à l'âge de trente-sept ans — ce qui est relativement jeune pour une telle vision, une telle clarté. Je comprends très bien, aujourd'hui, la leçon de poésie du professeur Turner, ainsi que sa question. Elle voulait dire : «Ne te demande pas pour qui ont été écrites ces lignes, elles l'ont été pour toi.» Elles l'ont été pour moi. Elles l'ont été autant pour chacun d'entre vous.

---

* On retrouve ce poème («Miracles») et d'autres, tout aussi remarquables, dans l'*Esquisse d'une anthologie de la poésie américaine du XIXᵉ siècle*, de Pierre Leyris, coll. «Du monde entier», Éditions Gallimard, 1995.

Construire un feu en été

Lorsque je suis revenu de ma promenade sur la plage, j'ai rejoint la maison de bois dans la forêt, et après avoir eu, comme chaque soir, une longue conversation téléphonique avec ma femme, restée à Paris, puis pris des nouvelles des enfants déjà partis en vacances, j'ai décidé de faire un feu.

Il n'y a rien de plus agréable et de plus gratuit que de faire un feu de cheminée en plein jour et en plein été. Un bon feu, c'est assez facile à construire.

Vous commencez par disposer plusieurs boules froissées de papier journal aux quatre coins du sol entre les deux chenets. Vous les recouvrez de brindilles ramassées dans la forêt, ou de bûchettes, de pommes de pin, d'écorces et de branches cassées en morceaux. C'est la moindre des petites choses, la couche de la jeunesse. Vous disposez ensuite, par-dessus cette couche, des bûches ou des rondins de taille moyenne, déjà solides, en prenant soin de les croiser, si possible trois par trois, et en laissant du vide entre chacun de ces croisements. C'est la couche de la force, la vigueur. Vous allumez. Les couches brûlent les unes après les autres. D'abord les jeunes brindilles. Ensuite, les rondins solides et denses. Lorsque ces deux couches ont bien pris feu, il suffit de rajouter des rondins et des bûches de plus en plus épais, de plus en plus lourds, de plus en plus longs à brûler et vous pouvez même vous offrir le luxe d'en choisir qui soient encore humides en leurs extrémités. Le bruit de l'eau qui s'écoule, qui s'élimine et se vide à mesure qu'elle brûle, a quelque chose d'amusant et de rassurant. Après quoi, vous pouvez prendre du recul, vous asseoir face au feu et le regarder.

Dans le spectacle des flammes défile l'éphémère de toute chose et danse l'image même de la vie : belle, multicolore, irrégulière et pointue, tout en montées et en descentes, dangereuse et fragile, insaisissable et pourtant présente, fugace et pourtant concrète, tout en aspérités et en rondeurs, déchirant l'espace et le vide autour d'elle, imprévisible et captivante, blessante et cruelle, parfois hésitante et parfois conquérante, et qu'il faut sans cesse alimenter, renouveler, entretenir, enrichir, soutenir, relancer, et qu'il faut aimer tant que durent les flammes, tant que l'on peut et que l'on doit nourrir les flammes, jusqu'au dernier éclat de la dernière braise, jusqu'à l'ultime rougeoiement sous le gris de la cendre, jusqu'à ce qu'il n'y ait plus que de la cendre, encore chaude, et que commence alors, peut-être, l'ultime et véritable traversée.

PROLOGUE

PREMIÈRE PARTIE
LA TRAVERSÉE

DEUXIÈME PARTIE
LA TROISIÈME FORCE

TROISIÈME PARTIE
NAÎTRE UNE DEUXIÈME FOIS

QUATRIÈME PARTIE
MATINS ET NUITS DE JUIN

CONCLUSION

DU MÊME AUTEUR

COLLECTION FOLIO

Dernières parutions

Composition Bussière
et impression Bussière Camedan Imprimeries
à Saint-Amand (Cher), le 26 janvier 1998.
Dépôt légal : janvier 1998.
Numéro d'imprimeur : 1707-1/2823.
ISBN 2-07-040407-2./Imprimé en France.